MW01295829

bare•bones
— *the* best *of* —

edited by Peter Enfantino and John Scoleri

Acknowledgments

Peter
For Paula
and for the three J's: Jack, John and Jose

John
For three friends who inspired me to take this leap
Peter Enfantino, Richard Christian Matheson and Richard Joseph Ricci
and always, Vonna

This book is dedicated
to all of the contributors who lent their talents to
*bare•*bones:

Whitney Scott Bain
David Allen Brown
Don D'Ammassa
Thomas Deja
Stefan Dziemianowicz
Robin Evans
Vince Fahey
Sean Farrell
W.D. Gagliani
Derek Hill
Gary Jonas
Jim Kingman
Allen Koszowski
Gary Lovisi
David J. Schow
Bob Simonson
David H. Smith
Bud Webster

and

Lawrence McCallum

whose column
"The Late Show"
was the longest running feature across
The Scream Factory and *bare•*bones

bare•bones
— *the* best *of* —

edited by Peter Enfantino and John Scoleri

Santa Clara, CA

Table of Contents

Your trusty editors, circa 1989 (top) and 2010 (bottom).

Dueling Editorial

Well, here we go again.

It might seem like we're breaking a *bare•*bones tradition by having a single editorial, rather than a pair of 'dueling editorials' as we did in most issues of the zine. But this is not unprecedented, which we'll get to, soon enough.

Chances are that if you're reading this, you're already familiar with *bare•*bones, or perhaps more likely her older sibling *The Scream Factory* (20 issues published between 1989-1997). 2019 saw the release of a 600-page collection from Cemetery Dance, **The Best of The Scream Factory**, and the warm reception to that volume led us to create this companion that you now hold in your hands.

We kicked off **The Best of** *TSF* with a 25,000-word history of *The Scream Factory*, and while we don't have nearly as much to say about our follow-on (*bare•*bones only ran four digest-sized and one magazine sized [double] issues), we thought a similar history was warranted.

John: As things were winding down with the final issue of *TSF*, Peter and I already knew that we wanted to continue doing something similar, and while we were excited to free ourselves of the strict confines of horror, as well as the costs and headaches involved with trying to maintain nationwide newsstand distribution, we didn't know exactly what form that would take.

Peter: *TSF* was our baby (and that of Bob Morrish) for ten years, but that baby had grown into a whining, needy, obese, and money-draining pre-teen by the time we had all had enough and put it up for adoption (where its moniker was kidnapped by several large companies—no, I won't go into that here). As documented laboriously in the introduction to **The Best of** *TSF* (did we mention that it was sold out on the day of publication?), there were some good times and there were some bad times but, in the end, what broke us up was a sense of stifling. I had had enough of reading vampire novels and wandered far afield into the genres of western, crime (especially 1950s), and digests (if that can be labeled a genre). It was becoming quite apparent that a horror magazine was not the proper venue to espouse the novels of Steve Frazee or Lionel White.

John: I don't think we put it up for adoption so much as we had it put down.

Peter: Long before the demise of *TSF*, John and I had been talking about a smaller bare bones affair where we could write about our various new hobbies without readers taking us to task. As I recall, these talks almost led to an offshoot of *TSF* while it was still being published. As it turned out, we soon found ourselves with lots of time on our hands anyway so we dove back into the publishing waters.

John: Just the thought of being able to cover whatever oddball interests that we had was exciting. Fortunately, we had a fair number of our *TSF* subscribers willing to take a chance on this new venture, so as long as we didn't kill ourselves (or each other) or go broke along the way, it was all good.

Peter: Only to find that things such as distribution, advertising, and deadlines were just as taxing as they were with a "big-time" publishing venture.

John: A large part of what made bare•bones possible was that I had recently come across a cool application for the Macintosh that would take documents formatted at 8.5″ x 11″, and flow them into page order so you could print out 5.5″ x 8.5″ saddle-stitched booklets (yeah, yeah, yeah… I know you can do that in InDesign these days. Remember this was twenty years ago!). I would create the layouts in Quark Xpress, would 'print' them through this app, and end up with a set of front and back pages I could take to Kinko's to xerox. With our trusty long stapler, we would collate and bind the issues ourselves. While this worked generally well for our needs, readers of the original magazine may recall the slightly stretched look to the contents, which was an artifact of the app reformatting the 8.5″ x 11″ original page to an aspect ration filling a 5.5″ x 8.5″ page. I like to think of it as an homage to how scope movies occasionally played on TV when they weren't being panned and scanned.

Peter: Yeah, whatever. Can we get back to the interesting stuff?

John: I guess it's worth pointing out that the magazine basically named itself. We wanted to set expectations accordingly that this would be a bare bones affair. I wasn't even thinking we'd have any supporting graphics at the outset (Pete loves a lot of small font text to know that he's getting his money's worth!), but that notion was quickly abandoned. For the logo, I italicized 'bare' because I wanted 'bones' to stand out as a reference to our horror roots (nobody realized that the skeleton on the first issue of TSF was our unofficial mascot!). So with TSF in the rear-view mirror, we began this foray with everything we needed. Except content.

Peter: I think the idea, in the beginning, was that we were going to sweet-talk a few of our regular contributors into writing for the new project but some had moved on to greener (or different) pastures. Stefan Dziemianowicz was busy collecting short stories from every corner of the Weird Tales world and doing a nice job pumping out collections with Bob Weinberg and Martin Greenberg. I remember we were seriously considering a massive project with Stef wherein he would read and write about every single issue of Weird Tales and we would publish it as a Deadline Press coffee table book. Unfortunately, that never happened. Lawrence McCallum was working on his **Italian Horror Movies** book for McFarland that came out late 98. But we managed to hang on to a handful of our regulars (Tom Deja, Bill Gagliani, among others) and welcomed aboard some new friends (Paperback Parade publisher Gary Lovisi, who inspired our first cover, and Midnight Marquee regular David H. Smith—more on him later). I see the first issue is cover-dated December 1997 and the indicia indicates we'd be publishing quarterly. That schedule was adhered to for a couple of issues.

John: Yeah, our first two issues were close to quarterly, but in retrospect, I'm just as thrilled that we managed to get out an issue each year from 1997 to 2001! As far as the contents were concerned, I thought we pulled together a decent mix of material for that first issue. In our "Dueling Editorials," written on Halloween, 1997, Peter set the stage for what readers should come to expect from bare•bones. On my side of the fence, I admitted that we changed our plans of making a simple, straightforward zine, right out of the gate. We couldn't see covering topics like vintage paperbacks without including covers, even if the reproduction left a lot to be desired. Fortunately, the extra effort with the layout went a long way towards improving the experience; at least making it seem more familiar to those who had been staunch supporters of TSF. It was perhaps a little light on the cinema/TV coverage, but that happened to be where my contributions fell in: an article on all of John Carpenter's films available on LaserDisc at the time, a writer's guide to plotting your own Escape From New York sequel, and what was designed to be the first in a series of articles exploring fear, focused on the memorable Zuni fetish from the TV movie Trilogy of Terror. We did realize a key segment of our market was heavily into paperback collecting, as we were, so it's no surprise we were well-stocked in that arena, including Gary Lovisi's article on bondage art in vintage paperbacks (which, as Peter noted above, we chose to showcase on the cover). We really wanted to make a strong statement to indicate that this wasn't just *TSF* with shrinkage. The issue also included Tom Deja's article on Lawrence Block's Tanner series, Bill Gagliani's article on John Sanford's 'Prey' novels, and an interview with Bill Crider. Rounding things out were one of Peter's exhaustive digest reference articles, this time on *Super-Science Fiction*, as well as another interview (Bill Warren - making this the *all*-Bill interview issue), and our first column carried over from the pages of *TSF*, *The ReFEARence Shelf*.

Peter: Morrish had gotten me interested in *Super Science Fiction* a couple years earlier when he mentioned they had run a few "All-Monsters" issues and so, in my usual fashion, I had to go hunt down a full set. This was in the very early days of eBay and so I believe I latched onto that full set through a guy who was selling digests through the mail. The weird thing is that it turned out the guy lived only a few miles from me and when I went to visit him he took me into his basement room (this was long before I'd seen **Zodiac** or else I'd have turned tail and run) and showed me a full set of *Ellery Queen Mystery Magazine*, which he sold me for peanuts. I flew through those seventeen issues of *SSF* in just a few weeks (a pace I wish I could still live up to) and usually had a smile on my face after closing each one, despite some odiferous material. I duked it out with a lah-dee-dah science fiction fan on some forgotten internet board around the time the issue came out (a guy with a stick so far up his ass it would have been nigh impossible to be surgically removed) about the merits of such "disposable" material as *SSF* when compared to the mastuhs like Pohl, Asimov, and Herbert. I'll take an 18,000 word *SSF* adventure by Silverberg starring Rand Norf of Galaxy VIII and giant tarantulas over a bloated carcass like **Dune** any day. Haffner Press put out a **Best of SSF** a few years ago with a decent selection of some of those wild adventures.

John: You later gave me a full run of *SSF*, which I still have. And for what it's worth, I enjoyed **Dune**. But to be clear, I'm not the stick-man referred to above.

Peter: I had a great chat with Bill Warren, whom I considered to be the be-all and end-all of science fiction movie critics. Then, a few years later we had a nasty falling-out over Forry Ackerman, of all things. But that was Bill. He loved a good fight.

John: I think you have an affinity for sparring as well… Avallone, Van Hise, Valley… I'm sure I'm leaving someone out. But I'll drop that before you get mad at me! We ran a few spot reviews by you, Vince Fahey and Sean Farrell to round out Issue #1, and to fill all remaining white space, I used anything and everything lying around me when laying out the issue: a photo of a skeletal bride and groom, which were from the head table at my wedding the month before our premiere issue was released; a photo of a pack of *Red Apple* cigarettes (an actual prop pack from Quentin Tarantino's films—seen most recently in **Once Upon a Time… in Hollywood**); and a photo of Sheryl Lee as Laura Palmer from *Twin Peaks*, wrapped in plastic. Why not! It was an opportunity to showcase all kinds of things that I loved!

Peter: I was really pleased with how #1 came out; we wanted something with variety and we definitely got it. But I also think we grew stronger from issue to issue and #2 certainly bears that out. The highlight, of course, was meeting up with Richard Prather at what must have been the 1997 Mission Hills paperback show (Interlude: We've discussed Tom Lesser's Los Angeles area vintage paperback show several times before, but it bears repeating, and I'd go so far as to say *bare•bones* would not have gotten off the ground if not for our love for the event and (*most of*) its inhabitants) and setting up the interview with Thomas Deja. At the time, Prather lived in Sedona, about two hours' drive from my place near Phoenix, and he invited me down to stay. Sadly, I never got around to it before Richard passed away in 2007. We did get to hand him a stack of #2 at the '98 paperback show and the author was kind enough to autograph copies for our subscribers; he seemed very happy for the attention.

John: I was hoping we might have a chance to do more signed specials as a thank you for our subscribers. These days, premiums like that are how publishers tend to offset costs. Obviously, financial gain was never a focus for us—we didn't even count our double issue as two issues towards our subscriber's commitments (the only reason I think magazines like Cinefantastique would do that so frequently). In our "Dueling Editorials," Peter talked about two important figures in his upbringing: Forrest J Ackerman (who he had interviewed for TSF #1) and horror host Bob Wilkins, who we interviewed in the issue. I pointed out that despite the nearly ten years that separated our ages, I too grew up with the same influences, though each at a different period in their life cycle (few consider the **Star Wars**-era of Forry's Famous Monsters of Filmland that I first experienced as its golden age, and I caught the tale end of Bob's run on Creature Features).

Peter: My "Annotated Index" entry this issue covered Michael Avallone's Tales of the Frightened, a short-lived digest that defied my expectations and contained some very solid material. My conversation with the one-of-a-kind Mike Avallone about TotF was chronicled in **Best of TSF** but I'll just add that Mike again promised to send me the manuscript for the unpublished **Satan Sleuth** for a future feature but it never showed up.

This was also around the time we befriended Bob (Robert) Colby, author of several incredible crime novels in the 1950s and 60s. Bob would sign every year at Lesser's paperback show and someone (I assume Ed Gorman) stuck a copy of **The Captain Must Die** in my face and ordered me to read it. I did, and I loved it.

John: I think the reason we actually went out of our way to introduce ourselves to Bob was due to the fact that our friend Dick Laymon had dedicated his latest book to a writer's group he had been in with Bob. The Laymon clan would normally attend the book show, but this particular year, they were leaving on vacation, and asked us to drop off an inscribed copy to Colby. When it came up that we had published Dick Laymon, I think Bob's eyes lit up.

Peter: I struck up a conversation with Colby while he was signing my book and he related that his career had pretty much hit the skids but that he would very much like some small press house to publish a collection of his "Paint the Town" stories that had appeared in Alfred Hitchcock's Mystery Magazine. He even had an uncollected story laying around that he'd add to the mix. John and I had been talking about expanding our publishing empire (like we had a publishing empire— JS) and this seemed like a natural way to get it going. Colby sent us copies of all the stories, we read them and liked them, and John formatted and printed the thing. That's how **The Devil's Collector** came into existence. It didn't sell particularly well, unfortunately, but it did get Colby's foot back in the publishing game. The next year, Ed Gorman bought a story of Bob's for one of his anthologies. John and I drove down to Bob's house and presented him with the finished books to sign. He had a fabulous glow in his eyes while he signed our very low budget project. Made the whole thing worth it. I never got into a fight with Prather or Colby, by the way.

John: I don't know how anyone could. Bob (Colby) in particular was an incredibly sweet guy. I'm glad we had a chance to work with him. Peter also provided an Index to Shell Scott Magazine to support the Prather interview, though I know he looks down upon it because it's not an exhaustive, annotated index to all of the stories in the true Enfantino fashion. Perhaps he'll find a market to scratch that itch someday. Shortly before the issue came out, Bob Wilkins, the local Creature Features host mentioned previously that Peter and I grew up with in the Bay Area, began selling a selection of segments from his show on VHS. I snapped up a set immediately, and finding myself with his contact information, realized that an interview in bare•bones would be a perfect fit! Bob was a wonderful, humble guy who really treated his fans with great respect. Didn't I have Bob sign a copy of bare•bones #2 for you at a local comic-con he was appearing at a few years later, Peter?

Peter: Yeah, you sold it to me a few days later.

John: He passed away due to Alzheimer's about 10 years ago, and that was a great loss felt by many, ourselves included. Back to the #2, I don't recall how I got word of it, though it must have been on some online forum, but I saw an essay comparing James Cameron's **Titanic** to the film **Somewhere in Time**, based on the Richard Matheson novel **Bid Time Return**. I thought it was a fascinating analysis by Bob Simonson, a member of INSITE (the "International Network of **Somewhere in Time** Enthusiasts"), that readers might find as interesting as I did. This issue also saw the return of Sean Farrell and Don D'Ammassa to the fold, the latter reviving his TSF column *The Overlooked Library*.

Peter: This issue also featured a piece on Jerry Warren, courtesy of David H. Smith, a writer I'd enjoyed in *Midnight Marquee*. As detailed in **Best of TSF**, John and I were putting together a book on Mexican horror movies of the 1950s and 60s and Smith was the first writer I contacted (thanks, I believe, to Gary Svehla's rolodex). The book project fell apart due to "creative differences" with Svehla but David was gracious enough to allow us to publish the piece in bare•bones. Props also to Greg Luce of *Sinister Cinema*, who sent us a boatload of Mexi-flicks to review for the book. That was a tough one to kill, believe me.

John: After our "Dueling Editorials," we mentioned ten articles that were forthcoming. It's amusing to note that only two of those were published, and both made it into this collection (Bill Gagliani's articles on Robert Lory's Dracula series and Richard Stark's Parker novels). There's also a mention of "a really cool column that we can't really talk about right now by a really cool guy whose name we really shouldn't divulge." I think Tom Monteleone's *MAFIA* column had already moved to Cemetery Dance by now, so I can only imagine we were teasing David J. Schow's contributions (he did have pieces in 3-4, 5 and 6). Did we have something else really cool lined up and I've just forgotten? Or did we run it, and I just don't know which of our other

contributors we were referring to?

Peter: It definitely wasn't Monteleone. That ship had sailed. In this issue, Bill Gagliani reviewed the entire "Expendables" series by Richard Avery. I had no idea what the hell this series was about when I picked up the four books in L.A. one year. I sure didn't want to read them but I was dying to read *about* them. Bill to the rescue! One of the other pieces we teased that I would have loved was Tom Deja's overview of DC Comics' "The Question," one of my favorite funny book series of the 80s.

John: Fillers this time out included a few LaserDisc reviews from me, a sidebar on a controversial Madame Alexander *Psycho* doll, the first tease of our 'rise from the dead' Deadline Press hardcover—Richard Laymon's **A Writer's Tale**, and an advertisement for *The Ultimate Caroline Munro Image Library*, which I had begun hosting online. That little site would lead to my maintaining Caroline Munro's official website for a few years, and also allow me to finally meet her on a trip to London in 1999. I consider her a dear friend. And examples of those high-res (in late 90s terms) unwatermarked Caroline Munro photos from my personal collection are still circulating on the internet to this day.

Peter: Every once in a while, John leaves his home theater to dump Munro magazine covers on the bare•bones website. I know they're there because the traffic always spikes.

John: Now that you mention it, the best of the *Caroline Munro Archive* needs to show up in print. In our "Dueling Editorials," Peter apologized for the year between issues. This was in part due to our efforts on the aforementioned **A Writer's Tale**. I had been introduced to a local printer (one who was at the time printing all the manuals for Apple Computer in Cupertino), and after using them for a bonus chapbook that shipped with the lettered edition of that book, I discovered that we could print a full-size, offset magazine for a very reasonable per-unit cost. We decided that it was time for bare•bones to grow up! These of course, were famous last words. While the printer did a great job with the magazine, and the per-unit cost was amazing (not to mention so much easier than going to Kinko's to copy, and then hand collate and staple hundreds of copies on our own), we ended up with far more copies of the magazine than we could ever sell. I sent cases back to Arizona with Peter (thankfully when he or his Mom had to drive to California for a visit), and years later I stacked several boxes out for curbside recycling... all of which makes those remaining copies even *more* valuable. In my side of our "Dueling Editorials," I apologized for changing format midstream (do you file them with magazines, or with digests, etc.). The one upside was that we were able to address one complaint we had received from a few folks, including one of our dearest followers, author Hugh B. Cave (affectionately referred to as 'Hubie' around the BB offices *(like we had offices— PE))*. Some folks didn't like the microscopic print of the zine. They loved the content; they just strained their eyes trying to read it. So if nothing else, our experiment with the bedsheet format (Pete will explain the reference) made at least one issue easier on the eyes of our readers!

Peter: You collectors out there will recognize the "bedsheet" reference if you've ever tried to amass a full collection of *Manhunt* or *Alfred Hitchcock's Mystery Magazine*. Both zines had begun life as digests and, in an attempt to grab hold of a precious place on the cluttered newsstand, had experimented with a larger (or "bedsheet" size) before throwing up their hands and returning to digest.

John: This issue included what had to be the most-requested article going all the way back to issue #10 of *The Scream Factory*, our "Worst of" issue. In that one, Peter wrote a fantastic article on *The Frankenstein Horror Series*. Ever since that piece was published, I (and numerous readers) looked forward to Peter's take on Robert Lory's Dracula series of novels. While Pete would ultimately hand over the reigns to Bill Gagliani, it still felt good to bring closure to that unresolved request from the *TSF* days.

Peter: We had someone on the hook to do a follow-up on Robert Lory's **Horrorscope** series, but it never happened.

John: Our pal Whitney Bain,

fresh off the boat following a trip to Jolly 'Ole England provided an overview on a 1998 Hammer tribute in London, as well as a pair of Hammer LaserDisc reviews. We interviewed another sadly overlooked class act, Robert Serling, brother of Rod and accomplished author in his own right.

Peter: *Shock Mystery Tales* was a riot to cover. Really sleazy stuff. I actually modified my format this time out and excluded star ratings since, as I said in the intro, "none of the stories deserves a star rating!" One of the best things about publishing a zine is that you get letters, and occasionally the writer doesn't take you to task for ignoring Mike Avallone on a "List of Greatest Detective Novelists" but, rather, contributes some helpful nuggets. Such was the case with a letter we got from Stephen T. Miller shortly after #3-4 appeared. Evidently there were more than the four digest issues of *SMT* I covered; in fact, there were two bedsheet issues that came out *after* the digests! Miller was kind enough to send me color scans of the covers as well as copies of the contents pages and we ran those in the letters page of #5. I have since latched onto one of those bedsheets and it cost me a very pretty penny. Still working on that last one.

John: Peter—why don't you go pop one of your favorite Elton John LP's on the turntable? Thanks! Okay folks, now that he's gone for a minute, let me just say that it would have been easy to put together a book comprised solely of Peter's annotated indexes to different digest magazines. And it's no surprise that almost all of those have been reprinted elsewhere online and in print (or both) since their original appearance in our zine. That said, it would have been a major oversight not to have at least one of these epic articles represented in this volume featuring *bare•bones* at its very best—so we agreed that *Web Detective* was the one to include. Oh, here he comes—say nothing.

Peter: "The Serial Box" was an idea I had come up with when I felt like covering just a few novels in a series; sometimes you can smell a series going bad after just a handful of books and you don't really want to commit to writing a 50,000-word treatise on **Death Merchant** or **The Penetrator**. I did later expand the **Sharpshooter** reviews, covering the rest of the series, and placed it in *Men of Violence* magazine. The plan is to tackle **The Marksman** next. Wish me luck. Gary Jonas gave me a hand with the column, pitching in reviews on **The Executioner**, **The Destroyer**, and Lawrence Block's Tanner. This is definitely a feature that will be resurrected in the near future.

John: This issue also featured our first contribution from David J. Schow, the tantalizingly titled, "In Search of the Chile Suppository." *Fangoria* readers were already familiar with Schow's entertaining non-fiction via his "Raving and Drooling" column, and I was pleased to finally pull him into our roster. **Wild Hairs**, his collection of non-fiction (including "Chili Suppository," which is not contained in this volume) is definitely worth your time. Derek Hill did double-duty this issue, with articles on Karl Edward Wagner's Kane as well as Amando de Ossorio's Blind Dead series. Lawrence McCallum's column "The Late Show" finally made the leap from TSF to *bare•bones*, and Peter interviewed Jeff Rovin, who had just released **Return of the Wolfman**, the first (and unfortunately only) book in what was to be a new series featuring the classic Universal Monsters (this one taking place after, and faithfully referencing the events of *Abbott and Costello Meet Frankenstein*!). My final contribution to this issue was a photo-essay on a new area of collecting that I had fallen into—Ann-Margret on the covers of vintage paperbacks! While our next issue would revert to digest size, it was our biggest saddle-stitched issue yet, weighing in at a whopping 68 pages! Peter used his side of the "Dueling Editorials" to offer up our explanation for returning to our *bare•bones* roots—namely the unreliability of wider distribution channels. I took the opportunity to talk about the annual paperback show that the issue was finished just in time to coincide with. I know we've belabored the point, but in addition to the good times we've always had seeing friends who come together from around the globe, there were also many great book-related scores to remember. Whether it was getting Richard Matheson and Robert Bloch to sign our books, or Peter finding me a long sought-after copy of John Russo's sequel novel to **Night of the Living Dead**... But at the end of the day, it's safe to say that if not for Tom Lesser's show, *bare•bones* would never have lasted as long as it did.

Peter: I see on the letters page that we promise a few things that never materialized. My overview of the Warner *Dirty Harry* novels ended abruptly at, I believe #4. I never finished it, but Gary Lovisi wanted it anyway so it popped up in *Paperback Parade* some years ago.

John: It just dawned on me that all of our covers, with the exception of this issue, reproduced a book or magazine cover featured inside (#3-4 also had a photo of Ingrid Pitt as a vampire). Because we were featuring the Richard Stark 'Parker' books with an excellent overview by Bill Gagliani, and touching on the new film adaptation with Mel Gibson (**Payback**), I decided to fabricate my own Permabook **Payback** tie-in.

Peter: I tackled an annotated index to a short-lived western digest called *Gunsmoke*, published by Flying Eagle, better known as the publisher of *Manhunt*. This was my first "annotated" foray into the western genre and it took me a couple decades to follow it up with a piece on *Western Magazine*, a digest that featured fiction by Richard Matheson, Elmore Leonard, and Steve Frazee. That monster appeared in *The Digest Enthusiast* a couple years ago. I had pretty much ignored the western in print (even while I always loved the western *film*) but what got me hooked was a novel by Steve Frazee called *He Rode Alone*. This was one of those random 4-for-a-buck grabs at *Black Ace Books* back in the early 1990s; I think the cover lured me in. What amazed me was that Frazee had essentially written a Gold Medal crime novel with western trappings and, by the time I was finished, I knew I had to seek out more material by this guy. One of the features that would have shown up in *bare•bones* was a massive piece on Frazee by a writer from San Francisco, a guy who was more obsessed with Frazee than I was and had amassed a complete collection of his novels and magazine appearances. I only got to see a bit of the overview and then the writer disappeared. Sadly, I learned a few months later that he had taken his own life.

John: With the arrival of Y2K, we decided to write about our top tens of the nineties (we previously did an 80s horror decade in review in issue #7 of *TSF*). We invited our regular contributors to join in, and we received a particularly enlightening piece from David J. Schow, which we led with as a feature article, and are proud to include in this collection as well. It's always interesting to revisit lists to see if your original appraisals held up over time. While most of mine did, I'll admit that I was wrong in picking **Pulp Fiction** over **Jackie Brown**...

Peter: Issue #5 saw our last contribution from Lawrence McCallum, a guy who had been with us since the start of *TSF* and who had just hit the big time with his McFarland hardcover on Italian horror films. I think that may have been one of my proudest moments, seeing one of our contributors sell his first book after taking the ride with us.

John: Which brings us to the final issue of *bare•bones* Mach I (or Volume 3 Number 1, as it's referenced on the title page). This time out, our "Dueling Editorials" became one. (*Told you this wasn't unprecedented!*) We were reeling from the sudden loss of our good friend Dick Laymon, who died of a heart attack on Valentine's Day, 2001. As we discussed in that shared editorial, we had been working with Dick on what would have been a follow up to **A Writer's Tale** for *bare•bones*, since things had really turned around for him in the U.S. since the book was published. While Dick's death knocked the wind out of our sails, we managed to squeeze out a last issue in time for the show. Peter delivered another great annotated index—this time for *Justice*. David J. Schow was back with more commentary,

and his review/article on Trevanian's **Hot Night in the City** was such a great intro to the author, we've included that as our closing piece in this volume.

While working on an unpublished project with David Allen Brown, I found out that he had gotten to know Dan Ross, author of the *Dark Shadows* paperback novels. I asked him to do an article on that series for us. Not only did he deliver a great article on the published books, he also included the proposal for an unwritten novel in the series. Just the kind of juicy morsel that I knew our readers would appreciate.

Peter: And it fit in so well with the type of material we were presenting. I don't have very many memories about this one. It's extremely slim so, as John alluded, I think the project started weighing us down. After this issue, my writing pretty much shut down for ten years. This was in the day before print-on-demand and it was getting harder and harder to get dealers to pick up small press zines. But... let me stress... *bare•bones* never became the albatross *TSF* had become. I loved every minute of it.

John: So here we are. Inspired by **The Best of *TSF***, we hand-picked the contents of the volume you now hold in your hands to represent *bare•bones* at its very best. And where do we go from here, you ask? Well, plans are already underway for a *bare•bones* revival. We've reached out to a number of our existing stable of writers, and folks are excited. We're getting the band back together. We've even got a few pieces that have been sitting in cold storage, just waiting for the return of *bare•bones*. Plus we've got our eyes on some new folks that we're hoping to bring into the fold. We do hope you enjoy this collection, and will consider checking out the new and improved *bare•bones* in the very near future!

— returning in 2020 —

bare•bones

bare•bones

Premiere Issue
December 1997
$3.50 U.S.

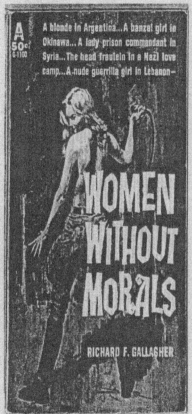

A blonde in Argentina...A banzai girl in Okinawa... A lady prison commandant in Syria...The head fraulein in a Nazi love camp...A nude guerrilla girl in Lebanon—

WOMEN WITHOUT MORALS

RICHARD F. GALLAGHER

UNEARTHING VINTAGE AND FORGOTTEN HORROR/MYSTERY/SCI-FI/WEIRD PAPERBACKS-FILM-PULP FICTION-VIDEO

THE TERRIFYING *NEW YORK TIMES* BESTSELLER!
"SANDFORD GRABS YOU BY THE THROAT AND WON'T LET GO...
TOUGH, GRITTY, GENUINELY SCARY."—ROBERT B. PARKER

RULES OF PREY

never KILL

JOHN SANDFORD

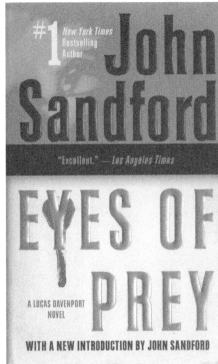

#1 *New York Times* Bestselling Author

John Sandford

"Excellent." —*Los Angeles Times*

EYES OF PREY

A LUCAS DAVENPORT NOVEL

WITH A NEW INTRODUCTION BY JOHN SANDFORD

The Electrifying *New York Times* Bestseller!
By the Author of *Rules of Prey* and *Eyes of Prey*

SILENT PREY

"Sleek and Nasty...
Superb!"
—*St. Paul Pioneer Press*

JOHN SANDFORD

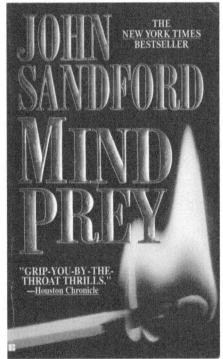

JOHN SANDFORD

THE NEW YORK TIMES BESTSELLER

MIND PREY

"GRIP-YOU-BY-THE-THROAT THRILLS."
—*Houston Chronicle*

*I love exhaustive overviews (I've penned a few myself). I had an Annotated Index feature scheduled to run in each issue, which would spotlight a short-run digest zine, and we wanted to include a similar article dissecting a novel series in each issue as well (high on my list, though never to materialize, was a piece on Dan J. Marlowe's "Drake" books). Bill Gagliani took to that task with a mighty vengeance. Of course, John Sanford's best-selling "Prey" series continues to this day (2019 saw the publication of his 29th, **Neon Prey**) and they seem to get better with each successive book. -Peter*

A DIRTY HARRY FOR THE NINETIES:
John Sanford's Lucas Davenport
by W.D. Gagliani

John Sandford added a new chapter to the book of noir fiction when he published his first Prey novel in 1989. Perhaps it says something about the impact of noir that each of the eight novels has been more successful than the previous. Perhaps it says something about society that we tend to like our heroes tough and macho and just a slight bit beyond right-wing, as long as their hearts are in the right place and they hesitate ever so slightly before slugging (or shooting) women. In a society where police are asked for increasingly repressive behavior and routinely given more latitude in dealing with alleged criminals, the Prey books seem to emphasize that police hands are hog-tied when dealing with suspects. The result is a collection of novels which, in most cases, advance an agenda decidedly right of center. The fact that the novels manage bestseller status eloquently points to the public's hunger for suspense, yes, but also their hunger for a strong and pro-active police force. And if some innocent people's rights are mangled in the process, well, they'll sort it out in the end.

John Sandford is the pseudonym of John Camp, a journalist for *The Miami Herald* from 1971 to 1978 and for *The St. Paul Pioneer Press* since 1978. He was named a finalist for the Pulitzer Prize in 1980 for writing a series of articles on Native Americans in Minnesota, and won the Pulitzer Prize in 1986 for a series on the Midwest farm crisis and its effects on a farm family. As Camp, he is the author of **Plastic Surgery: The Kindest Cuts**, and **The Eye and the Heart: The Watercolors of John Stuart Ingle**. Along with the "Prey" novels discussed in this overview, he has also written three other thrillers (both as Camp and as Sandford): **The Fool's Run, The Empress File**, and the newest, **The Night Crew**. Most have been bestsellers.

While one can't accuse Sandford/Camp of being a stylist, his straightforward prose cuts to the heart of a story in an appealing, uncluttered way. Writing instructors may continue to debate showing versus telling, but his journalist's tendency to describe simply—with no adornment or superfluous words—seems refreshing when compared to more impenetrable efforts, and more than likely accounts for a lot of his success with readers of all types. Unlike some authors who bask in the light of their own writing, Sandford tells a story in the most economical way possible. He lets dialogue carry major portions, with minimal use of annoying, overly creative tags; he jumps from scene to scene with generally unobtrusive transitions. Only occasionally does he stumble, and then it's usually a case of the scene having been trimmed with too sharp a razor—sometimes a few more words would help better orient the reader in the action. A small quibble, and one seen less and less in the later novels.

The Prey series stars Lucas ("... the guy's no couch.") Davenport, latest in a long and distinguished line of tough-guy macho cops doing their thing in the big city. Set in the relatively underused Minneapolis-St. Paul area of Minnesota, with occasional forays into northern Wisconsin, this isn't the typical big city of the traditional crime tale. Indeed, the setting is perfect for various kinds of narratives, since one can be in the middle of a major city one moment and deep in the North Woods on a remote lake within the hour. Lucas Davenport (LD from now on) likes to prowl the area in his decidedly un-police-like Porsche.

The flashy car makes him different, as does the killer's reputation—five or six bad guys ("Fuckin' Wyatt Earp," according to another cop), and his savvy ability to deal with the media. We learn nothing about his past, his childhood, or his origins, except that he is a lapsed Catholic. In **Winter Prey**, it almost appears as if he has a grudge against the Church or the priesthood, but the suspicion comes to nothing. Sandford prefers to deal in the present: LD's smile is described as scary, more of a grimace. In his spare time, he writes role-playing games and simulations, with which he has developed a nice side income (which allows him the car and expensive clothes). In essence, he is Sonny Crockett crossed with Dirty Harry, a cop for the Nineties, but no pretty-boy looks for him—he's big and his dark hair is just beginning to grey, and he has a wicked scar above and below his right eye (a fishing accident, of all things, in a neat twist on the cliché). He has a chipped upper incisor he never bothered to have capped, and a dark complexion—"He might have been an Indian except for his blue eyes." He inspires fear in the bad guys, and lust in the ladies. And what more does a hero need?

Occasionally, a hero needs helpful friends who are quirky enough to be interesting in themselves. LD is no different. There's Del Capslock (whose name "was taken off of a keyboard," according to Sandford), the undercover cop who was so good at playing a wino that he almost became one. There's Sloan, the fox-faced older cop who loves to drive LD's Porsche at illegal speeds. There's Sr. Mary Joseph, the former Elle Kruger, a high school chum who used to be beautiful but whose face was later marred by acne—she's in LD's gaming group now, and he consults her in matters of criminal psychology and ethics. LD's women have run the gamut from Jennifer,

news anchor and eventual mother of his child, to Carla (an artist), to Cassie (theater actress), to Weather Karkinnen, the surgeon who snares him in **Winter Prey** and stays with him through **Sudden Prey**, though the future is uncertain. Sandford has wisely decided to please cross-gender readers. LD is the prototypical womanizer—lusty, attractive, and desirable as all men wish to be—and gives male readers an image for which to strive and female readers an image with which to fantasize. This appears to have been a sound decision, as Sandford's books all sell extremely well.

On a more serious note, a favorite Sandford theme is the relationship between the police and the media, and how the typical media circus affects an ongoing investigation. LD is camera-friendly, and the chief of police is well aware of his appeal and more than willing to use it to the department's advantage. While this removes LD's anonymity for street work, it provides the authorities with a trusted and believable spokesman, and every major police force in the country wants one of those.

LD's willingness to deal with the media representatives, and mostly those from TV, comes from his—and Sandford's—understanding that the relationship is especially important given the importance of television in everyday life. News and information can be spread easily, to informants and often even to perpetrators, and basic facts can be manipulated for a variety of reasons. LD often shows Sandford's disdain of the TV media—he willingly trades information for favors, and occasionally plays TV stations like fiddles. This characteristic of the Prey series may be a curious bit of wish fulfillment—all law enforcement organizations probably have wet dreams about controlling the media (and all attempt it at one time or another), though they rarely succeed. Amidst all of that, LD remains acutely aware that ratings drive the market, and he dangles exclusives to just the right people at the right time. Presumably, Sandford draws heavily upon John Camp's experience as a print journalist, saving the sharpest barbs for the TV folks who labor in the ultimate environment of style over substance (anyone bother watching their local news lately?).

Sandford also has points to make about police department politics and its effects on investigations. Chief Daniel feels the pressure of an upcoming election. Chief Roux frets about her position because she is a woman in a man's world, and also because she has sights set on a Senate seat. Both chiefs shrug off experts' advice cavalierly, and both recant their opinion when faced with potential public outrage or political fallout. Both prefer to keep serial killer stories out of the media, since such stories produce public and political pressure and cast a department in a bad—ineffectual—light. One need not be an insider to sense that most major city police chiefs are driven this way, but Sandford/Camp has been on the inside enough to describe it in terms that are both ironic and vaguely appalling.

These themes, and others mentioned in the novel descriptions below, balance the action/suspense aspects of John Sandford's Prey books with enough real-world grounding to grant the series an informative sheen—though the earlier books were sometimes accused of weakness in the procedural descriptions, Sandford has clearly tightened up in that area.

After **The Night Crew**, Sandford plans two Prey novels in a row. If they follow the pattern, they will both improve on the formula which has made him a major player in the suspense thriller field.

Rules of Prey (1989) **1/2

Right from the start, Sandford paints Lucas Davenport (LD) in a light dappled with shadows. When we first see him, he is under police surveillance because someone in Homicide suspects he just might be the "maddog" killer who has murdered two women. Lucas is aware of the surveillance, but not the reason. He leads his watchers to the track, where he shares some inside information with the jealous cops --after all, how many other cops drive Porsches to work? Suddenly police chief Quentin Daniel calls off the surveillance. A third murder has just been committed, so Davenport can't be the perp. Might as well put him on the case. Before LD leaves the racetrack, he wins $22,000 in front of the shocked surveillance cops.

As the only cop in the Office of Special Intelligence, he is to run an investigation parallel to Homicide. From then on, LD uses his net of street contacts to hunt for this newly acknowledged serial killer, who chooses his female victims following a pattern no one has yet cracked. A young attorney in the county clerk's office, Louis Vullion—the maddog—spots his prospects during his daily routine and "collects" them later, after thorough surveillance and preparation. He leaves notes at the murder scenes: Never kill anyone you know, Never have a motive, Never carry a weapon after it has been used. Vullion kills because he likes it, because he gets a sexual thrill out of it, and he begins to taunt LD, who is visible in the media thanks to his reputation and car.

Though the back and forth between LD and the maddog is entertaining, it's not altogether novel. A bit of characterization that does work is the relaxed way LD falls into bed with Jennifer, a local news anchor (who will eventually bear his child but not marry him), and Carla Ruiz, an artist who survived a previous maddog attempt. LD juggles the two lovers with just enough guilt to be realistic, but ultimately without much remorse. Yet another shadowy area of his character is LD's use of yet another desirable anchorwoman as bait (and realistic is the way the maddog slips his surveillance and almost gets to her anyway—Sandford does not make cops invincible). Finally, LD's way of dealing with the maddog, preventing a potentially drawn-out trial, makes him a candidate for the Dirty Harry award.

Creaky at its worst, but engaging and told with just the right amount of zeal for the violence, this novel forms a good introduction to the LD character.

Shadow Prey (1990) ***

Three murders, three different cities. Same method—victims have their throats cut with an Indian ceremonial obsidian knife. Aaron and Sam Crow are on a spiritual warpath against racism, and the spirit has now given way to the outright murder of people who have been deemed enemies of Indians. But their assassins are falling prey to police one by one, and the Crows slowly come to rely on Shadow Love, the psychotic ex-con who might be one or the other's son. The problem is that even the Crows don't know his agenda, which includes eliminating those Indians he considers traitorous. Also on his roster is the murder of LD and Lily Rothenburg, a New York cop on loan to the Minneapolis PD because one of the original murders occurred there.

Lily Rothenburg is a beautiful woman who, as a cop, is everything LD might want. She carries a huge .45 semi-auto in her rigged purse—that's LD's favorite caliber, so it's true love even though Lily is married, albeit unhappily. In a firefight with one of the Crows' assassins, Lily uses the .45 to save LD's life and reduce the enemy's number by one. After that incident, LD and Lily are inextricably linked—and all the better in the eyes of Shadow Love. His attempt on Lily's life is almost successful, leaving her shot in the chest.

In the meantime, LD faces the Indian community's wall of silence, since most Indians at least tacitly agree with the Crows and their goals, one of which is to assassinate the current director of the FBI, a racist, Indian-hating pedophile named Lawrence Duberville Clay.

The novel boasts two climaxes. In one, the doomed Crows attempt to shoot their way out of a house in which they trapped FBI man Clay while he "entertained" a 12-year-old girl. The other climax occurs when Shadow Love, now a rogue assassin, shoots up LD's house when he goes for LD and his former lover, Jennifer. Both scenes are visual and written in the gutsy noir language Sandford doesn't always manage with total success.

According to an on-line interview with Sandford (available at the official Sandford web page), this novel was the least successful of the series. Perhaps it is too controversial, since the Crows are not entirely wrong in their motives, and LD's world is not so neatly packaged when his opponents make some valid points with

their generally illegal behavior. Indeed, the Crows come out of this novel with some semblance of nobility, while LD seems prejudiced and generally narrow-minded. LD believes other Indians should turn in the Crows because they are criminals—he can't comprehend the Indians' hateful silence, or how the offer of reward money is treated with disdain by even the poorest of the community. This theme is underscored when an agent of the Bureau of Indian Affairs, himself an Indian, is murdered by an outraged Shadow Love (who can no longer distinguish between friend or foe).

Shadow Prey is not painted in comforting shades of black and white, and may suffer as a result. LD is essentially an avenging angel, and comfort is to be had only when his instincts are true and his quest holy. Here, Sandford has made the equation more complex by offering multiple points of view and more rounded motivations. Yes, the Crows do act like crazed gunmen, going out with guns blazing in both hands—the Butch and Sundance imagery must be intentional—but their campaign is so clear-headedly political, their manifesto so convincing, that their deaths leave one hollow. The climactic battle between LD and Shadow Love is more comfortable to swallow, because this assassin is much more convincingly psychopathic. LD delivers the self-decreed death sentence, and all is right with the world.

Eyes of Prey (1991) ****

With this entry, Sandford reaches back into his bag-o- psychos and draws a doozy—pathologist Michael Bekker ... in love with his own beauty, referred to as Dr. Death while in the service, Bekker just wants to watch people die, and take notes. But he can't stand to leave their eyes whole, because he knows the eyes will haunt his dreams, watching, forever watching, keeping him from sleep and driving him insane. Therefore he destroys the eyes after death, knowing it's the only way he will avoid the restless ghosts. Most of his life is spent high on one illicit drug or another, often in such bizarre combinations that he himself isn't sure how they'll affect him.

Sandford borrows the Hitchcock device of the criss-cross, from *Strangers on a Train*, when Bekker uses Druze, a scarred young actor and acrobat, to kill Bekker's hated wife. In return, Bekker will kill Druze's biggest obstacle at the theatre, his employer. They will both mutilate the eyes afterwards, making it seem as though both murders are the work of the same killer. Since there is no connection between Bekker and Druze, the police will be too stupid to put it together. Of course, the corpses pile up as the situation spins crazily out of control and more murders are called for as cover-up. LD's sixth sense immediately pegs Bekker, but the doctor is wily.

LD is already on edge after the Crow incident, and here he almost kills a suspect who pulls a knife on him. Only his friend, undercover cop Del Capslock manages to keep him tethered. But LD's nerve is about to snap, and Chief Daniel assigns him Bekker's case to keep him busy. Plus, he's the department's ace media liaison—indeed, television newspeople love him, and anchorwomen flirt with him shamelessly. As mentioned earlier, LD understands the media's need for ratings so well that he is often able to manipulate local media to his advantage, either by give-and-take or by coercion. When dealing with a serial killer of Bekker's intelligence, it becomes necessary to work hand-in-hand with local media, even if both sides technically resent needing the other.

As the body count increases, LD begins to crack under the pressure. Not only is he tracking two killers, but there is also the knowledge that there was a witness to Bekker's wife's murder—her lover—who is willing to give anonymous hints, but won't come in because of his position. LD also begins a brief affair with a young actress who knows Druze, with tragic results. By novel's end, not only does LD mar Bekker's beauty with the rage of an animal, but he is also forced out of the department under threat of a media circus regarding brutality charges. He agrees to leave, but not before indicating that he knows the Loverboy's identity. The shocking finale reflects certain truths—trite as it sounds, good guys sometimes go bad and other good guys pay the price. These bits of unadorned truth make **Eyes of Prey** one of the best of the series, despite the standard psycho killer motif. Ending on a downbeat is gutsy in today's unambiguous climate, even if it's clear that LD (like James Bond) will return.

Silent Prey (1992) *1/2

This somewhat weaker installment screams to be turned into an incomprehensible movie starring a Baldwin brother (wait, that's been done before). On the surface, it should work—LD's best adversary to date, Bekker, recently escaped from prison and loose on the streets of Manhattan, luring innocent people to a cellar laboratory in which he can watch them die; Robin Hood, a cadre of cops who have been assassinating deserving victims (crooks and scumbags who got off scot-free) and have now escalated to include a fellow cop who could finger them; Lily Rothenburg, the woman cop whose gun is as big as LD's, now recovered from her own gunshot wound and assigned to hunt both Bekker and Robin Hood. No longer on the Minneapolis police force, and given that he captured Bekker in the first place, not to mention his experience in spinning the media, LD is called in to consult on the Bekker case—and to secretly help root out Robin Hood by using one investigation as a cover for the other. Lily's new lover, a highly-placed cop with a bad heart, may be Robin Hood's leader, but he is also the NY cop running Bekker. LD is partnered with Barbara Fell, partly to determine if she is a Robin Hood and partly as a device to give him some sack time while Lily is otherwise occupied.

While it's not quite a fish-out-of-water plot as the film *Coogan's Bluff*, Sandford consciously spins it as the tough-talkin' hick-from-Minnesota who packs a mean .45 proves himself on the streets of the real big city. Of course, LD must emerge not only unscathed but in the role of savior—the hick must show up the big city bullies. It's something of a cliché, and it burdens the book with an agenda almost too trivial to provide the suspense it needs—cops can't abuse their power, shouldn't take the law into their own hands, yadda yadda yadda. It's all too reminiscent of another Dirty Harry movie, *Magnum Force*, in which rogue motorcycle cops go the vigilante route. If **Silent Prey** had stuck with Bekker, instead of complicating things with his role as a witness to Robin Hood's cop-killing, the novel would have retained Sandford's usual focus. Unfortunately, too much side business tends to obfuscate an otherwise serviceable plot.

Winter Prey (1993) ***

The fifth installment of the LD canon carries with it a strange ambivalence— it is both one of the best, and yet the most frustrating of the series.

The Iceman invades the bleak north Wisconsin winter, arriving in a snowmobile and leaving behind a ruthlessly butchered family of three in a smoldering house. The Iceman is out to retrieve an incriminating photograph from a kiddie- porn tabloid. He has no luck finding it, so he disappears back into the persona of an innocent citizen outraged by the horrible crime.

Sheriff Carr, overwhelmed by the killer's cold- bloodedness, asks out-of-work LD to consult. LD is wintering in his Wisconsin lake cottage, so he ends up deputized and virtually in charge of the investigation, which is hampered by a small-town religious disagreement, among other things. Before long it becomes apparent that a kiddie-porn ring is operating in the area, and the killer is afraid he'll be recognized from the missing photograph. The Iceman, whose point of view is featured, begins killing both witnesses and co-conspirators. But who is he? As LD races from clue to clue, the Iceman is always a step ahead.

LD meets Weather Karkinnen, surgeon and part-time ME, and before long finds himself again in a relationship. The Iceman, meanwhile, fears that Weather could definitely identify him from the photo, so the doctor tops his hit list. LD manages to protect her but not others, and the bodies pile up in the frozen waste. Along the way, we see the Iceman interacting with teenagers "trained" in the ways of sex and pleasure, one of whom is a young girl who loves the Iceman because he's the only adult who's ever been "nice" to her. These scenes, though jarring, become crucial later.

Winter Prey is superb in the manner in which Sandford evokes a northern Wisconsin small town (in one scene, Weather describes the six local restaurant choices with dead-on accuracy) gripped in a typically dangerous winter freeze. The outdoor sections are so well-rendered that they are likely to induce chills even if read in summer. The novel is also significant because it is the only one of the eight structured as a traditional mystery. We may be privy to the Iceman's thoughts and moves, but his identity is not soon revealed.

Unfortunately, there is little shock value in the Iceman's true identity, though it seems there should be. The red herring of the suspicious ex-alcoholic Catholic priest is both obvious and ultimately somewhat distasteful due to LD's less than sensitive approach to the priest's demons—so insensitive, I mistakenly thought Sandford intended to outline LD's childhood abuse at the hands of a parish priest. LD's fascist outbursts, supposedly an ends-justify-the-means approach, here reinforce his Dirty Harry image without actually broadening the scope of his character. One senses that LD would likely have been a fine schoolyard bully himself.

Another disappointing aspect of the novel is LD's tendency to merely react to events. He is unable to prevent the Iceman from killing anyone on the list, with the exception of his new girlfriend, Weather. He does not truly "detect" the identity of the killer, but rather has it forced on him by the killer himself. Lastly, the novel is noteworthy also for the final scenes, in which LD is shot and Weather saves his life. This shooter's identity is actually shocking, thereby making the end more of a statement than what came before.

Winter Prey can be said to succeed if one considers that cops aren't Sherlock Holmes or Miss Marple types. A case could be made that these weaknesses are actually an unusual sense of realism—after all, police tend to be merely reactionary. Inasmuch as LD is a stranger in town, hampered by attitudes and the extreme weather, this is about all one could expect. Though it doesn't function as a proper mystery, **Winter Prey** manages to capture one of the realities of police work—cops are all too often left to do clean-up after the fact, and no amount of law enforcement savvy will change that. The surprise of the final scenes underscores this theme—even LD can lower his guard in certain situations.

Winter Prey also succeeds with its laser-like portraits of small town people and cops. For instance, Sheriff Carr realistically attempts to tread the fine line which separates his friendships from his official duties. Deputy George Climpt—LD's partner—represents an older version of LD, and the two get along because they share methods and mindsets.

While not perfect, **Winter Prey** shows Sandford at his frustrating best. If nothing else, it'll make you wear your mittens the next time you venture out in a Midwestern winter.

Night Prey (1994) **1/2

Koop is a bodybuilding cat burglar who moonlights as a serial killer, though no one has yet put the pattern together because his victims span several years and states. No one, that is, until state investigator Meagan Connell, an unpopular feminist who happens to be dying of cancer. She has made catching this killer of women her life's work, knowing she has little life left.

Rose Marie Roux, the new police chief, has appointed LD Deputy Chief of Intelligence, to work serial killers and other offbeat crimes. Now she assigns him to work with Connell, well aware the two don't see eye to eye—at least until some grudging respect is built.

The intense first scenes make Koop the cat burglar an intriguing opponent, as he invades a beautiful stockbroker's apartment. His inside info on Sara Jensen is superb—her movers have provided him with a key impression and cased her jewelry for him, for a cut. But as Koop steals through Sara's bedroom, he is smitten by her sleeping beauty. In one surprising moment, he leans over her and lightly licks her forehead. Then he takes her jewelry

and disappears. He is also led to acquire a key for the building across the street and sets up a post on the roof, from which he can watch her shower and dress.

Meanwhile, LD works on the Koop case and a strange locked-room murder case, as well as continuing his media spinning for the department. Even though he is still living with Weather, LD can't help but respond when Jan Reed, another lovely TV news anchor, begins flirting with him—his womanizing tendencies and urges are as much a part of his character as James Bond's. He remains faithful, if tempted, and somewhat defensive as a response to the guilt he feels.

Though LD masterminds a trap for Koop, it's Sara Jensen who willingly leads him to the authorities. By then she has reasons of her own to want the burglar captured or dead. In the end, it is Meagan Connell who delivers the novel's poignant ending by sacrificing herself to her cause and thereby fulfilling her life's purpose.

Night Prey is entertaining enough, but Koop is an unworthy opponent for LD, who seems bored. Sandford seems bored too—why else give LD a second case, and an ally more determined to catch Koop than he is? Plus, LD's game business is doing well enough now to afford him an ample second income, and his new position keeps him off the streets. Is it any wonder the novel's focus slips, causing it to drag? Koop makes a creepy enough burglar, but he lacks the charisma of Bekker, or even the maddog—who can forget Dirty Harry's opponent, Scorpio?—proving once again that the antagonist in the crime thriller is every bit as important as the sleuth.

Mind Prey (1995) ***1/2

Sandford rebounds hard and well with this intense novel of kidnapping and deadly games. John Mail, a deranged young gaming and computer freak, is the author's best antagonist since Bekker.

When Mail snatches psychiatrist Andi Manette and her two young daughters, everyone assumes it's a simple matter of ransom—Manette's family is moneyed and politically connected. But Andi recognizes the young convict she attempted to treat years before, when she worked at the state hospital for the criminally insane. He was the one who scared her by confessing his sexual interest in her. Now at his mercy, trapped in a farm cellar with her daughters and no way to escape, Andi attempts to call on her psychiatrist's insight to beat him at his own game. But when Mail comes for her the first time, it's clear that he is not motivated by money, but by sex and revenge. The nightmare begins.

LD investigates various members of the family—Andi's father, a downward spiraling political player; her ex- husband, a successful builder; her mother, quietly suffering through her husband's infidelity; and her business partner, an abrasive psychiatrist for whom Andi's death could be a windfall. Motives and motivations intertwine, until LD is forced to look elsewhere, all the while instinctively sure that the family is something to look at. But Mail has covered his tracks well, assuming a dead man's identity, and the connection between kidnapper and victim is not readily apparent.

Meantime, Mail begins to taunt and challenge LD directly, confident of his own computer skills and gamer's abilities. He has studied LD's games and simulations, which makes him a more formidable foe than at first thought. LD finds himself reluctantly admiring Mail's ability to lead them all by the nose. LD's game company is now worth millions and run by a professional manager, and LD brings the company and some of the programmers into the investigation as bait, knowing that Mail can't resist the challenge of playing against those who write the games he loves.

The novel twists and turns as LD and Mail thrust and parry. The authorities are not altogether sure Andi Manette and her girls are even still alive, but LD begins to drive Mail more than the kidnapper realizes. A mysterious informant who keeps Mail apprised of the investigation makes for a solid subplot. Meanwhile, Mail continues his sexual assaults of Andi and plans a finale in which she dies and he disappears.

The balance of the novel is just right, bringing it within range of the genre's Holy Grail, **The Silence of the Lambs** by Thomas Harris. Sandford plays all the cards in exactly the right order, when he's not holding them close to the vest. LD is as ruthless as ever in his quest, not so much to rescue the victims, but to win. He relishes the hunt, the game, and a worthy opponent like Mail—who enjoys the chase even though he is its subject.

Sandford layers in a couple of extra themes for good measure, but this time they don't detract. One is the philosophical debate regarding Andi Manette's confidential patient records—are they sacrosanct, though they could save her life? While rummaging through the files, cops find crimes confessed by patients but not reported (as by law) by Manette. Sandford speaks through LD often, and his stance might not be ACLU-approved but it does fit LD's right-wing lean, which is part of his "charm," as it were (again reminiscent of Harry Callahan). It's easy to side with him when he turns out to be right.

Yet another distraction is the fat engagement ring LD has bought Weather—he carries it in his pocket and twirls it, waiting for the right moment, or perhaps the decision that marriage is what he really wants. LD is essentially a lover of women—all women—and he's not at all sure he wants to change that. His dilemma, while sexist to the extreme, seems endearing rather than annoying. That Weather is completely aware of the whole situation provides sweet irony and humor.

In an ending right out of *Dirty Harry*, LD plays judge, jury and executioner in a subtle, fatal manipulation of Mail's claustrophobia. LD knows the system, and—in his world—the system can't be trusted to mete out justice, but he can.

Add up the quality of the antagonist, the *Dirty Harry* trappings, the themes explored, and LD's marriage fears, and **Mind Prey** rates high as a forceful thriller with enough ambiguity to mirror real life.

Sudden Prey (1996) ***1/2

The most recent LD novel takes a stripped-down approach and delivers a near-flawless bolero of death. If using a musical term to describe a novel seems outlandish, consider that the bolero is characterized by a repetitive motif which increases in volume and orchestration, creating a sense of intensity. In **Sudden Prey**, three gunmen out for revenge repeat the motif of almost casual death and murder.

LD's team tracks two women bank robbers and lays back, waiting. When the women shoot an innocent bystander, members on LD's team kill both women in a shoot-out. LD is criticized for manipulating the women into committing the robbery by not apprehending them sooner.

The women were the sister and wife of Dick LaChaise, a hardened criminal in prison for various violent crimes, as well as connections to the Seed (a sort of midwestern motorcycle gang/militia hybrid possibly styled after the Outlaws motorcycle gang). When LaChaise is allowed to attend the funeral of his women, he escapes from custody with help from two equally psychopathic buddies. Then they converge on the Twin Cities, where—armed with automatic weapons and even a compound bow—they start a campaign of death against three cops of LD's team. In a brilliant stroke of terrorism, the LaChaise gang (as they are referred to in the media) begins by targeting the cops' spouses. Two out of three assassination attempts are successful, and suddenly LD and Del and the other cops can only attempt to stay out of sight. Other spouses and girlfriends, including LD's fiancée, Weather, are sequestered in a "safe" hotel guarded by a legion of cops.

But LaChaise and his henchmen, Martin and Butters, seem suicidally fearless—they have already resigned themselves to a violent death (much like the Crows of **Shadow Prey**, though without the sheen of political ideals). Because they are ready to die, ready to make spur of the moment plans, and ready to change those plans, they become fearsome weapons of retribution. It's to Sandford's credit that his portrayal of the three gunmen rings true and occasionally edges into poignancy, when clearly showing how and why they became so cold-hearted. That the three retain some

humanity after their horrifyingly casual acts of violence is both amazing, and a tribute to Sandford's increasing facility with layered brushstrokes.

When LaChaise is wounded in a shoot-out with Del, they kidnap his sister-in-law, a horse rancher with some medical training. From then on, Sandy Darling is forced to play a game in which the police don't know if she is a willing accomplice or a hostage. To further complicate the different aspects of LaChaise's rampage, Sandford introduces a crooked cop, Stadic, who is blackmailed into feeding LaChaise information on the cops' spouses, and who then attempts to play a solo version of the game in order to clean up after himself—killing witnesses who can finger him, feeding both fellow police and LaChaise bad or spotty information, and generally making himself a nuisance the police just don't realize exists. Stadic even saves LD's life at one point, but his motive is really to make sure the gunman dies without a chance to ID him as the cop on the take. Hopped up on no sleep and eventually uppers to keep going, Stadic watches his secure perch unravel bit by bit, as his preventive strikes get out of hand and he spirals out of control.

Another complication is Weather's attitude at being confined and kept from surgery. It's easy to agree with LD's frustration in dealing with her, knowing that LaChaise is saving Weather and LD for last. This subplot will doubtlessly be explored in the next Prey novel, for it raises the ugly specter of Weather's independent streak clashing with LD's mostly conservative, somewhat chauvinistic attitude. Indeed, **Sudden Prey** has the most ambiguous ending of the series, at least in terms of LD's long-term relationship and its chances.

In an amazingly effective exploration of the media theme, LD and another cop are caught on videotape laughing uncontrollably over the body of one of the gunmen. Local television stations make mincemeat out of the police, running the brief clip over and over, while the community expresses its outrage at the police thugs' insensitivity. What the tape does not show is that LD and the other cop had just sent a fatally-wounded fellow cop to the hospital, and that their laughter (which they can barely remember) was merely an automatic reaction to the fact that the gunfight did not turn into a hostage situation even though the gunman had been cornered in a private home and held a family captive which he could have used as a bargaining chip. Once again speaking through LD, Sandford hopes to use the scene to show that the public's opinion of police and police work is flawed by a lack of understanding and empathy. The scene and its repercussions serve to make the point.

The final scenes are riveting and written with the tight control of someone who has learned to be comfortable with his primary characters. Sandford proves with this novel that he has found a groove, and that Lucas Davenport deserves to be considered a player in the stakes for memorable lawmen of noir and near-noir fiction.

Consulted for aspects of this article:

"John Camp/John Sandford," by David Finkle. *Publisher's Weekly*. June 29, 1990. 83-84.

An interview with John Sandford conducted by Sean Doorly on AOL (April 9, 1997), as available on the John Sandford Web page maintained by Roswell Anthony Camp. *(no longer online)*

The John Sandford Web page *(no longer online)*

I met Bill Crider through Ed Gorman, who told me Bill would be a great addition to The Scream Factory. *Ed, as usual, was right. Bill contributed a few spot reviews and a killer piece on horror westerns to TSF. Bill also sent us a list of "forgotten crime gems," novels that had not yet gotten the widespread approval afforded Goodis or Thompson. I hunted down all 14 of those recommendations and devoured them in no time. Bill was a very enthusiastic and giving man; he'd trumpet on his website the stuff John and I were doing without a nudge. As I recall, the following interview was supposed to run in* Paperback Parade *but I liked it so much I kept it for myself. Bill died in February 2018, but his enthusiasm and knowledge can still be enjoyed at billcrider.blogspot.com* -Peter

A TALK WITH BILL CRIDER
by Peter Enfantino

We first met Bill Crider at a World Fantasy Con in Chicago several years ago. Actually, we thought we were meeting Jack MacLane, but Crider showed up instead. Cliff Brooks, our co-editor in the pioneering early years of *The Scream Factory*, had become, well, enamored of Jack because of a tome known as **Goodnight Moom**. I have actual memories of Cliff performing a pirouette across his living room, a copy of aforementioned Zebra horror novel in one hand, and... well, never mind what he was doing with the other. He just really liked the book a lot. In fact, he put it on his "Top Ten Best Novels of the 1980s" list in *TSF #7* (which, by the way, is still available as a back issue elsewhere in this mag). So we met Jack/ Bill at the Con and were bowled over by how nice a guy he was. When it came time for us to do an article on Western Horror, the Bill half of the writing team was recommended by Ed Gorman as *the* expert on that subgenre. We caught up with Crider to find out what he's been up to recently.

bare•bones: You were one of the first to get involved in "paperback fandom." What was it like back then?

BILL CRIDER: I feel a little like a dinosaur answering this one. I got started in paperback collecting in the Jurassic era, before there was any organized paperback fandom. What interested me was paperback original mystery novels. I just started buying all I could find. Fool that I was, I didn't pay any attention to the condition of the book; all I cared about was the author. And of course I didn't care about covers or anything like that. I just wanted to read the books.

BB: Were there any kind of networks of fans to become involved with?

CRIDER: I didn't know anyone was collecting except me until I did an article on pb original publishing for a mystery fanzine called *The Mystery Readers Newsletter*, edited by Lianne Carlin. Several people who subscribed to that fanzine wrote me, including a guy named George C. Hoyt, who was also collecting pb originals. He had an extensive Want List, including a lot of Michael Avallone books, some of which I was able to help him out with. His collection was probably even more than his Want List. When I mentioned in a letter that the only John D. MacDonald book I didn't have a copy of was **Weep For Me**, he sent me one by return mail. No charge. That's what the hobby was like in those days. There were several others that I corresponded with, including Pat Erhart, who collected Jim Thompson. I sent her a couple of Thompson books. The Hillman **Nothing More Than Murder** was one of them, and it was later returned to me by someone who bought it from Pat's collection after her death. Bill Pronzini was collecting then, too. He wrote a letter to the fanzine about my article. All of this was in the late 60s and early 70s, so there was a network out there, and there were already collectors, though mostly people collecting certain authors or certain kinds of books (mysteries or SF, usually) rather than trying to get, say, a complete run of Handi-Books or every book with a Bonfils cover.

BB: You were involved with one of the first fanzines devoted to vintage paperback collecting, *Paperback Quarterly*. Tell us about the zine, and your involvement.

CRIDER: Billy Lee, who started *PQ*, got interested in collecting because of me, I think. I was always telling him about my books, and he got the bug. I was living in Brownwood, Texas, then, and Billy, Charlotte Laughlin (Billy's wife) and I used to travel all over the place looking for paperbacks. We'd go to San Angelo, Abilene, and anywhere else we could drive from Brownwood. Billy thought a lot of people would be interested in reading about paperbacks, so he got the idea of doing a fanzine. Right from the start he recognized the importance of reproducing the covers, and he printed the first issue of the zine on a photocopy machine so he could he shoot covers. The covers didn't turn out very well, but they were better than nothing. Catherine and L. Sprague de Camp visited Brownwood about this time, doing some research on Robert E. Howard, so Billy used them on the cover of his first issue. There was quite a bit about the de Camps and Howard in *PQ* after that, and Charlotte later became de Camp's official bibliographer. For the first couple of years, when *PQ* was struggling along, Billy, Charlotte, and I wrote most of the articles. (Billy used a couple of pseudonyms for some of them, as I recall.) Later on, we got some other contributors, and the magazine got a lot better. Bill Lyles, Tom Bonn, Michael Barson, and M.C. "Bunker" Hill are the names that come to mind. There was some pretty good stuff in *PQ*, and some great photos of covers considering the technology we had to work with. We even had color. Billy took photographs, had multiple copies printed, and glued the photos into every copy of the magazine that he sent out. There was one cover I especially remember, not a photo, that was done by Piet Schreuders. He drew a map of New York in the 1950s in the style of a Dell Mapback and located all the publishing houses on it. It was a wraparound, and I have one of them framed in my office at work. Billy even did a *PQ* calendar one year, with each month featuring a different paperback cover. I still have one of those calendars, too. Billy had some great ideas, but he was ahead of his time. Today you see pb cover art on all kinds of card sets and postcard books (some of them done by Michael Barson), and I like to think they're descended from *PQ*. I furnished a lot of books for Billy to photograph, wrote a lot of the articles, and even helped in the production of the magazine. After Billy stopped photocopying and started using more sophisticated equipment, he'd go down to the printing shop and do most of the work himself to save money. After each issue was printed, I'd help him fold and staple the print run. It was a lot of work, but we had a good time.

BB: Why was *PQ* discontinued?

CRIDER: For one thing, the circulation was never very high, and Billy was losing money. I guess there just wasn't enough collectors then, or at least not enough who wanted to subscribe to a fanzine. Too, Billy and Charlotte started a family and the kids took up a lot of their time. (They still do!) Billy still has his collection, though I think he'd love to sell it.

BB: Are you still active in pb fandom?

CRIDER: I still collect, though certainly not as avidly as before. I have most of what I really want in the way of pb originals, except for a few Ace doubles and a couple of really elusive Harry Whittington titles. Of course there are a few zillion things I'd like to have just for the fun of it, and if I ever win the Texas lottery, I'll indulge myself. I subscribe to both *Paperback Parade* and *Books Are Everything!* and read everything in every issue. Now and then Gary Lovisi or R.C. Holland can tempt me into writing something about collecting, but I'm reluctant because I'm awed by the scholarship that's on display these days. Billy Lee and I were really just amateurs compared to the writers on the scene now.

BB: Aside from the high prices, a price guide, and the advent of pb shows, what are the differences and similarities of fandom then and now?

CRIDER: Obviously the easy answer to that is the big difference is that there are a heck of a lot more people involved these days, and they seem to have a lot more money to spend. I cringe when I see the prices that some books are bringing, and I'm sure glad I got mine when I was paying a nickel or a dime for them, even if they aren't in "Gem Mint" condition. One of the similarities is that there still *seem* to be a lot of very nice and enthusiastic people in the hobby. Most people I've met through pb collecting are genuinely interested in sharing information and even books with one another, and they really seem to enjoy the hobby.

BB: What are your vices as a collector?

CRIDER: My major vice is still pb originals. I do collect reprints by certain authors (Hammett, Chandler, Ross MacDonald, John D. MacDonald, Harry Whittington), and I have a weakness for spectacular covers when I run across them. I like Dell dimers, and for sleaze I like the old Beacon books. I'm especially interested in "backwoods" books, whether written by Whittington or anyone else. (I did an article on that topic for *The Journal of Popular Culture* 12 or 15 years ago, with photos by Billy Lee.)

BB: Any exciting or rare finds on your trips?

CRIDER: When I started collecting, good finds weren't that unusual. I picked up copies of all Jim Thompson's books before I ever knew anyone else was interested in him. I ran across a whole box of like-new first printings of John D. MacDonald's books in one store, and Ace doubles used to be fairly easy to pick up. Billy Lee and I used to compete every year at a library sale in Brownwood to see who would come up with the best finds. I remember once that I grabbed a copy of the L.A. Bantam **Jokes and Wisecracks** right out from under his nose, and while I was gloating he picked up an unread copy of the first Avon printing of **Perelandra** that had been lying under the Bantam. I learned a good lesson about gloating from that episode. One of my favorite memories of Billy's collecting is from the time we went to Bouchercon in Milwaukee. I don't know whether this is still true, but at that time there was a used-book store in the Milwaukee airport. We stopped by while waiting for our return flight, and Billy bought two full boxes of books. I carried one on the plane, and he carried the other. Milwaukee at that time (about 1980) was a great place for old pbs.

BB: Give me a few "hidden treasures" that haven't been discovered yet, along the lines of Jim Thompson or **Black Wings Has My Angel**.

CRIDER: I guess I was the first one to write much about either Thompson or **Black Wings**, in that article in *The Mystery Readers Newsletter* that I mentioned. I'm not sure there's anything like that left around, though I can't for the life of me figure out why no one's seriously trumpeting the talents of Charles Williams. When it comes to story-telling, he tops just about everybody. I'd think all of his Dell First Editions or Gold Medals would be high on anyone's reading list. (My own favorite happens to be **River Girl**, which is a Gold Medal Giant, probably not that easy to find.) Lionel White and Ovid Demaris are two more Gold Medal writers you don't hear enough about. For my "undiscovered classic," though, I'd nominate a book called **The Hot Shot** by Fletcher Flora. It's an Avon from about 1956, and I think it's great. It's a crime novel, about gangsters and fixed basketball games, as told by someone who sounds an awful lot like Holden Caulfield. And it works. Anyone who has a copy and hasn't read it is in for a real treat.

BB: When you made the step from fan to pro writer, did you find yourself emulating any of your favorite writers?

CRIDER: The truth is that, as much as I'd like to write like my favorite authors, I can't write like anyone but myself. For better or worse, what you get in one of my books is pretty much me. I do use different styles in different books, but all the styles are my own.

GOODNIGHT MOON

He lusted for death by the light of the moon!

Jack MacLane

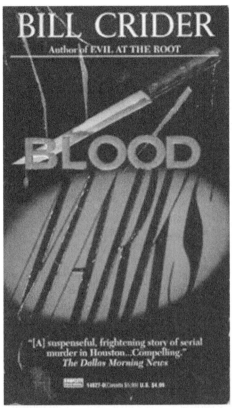

BILL CRIDER

Author of EVIL AT THE ROOT

BLOOD MARKS

"[A] suspenseful, frightening story of serial murder in Houston...Compelling."
The Dallas Morning News

A DAN RHODES MYSTERY

BOOKED FOR A HANGING

BILL CRIDER

AUTHOR OF THE TRUMAN SMITH MYSTERY SERIES

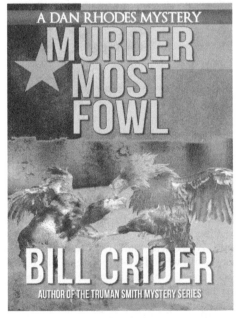

A DAN RHODES MYSTERY

MURDER MOST FOWL

BILL CRIDER

AUTHOR OF THE TRUMAN SMITH MYSTERY SERIES

BB: Since you write in all different genres, who are your influences in each? How about westerns?

CRIDER: In westerns, my strongest influence without a doubt would be Harry Whittington. *(ed. note: Bill has committed himself to an article on Whittington's westerns for a future issue of bare•bones)* I think I've read every western he ever wrote. But then I've also read a lot by Donald Hamilton, who wrote some darn good ones, and Elmore Leonard and Louis L'Amour and lots of others.

BB: Horror?

CRIDER: I'm not sure I've been influenced much by any one that I can name. I've certainly read a lot of Stephen King, but my books are nothing like his (probably to the detriment of my sales).

BB: Mystery and suspense?

CRIDER: Too numerous to mention, but I'll name some of my favorite writers: Raymond Chandler, Dashiell Hammett, Ross MacDonald, John D. MacDonald, Charles Williams, Harry Whittington, Donald Hamilton, Jim Thompson, Mike Avallone, Lionel White, Ovid Demaris. And that's just the beginning. You'll notice that most of those guys aren't writing anymore. I like a lot of the more recent writers, too, but I wasn't influenced by any of them as far as I know.

BB: You've written several horror novels under the pseudonym Jack MacLane (including the much-acclaimed **Goodnight Moom**). Why weren't these Bill Crider novels?

CRIDER: I didn't want to confuse the readers. Bill Crider is the guy who writes those nice books without very many dirty words and without any hot sex scenes. He writes the books that my mother can recommend to her friends. Jack MacLane, on the other hand, is a nasty boy. He writes about blood and gore and disgusting stuff like that, and there's even sex in some of his

stories. Jack and I are distinct personalities, and he writes entirely different kinds of books, in different styles.

BB: Your first novel (not counting your Nick Carter novel), was released in 1986. Why did it take you so long to get into the writing aspect of books?

CRIDER: Good question. I always wanted to write books, but somehow I just never got around to it. I was in school for a long, long time (four years as an undergrad, six in grad school), so I did a lot of writing, but all of it was in the form of term papers. I didn't have time for fiction, and to tell the truth I was intimidated by all the great writers I was studying. I had the idea that if you couldn't be William Faulkner, why bother? It took me a long time to get over that. After grad school I toyed with the idea of writing poetry, and I actually published poems in a couple of literary magazines. My first national sale was a poem, in a magazine called *The Runner*, which eventually merged with *Runners' World*. But I still had the idea of writing fiction in the back of my mind. I wrote a fantasy novel that was never published, and then a friend suggested we do a Nick Carter book. We sold that one, and I thought that maybe I didn't have to be Faulkner after all. I found out I could be happy being Nick Carter. So finally I got started doing what I'd wanted to do all along.

BB: You've written 9 novels set in the universe of Sheriff Dan Rhodes and his goofy deputies. The series is a little like *Andy Griffith* meets *The Rockford Files* in that it combines suspense (at times very dark) with a dash of humor (also very dark at times).

CRIDER: I'm not sure exactly what inspired Sheriff Rhodes, but I think Andy and Barney and Mayberry are probably in the mix. I love *The Andy Griffith Show*. My stuff is a little darker than that, though, because even though I enjoy writing humor, I have a twisted mind and Jack MacLane's always lurking in there somewhere. **Murder Most Fowl**, the 7th Rhodes book, opens with

Rhodes discovering a body floating down a creek in a portable outhouse. I just enjoy doing stuff like that.

BB: Another aspect of the Rhodes novels I found refreshing is a "continuing timeline," that is, the books do not ignore what happened in previous novels. In fact, each succeeding novel expands on incidents from past books. Such as Rhodes' continuing romance/courtship with Ivy Daniel.

CRIDER: Wow! I've been waiting a long time for someone to bring that up. You're the first one who's noticed, or at least you're the first one who's commented on this aspect of the Rhodes books. In the Rhodes universe of 9 novels, only a little more than a year has passed since the first book, though it's been 12 years in our world. I've taken Rhodes right through the seasons in chronological order. This was deliberate, as was the fact that characters from the earlier books keep turning up in the later ones. A lot of the characters from **Booked For A Hanging** turn up again in **Murder Most Fowl**, for example. Rhodes lives in a small town in a small county, and he keeps running into the same people, just as he probably would in real life. Not very much about the Rhodes books was planned from the beginning, but these things were. I'm glad someone finally caught on.

BB: **Blood Marks** is an excellent addition to the serial killer genre. Since it could easily be classified as horror, why wasn't this a MacLane book?

CRIDER: Originally, it was. It's a long story, but basically what happened was that in the middle of a two-book contract, Zebra changed editors on Jack and me. The new editor didn't want a serial killer book, so I told my agent to look for another paperback publisher. She thought the book was so good that she sent it to my hardback editor, who bought it immediately. I wanted to publish it under the MacLane name, but the editor didn't. The editor won. As it turned out, getting the book into hardcovers was the best thing that could have happened. It got better reviews than anything I'd done, it

sold to paperback, and it's had a couple of foreign sales. So it's done very well for me.

BB: In addition to Dan Rhodes, you've got two other series characters, English Lit Professor Carl Burns (autobiographical?), and P.I. Truman Smith. What sets these characters apart from the hundreds of other fictional P.I.s out there these days?

CRIDER: First of all, Carl Burns isn't really autobiographical (despite what my wife might tell you), even if he does have my initials (reversed, of course). He's an English teacher, but that's about where the similarity ends. What makes him different from other amateur detectives, according to some of the letters I've had, is that he always seems to be getting beaten up by women. How many detectives can make that claim? I think the supporting cast in the Burns books is also pretty entertaining, especially Boss Napier, a "Tuckerization" of Cap'n Bob Napier, who publishes a letterzine called *Mystery and Detection Monthly*. I like to think that Truman Smith is in the tradition of Chandler and Hammett, and *Publishers Weekly* said something like that in their review of **Dead on the Island**, though others may not agree. Smith gets scared when he gets shot at, and he doesn't like violence at all. He's not very good at it, which sets him apart from a lot of fictional P.I.s. I've always loved private-eye fiction, and the Truman Smith books are my feeble tribute to the writers I've admired for so long.

Following the publication of our premiere issue, Bill Crider wrote:

I've been remiss in thanking you for the interview in bare•bones, which was undoubtedly the best interview anyone's done with me. And the magazine is great, too. One of these days, I might even do that article on Whittington's westerns.

Best,
Bill Crider

BILL CRIDER BIBLIOGRAPHY

The Coyote Connection (a Nick Carter novel; in collaboration with Jack Davis) Charter, 1981

Too Late to Die (Dan Rhodes) Walker, 1986; Ivy, 1989.

Shotgun Saturday Night (Dan Rhodes) Walker, 1987; Ivy, 1989.

Ryan Rides Back (western) Evans, 1988; Ballantine, 1989.

One Dead Dean (Carl Burns) Walker, 1988.

Cursed to Death (Dan Rhodes) Walker, 1988; Ivy, 1990.

Galveston Gunman (western) Evans, 1989; Ballantine, 1990.

Dying Voices (Carl Burns) St. Martin's, 1989.

A Time for Hanging (western) Evans, 1989.

Death on the Move (Dan Rhodes) Walker, 1989; Ivy, 1990.

Evil at the Root (Dan Rhodes) St. Martin's, 1990; Ivy, 1991.

Medicine Show (western) Evans, 1990.

A Vampire Named Fred (juvenile) Temple, 1990.

Blood Marks (suspense) St. Martin's, 1991; Gold Medal, 1993.

Dead on the Island (Truman Smith) Walker, 1991.

Gator Kill (Truman Smith) Walker, 1992.

Texas Capital Murders (mystery) St. Martin's, 1992.

Booked for a Hanging (Dan Rhodes) St. Martin's, 1992.

...A Dangerous Thing (Carl Burns) Walker, 1994.

Murder Most Fowl (Dan Rhodes) St. Martin's, 1994.

When Old Men Die (Truman Smith) Walker, 1994.

Winning Can Be Murder (Dan Rhodes) St. Martin's, 1996.

The Prairie Chicken Kill (Truman Smith) Walker, 1996.

Mike Gonzo and the Sewer Monster (juvenile) Minstrel, 1996.

Mike Gonzo and the Almost Invisible Man (juvenile) Minstrel, 1996.

Mike Gonzo and the UFO Terror (juvenile) Minstrel, 1997.

Murder Takes a Break (Truman Smith) Walker, 1997.

Murder By Accident (Dan Rhodes) St. Martin's, 1998.

AS JACK MACLANE:

(All horror, published by Zebra)

Keepers of the Beast, 1988.

Goodnight Moom, 1989.

Blood Dreams, 1989.

Rest in Peace, 1990.

Just Before Dark, 1990.

AS CLIFF BANKS:

Tunnel Rats Popular Library, 1989.

AS JACK BUCHANAN:

Stone M.I.A. Hunter #10: Miami War Zone Jove, 1988

Stone M.I.A. Hunter #12: Desert Death Raid Jove, 1989.

Stone M.I.A. Hunter #14: Back to 'Nam Jove, 1990.

GIVING ME THE CREEPS
The Legend of He Who Kills
by John Scoleri

The Doll. The Zuni fetish. He Who Kills. Whether or not you know him by name, chances are you're familiar with him. He was the memorable star of Dan Curtis' *Trilogy of Terror*; an anthology film comprised of three adaptations of stories written by the celebrated grandmaster of horror, Richard Matheson, each starring Karen Black in a different role. The Zuni segment, titled "Amelia," continues to resonate with viewers decades after it first aired on March 4, 1975 as ABC's Tuesday *Movie of the Week*.

William F. Nolan adapted the first two-thirds of *Trilogy of Terror*: "Julie," based on Matheson's story "The Likeness of Julie," originally published in the anthology **Alone By Night** (under his pseudonym Logan Swanson to avoid two stories appearing in the same book under his own name), and "Millicent and Therese," based on Matheson's story "Therese," originally published in *Ellery Queen's Mystery Magazine* under the title "Needle in the Heart." Matheson had to know that Nolan didn't stand a chance of being remembered for the two stories that preceded his knockout punch. The author himself adapted his story, "Prey," originally published in *Playboy* in April of 1969. A young woman and her overbearing mother have an argument, after which the woman breaks a date with her boyfriend and ends up spending the evening alone in her apartment with a unique gift she had planned to give him. He Who Kills. An authentic Zuni fetish,

"Prey" story illustration from *Playboy* by Martin Hoffman.

with a scroll explaining that it contains the spirit of a Zuni warrior, held in check by a gold chain around its waist. When the chain accidentally slips off (oops!), hilarity ensues. For the next twenty minutes, this frenetic, maniacal creature terrorizes Karen Black.

The telefilm received a nice push from the network, and they made no effort to keep the doll as a surprise to the audience. Not only does he appear in the display ad for the show in *TV Guide*, he also garnered a two-page color spread in the magazine (see following pages).

While the original short story is very suspenseful, the telefilm succeeds thanks to the brilliant work of Erik von Buelow, the designer of the Zuni fetish props. In 1991, an original prop sold at

auction for $4,400—well over the $1500-2500 estimate. I've had the rare opportunity to hold one of the original prop heads in my own hands, and the little guy is pretty terrifying even when he's not scampering around the floor, nipping at your ankles.

I expect that most everyone who saw the original broadcast can still recall the state in which director Dan Curtis left them, as the titles came up on Karen Black's smiling, possessed face. That little doll

burned himself into my subconscious, and I'm sure was the cause of many restless nights and bad dreams of all the things in my room coming to life. Though I didn't know it at the time, it was just the first of many times the work of Richard Matheson would leave an indelible impression on me.

My wife will never forget her first experience, either. After the program aired back in 1975, she found herself babysitting for a family with an asthmatic

Sidebar and photos from
TV Guide March 1-8, 1975

What a Doll!

The churlish little chap you see menacing Karen Black at the left is a doll aptly named He Who Kills. He's a "Zuni fetish" creature who pursues the unfortunate Miss Black through "Amelia," a segment of *Trilogy of Terror*, an ABC TV-movie encompassing a trio of supernatural stories, to be broadcast this Tuesday (March 4). Getting an 8-inch-tall doll to chase someone around an apartment is a tricky job, even for TV's special-effects experts—especially since, in this case, the persistent critter gets kicked, beaten, drowned, stabbed, squashed and smashed but keeps coming back for more. Designer Erik von Buelow fabricates He Who Kills out of a plastic material that lets the doll maintain its original shape no matter what's done to it. For added charm, he gave it three expressions: ugly, uglier and ugliest (above). And he designed a wheeled model that was operated by a team of free-lance special-effects men from under a false floor. Later, because producer Dan Curtis was dissatisfied with the way the doll ran across the floor, designer von Buelow came up with a motorized version. The cost of running the little fellow through its paces was a not-so-little $15,000—more than many human guest stars are paid. But the producers had no choice in the matter—8-inch character actors are very hard to find.

Chihuahua. Imagine the raspy growl of a small dog scurrying across the linoleum floor, providing an all-too similar sound to our Zuni friend. She spent the evening on the couch with her feet up off the floor, just waiting for He Who Kills to get her.

The original telefilm was first released on home video from MPI in the late 80s, along with a special release of just the Zuni fetish segment under the title, *Terror of the Doll*. It was a thrill to finally be able to revisit the story on demand (a privilege lost on those of you who grew up in the home video era).

Fortunately, it's easier now than ever before for fans to revisit the legend of He Who Kills. Matheson's story "Prey" is one of several stories included in the TOR edition of **I Am Legend**, and *Trilogy of Terror* has not only has seen several DVD releases through the years (Anchor Bay in 1999, a special edition from Dark Sky Films in 2006), it is now available in a newly restored deluxe edition (both DVD and Blu Ray) from Kino Lorber (though shame on them for spoiling the closing shot of the telefilm with the cover art).

Of course, it was only time before the inevitable remake or sequel. If you wondered how William F. Nolan might have handled adapting Matheson's "Prey," you need look no further than *Trilogy of Terror II*. Broadcast on October 30th, 1996, the program was once again comprised of three stories directed by Curtis. Each stars Lysette Anthony, who had done a fine job as Angelique in Curtis' 1990 reboot of his classic *Dark Shadows*). The first two segments, Nolan's adaptation of Henry Kuttner's "The Graveyard Rats" and a recycled Matheson script, "Bobby" (previously filmed more effectively for the Dan Curtis anthology **Dead of Night**), are quickly forgotten as anticipation builds for the return of the doll. "He Who Kills," co-written by Nolan and Curtis, picks up shortly after where the original teleplay left off. The police have discovered the dead bodies of Amelia and her mother in her apartment. They also find the charred remains of our little buddy in the oven, where he was last seen in doll form in the original film, and they take him to the police lab to undergo Lysette's forensic investigation. As you might expect, all hell breaks loose. Sadly, the story is so derivative of the original that it's a disappointment.

Despite the change of characters and setting, all of the key plot points are there. The only thing Nolan and Curtis managed to leave out this time was the "terror" in the trilogy. Not even the new doll footage makes it worth watching. I can't imagine anyone introduced to the tiny Zuni nightmare by way of this offering seeking out the original. And while this segment doesn't really stand up on its own, since the plotlines are so similar, if someone did watch the original after seeing this, almost all of the suspense would be spoiled, having presented the audience with a blueprint of the original teleplay. If none of the original creators had been involved, perhaps *Trilogy of Terror II* could have been written off as a cash-grab by someone who managed to get their hands on a hot property. Surely Curtis and Nolan could have come up with something—anything—that would have played better than what was produced. On the bright side, the poor reception has thus far prevented a *Trilogy of Terror III*.

But it turns out that television wouldn't be the last rodeo for our Zuni friend. For **He Is Legend**, a 2009 Richard Matheson tribute anthology, writers were invited to create original stories set in Matheson's fictional universes, including sequels, prequels, and companion stories. Joe R. Lansdale delivered "Quarry" as his take on He Who Kills. It tells the story of a man who acquires a similarly packaged Zuni fetish from an antique shop (lest anyone think there was only one of these African souvenirs offered for sale). Lansdale does what he can to give the reader something fresh, but at the end of the day, it's the same basic premise. Zuni comes home. Zuni gets loose. Zuni goes on the hunt. Like the majority of the contents of the tribute anthology, it's an interesting, albeit unnecessary, curiosity.

My personal favorite tribute arrived out of the blue in an issue #26 of the *Animaniacs* comic book published by DC Comics. Our familiar Zuni graces the cover, which parodies the classic EC format with the title **Tales from the Tower**. It contains "Tickle-Me Evil," a six-page story written by Sen Carolan and Jennifer Moore, and illustrated by Leonardo Battic and Scott

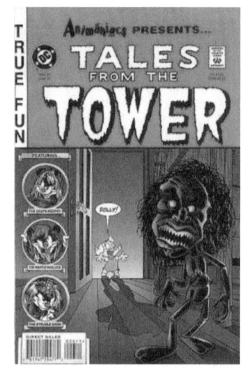

McRae, in which a little girl is given the Zuni fetish for her birthday. As she tosses him around, the Zuni mimics the popular *Sesame Street* Tickle-Me Elmo doll, laughing and pleading not to be tickled. Oblivious to the child, the doll comes to life and attacks, and gets into a very Looney Tunes cartoon-style fight with the family dog. The dog ultimately saves the girl, but the last panel of the comic reveals that she is now possessed; trademark sharp Zuni teeth and all.

For those of you (like me) who always dreamed of being the proud owner of a Zuni warrior, you're in luck. Majestic studios issued a 1:1 scale replica of He Who Kills about 15 years ago. It's a nice display piece, and was reasonably priced when issued, though prices in the secondary market have gone up considerably since then. More recently, Hollywood Collectibles Group offered a limited edition prop replica. While not cheap at $300, it's the finest Zuni that has been offered to date (that's him on page 34). If you do get yourself one, just be sure he doesn't lose his chain.

Trust me. He Who Kills is not dead. He's just waiting for the ideal moment to return...

bare•bones

Volume 1 Number 2   Spring 1998 $4 U.S.

**UNEARTHING VINTAGE AND FORGOTTEN
HORROR/MYSTERY/SCI-FI/WESTERN
FILM-PAPERBACKS-PULP FICTION-VIDEO**

RICHARD S. PRATHER

A novel of blondes and violence
by the creator of SHELL SCOTT

PATTERN for PANIC

BERKLEY BOOKS
G-98
35¢

COMPLETE
AND
UNABRIDGED

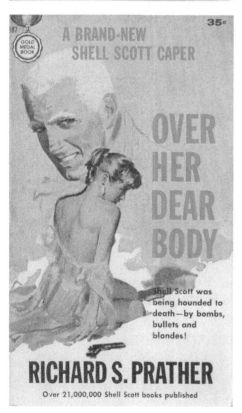

A BRAND-NEW
SHELL SCOTT CAPER

35¢

GOLD MEDAL BOOK

OVER HER DEAR BODY

Shell Scott was being hounded to death—by bombs, bullets and blondes!

RICHARD S. PRATHER

Over 21,000,000 Shell Scott books published

RICHARD S. PRATHER

25¢

GOLD MEDAL BOOK

DARLING, IT'S DEATH

Over 10,600,000 Prather books sold

More SHELL SCOTT Shenanigans

40

One of the things I desperately wanted to do with bare•bones was to chronicle the "Gold Medal Days" (as Ed Gorman coined it) of crime paperbacks. Ed had sent me down a rabbit hole of collecting years before and I was obsessed with the Gold Medal label. I think Richard Prather's love and frustration with the company that made him (and that he, in turn, made a lot of money for) come through perfectly in the following interview... -Peter

DIG THAT CRAZY 'TEC!
Richard Prather Interview
by Thomas Deja

You could make a good argument for Shell Scott being the most successful private eye of the 50's.

Unlike Mike Hammer, who has lived on in a series of films and television incarnations, Shell Scott might be an unfamiliar name to many newer fans of noir and detective fiction. What these fans don't realize is that during the 50's and early 60's, this creation of former Merchant Marine Richard Prather outsold pretty much everybody on the map. The books, with memorable titles such as **Take a Murder, Darling, The Scrambled Yeggs, The Cock-Eyed Corpse**, and **Dig That Crazy Grave** promised a heady cocktail of sex, violence, wild action and hip dialogue. And Shell, a six-foot-four giant with close-cropped hair, made an impressive host, noir detective as porn star. The greatest thing was, Prather *delivered.* The best Shell Scotts were shaggy dog stories that never let up. In the Scott novels, Prather seemed to be holding all the conventions of every noir detective, from Marlowe on down, up to a funhouse mirror. Whether the books feature defaced giant nudes, a costume party where our hero dressed up as a clown, or a presidential candidate whose speeches were lip-synched, you're guaranteed some of the strangest, most inventive—and fun— detective novels of all time. Richard Prather knew how to spin a yarn, and didn't disappoint throughout over forty novels.

Unfortunately, a bad experience with Pocket Books in the 70's caused Prather's output to dwindle. He seemed to disappear off the map until a renewed interest in Scott brought him back with two new novels, **The Amber Effect** and **Shellshock**. But then Prather split from his then-publisher Tor, and it looked like it was all she wrote for Shell Scott.

Luckily, that's no longer true. Borgo Press is in the process of publishing a career retrospective by Graham Andrews, **Two Just Men: Richard S. Prather and Shell Scott**. Furthermore, new Prather material will be surfacing in an anthology of detective fiction edited by Ed Gorman and Martin Greenberg, and a new novel called **The Death Gods** may be in the offing. For fans of the most famous resident of the Spartan Apartments, this can only be good news.

In the following interview, Prather discusses his entire career, from his determination to be a writer through his years with Gold Medal and Pocket and his present status.

*bare•*bones: What went into the creation of Shell Scott?

RICHARD PRATHER: I've thought about that over the years, because you don't really know where these things come from. It's like when you're writing and it's going very well, it's almost like the words and ideas are flowing through you from somewhere else. It came from a lot of places. I originally called him Brad Crane.

BB: Really?

PRATHER: Yeah, and I'm glad I changed it. I had a friend when I was in junior college, a guy named Brad Voight. He looked a little like my later description of Shell Scott, a good-looking guy, had sort of angled, blondish brows and hair, except his hair was long, very well built, very bright guy. All his mental attributes and muscularity, his daring and courage and ability to shoot people ... that's basically me. (laughs) If you buy that, we're on our way. You'll buy anything.

BB: I noticed the first handful of Scotts were fairly straightforward before they became the grand noir farces that we all know and love. When did you decide to have fun with some of the noir conventions?

PRATHER: This sort of goes back to the question of where I got Shell Scott. I had done a lot of reading in the (field of) mystery. I'm sure you already know that the biggest influence on me was Raymond Chandler, two of his books particularly.

BB: I don't think you can be a private eye writer and *not* be influenced by Raymond Chandler.

PRATHER: No, because he changed the field. Anyway, the first book I wrote, I called it **The Maddern Caper**, although it wasn't published under that name. Then came **The Case of the Vanishing Beauty**, **Bodies in Bedlam**, and so on. Very quickly, a little more humor and strange or wild situations Shell'd get into occurred, and it was never anything I planned. It was sort of an organic

development, just what appealed to me. And I was always looking, when I plotted a book, for something new, something that was fresh to me that nobody had done before. I just seem to gravitate to situations where Shell could be a little outrageous—under the bed with his pants off while Bull Harper's coming in to see his sweetie, that sort of thing.

BB: The titles were so distinctive, instantly memorable. How'd you come up with them?

PRATHER: Well, you can give credit to me for some, to my wife for **Bodies in Bedlam**, but most of them I can't take credit for. When I was with Fawcett/Gold Medal, in fact most publishers reserve the right to change the title. Well, I didn't like it, and I objected—it goes back to the first book I had published, **The Case of the Vanishing Beauty**. I called it **Laughter of a Cadaver**, and editors and publishers apparently think the public is illiterate. Maybe it is today, but it wasn't then. They changed my title, I complained, and that was my first lesson in how publishing worked, because they still called it **The Case of the Vanishing Beauty**. I complained because (Erle Stanley) Gardner was still big back then, and all of his books were **Case of** this and **Case of** that, and I wanted my books not only to have my title on them, but not to sound derivative. But the editors and publishers think more in terms of packaging, and they know more about packaging than I do. I know how to write the books, and they know how to sell them.

But many others—for example, **The Meandering Corpse** was originally called **The Peripatetic Corpse**. I guess they thought people wouldn't understand peripatetic, but if they don't understand peripatetic, they won't understand meandering. Several of the books are like that. **Take a Murder, Darling** is theirs, **Everybody Had a Gun** was mine, **Pattern for Murder** was mine, **Way of a Wanton** was mine—actually not quite. I had called it **Wanton's Wake**, and they changed it to **Way of a Wanton**. **The Wailing Frail** was their title, as was **Have Gat-Will Travel**, because

42

that was a take-off on *Have Gun-Will Travel*.

BB: How much input did you have in the packaging for Gold Medal, especially since in the 50's you were raking in the bucks for them.

PRATHER: Yeah, we were their biggest seller for many years, and overall I guess I was their biggest seller. I had nothing to do with the packaging at all. What happened in the early 50's, maybe '53 or '54, I talked to Dick Carroll, the beloved late editor (of Gold Medal) one time when he was out on the coast. You know, it bothers me to think I tried to avoid meeting him for as long as I could. I didn't want to meet editors or publishers or anything. He told me how (Prather Months) came about—I didn't know, all I knew was that they started printing more of my books and reprinting several others, putting on new covers and stuff. And he said that they checked all their authors and all their titles to see what had been their best sellers, and it turned out that my books had sold more than anyone else on their list. And I had given them more books than any other author. I kept turning them out like crazy.

BB: You averaged about two a year, if I remember right.

PRATHER: Yeah, and in the first two or three years I was working sixteen, eighteen hours a day and going to bed and getting up and working seven days a week. That's not the way I am now; I've been there, done that. But I had given them all those books and it'd turned out they were selling really well after a slow start. So that's when they began having what they called "Prather Months'." Particulary when they had a new book, they'd bring out the new book and would reprint all the old ones, or most of them. Of course that was great in those days, because writers were not then used to being paid on print order. You know how it is now—they pay you on what they call the net sale, but it's not a net sale, because no net sale is reported. This is one of the fights I've been in for a long time. But anyway, in those days they paid on print order, so

when they brought out a hundred thousand or two hundred thousand, they gave you a check for that amount.

BB: One of the things that made Shell Scott great was that he was almost the exact opposite of Mike Hammer and the other noir detectives.

PRATHER: Yeah, that was just coincidental, because I hadn't read Mike Hammer when I started. Have since then, and think Spillane's a good man, writes well with narrative drive and power. I'm not one of the guys who knocked him, because he's been knocked a lot.

I guess you can almost say (Shell and Hammer) are diametrically opposed. Even in appearance. I deliberately made Shell look different from anyone else I knew. Part of it might've been this friend I had, but it was mainly just trying to make him different from the average private eyes.

BB: Yeah, when we think of noir private eyes, we think of Humphrey Bogart, all dark and craggy --

PRATHER: Or Dick Powell. But Shell sort of started that way. I did like I do with all my characters, fill a page or two with description and background, things that don't even get into the book so that I know the characters pretty well. He just turned out to have short cropped white hair, angled brows and big 6' 2".

BB: You mentioned **Pattern for Murder**, which was written under a pseudonym originally and later was rewritten as a Shell Scott.

PRATHER: It was originally written as a Shell Scott. **Pattern for Murder** was the first book I wrote, called **The Maddern Caper**. I sent that to Scott Meredith, who I looked up in *Writer's Digest*. But that book didn't sell right away; it took two and a half years to sell. When it was finally published by Graphic Books in '52—I started and wrote it in '49—I had written, I don't know, seven or eight books. Gold Medal had brought out **The Case of the Vanishing Beauty**, **Bodies**

A RICHARD PRATHER BIBLIOGRAPHY

THE NOVELS

Always Leave 'em Dying (Gold Medal, 1954)
The Amber Effect (Tor, 1986)
Bodies in Bedlam (Gold Medal, 1951)
Case of the Vanishing Beauty (Gold Medal, 1950)
The Cheim Manuscript (Pocket, 1969)
The Cockeyed Corpse (Gold Medal, 1964)
Dagger of Flesh (Falcon, 1952)
Dance with the Dead (Gold Medal, 1960)
Darling, It's Death (Gold Medal, 1952)
Dead-Bang (Pocket, 1971)
Dead Heat (Pocket, 1963)
Dead Man's Walk (Pocket, 1965)
Dig That Crazy Grave (Gold Medal, 1961)
Double in Trouble with Stephen Marlowe (Gold Medal, 1959)
Dragnet: Case No. 561 (Pocket Books, 1956), as "David Knight"
Everybody Had a Gun (Gold Medal, 1951)
Find This Woman (Gold Medal, 1951)
Gat Heat (Trident, 1967)
Joker in the Deck (Gold Medal, 1964)
Kill Him Twice (Pocket, 1965)
Kill Me Tomorrow (Berkley, 1955)
Kill the Clown (Gold Medal, 1962)
The Kubla Khan Caper (Trident, 1966)
Lie Down, Killer (Lion, 1952)
The Meandering Corpse (Trident, 1965)
Over Her Dead Body (Gold Medal, 1959)
Pattern for Murder - aka **The Scrambled Yeggs** (Graphic Books, 1952), as "David Knight"
Pattern for Panic (Gold Medal, 1961)
The Peddler (Lion Books, 1952) as "Douglas Ring"
Ride a High Horse - aka **Too Many Crooks** (Gold Medal, 1953)
Shellshock (Tor, 1986)
Slab Happy (Gold Medal, 1958)
Strip for Murder (Gold Medal, 1955)
The Sure Thing (Pocket, 1975)
The Sweet Ride (Pocket, 1972)
Take a Murder, Darling (Gold Medal, 1958)
The Trojan Hearse (Pocket, 1964)
The Wailing Frail (Gold Medal, 1956)
Way of a Wanton (Gold Medal, 1952)

THE COLLECTIONS

Three's A Shroud (Gold Medal 665, 1957)
  Contents: Blood Ballot; Dead Giveaway; Hot-Rock Rumble.
Have Gat—Will Travel (Gold Medal 677, 1957)
  Contents: Sinner's Alley; Code 197; The Build-Up; Trouble Shooter; Murder's Strip-Tease; The Sleeper Caper.
Shell Scott's Seven Slaughters (Gold Medal s1072, 1961)
  Contents: The Best Motive; Crime of Passion; Squeeze Play; Butcher; Babes, Bodies and Bullets; The Double Take; Film Strip.
The Shell Scott Sampler (Pocket 55028, 1969)
  Contents: The Guilty Party; The Live Ones; The Da Vinci Affair; The Bawdy Beautiful; The Cautios Killers.

THE SHORT STORIES

Babes, Bodies and Bullets (*Shell Scott*, July 1966)

The Barbecued Body (aka Crime of Passion)

The Bawdy Beautiful (**The Shell Scott Sampler**)

The Best Motive (*Manhunt*, January 1953)

Blood Ballot (*Menace*, November 1954)

The Bloodshot Eye (*Shell Scott*, June 1966)

The Build-Up (*Suspect Detective*, February 1956)

Butcher (*Manhunt*, June 1954)

The Cautious Killers (*Shell Scott*, November 1966)

Code 197 (*Manhunt*, June 1955)

Crime of Passion (*Manhunt*, December 25, 1954)

The Da Vinci Affair (*Shell Scott*, February 1966)

Dead Giveaway (**Three's a Shroud**)

Death's Head (aka The Best Motive)

The Double Take (*Manhunt*, July 1953)

Film Strip (*Ed McBain's Mystery Book #1*, 1960)

The Guilty Party (**The Shell Scott Sampler**)

Gun Play (*Shell Scott*, August 1966)

Hard Rock Rumble (aka Hot-Rock Rumble)

Hot-Rock Rumble (*Manhunt*, June 1953)

Kill the Clown (*Manhunt*, June 1957)

The Kubla Khan Caper (*Shell Scott*, April 1966) *abridgement of Trident novel*

Lie Down, Killer (*Justice*, July 1955) *abridgement of Lion novel*

The Live Ones (**The Comfortable Coffin**, Gold Medal, 1960.)

Murder's Strip-Tease (*Thrilling Detective* Vol. 71/ No. 1, February 1953)

Nudists Die Naked (*Manhunt*, August 1955)

Pattern for Panic (*Manhunt*, January 1954) *later released as novel*

The Rival Act (*Manhunt*, October 1957)

Sinner's Alley (**Have Gat—Will Travel**)

The Sleeper Caper (*Manhunt*, March 1953)

The Spirit of the Convention (*Accused*, May 1956)

Squeeze Play (*Manhunt*, October 1953)

Trouble Shooter (*Accused*, January 1956)

in Bedlam, and **Everybody Had a Gun**, and because the books were beginning to sell well and Richard Prather and Shell Scott were Fawcett/Gold Medal property in a way, they felt I shouldn't sell a Shell Scott novel to anyone else. So the agreement was, we would change the name—my name became David Knight—and I don't remember, but I think it became a Shell Scott book.

BB: It became **The Scrambled Yeggs**.

PRATHER: That's right. So it had three titles—**The Maddern Caper**, **Pattern for Murder**, and **The Scrambled Yeggs**. I kinda like **The Scrambled Yeggs** now, even though it wasn't my title.

BB: Tell us about the collaborative novel you did with Stephen Marlowe.

PRATHER: Oh, that was **Double in Trouble**. Back in '50, I got a letter from Scott Meredith, who was both mine and Stephen Marlowe's agent. I had read Marlowe's Chester Drum books, but we had never met, never talked and never corresponded. But I guess he and Scott Meredith and maybe Dick Carroll came up with the idea. I didn't know anything about it. The idea was we would write a book with these two contrasting investigators, Shell Scott on one side and Chet Drum, who was more dour and quiet, on the other.

BB: Drum was more conventionally noir.

PRATHER: To make it short, I agreed to give it a try, warning Marlowe in advance about the way I plot. He wrote me, I wrote him, we sort of got together on what the plot would be about, and I did my own outline and he did his. But we wrote individual chapters—it started out with my chapter, and he got that and sent me the second chapter, and I followed on from that with three, making sure I picked Shell Scott up where he was at the end of chapter one. So I did one, three, five, seven, and so on, and Marlowe did the rest. It turned out to be easier than

I thought in one way. It was a difficult job, putting it all together and not incensing Steve and he not incensing me because we work so differently. But it turned out pretty well, and after about a year of voluminous correspondence and working out plot problems so we'd both be satisfied, he flew out to Laguna Beach where my wife and I were living at the time and we got together to work out the rough edges. Tina typed the manuscript while we were working on parts of it, put it together finally, dedicated it to Dick Carroll, and I guess it was a pretty big seller right off the bat. I'm glad I did it, but I don't want to do it again. I like just sitting in the office alone with my portable on my lap and hack away.

BB: Was there any interest in bringing Shell to the movies?

PRATHER: Well, that's one of the mysteries of my life. At one time, most of my books were (selling) over a million copies. In fact, for a lawsuit I listed the top ten authors who had written the most million-copy best-sellers and I'd done more than any of the others at the time. But on the list there were nine who had movies or television (made from their books) and there was me.

There were two deals closed, options taken that never went to fruition. In one case, there was a merger and the deal got lost in the shuffle. I know Marty Giraud and Dick Shepherd wanted to make **Find This Woman**, and that fell through. The upshot of it was there never was a movie or a television series, although it was projected and talked about. But it's never happened, and I've never been able to understand it. I'd think with all the books, somebody could make a fortune if a producer wanted to make a series.

BB: Tell me about the switch to Pocket in the 60's.

PRATHER: That was 1962. I'd been with Gold Medal Fawcett and doing fairly well, was very happy with them. But by September '62, we hadn't made much money—only about a fourth as much as the previous year—and I was just working on

a book and got a call from Scott Meredith. I had later discovered that he had been talking to other publishers about moving me. Not for me; I was happy where I was. He said he would come out to see me and asked me if I knew what it was about, you know, wondering if I had heard any rumors. I said, 'I dunno, is Gold Medal going to reprint all the books or something?' He said he'd tell me when he got there.

So he flew out with his brother Sidney and came to our home in Laguna Beach. He had a contract with Pocket Books written out, ready for me to sign if I wanted to. The thing is they were willing to pay me an advance against royalties—I won't get into the big rip-off; I sued them finally - but this advance against royalties, you naturally expect you'd get your advance and, as a little time goes on, the books will sell enough to exceed the advance. But anyway, they were willing to pay me $75,000 a year against royalties with no books in hand. I was supposed to do twenty-five books for them and they would pay me the $75,000 *plus* royalties.

This impressed me. I didn't really want to leave Fawcett, cause I was happy with them. They'd done a really good job with me and at that time they were using those marvelous McGinnis covers, which were the best I'd ever had. I, foolishly perhaps, felt that if Pocket was willing to pay me $75,000 a year with no books at all in hand, this expressed quite a bit of confidence in what could be done. Of course, Scott Meredith did a good selling job on me, too. The upshot is I met with Roscoe Fawcett, Charlie Rubes and Ralph Day, and they flew out to Laguna. We met at my home and talked about it. I was ready to go to Pocket Books, was hoping that Fawcett could match the offer, because they had twenty-two or three books by then. I was their best seller on the list. So I asked if they'd match the offer, thinking they would. I said, 'No way I'd leave if you matched it.'

Anyway, they declined to do that, so I went to Pocket and wound up suing them.

BB: Did you want to kill the guy who decided to feature photo covers with a guy

GOLD MEDAL BOOK

SHELL SCOTT grinned: "I want the facts, ma'am. Just the bare facts."

STRIP FOR MURDER

35¢

OVER 22,000,000 SHELL SCOTT BOOKS SOLD

RICHARD S. PRATHER

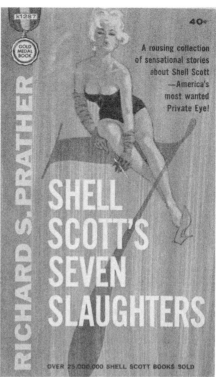

GOLD MEDAL BOOK

k1287

40¢

A rousing collection of sensational stories about Shell Scott —America's most wanted Private Eye!

SHELL SCOTT'S SEVEN SLAUGHTERS

OVER 25,000,000 SHELL SCOTT BOOKS SOLD

RICHARD S. PRATHER

GOLD MEDAL BOOK

s1051

35¢

She was a siren, all right, and I'm SHELL SCOTT... answering her call

THE WAILING FRAIL

OVER 23,000,000 PRATHER BOOKS SOLD

RICHARD S. PRATHER

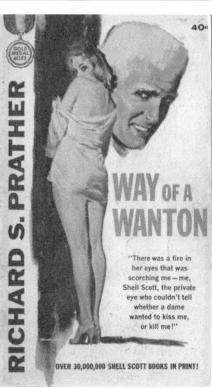

GOLD MEDAL k1382

40¢

WAY OF A WANTON

"There was a fire in her eyes that was scorching me—me, Shell Scott, the private eye who couldn't tell whether a dame wanted to kiss me, or kill me!"

OVER 30,000,000 SHELL SCOTT BOOKS IN PRINT!

RICHARD S. PRATHER

in a cotton ball wig on them?

PRATHER: Well, I didn't even like their first covers. Before the first book was published—that was **Dead Heat**—I didn't like it all, particularly when those (Fawcett) McGinnis covers had been so beautiful. Fawcett had been bringing out every reprint with a new McGinnis cover. The one I like is for **Strip For Murder**. I think Sheri Hite, who wrote **The Hite Report**, posed for that one.

Anyway, back to **Dead Heat**. It seemed like they just got worse until this sappy-looking guy with the flower in his hair on those photographic covers. It was very painful. It was more painful to get royalty payments that recorded ten thousand copies shipped and eighty-four hundred copies returned.

That was a very stressful time at the beginning, because in order to go to Pocket, I still had two books to do in order to finish my contract with Fawcett. I had to do those, which would be **Joker in the Deck** and **The Cock-Eyed Corpse**. Then I had to do one for Pocket, which was **Dead Heat**. Then in November of '63, I was writing the second book—that was **The Trojan Hearse**, which was my conservative view, opposed to socialism and so forth—when Kennedy was killed. I was sitting in my little room when that happened. It made it very hard to finish the book.

But I went on there. I only did a total of thirteen for Pocket, because by the time I got my second set of royalty statements I knew they were boning me. I knew something was extraordinarily amiss. Two of my books with Fawcett were paid, not on print order, but shipments minus returns, and I never had more than a fraction of one percent of returns. Then all of a sudden with Pocket, while Fawcett was still outselling what Pocket *claimed* to be selling, I saw these *enormous* returns— seventy thousand returns, eighty thousand returns. I later found out how they did it; it's all a shuffle on paper. At least I had two books on the Fawcett list that were still net sales to compare to Pocket, and I eventually had to enter into a lawsuit against (Pocket).

BB: I'm assuming the lawsuit was the reason why you stopped writing the Shells in the 70's.

PRATHER: Well, I initiated the lawsuit in '74, the lawsuit in '75, going back to New York for arbitration. I won the court case, but ended up getting screwed by some attorneys. I spent five years on that lawsuit full time. Whatever I'm doing, I tend to do it full-heartedly, whether it's writing a book or suing a publisher, so I didn't write anything at that time. Also, I knew Simon and Schuster/Pocket Books was the biggest publisher in the country and probably had about fifty attorneys on retainer, and it was just me and my one or two attorneys against them, so I couldn't afford to waste any time. Especially since, by the time we got to the lawsuit, Pocket had used its circuitous accounting to claim I owed them $350,000. If I had lost the lawsuit, I would've been stuck with them another ten years because, strangely, even though they were going bankrupt publishing me, they still wanted me at the same terms for another ten years. Only I would've started out in debt three hundred thousand dollars. And there was no way I could've earned that.

BB: Let's jump ahead to 1986. That was a big year for you, because you received the Grandmaster Award from the Private Eye Writers of America, and the first Shell Scott in ten years, **The Amber Effect**, had been published by Tor. How did you feel getting the award?

PRATHER: It just knocked me outta my tree. I was asked to come back to the Bouchercon in '86, and nobody gave a hint that the life achievement was in the offing. I had no clue whatsoever, not until I got back there. If I had been told I had forgotten; I thought I was just gonna appear and sign books, and of course **The Amber Effect** was coming out and this was good for sales. But as far as any kind of award, I didn't have a clue. I think Ed Gorman was very instrumental in my getting that. In fact, when I talked to him on the phone, I told him that was my knowledge so I owed him.

I remember I was appearing on a panel about private eyes, and I went back to sit down and said, "I can pretty much head for home." (LAUGHS) And someone started talking about the Life Achievement Award, and I'm thinking about getting outta there and having a smoke, you know. Then I heard my name. I started paying closer attention, and sorta went into shock, because it seemed that my editor at Tor mentioned my name and asked me to come on stage. They handed me this plaque and I started saying, 'My God, this is fantastic!' They told me later people were applauding, like they always do—you could say "this is Joe Zilch," and they'd go off—and I talked right through the applause and nobody heard a thing I said. (The plaque) is sitting up on the wall in here behind a stack of books; I can still see half of it.

BB: You also had **The Amber Effect** coming out at that time, as you mentioned earlier.

PRATHER: **The Amber Effect** was written while I was still under contract to Pocket. As a result of the lawsuit, I was given a nickel and a dime, but it also ended the contract, wiped out the money that Pocket falsely alleged that I owed them and returned to me all the rights to the books that they published and the one remaining manuscript, . That had been written in '73 or'74. I had that, and wrote another one after Tor had decided to publish **The Amber Effect**, **Shell Shock**. The only one we wrote specifically for Tor was **Shell Shock**, and then we had a falling out, too.

BB: You've just completed a new Shell Scott.

PRATHER: Yeah, it's sitting right here. It's about eight inches high, about a thousand (manuscript) pages. It's called **The Death Gods**, a book I've been working on forever, it seems like. It's a Shell Scott, but it's a long sucker, about three or four times longer than the original books. You know, those were about 60,000 words, the Gold Medals. But we'll wait and see. I don't like to talk about them until the final manuscript is ready to go.

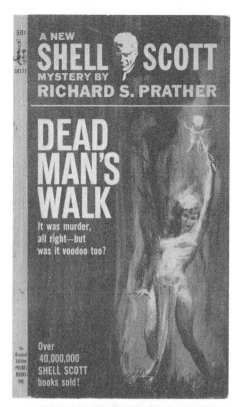

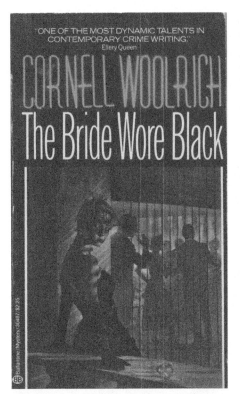

CORNELL WOOLRICH
The Bride Wore Black

THE INVENTOR AND ALL-TIME MASTER OF THE PSYCHOLOGICAL SUSPENSE NOVEL

CORNELL WOOLRICH
Rendezvous in Black

THE INVENTOR AND ALL-TIME MASTER OF THE PSYCHOLOGICAL SUSPENSE NOVEL

CORNELL WOOLRICH
The Black Curtain

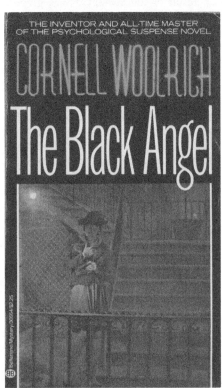

THE INVENTOR AND ALL-TIME MASTER OF THE PSYCHOLOGICAL SUSPENSE NOVEL

CORNELL WOOLRICH
The Black Angel

TWILIGHT OF THE MIND
The 'Black' Novels of Cornell Woolrich
by Derek Hill

A woman disappears, seemingly into thin air; a man is framed for the murder of his wife, and must race against the clock to clear his name; a phantom beast stalks the dark alleyways and narrow, shadow-haunted streets for souls to devour; a darkness, strange and malevolent, shrouds the city and all its inhabitants within a cosmic game no one could possibly win; a pair of lovers try desperately to flee the city before the creeping inevitable grinds them down.

Escaping the inevitable. That pretty much sums up the dark world of Cornell Woolrich's characters. Sometimes the clock is beaten and the hands of doom stilled. Most of the time, though, doomsday looms large and fierce, refusing to be averted without some blood shed. The race against time is fixed from the start; the path to oblivion paved from birth. Some people just learn to slip away from its grasp for a time. In the end, whether we have it coming or not, we all have to stare into the big black.

This philosophy of trying to escape the inevitable has never been better expressed than in Woolrich's novels of dark destruction, the so-called Black Series. Throughout the 1940s and 1950s, Cornell Woolrich crafted some of the finest, most suspenseful novels ever written, including **Rear Window** (1942), **Phantom Lady** (1942), **Deadline at Dawn** (1944), **Night Has a Thousand Eyes** (1945), **Waltz Into Darkness** (1947), **I Married a Dead Man** (1948), and the "Black Series" (1940-1948). Beginning with **The Bride Wore Black** (1940), and ending with **Rendezvous in Black** (1948), Woolrich perfectly documented the poetry of the night known as noir.

Smoky bars, deserted dance halls, darkened alleyways—the clichés of noir fiction— became psychological landscapes in Woolrich's hands, in which his characters are forced to come to grips with their own mortality and learn to somehow overcome it, sometimes within only a matter of hours. His characters prowl the colossal dark city searching for a way out of their personal hells. Sometimes that escape comes through alcohol, sometimes drugs, sometimes through the lonely passionless attentions of a total stranger. Sometimes, it comes through murder. But most of the time it doesn't come at all.

Woolrich peopled his stories with ordinary folks, luckless joes and janes with one foot pointed towards Park Avenue, the other already in a grave. They aren't always smart, nor are they particularly ambitious. Most of his characters are usually motivated by one of three things: sex, money, or love. But in the end, all that really matters is whether or not they escape the inevitable.

•

The Bride Wore Black (1940) was the first of the Black Series and the first to deal with the avenging angel theme which Woolrich returned to again and again throughout his career. And it is here, in what is considered to be his first real crime novel, that Woolrich also gives us a glimpse of a character who will commit any act in the name of love. Even murder.

The novel begins in New York City, where a young woman by the name of Julie is about to make her getaway. To Chicago, Julie tells a childhood friend of hers who has escorted Julie to the train station. ". . . I only hope I see you someday soon," Julie's friend says. But Julie responds with a resounding no. She has no plans to return. Ever. So she says.

Julie hops aboard the train headed for Chicago. But by the time the train screeches into the next station, she's off and running straight back into the maze of the metropolis' concrete canyons. She books a room at a rooming house using an alias. Once alone, she yanks out some photographs of five different men, studies them, brands them to memory, and subsequently burns them all. Having done all that, she can now get to business. Her destiny and that of five men are now fatally linked.

With that captivating, if enigmatic first chapter, Woolrich sets the stage for an episodic modern Greek tragedy. Characters move through the serpentine plot, manipulated by malignant forces. Julie Killeen hunts down each of the five men, ensnaring them into a cruel game of her own making. The reader is never sure—until the end, of course—as to why Julie is hunting these men. But before each man succumbs to her dark ways Julie always reveals her "real" identity, and just as the shocking realization dawns on them, so does oblivion.

One man dies in a fall from the top of a building; another is trapped in the crawlspace beneath the stairwell in his own house; another poisoned; another shot through the heart with an arrow.

Throughout all of this, Julie is being hunted down herself, by the obsessive Detective Lew Wanger. And ol' Lew desperately wants to dish out some karmic retribution served Woolrich style.

Though not as heated or psychologically compelling as some of Woolrich's other novels in the series, **The Bride Wore Black** is nevertheless a required text. It's perhaps a bit too mannered in parts and really lacks the paranoiac detail and almost operatic set pieces he later made his own.

•

The second novel in the series, **The Black Curtain** (1941), reads like a fever dream. Unlike **The Bride Wore Black**, which utilized the omniscient point-of-view to ill-effect, as if Woolrich was afraid to get too close to his characters' psychotic escapades, **The Black Curtain** is written in the first person. This almost-perfect black pearl of a novel is tough, paranoid, lonely, and perfectly explores the overused noir cliché of amnesia. In Woolrich's hands, it becomes nothing short of tragic.

In the opening chapter, Frank Townsend "awakens" to find himself flat on his back on the sidewalk. Some bricks from the top of a building just happened to come loose and fall just as poor Frank was passing by. When Frank regains consciousness, he has no idea where he is. A young boy runs up to him and hands him back his hat. But Frank—to his utter surprise—notices that the initials inside the hat are "DN", not his own. Frank points this out to the kid, but the kid is adamant that the hat is Frank's:

Sure it's yours! I seen it roll off you when you went down!"
Townsend cast his eyes doubtfully over the littered sidewalk and the gutter alongside, but there was no other hat in sight.
The kid was eyeing him askance. "Don't you know your own hat, mister?

With this brief tantalizing opening—a Woolrich trademark—the reader is hooked. Frank Townsend is a man out of time. He soon discovers, after reuniting with his still loyal wife, that he's been missing for the last three years.

This shocking revelation sends Frank—for the first half of the novel—on a quest to rediscover what he did for the last three years of his life. Ultimately he does find out, but only after re-entering the shadow life he once inhabited as Dan Nearing.

The last quarter of the novel, which focuses on Townsend's valiant quest to defend himself against a charge of murder he may or may not have committed as Dan Nearing, doesn't hold up as well as the first half. The story opens up a bit too much, losing much of the claustrophobic, tortured outlook of our hero. He regains his lost years a bit too easily through the assistance of Dan Nearing's plucky girlfriend Ruth. There is also the matter of the slightly implausible finale, which is practically a Woolrichean trademark. Woolrich's beginnings are usually taut, jolting blueprints in how to get the reader's attention. His stories never lull the reader into a fitful dream; they grab us by the neck and throttle us with action and suspense, daring us not to scream "What next? What next?" And because of that, with few exceptions, Woolrich can never quite pull off a satisfactory ending.

However, **The Black Curtain** still remains one of Woolrich's finest novels, due mostly to his brilliant, frightening, tragic evocation of what it would feel like to have "lost" three years of one's life.

•

For his next foray into the dark heart of humanity, Woolrich left the concrete towers of Manhattan and headed down to South America, where a mysterious killer roams the cobble-stoned streets and back alleys of a large city.

Having spent many years in Mexico City as a young boy, Woolrich obviously never forgot the cadences, the sensations, the slow spicy crawl of life. His South America is rich in detail and imagery—from its crowded cafes, noisy luxuriant plazas, to its quiet dusky cemeteries shrouded in old world superstition. You can feel the muggy night air coil up around you like a net of panic sweat. Perhaps it's a sensation Woolrich could never quite shake.

Black Alibi (1942) eschews many of the traditional noir themes and archetypes, and instead focuses on all-out horror and suspense. After an over-the-hill nightclub performer named Kiki Walker agrees to parade through the center of town with a fierce black jaguar (only after being urged on by her manager, a down-and-out American named Jerry Manning), the beast gets loose and disappears into the bowels of the city. Soon after, young women start turning up dead, ripped apart, seemingly victims of the great stealthy beast.

Woolrich pulls out all the stops. This novel delivers some of the finest bare-fisted goods, especially when showcasing any one of its five lengthy set pieces. Most notable of these is the scene in which beautiful young Teresa Delgado is forced to venture out into the night to fetch some charcoal for her father's fire. She has no choice but to face the nightmare stalking the streets. Woolrich's writing is in top form with this scene, conjuring up not only our primal fear of the dark, but of a young girl's coming-of-age anxiety and hysteria, and of her desire—even at the cost of her own life—to know what fierce beast awaits her and everyone in the dark.

She had to see, she had to know, her fright-distended soul could bear no more. The muscles of her neck started to tug, to pull her head around, to look behind her at the doom-pregnant entrance she had just quitted.

Another set piece in an old cemetery at night is also brilliantly done, but it can't match the hyper-realized suspense or diabolical frenzy with which Woolrich writes about poor Teresa's fate.

As we follow a team of detectives and Jerry Manning in their hunt for the killer jaguar, Woolrich again builds up our expectations so high that he can't possibly satisfy us. Alas, the ending of **Black Alibi** is such a letdown it borders on the excruciatingly unforgivable sin of telling the reader "it was all just a dream." Remarkably though, that the insipid, improbable ending doesn't tarnish what has come before is a major compliment to Woolrich's handling of the material.

•

Back to the city and all its many hells, Woolrich wrote **The Black Angel** (1943). It's another first person narrative, though this time told from the viewpoint of a young woman who is forced to clear her husband's name when he is convicted of murdering his mistress.

Alberta "Angel Face" Murray discovers that her husband is having an affair. This little revelation cracks Alberta's world so thoroughly that she plans on confronting her husband's mistress. One night, after a couple shots of gin, Alberta sets out to regain her husband once and for all. But when Alberta reaches the mistress's apartment she discovers that someone has already beaten her to it. The "other" woman is found smothered to death, and to Alberta's horror there is evidence linking her husband to the crime scene. So what does a dutiful wife do? Bury the evidence, of course.

But the cops are too quick and they arrest Alberta's husband on murder charges. He's soon facing the chair and it's up to Alberta to clear his name. The mistress, who was known as Mia, was a good time girl in more ways than one, and she entertained a lot of other men, too. Knowing this, Alberta takes it upon herself to sink down into the city's underworld of sex, drugs, and other sordid activities, to clear her man's name. She even ends up being the fave doll of a pushy, violent mobster.

Though ordinary in many respects, and lacking in any real memorable scenes, **The Black Angel** is a quiet burn of a novel. It never quite ignites into an explosion, but it does maintain heat as the naive and stalwart Alberta is forced to shed a few morals in order to preserve the sanctity of her marriage.

Perhaps the novel's major weakness is in Alberta's characterization itself. You're never in real doubt of her strength or valiant crusade to clear her husband's name. Nor do you really care. Her husband's a lying, cheating lout who doesn't really deserve Alberta in the first place. Granted, Woolrich was writing this in a time, and for a market that may not have seen anything amiss in Alberta's slavering devotion to her husband.

Nevertheless, **The Black Angel** is an interesting entry in the Black Series.

•

For the fifth novel in the series, Woolrich again headed down south, this time to Cuba, to give us one of the wildest books and one of the best. **The Black Path of Fear** (1944) is pure pulp fiction and all the better for it.

Two lovers—Scotty and Eve—flee the heady, violent air of South Florida, and hide out in the chaotic oasis of Havana. Eve is a gangster's moll who wants to get as far away from her present situation as she can, and Scotty is a chauffeur driver for Eve's "owner," the very scary Eddie Roman. But by the end of their first night soaking up the good vibes, the black tendrils of fate creep into the lovers' story. The woman is murdered and the man is framed for her death.

The first chapter is pure Woolrich. The two lovers swing and groove through the crowded Havana streets, drinking and trying to lose themselves within the city's magic and within their own love for each other. You can't help but twitch in discomfort as the creeping inevitable comes slithering in. Eve's demise is one of the strangest death scenes Woolrich ever wrote:

…I looked down at the floor under her. Small dark red drops were falling one by one, very sluggish, very slow. You couldn't see them drop; you could only see them after they hit. They made intricate little patterns, like burgundy snowflakes or midget garnet starfish on a beach.

Soon enough, before Eve's blood can even dry upon the beer-slick nightclub floor, Scotty is arrested for her murder and forced to clear his name. But all of the possible leads prove fruitless, and the looming threat of spending the rest of his life in a Cuban jail comes crashing down upon Scotty.

So what does he do? He escapes, of course, and flees into the dark shantytown sprawl of Havana. Soon after, he meets a beautiful and tempestuous woman who goes by the name of Midnight. She listens to Scotty's story and agrees to hide him from the police. Midnight hates the police, for reasons of her own.

Woolrich spins the reader through a city populated with gangsters, smugglers, opium dens, the noble poor, a mysterious Chinese shop owner, and other such stereotypes. But strangely enough, even though everyone comes off as two-dimensional, you never lose interest. Woolrich moves the story so quickly you never have time to realize its improbability. He challenges us to scream "this doesn't make sense, it's preposterous." But Woolrich isn't interested in formal naturalism. His literary world is stuffed with people who wear their neuroses on their sleeves.

You really want Scotty to clear his name and dish out some retribution. He's another of Woolrich's Everymen, the two-bit loser with eyes towards the stars. All Scotty ever wanted was what we all want: love, a little tenderness, a little peace.

Without a doubt the best scene in the novel—another hyper-real set piece—is when Scotty must infiltrate the "enemy" camp, and lure the bad guys out to follow him so that the cops can bust them. Unfortunately for Scotty's sake, the enemy camp is an opium den.

I was groggy with fright. I knew—or at least I hoped—that I was going to get over it in a little while; you can get used to anything, but it sure was on full right then. I could feel sweat pumping out all over my forehead, and it came out cold and oozy.

Scotty's fear is palpable, as he must fake experience with ingesting the potent drug. You're mesmerized as you watch a man sink deeper and deeper into the morass of someone else's making. You shake your head and wonder—with absolute sincerity—how in the hell poor Scotty ended up in this mess.

The Black Path of Fear is a wildly eccentric novel; melodramatic in that inimitable Woolrich style. One can't help but wonder what directors David Lynch or the Coen Brothers would do to this novel (or any of Woolrich's novels for that matter) were it to be adapted for the screen today.

•

To end the cycle, Woolrich returned to the "avenging angel" theme, though this time the punishment was to be meted out by a man, not a woman. Superficially, **Rendezvous in Black** (1948), is a retelling of **The Bride Wore Black**. But where the latter novel came off as cold and aloof, due to Woolrich's seeming aversion to stick his—and our—faces too close to the grime of his characters' misdeeds, **Rendezvous in Black** is anything but distant. It's a slow, tortured novel of a love lost, a post-WW II ghost story about a young man's desperate attempt to bring back from the dead the one thing that ever mattered to him.

It begins like most of Woolrich's other novels in the series: tragically. Johnny Marr and his girl Dorothy are two young lovers and they always meet for their dates in front of Getty's Drugstore. But one night Johnny is a little late in getting there, and when he races up to the spot, he's confronted with a large gathering of people milling about in front of the store. At first he thinks the drugstore must've gotten knocked over. But then it slowly dawns on him that no one in the crowd is talking. They're all silent, and staring down upon the road where a mangled, bloody form lies waiting to be identified.

Johnny moves closer to the edge of the sidewalk, closer to the edge of his very own life. His girl, pretty Dorothy is dead, the victim of a horrible hit and run.

From that moment on, Johnny Marr becomes a man frozen in the past. He will never forget that night and the way Dorothy's body looked as she lay crumpled in the gutter. And you can bet that he won't let the person—or persons—who caused this terrible mistake forget it either.

The opening chapter is captivating—as if that's anything new when dealing with Woolrich. It's hard to top such wonderful passages as this:

Every night now, all alone, a motionless figure stands waiting in the niche by the drugstore window where the lotions and the toilet waters are. A figure with patient, ever-seeking, haunted, lonely eyes. Waiting through the hours for eight o'clock, an eight o'clock that never comes. A lifelong stand-up, a stand-up for all eternity. Waiting in the mellowness of June, the sizzling violence of a July electrical storm, the star clearness of August and September nights — waiting in the leaf-strewn wind of October, coat-collar upended about his throat, shifting and scuffing patiently in the bite of November.

But for all its lyrical flourishes, **Rendezvous in Black** also contains some of Woolrich's most purple, overwrought prose ever. And that's saying something, considering how dizzy his prose could be. Even so, the novel is memorable due to its solemn, haunted tone.

The image of a ghost-haunted Johnny Marr slouching through the dark city, waiting for his girl to return, is a powerful one. He perfectly embodies all of Woolrich's literary obsessions and anxieties. We all hold something sacred in our hearts, Woolrich seems to tell us, something which, if stolen from us, will motivate us to commit even the most unpardonable sin. Johnny murders those whom he believes stole something from him. To Johnny, his acts of retribution are actually making something good again, a futile attempt to bring a little purity back into the world.

•

Cornell Woolrich was a bitter recluse and an alcoholic when he died in 1968, and his glory days as a writer were far behind him, but his legacy as one of crime fiction's best is undisputed. His tales are ragged at times, stylistically sloppy, and more than a little overblown. But they're also some of the most gut-wrenching stories ever written. The "Black Series" retains its power to chill after all these years because Woolrich was the master of drawing out minute details—bordering on the pathological—about his characters. No one was better at exploring the dark psychological landscapes of character; their obsessions, their paranoia, their need for love and acceptance.

In the last few years Penguin Books has reprinted two non-Black Series novels, **Waltz Into Darkness** and **I Married a Dead Man**. With any luck, they or some other publishing house will also reprint the "Black Series." With the resurgence of interest in pulp fiction and neo-noir, the time seems ripe to once again take a stroll through Woolrich's twilight of the mind.

Peter and I both grew up in the San Francisco Bay Area, and even though he's nine years older than I am, we shared a mutual affection for our local Creature Features host, Bob Wilkins. Bob was funny, interesting, and relatable. Because he was just Bob. He wasn't dressed up in a costume pretending to be someone else (until Captain Cosmic came along). I never developed an appreciation for costumed horror hosts. Blame it on Bob. He set the standard. He is fondly remembered, and thankfully immortalized in a handful of recordings of his shows that have survived. While Bob wasn't the biggest name we interviewed in bare•bones, he may very well have been the most important to us. -John

BOB WILKINS
The *bare*•bones Interview
by Peter Enfantino and John Scoleri

Chances are, unless you grew up in the San Francisco Bay Area, you have no idea who Bob Wilkins is. If you're a monster movie buff, you've no doubt heard of Ghoulardi, Zacherley, and Elvira; all late-night horror hosts. Bob Wilkins, the host of *Creature Features* for over a decade, was a lot like these other hosts in many ways: He told bad jokes; he broadcast from a set laden with cobwebs and skull candles; he played host to genre personalities like Christopher Lee, William Shatner, Leonard Nimoy, and Forry Ackerman; he ran lousy flicks. But Bob was different in one big way: he was cool; unruffled. Bob didn't get excited, jump around, or make an ass of himself. He'd enter his set to a tune straight out of a stripper show, sit in his rocking chair, light up a big fat cigar, and say something like, ***"Horror of Party Beach**. Makes you wonder why you turned to this channel, doesn't it?"* We caught up with Bob to get his views on TV, movies, and the general state of horror today.

bare•bones: How did you get into broadcasting?

BOB WILKINS: I was just out of Indiana University with a degree in marketing and advertising. I went up to Chicago and got a job in advertising... had to start in the mailroom actually because nothing was available. After a couple weeks in the mailroom, I got a job in the marketing department. After working there for about six months with a lot of statistics and things of that nature, I started to pal around with the copywriters and the creative people who make ads. This was an area that intrigued me. Eventually I got into that department and became a copywriter. There were probably ten of us on the staff there and I was the youngest at the time and learned a lot from the older guys (they were all men in those days). I had a ball there, really. I was in the Chicago area for about three years and on various vacations I would journey out to Sacramento, California to visit a friend of mine that I went to IU with. This part of the world seemed a lot better than cold Chicago, so in the early sixties, I jumped into an old Oldsmobile I had and I drove cross country to Sacramento and immediately began looking for a job in that city. Just by chance, after being there for just a couple weeks, I was looking to hook on with another advertising agency, but somebody told me that there was a position open at a TV station in town. They were looking for someone to write and produce television commercials so they could act as their own in-house ad agency. These were the days when the local retailer still used the newspaper and radio format. Not many of them had hooked up to local TV yet. The Kelly Brothers, two young guys owned

WEEKLY LISTINGS 1977

TV TIMES
SEPT. 4 · SEPT. 10

BOB WILKENS—
Featured Creature of
'Creature Features'
Story on page 2

Channel 3 (KCRA) in Sacramento, an NBC channel, and that's where I got my first venture into television.

BB: How did you gravitate towards horror movie host?

WILKINS: There were always going-away parties at the station, especially for the on-air talent. They were given a farewell luncheon, just the people from the station were invited. People would get up and tell stories. One day, I hadn't been at the station very long, I went to one of these parties, and the sportscaster was leaving to take another job in Chicago, and all of a sudden (the sportscaster) calls on me to give his farewell address. I hardly knew the guy, but I got up in front of everyone and did a four or five minute monologue, sort of off the top of my head, and I guess that made an impression on management because shortly after that (management) called me in and asked me if I wanted to host a late night movie on their

58

TV station. I was taken back a bit. I asked them what they had in mind, and they said, "Well, we want you to take a couple movies home, these will be horror and science fiction movies, and we want to see what kind of ideas you come up with and maybe you can have some fun with it." I took the movies home. The first one I watched was *Attack of the Mushroom People*. Now, I, like every other person maybe growing up, had seen all the classics—Karloff, Lugosi—and I never knew that these Japanese-type films existed. There was no way I would have paid money to see that in a theater anyway, but I thought it had a hilarious title to it— *Attack of the Mushroom People!*—and I thought I could certainly have fun with it. I had probably a two week period where they wanted me to come up with the format and see what kind of ideas I had, and did I indeed want to do this? I told them I was interested and I would give them an honest answer. These were the days, this is probably in 1964, after the 11:00 news they played the National Anthem and went to black. All the stations across the country. There was no cable, no all-night programming, so this was going to be an extension after their news. The show would come on at 11:30 and I would be the only thing on the air. After watching *Attack of the Mushroom People*, I didn't see how I could honestly tell people to watch it because they would tune out and go to bed after they'd seen ten minutes of it. So I did just the opposite. I told them not to watch it. I think we had an unusual guest on. Basically that was the format: we had an unusual guest, we had conversations, we had amateur films on, we had all sorts of things on during the early years of the show. I was never told by management whether they liked it or disliked it—we never had any conversations at al. It was just a ball for me because here I was hosting a show and doing anything I wanted to and nobody was directing me in any direction. So that's how this whole *Creature Features* business started. It was called *The Bob Wilkins Horror Show* early on. What I found out was that a lot of young people at the time were shooting 8mm movies and some of the stuff was just unbelievable—I mean kids, thirteen, fourteen, fifteen years old.

(The show) was tailor-made for a youthful audience, but once the show started to roll, we booked every good horror film available, and no other station had bid on them so they came very cheaply. We played some great films along the way. From there, I got an offer while I was on Channel 3 from Channel 2 (KTVU) to host a show there. I almost had to give up my full-time job, which was writing and producing commercials. I had to eventually give that up because I was going to Channel 2 once a week to do that show and then hosting the one in Sacramento. I really couldn't devote all the time to the other job.

BB: Why didn't you use a gimmick? You never wore a costume or used big-breasted women for props.

WILKINS: I really had to be my self. I'm not an actor nor do I have the ability to act like someone else. I've been told I have a sense of humor and I thought I could certainly make fun of most of the films I had on or make the show worthwhile with the laughs that we were able to provide (the audience). We did a lot of crazy things. We had a serious show one night talking about pay toilets. The new airport in Sacramento was going to have pay toilets out there and we made like it was a big issue. Tongue in cheek things like that, things that other stations wouldn't dare think of.

BB: Did you have a knowledge of horror movies or did you depend on an assistant's knowledge?

WILKINS: I was not really a fan of horror films, or western films, or a fan of anything when it came to movies. I did have a couple of people in Sacramento who would fill me in on various entertainers. I would give them an advance list of the movies were coming (on the show). Many times they would appear as guests on the show. One was a young Bob Shaw, who now works for Channel 2 as entertainment editor. He interviews stars all across the country. Bob used to write me letters, I invited him on the show one day and we became friends. When I got the job at Channel 2, he came on the show and talked about this and that and eventually ended up editing movies for television at Channel 2. There were maybe a half dozen experts who were always calling me to do this and that. If I got something wrong on the air, they would let me know and I would correct it the next week.

BB: Were ratings important to the show?

WILKINS: In television the ratings system is very important. That tells you how long your show is going to be on. If you start to get low ratings you are pulled off the air. In the old days, you'd have some time, but today with the sophisticated ad agencies who are rating shows—who make the buys on television—you have to really be on the ball to keep a show on any length of time. So, with my background in marketing and research, I was familiar with the ratings system. I bought television programs when I was in advertising for clients. I knew when the ratings were happening and in the early days when I was on television, the ratings might come once every quarter. When I was finishing up television in the Bay Area and had been on the air for almost a dozen years, ratings were coming on a monthly basis, sometimes twice a month, sometimes three times a month. That was really carrying it too far. I'm sure that today they can punch a computer and find out what the show did last night. All this was the handwriting on the wall. Being a marketing man, I think, lengthened my career because I just wasn't a talent who got in front of the camera every Saturday night. I researched it. I helped book the movies with the program director. I think that extended my length of service there in television. I'll give you a classic example: when I was at (channel) 2, the program director wanted to schedule the original *Invasion of the Body Snatchers* to coincide with the newer version, which was opening up in theaters. I convinced him to wait two or three weeks. I kept telling people (on air) to go see the new movie, because we were going to play the original one and I wanted them to compare the two movies. We even had a contest on why they liked the original one versus the newer one. What happened was, when we

played it two or three weeks later, we got a tremendous rating. It just doubled anything we'd been doing in recent times. It really gave the show a nice little boost.

BB: How were the ratings?

WILKINS: The ratings were always very, very good. Again, I think a lot of it had to do with my background in marketing and research. Even if we had a weak movie, we might have a guest that I had filmed, that we had "in the can." I would start to promote, "Hey, we're going to have William Shatner on the show in two weeks, so mark that down on your calendar." Maybe that would coincide with a movie that was not quite as strong as I would have liked, but the Shatner interview would give it a shot in the arm.

BB: Were there any particular favorites among all the films you aired?

WILKINS: Good science fiction films always seemed to do well. The film that always had great ratings in the Bay Area was *Night of the Living Dead*. We had (director) George Romero fly out from the East and be on and answer questions about the movie.

BB: Were you involved in the production of the show?

WILKINS: Yes, I wrote the whole show in advance. I talked to people if I needed props, sound effects and so forth. The Saturday show started on a Monday, when I came in. I was at Channel 2 and Channel 3 almost every day of the week and they're working on the show, calling people and lining up guests. So I was very active in the show, not that I didn't take suggestions from some of the other people, but all the (hopefully) funny bits in between the movie, the breaks, were all written by me. If it was funny, it got on.

BB: Why did you finally walk away from the show? Do you have any regrets?

WILKINS: No, I don't really have any regrets. I did it in both markets for a combined 17 years. Once I left for (Channel) 2, I really didn't have much contact with (Channel) 3 except coming back once a week to do (the show) and I think that rubbed the management (of Channel 3) wrong and I did not do the show there much longer after that. I could never put my finger on it, the show was doing real well there, but top management there really liked to control things and, all of a sudden, I was an independent contractor and no longer an employee there. We parted company in good terms, but they wanted to end the show. I immediately got an offer from Channel 40 in Sacramento and did the show there for twelve years, so I was always doing two shows a week for most of my career in that area. When you get a job in television, you just know that it's not going to be for the rest of your life, okay? It's more true today than it was in the past. If you're on the air, I don't care if it's *Home Improvement*, one day they're gonna knock on the door and say it's over. That's because of the ratings. They can tell when a show is starting to go downhill. They may try to do various things to pump it back up, but there's so much television and so many choices that all of a sudden you grow weary of a show that you've been watching for a long time and you go somewhere else. I wanted to walk out of there, to quit, while I was ahead. In preparation for that, I talked it over with my family. I wanted to get back into advertising. I always wanted to start my own agency and if I could handle two accounts, handle their advertising, I would pick the following two people: George Lucas and Nolan Bushnell. Lucas had not put **Star Wars** out yet. Bushnell was the owner of the "Pong" electronic game. I had met Nolan at a big bash that he had at his house in the San Jose area. He had just opened up several "Chuck E. Cheese" pizza parlors. So, I had an audience lined up with these two individuals hoping that I could line up a job with them, hopefully where my advertising agency would be involved. I left Channel 2. I still continued to do the show in Sacramento but I knew that one would wind down or I could quit at any time and there wouldn't be any hard feelings about it. So I met with George Lucas. Lucas,

I had met at a Hollywood event where we were flown down there to interview various people. He was getting out of a big limousine and we just sort of bumped into each other. He told me at that particular time that he knew who I was, that he used to watch the show when he'd lived in Modesto, where he grew up as a youngster. I told him that I might be contacting him someday. He said fine. So I met with Lucas. He had a small Victorian house in Marin County. I had a meeting with him where he sketched out on a yellow sheet of paper his dream to have the ranch, as he called it, where all the production of his upcoming films would be done. He wanted me to be on his staff, wanted me to handle all his PR. To talk to all the various people who wanted to talk to him. George does not like talking to people. He's very shy, an introvert, and he wanted me to handle the press. He said "There's only one drawback. You'll have to go live in Los Angeles for two to three years because that's how long it will take to build the ranch." I said, "George, I can tell you right now that I would never take my family to Los Angeles." Of course, this was in the days of all the smog, the traffic. I think the smog problem has cleared up considerably today! So I turned him down, and we left it open that when the ranch was built that maybe I could fit in somewhere. So I went to Nolan Bushnell and he was anxious for someone to take over the advertising. I gave him the ideas I had for Chuck E. Cheese. I got his account and that made my agency. I held the account for three years. My timing in that case was very good.

BB: This is where John Stanley entered the picture?

WILKINS: When John Stanley took over, he said, "Bob, why are you giving this up?" I said, "John, one day they'll knock at your door and tell you it's all over. You won't have any warning. You'll think things are rolling along just fine..." I never wanted to put myself in that position. I said "I want to wish you well, but don't count on this job for the rest of your life because it's not going to happen." Sure enough, a number of years later (Stanley) called me, he was very upset, and I guessed what had happened. He said "Bob, you were right. They knocked at the door and told me the show was going off. They gave me one or two weeks in advance to say goodbye." He was just heartbroken. At the same time, he worked for the (San Francisco) *Chronicle*, he was a very good writer, shortly after that the *Chronicle* let him go. Nothing is for sure out there.

BB: Did you follow the show after you left?

WILKINS: I never really did see John on television. That was part of my life that I gave up. Nothing on John, he certainly had a different style. I think that's why he lasted as long as he did. He did things differently than I did and he probable gained a new audience for the show, people who didn't necessarily like what I was doing.

BB: Is there room for a *Creature Features* -type show in today's TV climate?

WILKINS: I don't know. There might be. If it doesn't come to (TV station management) in a can to the front desk where they can just go back to a machine and air it, they don't do it. The news is the only thing they have a staff for to go on the air. Local shows of the nature of *Creature Features* doesn't exist anymore as far as I know. I think it could if they came up with some kind of gimmick or style to make the people tune in. I think it will come back one of these days and when it does more stations will start copying it and you might see more programming that's originated locally make it on the air.

BB: Have you kept up with the horror scene in general through the years?

WILKINS: I certainly don't go to the theaters to watch it too much. When I was ready to quit the show, all these "Jason" movies were playing. They were programmed as horror, but it was a real killer, a real person, and I commented to Bob Shaw at the time I was about to quit, "You know, I'm getting out just in time. I would not play movies of this type." Sure enough there was a whole wave of that stuff and it continues today. You know, in the old days, you'd watch a monster movie knowing that monster didn't exist. There was no real Godzilla, thank goodness!

BB: How did your *Creature Features* tapes come about?

WILKINS: The tapes are selling real well. What happened was, Channel 2 had a retrospect with Bob Shaw interviewing me. It was a two-part series on their 10 O'Clock News, "Whatever Happened to Bob Wilkins", or something like that. I went down to 2 and Shaw asked me if I had any tapes at home that they could use to get some scenes out of. I had just a handful, so they were looking all over the station for tapes. Let me point out that the show was always taped on two-inch tape. The following week, when he were to tape a new show they would simply erase the old show, so I didn't think they were going to find much and neither did Bob (Shaw). Much of the tape had become obsolete. Many 16mm films, feature length films, were put in the dumpster when 16mm was no longer used by television stations. Anyway, Shaw and a group of people looking through the station found about 10 to 12 hours of old tapes of my show. We don't know who put them there or why they put them there, but there they were. (The tapes) were all in good shape. They dubbed them all down and eventually I got copies of them. It's a lot of the intros to the shows and the closes, the segments and the interviews from *Creature Features* and also from *Captain Cosmic*. It was really quite a find and it brought back a lot of pleasant memories.

BB: Of all the guests you had on your shows, any that stand out?

WILKINS: I remember Larry "Buster" Crabbe coming in from Phoenix to be interviewed. He was promoting his book on exercise. He sat down and we talked for a half hour about the old serials he did, **Flash Gordon** and **Buck Rogers**. He was an Olympic swimmer, second to Johnny Weismuller in the thirties. That was one of my favorite interviews. It was as if we had known each other in high school

or something. Very easy man to talk to. Another was Christopher Lee, who came to the studio and was really quite a gentleman. He had one of the most beautiful women in the world, Maud Adams, with him and also Herve Villechez. (Lee was promoting) the Bond film, *The Man With the Golden Gun*, and the three of them looked so odd being interviewed. Lee was kind enough to stay afterwards and do an interview on horror and science fiction. One of the things that I will treasure is... I would go to Hollywood on occasion to interview people and on this one venture someone said, "Would you like to interview Boris Karloff?" I was with another fellow, Harry Martin, who worked in Sacramento, and Harry was there doing the interviews. Of course, we jumped at doing Boris Karloff. It was one of those very hot, hot days in L.A. No wind at all, very smoggy, just not a good day to be outside. They wheeled out Boris Karloff in a wheelchair and he could hardly speak. He had respiratory problems and could hardly breathe and we thought how wonderful it was for him to take time out to give an interview. It was obvious he was not a well man and about ten days later he passed away.

BB: Do the stations still court you?

WILKINS: I have gone back to make periodic specials. I'm flattered that the stations think of me and the fans still remember. I never have any plans to do those things, but I would probably accept them when they come along. I'm not counting on them and I'm not disappointed when I don't hear from anybody. It's always nice to be remembered. I bump into fans all the time and I've always answered the fan letters because the fans are really what kept me on the air.

BB: You also filled a lot of different shoes at KTVU. You were a weatherman and Captain Cosmic. Was this simply station economics or was this Bob Wilkins having a good time?

WILKINS: I started *Creature Features* at Channel 2 and the ratings were very high and management then starts to think, "Where else can we put Bob where he can help us in certain situations in the ratings. They had brought in a fairly new team for the 10 O'Clock News, and they offered me the weatherman position. Now, I had no background in weather but they felt I could handle the situation. It was a big move because I was commuting from Sacramento where I lived and my wife and I had a young son at the time, but I took the two-year commitment and tried to have fun with the weather. It worked out, but after two years I didn't want to do it anymore. I'm a daytime person. All my energy is during the day. At 10 O'Clock I'm ready to go to bed (laughs) and here I'm going on television at that hour. So we parted company with that and they understood and Pat McCormack filled in for me and did a good job for a number of years.

BB: How about *Captain Cosmic*?

WILKINS: This is really why I liked Channel 2. When they called me in on *Creature Features*, they didn't say, "Here's what we want you to do"; they left the creative part up to me. It was the same thing with *Captain Cosmic*. I got called in right after **Star Wars** came out. The kids are lining up, seeing the movie over and over. Tom Breen, who hired me to do *Creature Features*, came to me and said, "We've got a chance to lock up a lot of Japanese animation and we want to take advantage of the **Star Wars** popularity. We want to have an afternoon show for kids and we'd like you to host it. So let's see what you can come up with." I took some of the animation home. I asked my kids to watch them with me. My kids loved most of it. If they didn't like it, they'd tell me why. So I got a general idea of what was going on then. I figured the kids who were going to watch (*Captain Cosmic*) weren't going to know who Bob Wilkins was. They didn't stay up that late. Just to have fun with it, we came up with *Captain Cosmic and his Wonder Robot, 2T2*. That was the title of the show. The kids were always fascinated by the robot. I presented all this to management and they bought it without any changes and we had fun with that show for a number of years. The costume was made in Berkeley. *Captain Cosmic* became the number one show in that time period, which I believe was 2:30 in the afternoon 'til five. When you think about it, only the independents could do something like that. The network stations have programming in that period that is really suited more to an adult woman. Strangely enough, what killed it is that there was no more product than what we showed. You'd eat up that stuff real fast because you're on the air five days a week, so we replayed it several times and the ratings started to slip a little bit. We even tried **Flash Gordon** and **Buck Rogers** in there, which the kids did not like.

As Peter mentioned in the editorial, this piece was originally written for a book on Mexican Horror Films he and I were editing. When that project fell through, we were happy to be able to give it a home in bare•bones. In the magazine, Peter prefaced the article with the details of its origin, and offered up our first (and only) 'Golden Bone' award to David for letting us run the piece. After publication, he wrote that he was happy how the article turned out, and honored to receive the aforementioned 'Golden Bone.' Sadly, during the development of this volume, we discovered that David H. Smith passed away in 2007. We'd like to think he'd be pleased that the article finally saw publication in book form. -John

COGNITIVE DISSONANCE:
The Horror Career of Jerry Warren
by David H. Smith

"It is commonly said...that ridicule is the best test of truth."
-- Earl of Chesterfield (1694-1773)

Cognitive dissonance, a mouthful of a term, describes the holding of two incongruous beliefs in your mind at the same time. It is often linked to politics.

We Americans are particularly vulnerable to it. We want respect for life and we also want freedom of choice. We want to cut taxes and we also want more government services. We want to "live free or die" and we also believe that "there ought to be a law."

A poignantly amusing example of cognitive dissonance is the quartet of Hispanic horror films prepared for U.S. release by Jerry Warren (1923-1988) in the mid-Sixties. Their exploitative titles are infamous—alphabetically, ***Attack of the Mayan Mummy***, ***Creature of the Walking Dead***, ***Curse of the Stone Hand***, and ***Face of the Screaming Werewolf***—and frequently turn up as anathemas for genre authors to cite as they carp about the perfunctory dubbing of foreign-made monster movies.

Purists insist foreign films be shown in their original form, with English subtitles being the only obtrusions allowed. But the idea is more honored in the breach than in the observance. The finicky mainstream market rarely supports such art-house releases, and the idea that such a venture would be considered in the 1960s with derivative (if not downright hokey) Mexican monster movies is silly.

In 1965 about 15 percent of annual U.S. film grosses were attributed to foreign films (30 years later it is less than five percent). But critical respect was a commodity reserved for the influential European works of Fellini, Antonioni, and Bergman, certainly not the exploitative Mexican fare of Salazar, Morayta, and Urueta.

Hence, the handful of horror movies imported from south of the Rio Grande—to satisfy television's demand for inexpensive product to air during late-night non-competitive time slots (when commercial rates were nominal) and to provide fare for the dwindling number of Saturday matinees in the "nabes" (neighborhood theaters)—were all Anglicized in the most economical manner possible.

And Jerry Warren, offering no excuses and allocating no blame, was the cheapest procurer of them all. But each of the Hispanic films he did prepare and release holds an interest for credulous genre fans too ready to take critics' passing remarks dicta for gospel.

Warren grew up in Los Angeles, and, initially for his acrobatic dance routines, had earned "extra" parts in movies like *Anchors Aweigh* (1945) and *Unconquered* (1947). He is most notably visible alongside child actress Margaret O'Brien (b. 1937) in *The Canterville Ghost* (1944). Warren wisely realized his limitations as a film performer before casting agents did.

According to a posthumous interview with his widow, Warren then formed a music combo with himself on piano and vocals and made records for the Arwin Records label, including a number one hit at a Florida radio station. However, the full details of his recording career may remain a mystery. A number of sources compiling song-writing and performance credits fail to yield a mention of Jerry Warren; Marshall Bialosky, the president of The National Association of Composers/ USA was "unable to furnish...any information whatsoever on Jerry Warren" for this retrospective.

Warren found what he thought was his true calling behind the camera in the mid-Fifties, releasing *Man Beast* in December of 1956, a passable but cheap-jack interpretation of the Himalayan Abominable Snowman legend popular in the newspapers and magazines of the day. The film's low cost made a profit inescapable, and therein Warren saw his show business future. By assembling the barest minimums in every facet of production, any film he made would inevitably prove lucrative enough to not only finance his next production but also provide a livelihood—common business sense utterly lost on Warren's more notorious comrade of the era, Ed Wood (1922-1978).

But whereas Wood, through his naive excesses and goofy exuberance, has grown beyond cult status and achieved a kind of renown with audiences for his unswerving dedication in producing his warped visions for the masses, Warren has long been dismissed as a greedy pasticheur with, if it's possible, even less talent. Kim Newman, in **The BFI Companion to Horror**, went so far as to say "Warren deserves the title of world's worst film-maker."

By his own admission, Warren was only interested in putting out a product that was "playable." This self-effacing nature does much to explain why his name does not trip off the tongue as readily as does Ed Wood, Herschell Gordon Lewis, or Andy Milligan in discussions of low budget filmmakers. Walter L. Gay, writing about scurrilous Spanish film auteur Jess Franco in **The Sleaze Merchants**, made a non sequitur comparison between the two men's output, saying Franco's off-color films "as a whole are darkly lit, poorly paced, and filled with enough technical gaffes to give... Jerry Warren a run for his money."

After *Man Beast*, Warren made a handful of wholly original films, each a superficial likeness of the modest (but comparatively lavish) drive-in fare being produced by American International Pictures at the time. *Teenage Zombies* and *The Incredible Petrified World*, both released in 1960 (but made years earlier), ingeniously mimicked the kind of sensationalistic titles that AIP had made itself a name with. Again, Warren's ledgers were in the black enough for another leisurely hiatus, his career resuming in 1962 with *Terror of the Bloodhunters*, *Violent and the Damned*, and *Invasion of the Animal People*.

The latter two films served as prototypes for the bulk of Warren's future output. The first was a 1954 Brazilian film, *Maos Sangretas*, that Warren "presented" in a dubbed version of its 1959 re-cut re-release; the second was an ignoble retooling of a four-year-old Swedish film called *Terror in the Midnight Sun*. Although beautifully photographed and boasting an English language soundtrack, the movie had little hope for U.S. release with its brief (under an hour) running time. Sensationalist Warren bought the rights for $20,000, re-titled it, and inserted some extraneous lectures and voice over narration by John Carradine (1906-1988), padding the length by over a quarter of an hour ("Monsters Walk the Earth in Ravishing Rampage of Clawing Fury!" overstated the poster). Naturally, it made money.

Whereas other filmmakers took the same route as Warren in presenting foreign films on these shores, none have been as vilified. The very first Godzilla movie (*Gojira*), purchased by producer-promoter Joseph E. Levine (1905-1987), went through massive re-editing and had new American footage with future *Perry Mason* star Raymond Burr (1917-1993) seamlessly added before reaching the U.S. in 1956, two years after its Japanese release.

Other Japanese *kaiju eiga* were similarly amended with U.S. scenes by a variety of distribution companies, among them *King Kong tai Gojira/King Kong vs. Godzilla* (1962/1963), *Gamera/Gammera the Invincible* (1965/1966), and *Gojira 1984/ Godzilla 1985*. Still others received major overhauls, with the various reconstructions creating wholly new plots and finales. These include *Jujin Yukiotako/Half Human* (1955/1958), *Dailkaiju Baran/Varan the Unbelievable* (1958/1962), and *Nippon Chiobotsu/Tidal Wave* (1973/1975).

When NBC-TV first telecast the British-made *The Evil of Frankenstein* (1963), about 15 minutes of new, barely related scenes filmed in Hollywood were added to fill the time slot; the same tack was taken with *Kiss of the Vampire* (1963) and with *Hands of the Ripper* (1972).

The technique was not limited to horror and science fiction films with no-name casts. *Secret Ceremony* (1968), starring Elizabeth Taylor, Mia Farrow, and Robert Mitchum, was revised for television suitability, with new scenes added to replace those deemed too adult in this psychological melodrama.

Back in the theaters, Independent-International tried the same route, first by amalgamating Philippine caveman-cum-vampire footage with an otherwise threadbare outer space saga to create *Horror of the Blood Monsters* (1971), then with the cutting of *Psycho-A-Go-Go* (1965) to create *Fiend With An Electronic Brain* (1969) and the re-cutting of that to unleash *Blood of Ghastly Horror* (1971).

The Yugoslavian production *Operacija Ticijan* (1963) became an unwitting donor to a number of films, re-cut and re-dubbed over and over for *Portrait of Terror* (1965), *Blood Bath* and *Track of the Vampire* (both 1966).

But other, more redoubtable films and filmmakers have gone the same route, yet escaped the critical barbs usually thrown with such reconstructive methods.

Buying the rights to several acclaimed Soviet science fiction features, executive producer Roger Corman (b. 1926) first gutted *Niebo Zowiet* (1959) (with the help of neophyte Francis Ford Coppola) of its Russian propaganda and released it as *Battle Beyond the Sun* in 1963, but the Americanized names of its foreign cast of unknowns fooled no one. As the haughty Briton huffed in *Cluny Brown* (1946), "So many foreigners have foreign names." *Battle Beyond the Sun*'s box office returns were disappointing.

Thus enlightened, Corman decided to supplement the similarly top-notch effects footage of space flights and alien worlds from *Planeta Burg* (1962) with American actors and gave it to director Curtis Harrington (b. 1928) for overhaul. Harrington (as "John Sebastian") wrote and directed new scenes of waning star Basil Rathbone (1892-1967) as the Earthbound advisor to an interplanetary mission gone awry, with lustrous Faith Domergue (b. 1925) as his space station intermediary, and came up with *Voyage to the Prehistoric Planet* (1965), which AIP sold directly to television.

Corman, ever mercenary, enlisted novice Peter Bogdanovich (b. 1939) to scavenge the leftover special effects footage for another film. For the gauche *Voyage to the Planet of Prehistoric Women* (1966), Bogdanovich, pseudonymous as "Derek Thomas," cast Fifties blonde bombshell Mamie Van Doren (b. 1931) as the leader of a race of alien women who never come into contact with the Russian leads, despite the story's hinging on their accord. American International evidently thought more of this dross than the first effort and, contrary to claims of its immediate sale to TV, gave it a limited theatrical release.

Unbelievably, the cunning Corman was still trying same methods with the consumer demand in the early Nineties by video stores starved for product, cannibalizing his own New World releases for *Ultra Warrior* (1992) and 80 minutes of incomprehensible tedium.

These are just a handful of the

instances where "name" technicians are forgiven their early faux pas by virtue of their later successes. But Jerry Warren, more sinned against than sinning, remains the touchstone for the most unrespected kind of filmmaker, plundering others' works (however legitimately acquired) for his own gain.

In keeping with H. L. Mencken's observation that no one ever lost money underestimating the taste of the American people, this modus operandi employed for *Invasion of the Animal People* appealed to Warren greatly. He could acquire a completed film, pare it down to just its most exploitable imagery (chases, fights, creepy visuals, monsters, etc.), and narrate over (rather than dub) or even delete entire portions of character dialogue. On sets looking like Sears floor displays of beds and night stands, Warren could fill in any blanks by shooting new exposition scenes with low cost American actors. And Warren saw the recent glut of Mexican horror films as the perfect vehicle.

Mexican writer Octavio Paz, winner of the 1990 Nobel Prize for Literature, wrote of his countrymen's affinity for the morbid: "The Mexican is familiar with death, jokes about it, caresses it, sleeps with it, celebrates it. It is one of his favorite toys and his most steadfast love." Deprived of comparable indigenous films, horror movies imported from the U.S. had enjoyed phenomenal success south of the border beginning in the Fifties. It was inevitable that Mexican audiences, bored with their own film industry's reliance on dreary, sentimental dramas or lowbrow slapstick comedies, demanded their native product emulate the Americans' slick and scary fare.

This emulation which, according to Walter Kendrick's **The Thrill of Fear**, "signaled the birth of an international horror-movie industry" began with Fernando Mendez's *El Vampiro* in 1956. That film, its sequel *El Ataud del Vampiro*, and scads of other Mexican horror movies went so far as to counterfeit the English literary sources and European legends that Americans derived their most famous screen monsters from.

Furthering the resemblance, the Mexican movies' heroines, instead of the fringed shawls, flouncy skirts and big bangle bracelets worn before, were now attired in conservative dresses like their American counterparts. Sombreros made way for fedoras on the men. It made their importability to the north all the easier.

As a friend of the president of Azteca Films, Warren was given access to the product imported for the Mexican movie circuit flourishing in Los Angeles. American International had earlier snatched up a number of these films for sale direct to television, creating, along with sword and sandal epics (called *peplums*) from Italy, a whole package of indifferently dubbed monstrosities. Whatever their failings, the films became a very important development in the history of horror movies in America. They helped to expand the demographic of the fan base and demonstrate the diversity of the medium.

Progressive entrepreneur Warren further tested the waters of releasing foreign films with the November 1963 release of **Bullet for Billy the Kid**, a Mexican western to which he added expositional dialogue and peripheral scenes with American actors (similar to *Invasion of the Animal People*), Satisfied with the returns, but aware of the stronger market for horror films, Warren latched onto four of the supernatural thrillers scorned by AIP that he saw theatrical possibilities with and set to work.

Because of their low profiles, if not actually prepared at the same time, it is difficult to be sure which of the four films was actually made ready for gringo consumption first. *TV Guide* still credits **Attack of the Mayan Mummy** with a 1963 production date when it lists the movie for telecast.

But other factors make this figure seem unlikely. All four of the movies bear a 1964 copyright (in chiseled Roman numerals), and in Barry Brown's interview with and essay on actress Katherine Victor in **Scream Queens**, she states that, as she was filming her scenes for *Curse of the Stone Hand*, right next door was a setup for the mummy movie.

Thus confounded, for any sort of equability, the films must be discussed alphabetically; qualitatively, one must reach his or her own conclusions. Of Jerry Warren's input, think on this: Anyone who worked as hard as he did, Johann Sebastian Bach is supposed to have said, would have accomplished as much.

1. *Attack of the Mayan Mummy*

"Many woman has a past, but I am told that she has at least a dozen, and that they all fit."

—Oscar Wilde (1854-1900)

In 1952, an amateur hypnotist named Morey Bernstein allegedly took Ruth Simmons, a young Colorado housewife, back to a past life of a vivacious girl named Bridey Murphy, who had lived in Ireland a century earlier. In the course of five sessions, Ms. Simmons, in an authentic-sounding brogue, gave a detailed description of her life in the island republic. Mr. Bernstein later tried to verify these facts with the help of other persons and organizations in the United States and Ireland, and published a best-selling book from Doubleday. Ultimately, his results were disputed; before Ms. Simmons died in 1995, she confessed it had all been a hoax.

Nevertheless, the story, with its hypnotism and reincarnation angles, fascinated the public. Paramount adapted Mr. Bernstein's book in a low-key 1956 film starring Teresa Wright and Louis Hayward. It was a box office dud.

Universal modified the theme slightly for *I've Lived Before* that same year, with an airplane pilot (Jock Mahoney) believing he is the reincarnation of a pilot killed during World War I.

Also in 1956, AIP used the theme as the linchpin for *The She-Creature*, wherein a sideshow hypnotist (Chester Morris) regressed his female assistant (Marla English) into a weird prehistoric beast (Paul Blaisdell). A year later, with the public's interest in the Bridey Murphy case fading, director Roger Corman took a Charles Griffith script dealing with regression, *The Trance of Diana Love*, and, in a supermarket sound stage filled with fog machines and prop trees, goosed it up with time travel and Satan himself, and delivered *The Undead* to Allied Artists, starring the ravishing Allison Hayes.

In Mexico, director Rafael Portillo used the past life recollection idea as the basis for a short-lived film series featuring a warrior's mummy wreaking vengeance on the desecrators of his tomb, fusing Hollywood platitudes with Mexican history. All three entries filmed in 1957 in two months' time, the series of *La Momia Azteca* movies certainly cast a new slant on the familiar shambling corpse features made by Universal the decade before. Historically the films played fast and loose with true Aztec beliefs of life after death, but were certainly no more inaccurate than the Americans' interpretation of the ancient Egyptian precepts.

Florida-based distributor K. Gordon Murray snatched up the last two entries in the series for dubbing and release, *The Curse of the Aztec Mummy* and *The Robot vs. the Aztec Mummy*. Both were filled with enough flashbacks from the first one to explain what had transpired without too much audience collective head scratching.

But Jerry Warren, wise to the possibility that audiences might avoid just another stock sequel, chose to radically re-cut the first film. He interpolated new American protagonists (killing off the Mexican principals one by one off camera), transmuted an entire Mesoamerican civilization, and drastically changed the ending. His duplicity was a financial success.

A peculiar news story leads a skeptical Los Angeles newspaper editor (Bruno VeSota) to interview Dr. Frederick Munson (George Mitchell), who insists he has relevant information. The scientist relates his troubled relationship with the Cowan Research Foundation, a think tank headed up by his selfish brother-in-law, Dr. Edmund Redding (Ramon Gay), and their inquiries into the regression principle.

Munson has recently been forced out of the group, and makes his living as a widely syndicated television science commentator. He knows of the corporation's success in regressing one particular subject, Ann Taylor (Rosita Arenas), back to her life as an ancient Mayan priestess. Secluded from the outside world, Ms. Taylor lives in the research facility with her asthmatic little sister.

Keeping in close ties with the daily goings-on via clandestine meetings with his teenage nephew Timmy who also lives there, Dr. Munson learns the details of Dr. Redding's sessions with Ms. Taylor. Anesthetized and seated before a light of concentric neon tubing, she relates how, centuries ago in Mexico, she had been branded a heretic for entering a sacred pyramid's inner chambers for a furtive rendezvous with her warrior lover ("a great chieftain who approaches in elegant splendor"), and ritually sacrificed.

Dr. Redding believes Ms. Taylor's innate knowledge of the Yucatan pyramid will allow her to lead him to a hidden cache of gold which "would represent such wealth that it could actually affect the gold standard." The group heads for the Mexican historical site and enters the pyramid through an aperture only Ann Taylor knows of. She grows fearful "based upon intuitive feeling that in some way a dreadful force of dark evil would exert itself on all those present for entering into the catacombs and chambers that were forbidden to all but the Mayans themselves."

Sure enough, inside the pyramid, the moldering mummy of her lover from a past life emerges from out of the shadows and crushes Dr. Redding. The others manage to subdue the revived monstrosity "through the aid of gases that were brought along to test mineral content," truss him up and, violating a few Federal laws concerning smuggling of antiquities, head back to their California institute.

With the death of Dr. Redding, Dr. Munson hopes to legally wrest control of the institute from the surviving expedition members, but fears they may hide the mummy away before the courts recognize his authority. Dr. Munson enlists the aid of a mercenary colleague visiting from Hong Kong whose connections extend to the underworld ("I'm still well-connected in this city with people who deal in business that's sometimes rather sticky."). Agreeing to a fifty-fifty split of the gold hoard, the shady character hires a thief (Steve Conte) to steal the mummy from the compound.

The mummy bursts free as soon as the thief opens the door to the holding cell. Stunned, the criminal staggers back to his car and attempts a getaway. The mummy shambles across the compound, fighting off a groundskeeper as he instinctively seeks out his gold breastplate and bracelet. Further on, the mummy recognizes Ann Taylor as his reincarnated mistress through a lap dissolve, and carries her off in the customary lumbering-monster-and-dazed-heroine movie fashion. The woozy hit man plows into them, overturning his car and killing all concerned. The surviving members of the expedition, nephew Timmy included, go into seclusion; the think tank lock its doors; the mercenary colleague flies back to the Orient.

Coming full circle back to the newspaper editor's office, Dr. Munson finishes his tale with the realization no one can substantiate it. "Kill the mummy story!" the editor bellows into his intercom, then crumples a mock-up of a lurid front page with a headline about the living mummy and tosses it into his wastebasket.

Contemporary critiques of *Attack of the Mayan Mummy* are far and few between, and even nowadays little more than capsule reviews make mention of it. A "Dishonorable Mention" in *The Monster Times* #30's "The World's Fifty Worst Monster Films Ever" by Jason Thomas and Joe Kane accounted for the bulk of its notoriety for years before genre guidebooks began to scorn the film with regularity.

Donald C. Willis, in the first volume of his innovational **Horror and Science Fiction Films: A Checklist**, called it "a primer on how to avoid dubbing and how not to make a movie." Willis was stupefied by the "incredibly nihilistic ending," but overall found *Attack of the Mayan Mummy* "almost fascinating in its primitive techniques."

Since then, little else has been written to contradict those untoward sentiments. **VideoHound's Worst**

Nightmares, a slim primer on horror films, found it a "gleeful woofer [that] recycles much bad Mexican-horror footage." John Stanley, in his valiant but ultimately futile attempts to update his **Creature Features Movie Guide**, has so far dismissed the movie four times as "utter nonsense" with the new scenes helping not a whit.

In *Monsterscene* #2, Frank Kurtz conceded the original Mexican movie was "decent," but thought Warren turned it into a "viewer death-to-the-brain fest" with "the less said about [it], the better." Indeed, *Attack of the Mayan Mummy* has its faults, but resourcefulness on Warren's part cannot be counted among them.

Dr. Munson, at first sympathetic in his desire for the truth to be told, gradually becomes an insensitive cormorant through his own words. Despite his professed kindred affection, Dr. Munson can't even remember whether his nephew's name is "Timmy" or "Jimmy." He is such a cheapskate he is reluctant to splurge for a Coke when the boy's girlfriend shows up in his place for a secret meeting at a malt shop. While the fish out of water aspect of Dr. Munson's clandestine meeting affords a smile, in these days of pedophiles hanging around teen hangouts it seems hopelessly dated, never mind the precocity of the Mexican original's "Timmy," scarcely older than an elementary schoolboy, having a steady teenage girlfriend.

The rollicking background music in the malt shop scene may be one of Warren's own combo records from his earlier career— it certainly wasn't appropriated from the original Mexican soundtrack, which is amusing in itself with its leitmotif of a muted trumpet bleat and a crashing gong every time the mummy appears. The tune blaring from the jukebox doesn't sound like any of the familiar "library" music Warren could appropriate, and it sure isn't any Sixties rock-'n'-roll that youth would frug to like they do here.

Dr. Munson is more than ready to split the gold with his shady colleague to achieve his ends, showing far more interest in the possibility of an actual living "embalmed creature" than in monetary gain. But in the end, he confesses he has given up his cushy TV job to pursue medicine full-time (he helps out at a free clinic twice a week), and seems almost destitute in the editor's office. When the shortsighted newspaperman dismisses his story without sending so much as a cub reporter to follow it up, Dr. Munson is flabbergasted.

To those at all familiar with the original *La Momia Azteca* (or even its Anglicized sequels), Warren's rewrites are startling. Family relationships are altered and personalities completely changed. In the original, imperious Edward Redding was heroic Eduardo Alderan, as altruistic a movie scientist as there ever was. After Warren's rewrite, Dr. Redding has become a lousy parent, who "never had the time to give the boy the companionship to overcome the usual stepson problem." Ann Taylor, originally Flora, was his fiancé besides being his conduit to the Mayan (originally Aztec) civilization.

It was a purely archeological quest that uncovered the mummy in the original, not some race against time before an ousted board member could reassert control. The villain of the original film, *El Murcielago*, can be glimpsed in the scene of the press conference, sitting anonymously among the gathered media and scientists. In *Attack of the Mayan Mummy*, the title monster is a ragamuffin clod (and hardly a formidable one at that). In *La Momia Azteca*, he was, like the corresponding Universal mummy films, a noble warrior and unlikely tragic figure, undone by love, entombed alive to guard the secret treasure storehouse.

Even with its peccadilloes, *Attack of the Mayan Mummy* has earned Warren far too much disrepute. The fawning puppy dog fans of walking dead movies turn into snarling Rottweilers at its mention, though most have never seen the Mexican original. Most are too ready to accept the critiques of it as Hobson's choice for their own opinion.

"A mistake is something we can correct in time," the editor says at one point, "even though in some cases we're tempted not to." Without apology, opportunist Warren made the best of the meager situation offered him. *Attack of the Mayan Mummy* is nothing more than a bastardization if an amiable garden variety monster movie from

Mexico. It is a bad movie, without a doubt, but hardly a touchstone for the genuinely fulsome horror films out there still being scrutinized for hidden meanings in their misogynous torture and splattering offal.

2. *Creature of the Walking Dead*

"My soul, do not seek immortal life, but exhaust the realm of the possible."
—Pindar (518-438 BC)

Examining Jerry Warren imports is remindful of a line from a Bruce Cockburn song : "Your hands are full of thorns but you can't stop grasping for the rose." The few film fans who might sheepishly concede to enjoying one or more of Warren's quartet are hard-pressed to pick one as commensurably superior to the other three.

But if there is a first among equals, it has to be *Creature of the Walking Dead*, the most cohesive and coherent of them all. Derived from a 1960 release, *La Marca del Muerto* (which saw release to Spanish-language theaters in the U.S. in February 1962), *Creature of the Walking Dead* still manages to maintain its original themes of immortality and of unwitting complicity in murder by an evil twin, even with the cutting of several key scenes.

Before its release, fantastic films that did deal with the Doppelganger subject were usually Faustian horror stories of identity exchange or dark Jekyll-and-Hyde fables of personality transformation. Here it was again science gone mad, and *Creature of the Walking Dead*, with its moody photography, earnest performances, and mature handling of said themes earns higher marks than comparative serial fare like *Attack of the Mayan Mummy*.

"An Experiment in Terror! A Result of Horror!" screamed the ads. Unlike the other three imported films, Warren left the plot of the Mexican original intact for *Creature of the Walking Dead*, rather than changing it to accommodate his bombastic rewrites. And, as familiar as that plot may seem to genre fans, *La Marca del Muerto* stands as a sincere horror film that does not shortchange its shocks (and there are several) with a *deus ex machina* reliance on masked wrestlers grappling with the supernatural or with second-rate comedians inefficaciously enacting heroic roles.

In a flashback to 1881 ("when science had found the first leaves in the great volumes that were to follow"), Dr. John Malthus (Fernando Casanova) has figured out a way to transfuse the blood of young women to make himself immortal. The police catch up with him and, in a beautifully photographed scene transcendentally backlit (with a heavenly choir singing), he is led to the gallows and hanged for his crimes.

Flash-forward 80 years and his grandson Martin (Casanova again), also a doctor, inherits the family estate and quite literally stumbles upon his grandfather's secret lab (complete with the shriveled remains of his unwilling donors) and comes to realize his forebear's treatments may have allowed him to survive the hangman's noose.

Martin steals his grandfather's body from the family crypt and, with the lab newly accoutered with electric fixtures and the 19th-century victims' husks cleaned out, sets to work reviving the old murderer. With the blood of a kidnapped maid, Martin carefully transfuses just enough to resuscitate his grandfather and not kill the young woman in the process. John Malthus awakens, his wizened features and shock of thick white hair slowly disappearing to reveal himself an exact double of Martin. The elder scientist chides his grandson for lacking the courage to kill, but grudgingly accepts Martin's use of plasma stolen from the blood bank to maintain his vigor.

Ultimately, the plasma compounds are not enough, and John reverts to his decrepit true age. He overpowers his grandson, withdraws enough of his blood to effect the rejuvenation. John locks him up in one of the convenient cells in the back. Intending to take over the younger man's identity with a fast shave of his muttonchops and wearing a cravat to hide the rope burn of the executioner's noose, John insinuates himself into Martin's life by courting Beth (Sonia Furio), the younger man's fiancé.

Beth unties the scarf out of curiosity. The scar frightens her, and John

runs back to the lab even as his youth wastes away again. He kidnaps a young woman (Aurora Alvarado, the heroine of the four Mexican Nostradamus vampire "features") leaving church services (just as he had the century before) and drains her as well, though not enough to kill her either. From the next room, his imprisoned grandson berates him for his evil ways and for his misguided transfusion methodology ("The blood types won't mix the way you think they will!").

Later, his youth fleeting, he calls Martin's fiancé and begs her to join him at the lab, intending to exsanguinate her too.

Meanwhile, Martin and the two captive women manage to reach the keys and free themselves. Just as John is about to insert the catheter into the chloroformed Beth, Martin wrestles him away and, as the other two captives escape, fights his grandfather in a slam-bang free-for-all. A fire erupts from spilled chemicals, and Martin carries his swooning fiancé out as the flames consume his bloodied grandfather, still ranting about immortality as the heavenly choir swells again.

Creature of the Walking Dead, despite a couple of discursive inserts of people discussing the case (both in 1881 and present-day), holds up remarkably well. Warren had purchased a film of striking visuals that, when it did rely on dialogue, kept the characters in shadows deep enough to disguise the mismatched lip synch of dubbing. Warren also retooled the film as a narrative told by Martin. This measure allowed him to "talk over" the homey stretches of Martian's fiancé and her mother, as well as a scene of a medical colleague come to call and voice concern over Martin's unauthorized visits to the hospital blood bank (in *La Marca del Muerto*, this colleague was actually Martin's valet).

The biggest erasure from the Mexican original comes early on, as a priest goes to the mad scientist's death row cell to perform absolution. He is instead confronted by a wrinkled madman (the effective makeup strongly resembles Boris Karloff's beauty clay masterpiece from 1932's *The Mummy*) proclaiming his physical immortality, never mind his soul.

The shock effect of the suddenly aged Dr. Malthus emerging from the shadows is potent, and the matter-of-fact revelation of his mummy-like corpse disinterred in *Creature of the Walking Dead* is the only significant difference between the two versions.

What is left intact is the pronounced religious symbolism, evidence of the film's country of origin, at the time more than 90% Catholic. The voices of a religious choir are integral in several scenes, as the evil John (Gustavo in the original) stalks his victims leaving church services in two different eras; the hymn crops up again as the flames consume him at the end. A supernatural force slides the door bolt closed, making sure he cannot escape. When his grandson breaks the seal of his sarcophagus, the lid snaps up like a jack-in-the-box, with the crucifix welded to it, filling the screen.

To fill in the blanks left by editing the death row scene (as well as another of the priest talking with the prison warden), Warren filmed one prolix sequence (almost eight minutes long!) of an 1881 police inspector (Bruno VeSota) discussing the case with his masseur and another interested party. Warren's direction is wretchedly sparse here, with the masseur endlessly kneading VeSota's fleshy arm and shoulder (in 1959's *Daddy-O*, an assistant similarly massages him).

Though he later dismissed them as gobbledygook filler, Warren's contributions seem laced with an ingenious blend of metaphysics and mysticism, as if seeking answers to the most profound questions of human existence. There is epistemology ("The insurmountable quest of science has been to answer the unanswerable, to question the unknown, and delve into the black regions of darkness which surround the mysteries that make up the small world within man's limited perception."), ontology ("Is the world real? Is thought essentially a true reflection or merely an illusion brought about by a mind separate from the ultimate reality?"), existentialism ("Are you referring to a state of mind or realm beyond our comprehension?") and cosmology ("The degree of comprehending the so-called `mysteries of life' varies in each individual."). The characters' discussions do little to propel the story along, but, for the juvenile target audience, the gibberish was remarkably heady stuff, making *Creature of the Walking Dead* seem far more intellectual than it really was.

Creature of the Walking Dead seems to be the Jerry Warren film most reviewed by critics who either were not paying attention or (more likely) simply assumed, by virtue of consubstantiality, that it was just as choppy and eccentric as his other films. Donald C. Willis, in the second volume of his checklist, found it "another marvel of recycling," paying especial tribute to the "dandy musical motif' as "a classic of its kind." John Stanley claimed it all was "dreary stuff," originating from a Spanish [sic] film, with Warren adding "new turgid footage and [releasing] it as a neoturgid torturer."

It also seems to be the Warren film most familiar to the mainstream reviewer, Both Steven H. Scheuer and Leonard Maltin list it in their respective guides, calling it a "far-fetched horror thriller" in the former's and an "impoverished horror quickie" in the latter's.

Genre scribes denunciate *Creature of the Walking Dead* as well. Michael Weldon, in **The Psychotronic Encyclopedia of Film**, said the film, "in the best Jerry Warren tradition, makes little sense."

Bryan Senn and John Johnson, in their **Fantastic Cinema Subject Guide**, went even further and declared it a "boring, incoherent mess of a movie."

The *Castle of Frankenstein* 1967 Annual called *Creature of the Walking Dead* "inept" and "stupefying grade-D tedium [with] rank acting," but did concede there were "a few seconds of good photography." **Cult Horror Films** author Welch Everman, after a generous plot synopsis and a compliment of fine stills, still rationalized, "This is a bad film. This is a very bad film, and even if you have a high tolerance for bad films, you'll still find this one pretty hard to take."

Film writers still recognized the worth of *La Marca del Muerto*, even with the Warren interruptions. Phil Hardy gave a prudish slant to his entry for the Mexican original in **The Overlook Film Encyclopedia: Horror**, calling it "a routine rejuvenation picture which exploits its female cast members for additional sexual thrills." In the film itself, both of the doctors meticulously cut open their donors' décolletage just enough to allow the catheter to be inserted above the sternum, with nary a bosom in sight. Mr. Hardy continues with the "pedestrian direction [by Fernando Cortes] fails to endow the banal story with the sense of...perversion it so badly needs." You can't have your cake and eat it too, Phil.

Joseph Parda, in *The Exploitation Journal* #8, saw the merit of the 1960 original undone by the 1964 modifications. "By no means was the original Mexican version a masterpiece," he explained. "But with its atmospheric lighting and moving camera, Cortes makes it passable. Jerry Warren's harsh lighting, stationary camera and typical lack of effort make it unbearable."

At least, even with allowances, one critic saw the value of *Creature of the Walking Dead*. Lawrence McCallum, in *The Scream Factory* #10, discoursed that, despite Warren's changes, the movie "still emerges as a reasonably enjoyable thriller. Director Fernando Cortes creates a number of creepy scenes set in graveyards and darkened rooms, while also managing to provide several exciting action sequences."

Mr. McCallum was the first to recognize the film's antecedents: "Although the script seems to be a conscious imitation of Hammer's far better *The Man Who Could Cheat Death* (1959), there are enough good ingredients in *Creature* for the film to deserve attention." The Hammer movie cited, the second filmed version of Barre Lyndon's play "The Man in Half-Moon Street " (1939), was a thriller concerning the use of gland transplants to gain immortality.

Curiously, the title characters in *La Marca del Muerto* seem to be named after Thomas Robert Malthus (1766-1834), a British economist best known for his warning that, unless population growth was controlled, the world's population would grow faster than the world's food supply. Imagining a world of immortals, immune to effects of age (and even capital punishment), begs one to consider the possibilities of a big-budget post-apocalypse epic with a world of vampires murdering one another in search of blood "fixes" to survive.

Creature of the Walking Dead, with Warren's changes, is a dimidiated success. On one level, its genre ambiance, fluid photography and creepy music score par excellence more than equal comparable Sixties fare; on another, Warren's inserts make it akin to Forties radio melodrama that, while hampering the flow of the movie, are integral and provide the exposition the film requires for U.S. eyes and ears.

Creature of the Walking Dead rightfully belongs among the hierarchy of mad scientist movies, and is a sadly neglected thriller past due for more open-minded reappraisal by genre fans and critics alike.

3. *Curse of the Stone Hand*

"This living hand, now warm and capable
Of earnest grasping, would, if it were cold
And in the icy silence of the tomb
So haunt thy days and chill thy dreaming nights..."
—John Keats (1795-1891)

Nowadays the most elusive of Jerry Warren's imports, *Curse of the Stone Hand* gets most of its notoriety for that very mysteriousness. Long assumed by genre fans (and even the AFI catalog) that the two-part film was cobbled together from a couple of Mexican shorts filmed in the 1950s, the truth is much more complex.

The first half of the film is derived from a 1946 Chilean adaptation of Robert Louis Stevenson's "The Suicide Club" called *La Dama en la Muerte*. The second, unrelated half, long assumed to be a forgotten Mexican short at least a decade newer, of Chilean origin as well, comes from *La Casa esta Vacia* (1945), directed by Carlos Schlieper. Thus, unlike the others under reconsideration here, *Curse of the Stone Hand* has to be evaluated as a film unto itself, rather than in comparison with its archetype.

Technically, *Curse of the Stone Hand* may be Warren's chef-d'oeuvre. His input in the first story is minimal, and what little he did contribute to the second seems to be trying to make sense of a meandering story that seems to be heading nowhere at a snail's pace.

An artist is interrupted while painting a picture of an enormous Gothic Mansion. A thunderstorm threatens, and an old man (Ernesto Vilches) offers him shelter inside and to tell him of the subject edifice. He points out the artist a number of hands sculpted of stone placed throughout the house and arranged about the grounds.

The old man admits to the younger man he cannot imagine why the builder had the hands installed everywhere, leaving "not one area that had been overlooked in the placement of that which was to bring about the terror to each succeeding generation"; only that he is certain that the *objets d'art* bring about "a violent curse upon each and every owner of the house."

The first owner was a newlywed couple who saw their fortunes disappear as soon as they took up residence. Robert Braun (Carlos Cores), the husband, goes into the nearby city to try and win something by means of gambling the "house money" his wife (Judith Sulian) has stashed away.

An acquaintance invites Robert to join an exclusive club with high stakes, but he loses it all. He has to sign a standard contract that allows the club to perpetuate itself via insurance policies cashed as losing parties who fail to repay their losses in three days' time. The losers are all dealt cards until two are chosen to be slain by fellow members chosen the same way.

Sure enough, Robert and another man draw the cards marking themselves for death. The second unlucky fellow stays behind as the club members withdraw for cigars and cognac: he shoots himself, preferring to avoid the suspense of his own inevitable murder before the deadline comes.

Robert tries desperately to raise the cash to save himself, finding himself under the watchful eyes of the other club members at every turn. When he goes so far as to complain to the police, Robert is escorted into the chief's office to relate his story, only to find himself facing the man who dealt the cards.

At a loss, Robert finds solace with the acquaintance who first introduced him to the gambling club, thinking himself safe as the deadline approaches for the sentence to be carried out. The acquaintance shoots Robert dead, revealing his card requiring him to do the deed.

Aside from a lugubrious reading of the "Suicide Club" contract typed on plain bond paper, Warren's influence is absent in this story, and none of the plot is changed to accommodate voice-overs or delete dialogue. It is a remarkably well-photographed and -directed segment, with a palpable suspense that builds as the story progresses.

The card selection scene is especially masterful, as each player shows a different reaction to the pasteboard dealt him: One is a giggling nervous wreck; another straight-faced and deathly serious; another, engrossed in a book, wholly indifferent; and so forth.

Hopeful and desperate, Robert visits a bank in search of funds from a forgotten account; he then becomes terrified as fellow club members make their presence known, manipulating the viewer into sharing those emotions.

Donald C. Willis acknowledged there were "creepy moments" in this portion of *Curse of the Stone Hand*. James O'Neill, in **Terror On Tape**, liked the atmosphere of "certain Expressionistic scenes" of the segment. Written in the spring of 1878, Robert Louis Stevenson's "The Suicide Club" is a remarkably durable story, first adapted to film in America with a five minute silent version in 1909. Since then, it has been filmed at least five other times, from Germany to England and back to America again, featuring such stars as Paul Wegener (1931), Robert Montgomery (1936), and Mariel Hemingway (1989).

The Chilean film's director, Carlos Hugo Christensen, receives equal billing (minus the Hispanic given name) with Warren in the opening credits, a magnanimous gesture by Warren doubtlessly conceded because of the ease of adapting the film for the U.S. market. Apart from the prosaic legal discourse and a handful of explanatory dialogue (with the speakers' backs turned at opportune moments or out of the frame entirely to ease dubbing clumsiness), Warren had little to do but sit back until the second segment got underway.

Now, Warren detractors, ammunition loaded and hammers cocked to fire their pejorative guns, truly have a worthy target. The second half of *Curse of the Stone Hand* starts out promisingly enough, but soon deteriorates into a plotless imbroglio that eats up running time and, to hear critics tell it, brain cells as well.

After the widowing of Robert's new bride, the house is bought by a couple and their three children. The eldest child, Charles, dominates his little sister and brother with his cruelty and sadistic ways. When their parents drown "in a boating excursion," he becomes master of the house and the three grow up as wards of their uncle at the mansion, evidently inheriting great wealth from their parents' accidental deaths.

The younger boy, Jamie (Horacio Peterson), gets engaged to a girl (Chela Bon) from town before he goes off to college. When he returns for the Christmas holiday break between semesters, her finds Charles (Alejandro Flores) has married the girl himself. Jamie and the girl meet in secret, where she confesses she doesn't know why she married his evil sibling, and promises to run away with Jamie as soon as she can.

Overhearing all this by means of surreptitious Warren inserts is the estate's gardener (John Carradine), who then goes to town and tells a female friend (Katherine Victor) what he eavesdropped. The woman is dismayed, because Charles used to call on her sister before his marriage, leaving her a physical and emotional ruin each time (implying sadomasochistic sex, daring subject matter in the mid-Sixties). She fears the visits to her sister will resume when his nuptials dissolve.

Even after disparaging him from a second story window as he cavalierly walks by, the woman confronts Charles (actually a cloaked stand-in in best Ed Wood/Bela Lugosi/Dr. Tom Mason fashion) and demands he leave her sister alone. "Is there no part of you that can show for

77

once a semblance of human decency?" she beseeches him, surely not the most tactful nor syntactic of entreaties. In response, something unseen happens to him and she screams in fright.

The woman turns up later unscathed and tries to warn Jamie's beloved of something or other. The gardener talks of Charles' power: "Hypnotism or whatever you will, but it hasn't the degree of penetration with some people that it has with others." He also tells an assistant (Lloyd Nelson) of a mysterious locked room in the forbidden basement of the mansion.

It all moves along with the speed and finesse of a harbor dredge until the narrator of the tales is revealed to be the orphans' *in loco parentis* uncle when he is escorted from the deserted house by Charles' and Jamie's sister. The artist who had been listening to the tales goes down to the basement and breaks into the secret room. Inside, he discovers a portrait of Charles with hirsute werewolf features.

Then Charles' sadism is somehow tied to a weird "Dorian Gray" quirk, right? But he had been like that since childhood, so then, what does it really mean? How do stone hands have "a most devastating effect upon the estate and all its occupants" in any of what has gone on?

With the verifiable Chilean origins of both halves, the inclusion of *Curse of the Stone Hand* in Mexican horror cinema listings is no longer appropriate. Unfortunately, the military coup of September 1973 closed the Cinemateca Universitaria, formerly the main archive of Chilean cinema, and many films and documentaries were destroyed. The existence of the originals (for comparisons' sake) seems unlikely today.

The late Barry Brown reproved *Curse of the Stone Hand* in his adulatory biography of Katherine Victor, calling it "a mess, even by Warren standards. Mexican film footage, interesting in itself, is spliced into poorly written expository scenes." Mr. Brown quickly glosses over the fact that only because of Jerry Warren's "slipshod production values, uneven sound and atrociously expeditious editing" has Ms. Victor earned a chapter in the book at all.

In magazine interviews, Katherine Victor comes across as a charming and gracious woman, defending Warren and his disparate efforts without fail, no matter the stigma attached by participating in five of them. Of course, "the sight of Ms. Victor clad only in a slip [in the non-Warren *Cape Canaveral Monsters* of 1960] was a high point of preadolescence" for John Benson of *Not One of Us* magazine, and those readers with eyeglasses and receding hairlines will undoubtedly concur.

Donald C. Willis remarked it all came down to its "hilariously inconclusive conclusion." Don G. Smith got sidetracked with it in **Lon Chaney, Jr.: Horror Film Star, 1906-1973**, labeling it "an abortion" and "an abysmal testament to chaos." (*Curse of the Stone Hand* was released on a double-bill with Chaney's *Face of the Screaming Werewolf* in April 1965.) Michael Weldon softened Don G. Smith's metaphor, acclaiming the melange of old Mexican and new American footage resulted "in amusing chaos."

With his usual wordplay, John Stanley idiosyncratically tagged it "accursed viewing." James O'Neill, despite his grudging approval of the first half mentioned earlier, found the second half "a riot" and *Curse of the Stone Hand*, aggregately, to be "pure fool's gold and the definitive Warren cut-and-paste job," with the ending "totally pointless." Evidently a viewer of one of its late, late night broadcasts, O'Neill summed up, "This is best viewed while not completely conscious."

VideoHound's Golden Movie Retriever rightly saw it as "a mutation" of two separate films "purchased and monster-mashed into one by Warren."

Ed Naha, in **Horrors! From Screen To Scream** dismissed it as a "small budgeted Mexican horror film with little or no interest with American footage added to confuse the already hackneyed gore." Mr. Naha's definition of "gore" is extremely generous— nary a drop of blood is shown, the plume of smoke from a fired derringer constituting its violent content.

The earliest alphabetical guide to horror films, in *Castle of Frankenstein* magazine, summed up *Curse of the Stone*

Hand in its seventh issue, citing its origins and finding it "re-titled and 'revised' by American Jerry Warren so that it makes no sense at all. Addition of poorly shot scenes with American actors to tie it all together only makes it even more incomprehensible." It was a "completely incoherent jumble."

The second half, to be sure, is a muddle, but there is that first story to almost compensate for it. And both halves boast a strong fortissimo musical score by Jorge Andreani that can easily stand, if not alongside genre winners like James Bernard and Hans J. Salter, then surely cheek by jowl with placers like Albert Glasser and Richard Band.

In art films, *outré* images and nonsensical dialogue must frequently be interpreted by the viewer to make sense of a scene, making the filmgoing experience extremely subjective and the intent of the filmmaker open to conjecture. With *Curse of the Stone Hand*, reading between the lines is of no help, and even if the viewer would cross his eyes, hold the lines up to a mirror, and then read between them, it would still be pointless.

"Don't play what's there, play what's *not* there," musician Miles Davis once said. Alas, with *Curse of the Stone Hand*, subscribing to even the jazzman's motto is still not enough.

4. *Face of the Screaming Werewolf*

"If the changes that we fear be thus irresistible, what remains but to acquiesce with silence..."
—Samuel Johnson (1709-1784)

Sigh.

If only a smidgen of appreciation has been engendered by re-appraising Jerry Warren's films up till now, the *Face of the Screaming Werewolf* will undo even that. Horror film prigs bemoan the prostitution of Karloff out-takes from *The Terror* (1963) in *Transylvania Twist* (1989) and the employment of unused Lugosi footage in *Plan 9 from Outer Space* (1959); in the directors' meager defense, the scant footage was historically interesting, and the resultant films emerged as vapid but inoffensive, with the actors' marquee value really their only selling point.

But *La Casa del Terror* (1959) afforded Warren not only prime footage of Lon Chaney, Jr. in a reprise of *The Wolf Man* (1941), his most famous screen role, but also a wealth of moody visual material on a par with or exceeding the Universal classics of the Thirties and Forties. That is, until he sat down at his Moviola and undid what there was. Warren, purely, simply, and without excuses, blew the opportunity to partially redeem himself and ingratiate at least one of his films with fans.

The film was considered virtually lost for many years until its revival on the home video market in the Nineties. Its scrimpy running time (just shy of an hour) made it virtually unsalable to television, with that market's unequivocal 90-minute and two-hour movie time slots. Whereas Warren had padded the other films with longeurs to stretch their running time and thus ensure their practicality, he was strangely negligent with *Face of the Screaming Werewolf*.

In the intervening years, fans' curiosities had to be satisfied with magazines' and books' occasional mention of the frenzied title and the tantalizing photos of Chaney, not only wearing his Wolf man ensemble (minus his furry footwear), but also made up as a rather lumpy Egyptian mummy. Rumors ran rampant, frequently erroneous at that.

Rose London, in **Zombie the Living Dead**, referred to *Face of the Screaming Werewolf* as a "mish-mash," with Chaney essaying *three* roles, as a werewolf, a mummy, *and* a zombie. Said fans (myself among them) overestimated those stills in their minds, convincing themselves the movie just had to be about the greatest since the spinning glass globe of Universal was supplanted by the more topographically correct model of the Fifties.

How disappointed they must have been, and how disappointing *Face of the Screaming Werewolf* is.

Synopsizing the film is almost irrelevant. As Ron Haydock wrote in *Monsters of the Movies* #4, *La Casa del Terror* was "the kind of curious film only the Mexican film industry can seem to produce," a frothy musical comedy with some incongruously macabre scenes of a mummy-cum-werewolf's electrical revivification and of the inevitable carnage that ensues. With *La Casa del Terror* as a template, Warren took the bulk of Chaney's werewolf swatches and inwove mismatched footage from *Attack of the Mayan Mummy* and, hence, *La Momia Azteca* to create a tattered crazy quilt of a plot.

The press book hyperbole showed far more creativity in its sentence structure than did the film itself. "This one combines the talents of many of the finest actors of the field including Landa Varle, Lon Chaney and Raymond Gaylord," it ballyhooed, Anglicizing the names of two of the principals (one of whom shows up only in the old *La Momia Azteca* footage). "Great pains were taken in the production of the thriller to bring to the audience a continuous flow of excitement along with many moments of suspenseful and unusual terror."

Dr. Redding and party again journey to the Yucatan peninsula, now in search of historical artifacts only, rather than acquisitively hunting for gold. With Ann Taylor again guiding their way via recollections of her "Mayan" incarnation, the expedition into the catacombs of the pyramid leads into a confrontation with the living mummy. The outcome is a happier one this time, however, as Dr. Redding easily bests the monster with the toss of a handy cross (which bounced away harmlessly in *Attack of the Mayan Mummy*) and a fast cutaway.

In an incredible Mobius strip of Warren's invention, back in Los Angeles (again ignoring violations of international law and diplomatic brouhahas) good old Dr. Munson tells his rapt television audience of the exciting trip. It is obvious Warren shot this segment at the same time as *Attack of the Mayan Mummy*'s; with back-to-back viewings, it's fascinating to see the man's thrift with editing and use of footage.

Dr. Munson justifies the appearance of the raggedy mummy from *La Momia Azteca* alongside Chaney's far huskier form with a cool composure: "Dr. Redding has brought back with him not one but two embalmed creatures that were discovered in the level of the pyramid located with the help of Ann Taylor. The way it was explained to me: One is an actual mummified inhabitant of the ancient civilization preserved by a formula unknown to our generation; the other is that of a modern man, placed in the pyramid only recently after an exchange of body fluids with the mummy in an effort to achieve an apparent state of death."

The casual "body fluids" observation lends itself to all kinds of scatological humor. But with one matter-of-fact dissertation Warren not only clumsily explains the reanimation of the Mexican mummy, but also addresses one possible final fate of Larry Talbot, the original Wolf Man.

When last seen in 1948 tormenting a couple of baggage clerks in *Abbott and Costello Meet Frankenstein*, Talbot, in werewolf form, had launched himself off a balcony to tumble headlong into the waters off the Florida coast. As the fall was probably nonfatal to such a supernatural creature, it is reasonable (with that suspension of disbelief all horror films require) to assume that he made it to shore and, with the dawn, again resumed his search for final peace from the cyclic metamorphoses that cursed him.

That search may have led Talbot south of the border to Mexico. Remembering Dr. Mannering's solution to his unwanted immortality by draining the life-force from him via electrical egress in *Frankenstein Meets the Wolf Man* (1943), Talbot (an educated and intelligent man as depicted in the early scenes of *The Wolf Man*) may have adapted the method, modifying the galvanic energy exchange to a liquid one.

Of course, it's all farfetched and purely hypothetical, but separating what little wheat there is from so much chaff does predispose a fan to extremes. And, despite the illogic, the continuity does explain a lot, down to why Chaney has shriveled into a mummy-like figure entirely dissimilar from the other creature in the pyramid.

Back to *Face of the Screaming Werewolf* now. Dr. Redding is introduced at a news conference (with the supine Chaney-mummy glimpsed in the background) with more of Warren's run-on sentence flair: "Gentlemen, I was told earlier by Dr. Redding that the second creature must be kept under lock and key and so, of course, could not be brought along this evening. You will fully understand, I'm sure, as I present to you the man whose discoveries can be related I think best in his own words."

A man attending the lecture (the first real footage from *La Casa del Terror*, aside from a second's glimpse of Chaney back in the pyramid) switches off the lights and a shot rings out. When power is restored, a voice cries out that Dr. Redding is dead and the mummy has been stolen. This is an ugly parallel to real life and the actor portraying Dr. Redding: Ramon Gay was a popular leading man in Mexico for several years, playing the lead in all three of the "La Momia Azteca" films; his career was cut short in May 1960 when he was shot to death by the estranged husband of a Mexican actress he was seeing.

Now, almost a half-hour into the film comes Warren's utilization of *La Casa del Terror*. The thieves put Chaney into a station wagon and elude the police in a long chase through the streets of "Los Angeles." They go to a lab hidden behind the walls of a wax museum and set to work restoring the "mummy." First they heft his bulk into a steam chamber to restore his desiccated flesh (as was done to Glenn Strange's thawed Frankenstein Monster in 1944's *House of Frankenstein*); suitably rehydrated, the body is transferred into a giant centrifuge to stimulate circulation and restore life. The doctor's efforts are thwarted by the inadequate power supply, and he and his lackeys leave the body on an operating table to ponder their dilemma.

The preceding *nudis verbis* description of the lab scene hardly does it justice. It unquestionably rivals the finest set designs from the Thirties and Forties, with the most Gothic-style lighting and ambiance since Hollywood took to economically modernizing the mad scientist storyline. Inky shadows abound, the lab accouterments utilitarian but as ominous as any alchemist's lair.

The muteness of the scientist (Yerye Beirute) and his aides maintains the eeriness throughout the scene. Each has his own job to do, and there is no time frittered away with useless conversation. It seems as though time is truly of the essence. For his part, there was no dialogue deleted by Warren, only a dubbed concession of defeat at the finale. The sound effects of the lab equipment were cribbed from the "electronic tonalities" by Louis and Bebe Barron and their score for *Forbidden Planet* (1956), with the theremin playing squiggles, slow siren glissandos, and long stationary tones.

A providential thunderstorm sparks the equipment (as in *The Curse of Frankenstein* a few years before), and "Talbot" awakes with a start. Without dialogue (save for a muttered "No!"), Chaney lets his character's emotions be known through facial tics—confusion at his circumstance, realization of his location, and then horror at the sound of a dog's howl outside.

The storm passed, the full moon emerges from behind the cumulonimbus clouds, and, in adequate time-lapse photography, "Talbot" transforms into a respectable facsimile of the Universal Wolf Man.

The scientist and his aides reenter the lab. One of the lackeys has his throat bloodily torn open by the werewolf before the doctor can subdue the monster with his "pistolero atomico," a nod to the modern era with nuclear silver bullets.

Eventually, after more cannibalization of *Attack of the Mayan Mummy* with its corporate shenanigans and the final fate of the other "embalmed creature," another full moon (werewolf movies notoriously ignore astronomical convention) shines in on the encaged "Talbot." Transformed, he proceeds to kill the remaining medicos and run through the city traffic. After stalking a pretty young woman (Yolanda Varela), the werewolf climbs the outside of the building she enters, walks into her apartment, and carries her back to the waxworks.

The handyman (German Valdes "Tin Tan") from the wax museum comes to her rescue, bravely beating the werewolf over the head with a torch. The flames engulf the monster, leaving the girl cowering in the handyman's heroic embrace. A pair of Warren-inserted police detectives survey the situation. "Take a look," one says, gazing indifferently at the smoldering corpse. "They talk about monsters and werewolves. Huh! Just an ordinary guy."

"It's great what the imagination can do, eh?" his partner replies. And it takes a lot of that to see the worth of *Face of the Screaming Werewolf*. Chaney's scenes (which Darryl Mayeski couldn't bear to watch in *Screem Magazine* #8) are effective and well-done. Despite the encroaching years and the ravages of chronic alcoholism, Chaney still looks the part, and he clearly gives it his all. Unfortunately, aside from the two metamorphoses and the first bit of carnage in the lab, it's pretty clear the remaining werewolf footage was of a shorter and slighter stand-in wearing the make-up.

Claims of Warren shooting new footage of Chaney for the U.S. release, as well as rumors of Ed Wood handling the werewolf's scaling of the apartment building for an unproduced horror movie, are categorically absurd. Behind the camera, the origins of *La Casa del Terror* were wholly Mexican, and all of the footage of Chaney in *Face of the Screaming Werewolf* comes from that film.

Tom Weaver, in *Fangoria* #129, stated that Chaney shot all his scenes in a two-day marathon of filming of 12 to 14 hours each. But, given the myriad reports of Chaney's inability at the time to handle such work durations without some of his personal "iced tea" to ease him over the rough spots, Weaver's assertion must be taken with a grain of salt (or salsa).

Chaney's participation in *La Casa del Terror* was seen as "its only redeemable quality" by Don Glut in **Classic Movie Monsters**, but it suffered from "one of the most fatuous scripts in horror movie history."

A few writers have attacked *Face of the Screaming Werewolf* on the basis of Chaney's presence in it. John Stanley found his performance "clumsy and inept by any standards."

Sam Gafford, in *Chiller Theatre* #2, remarked that Chaney starred in the film

"in his quest to replace Bela Lugosi as the horror star who fell the furthest."

Ed Naha grumbled that the actor got "a chance to look inept in several characterizations (including the wolfman) in this Mexican melee of junior frolics."

Other writers felt sorry for Chaney. Eric Hoffman enjoyed the nostalgic look to it, and commented in *Famous Monsters of Filmland* #205 that "Chaney's first transformation in the film is in the best tradition" and reminiscent of his Larry Talbot heyday.

The Dark Side #53 had a review of the film, proclaiming Chaney "at the nadir of his career," with "pretty good" werewolf makeup.

Frank Kurtz allowed that Warren "came up with one of the most confusing and still entertaining messes to feature a faded horror star."

Psychotronic Video #5 recognized that it was "fairly bloody for the time, and must be the best mummy-in-a-wax-museum-that's-really-a-werewolf movie ever made," and reprinted the review in **The Psychotronic Video Guide**.

But one big-name star is scarcely enough to salvage a mediocre film. Bryan Senn and John Johnson dismissed it as a "no-budget pastiche," while Calvin Thomas Beck found it "grotesque" in **Heroes of the Horrors**, "a semi-remake of the Wolf Man, spiked with tequila."

Ted Okuda, in *Filmfax* #47 (and again in #57), tagged it "incomprehensible and inept—in other words, your run-of-the-mill Jerry Warren effort."

Ignoring even the historically interesting presence of Chaney, the film has been relentlessly gutted by writers for the Warren retooling. Don G. Smith could describe it as nothing other than a "mess."

James Robert Parrish and Michael R. Pitts wrote in **The Great Science Fiction Pictures II** the "pasted together sci-fi/horror thriller was ... nearly incomprehensible," sentiments echoed by James O'Neill, who said, "this minimally dubbed version makes absolutely no sense...and leads to nothing—much like the career of Jerry Warren."

Lawrence McCallum called it a "third-rate Jerry Warren clinker" in *The*

Scream Factory #15, while **VideoHound's Golden Movie Retriever** said, in all, there's "not much to scream about."

A couple of learned scribes embarrass themselves, not for their lack of firsthand knowledge, but for failing to admit it. Gene Wright, in **Horrorshows**, declared *La Casa del Terror* was "decorated with partially nude females," though such a concupiscent feature does not exist in any version.

Prim Phil Hardy seemed to be trying to make excuses for it, reviewing it as the musical comedy it was but, like Wright, subscribing to rumors of risqué content. "The picture is slapdash rather than slapstick, with banal erotic dream sequences and musical interludes to further spoil the rhythm of a story that requires a relentless pace and expert timing to work at all." At least.

Castle of Frankenstein reviewed it twice, but the outcome was the same in both instances. In issue #7, *Face of the Screaming Werewolf* was deemed "another hacked-up, plotless Mexican mishmash," that it was "crude" and had "awful dubbing." Two issues later, the magazine elaborated that it was a "plotless, foolish item" and low-grade."

Tongue in cheek, Michael Weldon wondered in **The Psychotronic Encyclopedia of Film** if Warren had succeeded in getting all of the comedy out (the slapstick scene of the handyman's miraculous survival of a multistory fall by bouncing off of an awning was left intact by Warren for the sake of expedience).

"This is one awful movie," summarized *Santo Street* #4, and few can disagree. Trying to figure out a linear plot for the film is difficult (though not impossible as some critics infer), with none of the trademark expository dialogue or the overweening narration that might have salvaged the film.

Fewer than 25 of *La Casa del Terror*'s 82 minutes of running time were retained by Warren, and the haphazard insertion of *Attack of the Mayan Mummy* footage to give *Face of the Screaming Werewolf* some semblance of continuity is futile and even a little pathetic.

Further enumerating the failings is equally disheartening. The scientist who revives Chaney is a characterless, motiveless cipher on the screen; the reasons for his lab's weird locale, his ultimate goal, his methods—even his name—remain a mystery. The waxworks handyman is a narcoleptic do-nothing in the Mexican original, mistaken for a psychiatrist in one protracted scene, and inexplicably part of an *affaire d'amour* with a gorgeous waitress who works near the museum. In one scene, the two pause to serenade one another in the back room of the waxworks as the werewolf peers at them from behind some packing crates. This was the only monster footage Warren could not incorporate into his film without a major overhaul.

Face of the Screaming Werewolf has become the most overanalyzed of Warren's imports for three very good and very different reasons. First, for the appearance of a bona fide American star in the original Mexican movie, and a famous genre one at that; second, as a fond farewell to the type of film that so delightfully haunted young minds from matinee visits and subsequent television reviews; and third, for the bastardization of that movie, leaving fans of Mr. Chaney and of horror movies in general with a bitter taste in their mouths, for what he and the entire genre were stooping to in the increasingly bloody and violent product being released at the time.

Jerry Warren did not originate the crude re-editing, invent the blunt revisions nor first oversee the atrocious dubbing of foreign films. But *Face of the Screaming Werewolf* certainly embodies all those aspects. Like werewolves, the half-man, half-wolf creatures that have stalked their way through folklore for about as long as human societies have existed, so too shall this film lope through fans' minds forever as the most hated werewolf movie of them all.

Not for what is, or for what it was. But for what it might have been.

"Let fame, that all hunt after in their lives,
Live register'd upon our brazen tombs..."
—William Shakespeare (1564-1616)

After the lucrative release of the four "Mexican" films, Warren's spirits were buoyed enough for him to try one more wholly original film in 1966. Hoping (according to the press book) to "reap immense results at the box office from both its own merit as entertainment and, of course, the built-in national publicity" from the *Batman* television show, *The Wild World of BatWoman*, "One of the wildest, grooviest and far, far outest motion picture features" began to fall apart even before the cameras rolled. A protracted lawsuit by National Periodical Publications (later DC Comics) caused skittish investors to renege on their promises and the budget summarily diminished.

When *The Wild World of BatWoman* did come out, only the perpetual hope of hormonal fourth graders for super-heroine Katherine Victor to spill out of her bustier and one incongruously stylish film *noir* mugging emerged to act as saving graces not up to the task. The few fisticuffs thrown in the quest for a stolen atomic hearing aid (!) would scarcely make anyone confuse it with the popular TV show. Michael J. Nelson, in **The Mystery Science Theater 3000 Amazing Colossal Episode Guide**, quipped upon seeing it, "This film hurt."

In the end, only a snippet of the monsters from *The Mole People* (1956) and the villain's threat ("Do you like monsters?") to breed the legion of "Bat Girls" with them gave *The Wild World of BatWoman* a wisp of the comic book reductio ad absurdum it strove for. A nonsensical prologue about drinking blood was appended for Warren to justify re-titling it *She Was A Hippy* [sic] *Vampire* in a desperate bid to recoup costs with a surreptitious limited release.

But, even with a codicil in the opening credits stating the comics company's disavowal of the film, it all came to naught. Disenchanted, Warren left the business and retired to a ranch in Escondido, periodically renegotiating distribution deals for his earlier films for continued income.

His outlook renewed after a long hiatus, Warren reemerged in the early Eighties for one last go of it with *Frankenstein Island*. It was a quasi-remake of his own *Teenage Zombies*, complete with a reunion of several of his key players from his Sixties triumphs, ersatz Amazons in leopard-skin bikinis and the exploitable appearance of the most famous movie monster of them all.

Introduced to the wonders of peroxide in the 15-year interim, former brunette Katherin [sic] Victor starred (albeit billed ninth) alongside *The Incredible Petrified World*'s Robert Clarke. But even with overwrought cameos by genre familiars John Carradine and Cameron Mitchell (1918-1994), there was no hope of deciphering the outlandish script, and the ingenues looked more embarrassed than seductive. The spastic Frankenstein Monster, ineffectually flailing his arms about during the heroes' melee with the zombie henchmen, was less imposing than a child in a Ben Cooper costume.

Out of the business so long, Warren failed to recognize the growing sophistication of movie audiences. With its reliance on plastic skulls and Halloween pitchforks for macabre effect, stock footage of hot-air balloons, and impoverished look to the crucial lab scenes, *Frankenstein Island* was clearly out of touch with the times.

Reminiscent of the Mexican imports, Carradine's sporadic appearances (in his pajamas) as a hologram, bellowing mumbo jumbo ("Oh, Disciple of the Golden Thread, the power ye seek shall be given! The power—the power!"), seem to bear no relation to the film at all. They look left over from some other, unfinished motion picture. Not surprisingly, *Frankenstein Island* failed utterly at the box office. (Gene Siskel and Roger Ebert even made it their "Dog of the Week" on their *Sneak Previews* TV show on PBS.)

Warren died of chest cancer at his Escondido home in August 1988 at the age of 63, content with his career but perhaps frustrated at the lack of critical favor. In an interview with his widow Gloria, she reflected on the basis for her late husband's disfavor with fans and the animus his

HER THRILLS RIP FORTH
IN WIDE WILD ADVENTURE!

BATMANIA!
IN ALL NEW BIG SCREEN!

BLAM!

THE
WILD WORLD OF
Bat
Woman

starring
KATHERINE VICTOR · GEORGE ANDRE · STEVE BRODIE
LLOYD NELSON · RICHARD BANKS · the YOUNG GIANTS
original screenplay directed and produced by jerry warren
an adp international pictures presentation

films inspire. "His problem was that his movies were never so bad that they were laughable," she reasoned.

Frequently unpolished, alternately soporific and thoughtful, and ultimately absorbing for the fascinating foreign film footage on display, the four Hispanic horror films handled by Jerry Warren will never grow in repute. The misguided animosity is too strong, and no retrospective or analysis will undo years of disparagement.

In **Cut: Horror Writers on Horror Films**, John Skipp and Craig Spector describe truly bad films as being "movies so retarded, so utterly clueless that intellectuals are literally forced to hallucinate deeper meaning in them...[because they] can't believe, much less accept, that anything could actually be that...stupid." In these four cases, the cognoscenti needn't embarrass themselves by hyperbolizing.

The unfeigned beauty of *Attack of the Mayan Mummy, Creature of the Walking Dead, Curse of the Stone Hand,* and *Face of the Screaming Werewolf* is that there are no philosophical insights, no profound subtexts to them, no *arriere-pensees,* no crises of morality. Each film's face value is its full worth.

Purely and simply, they are low-budget monster movies from Mexico that, without Warren's enterprise, would exist today only as prepossessing titles in foreign film listings.

Since the quartet's release more than 30 years ago, America has witnessed the disgrace of one president and the assassination of its leaders. It has witnessed battles over civil rights and equal rights, shame over the Vietnam War, the collapse of the Soviet Union but the rise of domestic terrorism. It has witnessed women and men in changing roles, a sexual revolution and a sexual plague, massive job loss, the decay of the inner cities and an explosion in violent crime and destructive drug use.

Similarly, through assassinations, the collapse of the peso and bizarre scandals, tough times have made many Mexicans willing to believe the worst about Mexico of late. Despite recent and justifiably acclaimed films like *El Mariachi, Like Water For Chocolate* and *Cronos* (all stateside critical and commercial hits), the future of the Mexican film industry seems bleak. Thankfully, the pococurante efforts of Jerry Warren remain to remind us not only of simpler, more innocent times in both countries, but of more tolerant, less xenophobic audiences on either side of the border.

To applaud the entrepreneurial spunk that made *Attack of the Mayan Mummy, Creature of the Walking Dead, Curse of the Stone Hand* and *Face of the Screaming Werewolf* is a naive conceit, perhaps. But the man took the four (five) ignored movies, invested his time and made them his own. He offered up no excuses, received no plaudits, yet still turned a profit. In a quirky way, Jerry Warren is the American work ethic personified.

Gracias, Jerry. *Descanse en paz.*

bare•bones

Volume 1 Number 3/4

Spring 1999 $7.50 U.S.

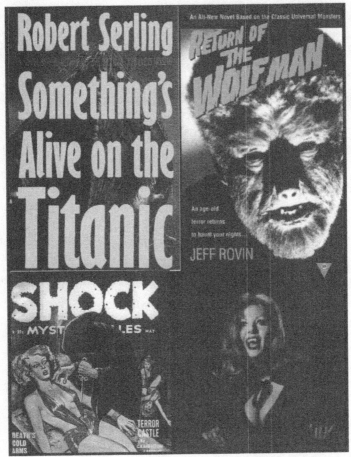

**UNEARTHING VINTAGE AND FORGOTTEN
HORROR/MYSTERY/SCI-FI/WESTERN
FILM-PAPERBACKS-PULP FICTION-VIDEO**

THE DRACULA HORROR SERIES #1

Dracula Returns!

by Robert Lory

Professor Harmon's visit
to ancient Transylvania
begins a new expedition
into the bloodthirsty realm
of the world's most fearsome
character!

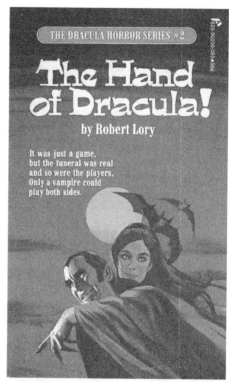

THE DRACULA HORROR SERIES #2

The Hand of Dracula!

by Robert Lory

It was just a game,
but the funeral was real
and so were the players.
Only a vampire could
play both sides.

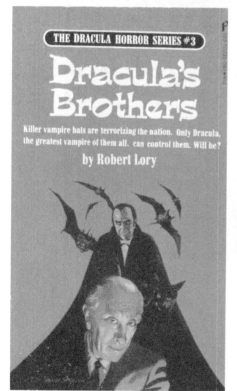

THE DRACULA HORROR SERIES #3

Dracula's Brothers

Killer vampire bats are terrorizing the nation. Only Dracula,
the greatest vampire of them all, can control them. Will he?

by Robert Lory

THE DRACULA HORROR SERIES #4

Dracula's Gold

A spine-tingling treasure hunt through the
wolf-haunted tunnels of Dracula Mountain!

by Robert Lory

I'm a sucker for series books. Particularly books with a matching trade dress—it's like collector's catnip. That said, I tend to collect far more than I have the time to read, which is why we regularly featured series articles. As I noted in the editorial, many readers were hoping Peter would tackle Robert Lory's Dracula series as a follow-up to his fantastic article on the Frankenstein Horror Series. While Peter wasn't willing to submit to the perceived punishment, he convinced Bill Gagliani to do so. Perhaps more than any other, this piece tied us directly back to our Scream Factory *roots. -John*

DRACULA LIVES AGAIN (AND AGAIN AND AGAIN...)
Blending Genres in Robert Lory's Dracula Series
by W.D. Gagliani

Genre-blending is all the rage right now, but it wasn't always the case. There was a time when solid lines delineated the parameters of all the popular genres, and to stray outside those lines meant certain banishment—or, at least, that an irate editor was forced to help the writer work the sinful themes from his or her novel. It was well-known that readers of such questionable genres could not handle variations from the strict boundaries set forth long ago, that they could not fathom such departures from the familiar and, indeed, that any such dilutions would weaken the genetic make-up of all genre novels. The end of genre publishing as we knew it.

Exaggeration? Well, yes, somewhat. The fact is, all the pulp publishers had been quietly blending genres for decades. They just didn't make a fuss about it. Science Fiction and noir thrillers had been married for years, both in publishing and in the movies. The supernatural often showed up in thrillers that on the surface seemed to be straightforward. And when Abbott and Costello met all the famous movie monsters and the classic actors who portrayed them, they proved that even widely divergent genres could blend with satisfactory results. You laughed at the antics of Bud and Lou, and you feared Dracula and the Wolfman—

it should have been a doomed effort, but it worked. Perhaps movies were responsible for accelerating the process, so more and more borrowed elements began showing up in novels. While this quiet revolution didn't wipe out the strict genre definitions, it did loosen them enough to pave the way for the likes of Robert Lory's Dracula Horror Series.

I read the first book of the series, **Dracula Returns**, when it was published in 1973. I was attracted by its cheesy cover painting—a very nice skull fading into the usual bat caught in flight before a full moon, with the background made up of a grim-looking Dracula complete with cape and Munsters haircut. I was going through a vampire appreciation phase, so it stood to reason that I would pick up this new book based on its premise alone—Professor Damien Harmon travels to Transylvania and awakens Dracula, turning him into some kind of slave. The back cover blurb was in First person, and that attracted me as well, for I always gravitated toward an active narrative voice. Strangely, the books are not written in First person—only that first cover blurb. I had never heard of Robert Lory and, to tell the truth, I haven't heard much about him since. His listing in **The Encyclopedia of Science Fiction** is skeletal at best—Lory was born in 1936 and still lived upon its

89

publication in 1993, his collection **A Harvest of Hoodwinks** was published in 1970, and he published several SF series. As for Horror, besides the Dracula series, he also published four novels as the Horrorscope sequence (See list). His SF and Science Fantasy novels are called "undemanding" and "unambitious but competent." Still, not a bad output for a mere "public relations adviser."

What attracted me to that first book, besides the First person blurb and the cover? It was the promise of a horror novel tinged with science fiction. Even then I craved the genre blending we take for granted now, but which was mostly unannounced and nearly hidden. Alas, I wish I could report that I fell in love with the series, but the truth is that—though I finished the first installment—I was not drawn into the rest. Now having been given the chance to catch up with the other eight novels, I find a strangely ambivalent feeling in trying to assess them. On one hand, I appreciate their simplicity and their use of well-recognized (and certainly overused) horror tropes. On the other hand, Lory's writing seems wildly uneven, straightforward at times and overtly pompous and eerily empty at others. Occasionally, one can spot the mechanical aspect of the writing machine that cranked out fifteen novels in three years. The overuse of horror conventions alone is not sufficient to damage the viability of a whole series, for we tend to accept the familiar with little question—if not, would so many TV series seem so alike? But when the writing turns cynical in its stamped-out approach, as often seems to happen in the later books of the Dracula series, it's just as likely that an audience will lose interest. A certain degree of conviction in the narrative voice helps to quell sudden bursts of disbelief, or even contempt. Had the novels been written in First person, as that first back cover blurb implied, I feel that the books would have stood up better and held interest longer. By using an inconsistently shifting point of view, Lory was unable to capture and hold attention. More on this subject later.

•

Dracula Returns (Pinnacle, 1973)

begins the series with a fair amount of style and success. In a two-part prologue, an unnamed Van Helsing and his cronies manage to stake Dracula in his coffin in 1883, and in 1938 Damien Harmon is beaten with a lead pipe on a New York pier and left for dead after having been rolled into the water. As the novel begins, the time is the present. Professor Damien Harmon survived the murderous thugs, but his career as a police officer ended not only because he was confined to a wheelchair, but also because he had disobeyed orders and attempted to work undercover. His two previous college degrees and a considerable family fortune allowed him to teach at a respectable university and eventually retire to continue his two main interests: dealing with criminals who managed to beat the court system, and researching the paranormal and occult sciences. Like Batman, Harmon has had his revenge on those who paralyzed him, and has sworn vengeance on all criminals who elude justice. He is ripe for a new weapon to bring to bear in his never-ending and illegal struggle against crime.

Lory then introduces Cameron Sanchez, the latest in a long line of assistant/partners who have done Harmon's bidding as executioners of criminals. Sanchez, a former cop jailed on a trumped-up charge, was saved from a life sentence by Harmon's vast financial and legal backing, and is now employed by him, ostensibly as his chauffeur and assistant. A bald giant of a man with martial arts training and a penchant for electronics, he shares Harmon's New York brownstone when he's not killing some low-life thug or mobster. Lory makes Cam a major Third person viewpoint character right from the start, though others' POVs are also utilized throughout the series. Cam would have made a superb First person narrator, based on some of the sections which feature his POV, playing Watson to Harmon's rather distant Holmes. If Lory thought to avoid the cliché, it was the only one—and one he should have embraced.

The plot shifts into gear as a handsome, elderly woman comes to visit unannounced and attempts to recruit Harmon by telling him she knows of his activities, and offering power he cannot imagine. The power of an unimaginable weapon. Leaving the same way she arrived, as a black cat, the woman also makes sure that Harmon will read certain passages from an ancient book and find yet another thin book he does not know he owns, "The Runes of Ktara," in which verses tell the story of the fall of Atlantis and what happened to one who survived its end. His name, Son of the Dragon, or Dracula.

After a jarring time compression, the three are headed to Transylvania, where Harmon will attempt to revive the vampire. Ktara's very existence depends on finding someone to pull the stake from her Master's heart, for she ages like a human when he lies in his coffin, but is as immortal as he when he has been freed. Indeed, she is not only able to come and go as a cat, but can also read minds and communicate with her Master and others telepathically—all except for Professor Harmon, whose run-in with the lead pipe in 1938 also left him wearing a steel plate in his skull. It soon becomes apparent that while it is in Ktara's interest to convince someone to remove the stake from Dracula's heart, that hardy soul's fate is out of her hands—Dracula routinely feeds on whoever she has brought to do her bidding. In this case, however, Harmon and Cam have devised a weird safeguard they hope will give them control of the vampire. An electronic implant in Dracula's chest, containing a sliver of the stake which held him prisoner, will be controlled by Harmon's small but growing telekinetic power—he is able to mentally withdraw or release the sliver in Dracula's chest. And if the professor's heart were to stop beating, his transmitter implant would send the message to stake Dracula as well, as a safeguard. Though the fact of Harmon's telekinesis is rather a stretch, the rest of the plot is not exactly grounded in reality either, so it's not that huge a stretch after all. It's a more complex arrangement than necessary, but it allows for some interplay between the four main characters' minds. Harmon's mind cannot be breached because of the steel plate, so his control over the vampire is likely to succeed where a mere electronic device would fail. Lory plays this card often in the series, whenever the issue of control is broached—Ktara is also able to influence people's will by entering their minds, but cannot do so with Harmon.

The climb to Dracula's mountain, the planting of the device in Dracula's chest, and the vampire's subsequent rude awakening form the novel's best moments. Lory manages to capture a suitably creepy atmosphere while using dialogue and imagery vaguely reminiscent of Polanski's *Fearless Vampire Killers*, but with clear intent. Harmon must teach the vampire that he is in charge, and so it is done with predictable but entertaining results. Cam is amusingly squeamish about the whole thing, and Ktara seems to be playing her own game—after all, she knows Harmon's motives, but allows him to control her Master so that she may be young again. Motivations swirl nicely here, and Lory's crowning achievement is to make the whole thing fun and believable in a goofy, TV-movie sort of way. Harmon's old professor pal, the Rumanian Alexandru Thorka, first appears here, helping the gang get into and out of the country without Customs hassles—though the long, heavy crate they take with them does arouse his curiosity.

The next part of the novel unfortunately lost me when I read it in 1973, as Harmon unleashes his slave vampire (whose ego is understandably huge) against stereotypical mobsters who have stolen a crate containing the means with which the implants' batteries can be recharged. On rereading it for this article, I can report that it reminded me of (John Landis's) *Innocent Blood*, the movie in which Robert Loggia plays a mobster who, when vampirized, sees the potential and turns his lieutenants and thugs into vampires as well. In that new light, Lory's earlier efforts appear more original.

This first novel of the series boasts a few fine moments and provides a fair amount of entertainment while building the basis for the books to come. The characters are engaging, and the plot—though far-fetched and often somewhat unintentionally comical—holds one's interest. The blending of horror, science fiction, fantasy, and hardboiled thriller is mostly effective, even if at some point the absurdity of the plot connections finally red-lines. The novels to come would prove widely divergent in these elements.

•

The second novel, **The Hand of Dracula** (Pinnacle, 1973), is ludicrous if studied too carefully, but works reasonably well as light escapism. Professor Harmon's niece, the beautiful and impetuous Jenny (a blonde California girl, totally straight even in those wild early Seventies) is convinced a friend is innocent of murder. There's a weird beginning in which a college kid is on a strange scavenger hunt just before his death. Jenny's friend was known to have threatened the victim, so he's now the prime suspect. Turns out both were members or prospective members of a pseudo-religious cult in which the leader, a drugged-out hippie type, practices human sacrifice to keep his flock at bay at a Manson-like farm (he has film-type special effects built into the "chapel" so he can appear to have paranormal powers). But in a surprising-yet-trite twist, the victim was actually killed by a crooked funeral director because the kid had stumbled onto the 2-for-1 burial scheme for the mob. In other words, the whole cult business is a red herring, though that doesn't help the cult members much—Harmon unleashes Dracula on them and he feeds well, after which a fire covers up the evidence. While full of convenient plot devices (the fire, edited tapes to prove the suspect's innocence, etc.), the novel manages to keep a certain rhythmic pace and, thanks to a smirking sense of perhaps intentional humor (the ageless Ktara refers to an "expected bonanza," and a ghoulish scene "would have been laughable," we're told, had it appeared in a movie), proves as entertaining as the first.

•

The winning streak ends with **Dracula's Brothers** (Pinnacle, 1973), an effort weak enough to undermine the whole series. There is some silliness about identical twins, one a magician and the other a scientist, and a game played as to which of the two has trained hordes of vampire bats to attack buildings and specific individuals. A rather ridiculous pitched battle between cops and vampire bats erupts on the roof of the United Nations, and Cam gets to try some electronic gadgets along with more traditional flame-throwers. The madman (but which one?) is holding the city ransom, you see, until respect and money flow his way. A scheming Dracula, under Harmon's control, is employed to trail the bats and locate the madman's hideout. Lory gets carried away with bad horror movie clichés in this one, making the dialogue as cheesy as a Kraft box meal. Two characters who will make further appearances are introduced in this novel—Hank Navarre, the tough cop who has it in for Cam Sanchez because he believes Harmon bought his freedom, and Proctor, an old cop friend of Harmon who's retired now, but still in position to help with unseen clout and/or the ability to ask for Harmon's unofficial help. Navarre mainly seethes as Proctor gets Harmon and the Drac team out of trouble, time and again. This installment is also notorious for two other cheesy confections: asterisks direct the reader to footnotes which refer to prior books in the series, so Lory's concise summaries don't become too confusing—a feature that seems somewhat pompous in this context; and Pinnacle's ads at the back of the book advertise a Dracula series by Robert Lory in which "Professor Charles Harvey and his assistant, Eric Fromann" resurrect the vampire. This rather embarrassing error is continued—amazingly—through each and every remaining volume of the series! Add to these indignities the Halloween orange front and back covers, and the one star rating seems almost generous.

•

The fourth installment, **Dracula's Gold** (Pinnacle, 1973), finds village youths murdered on Dracula Mountain, at the foot of the ruined remains of the castle. No one knows why they wandered there at night, but it may have something to do with an archeological dig that some distant Dracula relative has begun, using local labor. Dr. Thorka writes Harmon and requests his help in solving the case, knowing well that Harmon has some secret knowledge.

THE DRACULA HORROR SERIES #5

The Drums of Dracula

The throbbing of drums shatters the night as Professor Harmon's niece is kidnapped by devilish voodoo slaves!

by Robert Lory

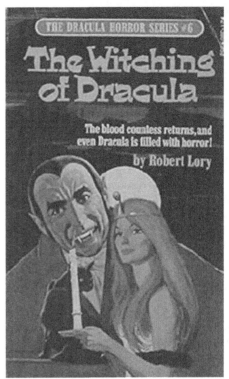

THE DRACULA HORROR SERIES #6

The Witching of Dracula

The blood countess returns, and even Dracula is filled with horror!

by Robert Lory

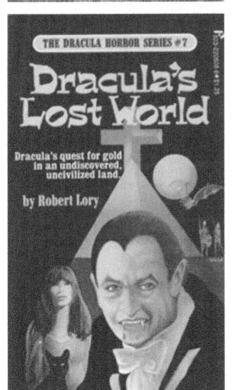

THE DRACULA HORROR SERIES #7

Dracula's Lost World

Dracula's quest for gold in an undiscovered, uncivilized land.

by Robert Lory

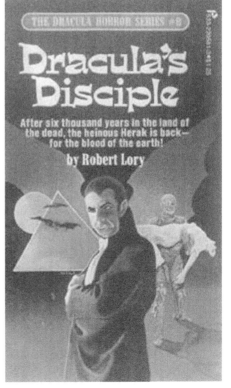

THE DRACULA HORROR SERIES #8

Dracula's Disciple

After six thousand years in the land of the dead, the heinous Herak is back— for the blood of the earth!

by Robert Lory

Besides, the mountain has been overrun with wolves since Harmon and his crew dragged something long and heavy out of the area. Harmon has no trouble convincing an angry Dracula that they should travel back to the old country—the vampire's fabled treasure must be the impostor's target, though it turns out that this is merely one of many hoards Dracula has secreted around the world in preparation for some secret purpose. When they are all back in Transylvania, standard Hammer film stuff happens—villagers wander too far at night, wolves give chase, villagers die, are found drained of blood, and so on. More unintentional humor abounds. The seal on Dracula's treasure room reads: "Break not the seal, open not the door, / Enter not within my room, / Else you this very night shall find, / Within, your night of doom." At one point, the evil woman actually behind the killings gets naked and plays with the gold: "filling her hands with coins, pressing them to her breasts, then lifting them over her head and giving herself a golden shower." Indeed! Joking aside, there is one creepy scene in which a vengeful Dracula commands the impostor to rip out his own tongue, all rendered in delightful detail. Between ripped out tongues and golden showers, **Dracula's Gold** is mildly amusing at best.

•

A rather superior effort is **The Drums of Dracula** (Pinnacle, 1974), which, for all its flaws, shines here as one of the better representatives of the series. The beautiful and much too wholesome Jenny Harmon invites herself to the island estate of Atwood Garth, an old friend of her uncle's, to study voodoo practices. Unfortunately, she immediately runs afoul of the local voodoo priest and his hench-people, who kidnap and hold her for ransom, forcing the Drac team to come running to the rescue. The voodoo scenes are spooky in a bad movie way, and there is considerably more nudity and sex than in most other volumes, a definite plus. Jenny, who is smitten with Cam Sanchez (he has the body of a god, after all) gets to spend some quality S&M time chained next to him, both naked. Daddy Bones, the voodoo priest, turns out to have some real powers,

but they are nullified by a particularly sadistic Dracula, who has begun to crave some Jennifer himself. Possibly inspired by scenes from the climax of **Live and Let Die** (the first Roger Moore James Bond movie), this adventure clicks along nicely and boasts a decent twist ending. It does, however, refer to islanders as "backward," "primitive," and "ignorant," and wins no prizes for its portrayal of the local patois. All things considered, however, this one is a highlight of the series.

•

The Witching of Dracula (Pinnacle, 1974) forms the other side of the sine wave of quality which characterizes the series. The beautiful witch Sabor (in this revisionist version, the true source of the legend of Elizabeth Bathory—the Blood Countess), returns to seek vengeance on the tall, dark and powerful man who sealed her into a glass coffin for eternity. Now awakened by yet another ignorant villager, the red-haired sorceress tramps around the mountains and makes life difficult for Alex Thorka, Harmon's hapless old friend. After yet another flight into the old world, the Drac team bumbles around while Sabor sucks the brains of various peasants and tourists, resulting in empty-skulled robotic slaves (intentional sexual metaphors? who's to say?). After taking over a resort castle, she becomes amused enough with Cam to plot a little tryst after he's been tortured and branded with her symbol, a stylized S. Lory seems to have descended into S&M wish mode (that's okay, all our stories are wish fulfillment) by making the evil witch so alluring. As usual, this witch loves to hear herself talk, awaiting both Dracula and Ktara with glee. Ktara, who for the first time seems a little smitten with Cam herself, manages to use her powers to protect him from illusion warriors and robotic slave warriors and the majority of the torture, but a power-sapping fire almost does her in. Sabor uses Harmon to taunt Dracula by forcing the vampire to save the old man, whose death would otherwise cause the vampire's staking. The magical duel continues until the unwitting Alexandru Thorka appears, creating a diversion, and one by one Sabor's enemies neutralize each

94

of her powers, until Dracula can feast on her blood. The protracted final battle rings with the boastful words of every bad movie ever made—where the bad guys always talk too much instead of wiping out their enemies. Sabor winds up at the bottom of a lake in yet another sealed glass coffin—in Lory's universe, all the bad guys have come back more than once. Light and amusing at times, this novel's over-the-top climax seems like yet another goulash of trusty clichés.

•

Dracula's Lost World (Pinnacle, 1974) is a marginally better effort, once again revolving around a secret Dracula hoard of gold, this one hidden in the Amazon, up a nasty river past tribes of unfriendly natives. A trio of crooks are clued in to the existence of a manuscript in which the location of the village is spelled out by an ancient Spanish sailor who survived capture there, and they murder several innocents in their quest to own it. Unfortunately, two bear a passing resemblance to Cam and Ktara, leading the vengeful cop Navarre to arrest Cam. Of course, the only way to clear the faithful giant is to track the bad guys to the lost City of Gold referred to in the manuscript and there to defeat Dracula's old protégé, an immortal named Kabaya. Yet another sadist, Kabaya suspends poor old Professor Harmon inside a pit full of piranha-infested water and links the length of the rope directly to his repeated sexual encounters with the Ktara look-alike, a creep who eagerly feeds her knife-wielding husband to the hungry fish. Here again, Dracula is expected—Kabaya has built a huge golden cross to keep the Master from checking up on his pupil. But the Drac team wins in the end, bringing home the Ktara look-alike so she can recite Drac-influenced testimony to Navarre in order to clear Cam. It's all so much ridiculous tripe, but the blend of luck, coincidence, and magical powers seems to work well enough here. Some good jungle scenes make this novel a more delightful read, even though the supposedly ancient manuscript is poorly written and thoroughly unconvincing.

•

The penultimate entry in the series, **Dracula's Disciple** (Pinnacle, 1975), is also one of the best. This time Lory uses the varied mummy canon around which to build his Drac team adventure, starting with the release of Herak from a metal jar prison. Six thousand years ago, Herak was imprisoned there by—who else?—an immortal Dracula, survivor of Atlantis. Suddenly freed by students participating in an Egyptian dig, Herak immediately begins inhabiting the bodies of students. One of the better-drawn enemies of Dracula, Herak captures some of the sense of wonder one would expect of a six-thousand-year-old disciple. Lory manages some of the same pathos often associated with mummy movies, especially the original, *The Mummy*, though he is not, strictly speaking, a mummy himself. Herak can, however, raise dead mummies and make them slaves, and they make much better adversaries for Cam than did the pike-wielding tourist slaves of Sabor. Though the plot revolves around the Old Ones, the race of Masters of which Dracula was a part and whom he was able to banish to another planet (or plane), it is Herak's struggle to learn about the modern world and make sense of what has happened to him, as well as gain his revenge, that makes this installment stand out in the series. Jenny Harmon has once again unwittingly forced herself onto the Drac team, and she conveniently becomes a prize for Herak, who requires fresh virgin blood for his rituals. His amazement at the difficulty of finding virgins in the modern world is almost endearing. Harmon gets a chance to do something more than just become bait for Dracula—his marksmanship helps clear the way for Cam and the vampire to attack Herak's Cairo headquarters. Cam has to fight mummies, who fall apart in gruesome ways, and Herak comes to covet Cam's body even more than Jennifer's blood and feminine charms. Even the usual over-the-top climax can't damage this, possibly the masterpiece of the series.

•

Finally we come to **Challenge to Dracula** (Pinnacle, 1975), in which Lory proves that a writer can indeed become jaded and treat his characters with disdain. First, the cover is by a different artist and contains a major error—the mighty Ka-

Zadok is portrayed as a red-haired Viking type instead of the black-haired Mongol he is supposed to be. This omen does not bode well for the rest of the book. The Drac team races to Tibet (a nod to **Lost Horizon**) to face yet another evil-doer shamefully defeated by Dracula. Ka-Zadok has sat frozen on a throne, guarding one of Dracula's hoards, for thousands of years. Now awakened, he uses his own magician's powers plus the advice of the Old Ones to draw Dracula to him. This mélange features the team's Indiana Jones-style flight to Tibet, complete with magical control of the aircraft, as well as more illusions—for instance, Ka-Zadok's mighty castle is a magical construct that's not really there (and it takes a lot of power for him to keep it visible). Not to mention suddenly appearing yeti, some real and some not, and more illusions than you can shake a stake at. Cam gets a chance to show off his warrior side when he challenges some of Ka-Zadok's denizens in a well-choreographed fight mano a mano. The climax is again talky and overdone, and ends the series with more mention of the Old Ones, but no more books to come. A slight effort, not nearly as effective as its predecessor.

Robert Lory's interesting take on both the Dracula legacy and, to some extent, every other major genre theme will likely be remembered for the good-natured frivolous fun it is—not literature, perhaps, but able to fill a niche left by the pulps. Though the science in Lory's works is decidedly dated, his success varying the routine brush strokes of the period at least grants his series a special appeal that often transcends its mediocre mechanics.

Dracula Returns (1973) **1/2
The Hand of Dracula (1973) **1/2
Dracula's Brothers (1973) *
Dracula's Gold (1973) **
The Drums of Dracula (1974) ***
The Witching of Dracula (1974) *1/2
Dracula's Lost World (1974) **1/2
Dracula's Disciple (1975) ***
Challenge to Dracula (1975) *

(Note: ratings are comparative within the series, forming a relative scale.)

THE DRACULA HORROR SERIES #9

Challenge to Dracula

The mighty wizard, Ka-Zadok, returns from the dead to seek dreadful vengeance against the Son of Dracula

by Robert Lory

Other novels by Robert Lory:

THE TROVO SERIES
The Eyes of Bolsk (1969)
Master of the Etrax (1970)
A Harvest of Hoodwinks (collection, 1970)

THE SHAMRYKE ODELL SEQUENCE
Masters of the Lamp (1970)
The Veiled World (1972)
Identity Seven (1974)
The Thirteen Bracelets (1974)

THE HORRORSCOPE SEQUENCE
The Green Flames of Aries (1974)
The Revenge of Taurus (1974)
The Curse of Leo (1974)
Gemini Smile, Gemini Kill (1975)

*Everyone knows Rod Serling. Far fewer knew his brother Bob was also an accomplished writer. My recollection is hazy, but I think that Peter first suggested that we track him down for an interview after reading his latest novel, **Something's Alive on the Titanic**, and loving it. I seem to recall that I worked on the questions with Vince, and he conducted the interview with Bob in Arizona. I also remember some follow up communications with Bob, and being impressed by how kind and accommodating he was. It's sad to note that all of the interview subjects included herein have since passed on. We hope that reading these interviews will encourage you to seek out their work. -John*

FROM THE FRIENDLY SKIES TO TITANIC DEPTHS
Robert Serling Interview
by Vince Fahey and John Scoleri

Robert Serling is the author of numeous airline histories and several novels including **The President's Plane is Missing** *and* **Something's Alive on the Titanic**. *His brother Rod was the television pioneer responsible for the* Twilight Zone. *He lives in Arizona, where he took the time to talk with* bare•bones *about his life and work.*

bare•bones: You've written several non-fiction books and the majority of your novels about airlines. How did you get involved in writing about aviation?

ROBERT SERLING: From boyhood. I used to collect pictures of military planes and build models. They were lousy but I built them. I have the manual dexterity of a sick goldfish. And then, I went into the Army and taught aircraft identification. Then, after the war, when I was with the United Press in Washington, I covered my first crash... a Pennsylvania Central Airlines DC-4 that hit a mountain in Virginia. From that, I got fascinated by the technique of accident investigation, so I went down to the Civil Aeronautics Board which used to investigate accidents... this was before the NTSB was even born, reading accident reports and to me they were like a mystery novel. So I started covering the airlines on my own time and eventually I quit my job in management and became aviation editor for UPI. That's how I got interested in airplanes.

BB: Was it through contacts made at UPI that allowed you to move into the writing of fiction and non-fiction?

SERLING: Well, I had written two books, the first of which was **The Probable Cause**, which was the study of air accidents and how they're solved and what we learn from them. Then I wrote my first novel, **The Left Seat**, about an airline captain, based on a true accident that I had covered and the chief character was based on an airline pilot I knew well. He was killed in a crash. And then, one of my jobs as the aviation editor for UPI was going out to Andrews Air Force Base and covering arrivals and departures of Air Force One. Driving home one night, after seeing the President off, I got to thinking, how would I cover something that happened to Air Force One? I imagined myself going out to Andrews Air Force Base, waiting for the plane to come in. It was late and kept getting later and later. An officer comes out and says, "I'm sorry. The President's Plane is Missing." That phrase stuck in my mind because I knew that would be the flash I phoned in. Then I thought, "God, what a title for a book."

I sent just the title in to my editor at Doubleday and she called me and said that it was one hell of a title if I could come up with a plot. They gave me enough money that I would be able to quit UPI if I wanted.

THE PRESIDENT'S PLANE IS MISSING

Robert J. Serling

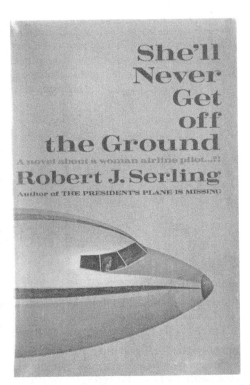

She'll Never Get off the Ground

A novel about a woman airline pilot...?!

Robert J. Serling

Author of THE PRESIDENT'S PLANE IS MISSING

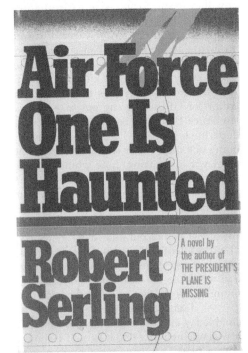

Air Force One Is Haunted

Robert Serling

A novel by the author of THE PRESIDENT'S PLANE IS MISSING

Robert Serling

A NOVEL BY THE AUTHOR OF *THE PRESIDENT'S PLANE IS MISSING*

Something's Alive on the Titanic

So a week later I sent her an outline. She accepted it, but said she needed the book done in six months. So I quit UPI, $7,000 in debt at the time, with no job and no idea how the hell I was going to live as a freelance writer. But I took a chance and turned the book in and it turned out to be a smash bestseller. It got as high as number five on the New York Times list. So I was in business, and though this was actually my third book, it was my first as a freelance writer.

BB: For books such as **Air Force One is Haunted** and **The President's Plane is Missing**, what kind of research did you do?

SERLING: Well, of course, for **Air Force One is Haunted**, with UPI, I knew a hell of a lot about Air Force One... what the airplane looked like inside, how it was handled and flown, air traffic control communication... that part was simple. After I wrote that, an airline contacted me and asked if I'd be interested in writing their history. That was easy too, because I'd covered the airline for a long time. So then, I started writing airline histories. As each one came out, some other airline would contact me, telling me I'd done a hell of a job and would I like to write their history. So I wound up writing six of those. I tried to alternate between fiction and non-fiction because when you do a non-fiction book you get a little bored and tired with the research because it takes so damn long (laughs). It usually takes about six months to research a non-fiction book and then six months to write it and rewrite it. With all the background that I had with airplanes because of my experience with UPI (which I was with since before World War II), I had a hell of a lot of background in the commercial airline industry. So my novels turned out to have airline backgrounds. I wrote one called **Wings** which was really the story of the airline industry from the 1920's. **The Probable Cause**, of course, is self-explanatory. **She'll Never Get Off the Ground** was a novel about a woman airline pilot and I wrote it when there weren't any. I never really had much trouble with research because my background was so solid.

BB: What led to writing **Something's Alive on the Titanic**, as while it fits thematically with your other ghost books, it has nothing to do with aviation?

SERLING: The Titanic was another of my boyhood fascinations. I loved reading about that from about the time I was ten years old and I always wanted to write a book about it. As a matter of fact, after I left UPI, I was tooling around with the idea of doing more research on the Titanic because nothing had been written about it in years. Just as I'd decided to write it, Walter Lord came out with **A Night to Remember**, and that killed it. Later, I had written **Air Force One is Haunted**, which was the sequel to **The President's Plane is Missing**, and used some of the same characters. It was a ghost story... the ghost of Franklin D. Roosevelt appears on Air Force One. And I got fascinated with the bizarre, the horror aspects... sometimes I wonder if my late brother Rod didn't put some of these plots into my head (laughs). This was the kind of book he would have written. With the Titanic, I knew I couldn't write another non-fiction book, there were too damn many good ones out by then. But I thought, "Boy, what a novel." So, that's how it got started. As an author, I don't always remember when I first thought of a story, especially this one that the Titanic could be haunted. I didn't have to do an awful lot of research with the Titanic to write a novel because so much had already been written about it in non-fiction. I already had a great background in reading non-fiction books about the Titanic that it came naturally.

BB: Since the book was published, have you had the opportunity to meet or speak with Robert Ballard (the man who discovered the wreck of the Titanic)?

SERLING: Ballard's discovery of the Titanic really was a godsend to me because that showed the world what the Titanic looked like today. Otherwise, I would've fallen into the same trap as Clive Cussler who had the ship in one solid piece. I've never met him though my feelings were a little hurt because I dedicated the book to him and he got galleys and I never heard from him.

I had a chance to meet him when he came to a Tucson Medical Association dinner. My doctor invited me to go but I was still pissed off so I said no.

BB: You list several reference works you used in the researching and writing of **Something's Alive on the Titanic**. I understand you also built a mock-up of the ship. Is this something you had done for any of your other novels?

SERLING: I built a hell of a model... a $50, three-foot model made out of plastic. It's my proudest achievement, and like I said I have absolutely no skill whatsoever with my hands but that one was a labor of love. I never did it for any of my other novels. When I wrote **She'll Never Get off the Ground**, a reader sent me a beautiful model of the Boeing 737, painted in the colors of the fictitious airline that I used in the book, and that was a real joy. Unfortunately, we moved and now I can't find the damn thing.

BB: What is it about Titanic that fascinates you?

SERLING: That's like asking me to describe the color red. I think one of the reasons the sinking still has so much effect on everybody is that anybody who's interested in that story can't help but put themselves in the same position. In other words, "Boy, if that had happened to me, what would I have done?" That's the first. Secondly, is the mystery of it. Why did it happen? What was wrong with the unsinkable ship? What mistakes were made? The very fact that there was such a tremendous loss of life, one of the two or three great sea disasters in history. Also, that it was the maiden voyage and there was such a cross section of society aboard the ship at that time. I think the whole darn story is incredibly fascinating from almost every respect. I think a marine engineer, a father, a mystery buff, anybody would be fascinated by all the aspects of this tragedy.

BB: Was it a difficult sell, or did the interest of the discovery a few years earlier still exist in the public at the time the book was published?

SERLING: Not this one. I had a good editor at St. Martin's Press who had loved **Air Force One is Haunted**. Then I had the good luck to have Boeing ask me to write the history of their company on their 75th anniversary. Because St. Martin's was my publisher at the time, I worked out a deal between Boeing, myself and the publisher that was extremely lucrative for the publisher.

Boeing bought something like 275,000 copies of the book before it was ever written. So, I think I had something of a foot in the door with the Titanic novel. **Air Force One is Haunted**, which didn't do nearly as well as **The President's Plane is Missing**, sold well enough that he took a chance on the Titanic novel. It turned out as well that he was a Titanic buff as well as a deep-sea diving salvage expert, so he gave me a lot of technical stuff that I normally wouldn't have known about. I think it was as much his labor of love as mine that sold the book.

BB: How well did the book do? What kind of response did it receive critically, or from any readers you heard from?

SERLING: It got good critical reviews but sold very poorly. The publishing industry has changed so, that you don't work with editors anymore... the sales department is king now. I don't think, and you can quote me, that the average American publisher could sell a cooling system in the middle of the Sahara Desert at high noon. They don't know how to market books, their sales, promotion, and advertising practices are just a collection of acronyms.

BB: **Something's Alive on the Titanic** deals quite strongly with those who pillage the underwater memorial. Do you have strong feelings about treasure hunting of the Titanic?

SERLING: My thinking has changed a little. I used to think the same way as Ballard did, "Leave the wreck alone, it's a graveyard," and I felt that way when I wrote the book. Now I keep thinking, with all the evidence that the ship is disintegrating, that if they can bring up artifacts, I no longer see any harm in it. Most of the stuff taken to be used

Robert J. Serling (1984) *photo by George Janoff*

as artifacts, mostly by the French, was found in the debris field between the fore part and the aft part of the ship... and there's nothing wrong with that. They didn't go in and strip the inside of the ship, so no, I don't find anything wrong with it now.

BB: When it was announced James Cameron was doing a film on Titanic, it seemed that your book would have been more in line of a James Cameron film than what he eventually developed. What did you think of the film?

SERLING: I loved it. I thought it was terrific. I think it belongs up there with *Gone With the Wind* as a classic spectacular. His attention to detail, despite one that I was nit-picky about, was incredible. I didn't know that he had carpet specially made to totally copy the ones used in the Titanic. The furniture, everything, was incredibly authentic, from costumes, to the weave design in the carpet, the color of the furniture, man, it's no wonder it cost $200 million. I wrote Cameron a letter, praising the movie, but also pointing out that they had one great technical error in it... the longshot from the ships showed smoke coming out from all four funnels, but the fourth funnel on the Titanic was a dummy. It couldn't have any smoke coming out of it. I also suggested that if he ever wanted to another movie about a great sea disaster, to do the Lusitania, since it's never been done. It's a story that's almost as sensational a disaster as the Titanic, and in the terms of history it was even worse because it caused us to enter World War I. I never got an answer from him either.

BB: Because you had such a strong interest, and a good knowledge of the ship and everything surrounding it, were you surprised by the number of people who saw it, the length of time it was in theaters, and it's popularity?

SERLING: Surprised is the wrong word. Overjoyed, because it confirmed my belief that a really great film about that ship would draw a hell of a lot of interest. I felt that way, overjoyed, because of the way the publisher had handled my book, without taking advantage of that basic interest of people who weren't even born when the Titanic went down.

BB: Has **Something's Alive on the Titanic** been optioned for film or television? Have you given any thought to whom you think would be an ideal director, or actors for the main roles?

SERLING: No, never optioned. I thought at the time that it would make a hell of a movie but I thought it'd be too expensive (laughs). I think, however, that Cameron made a better movie with *Titanic* than he would've with my book. He recounted history and my story would've been 75% fiction, which is why I thought his movie was better. I hate to say that because you can imagine how wealthy I'd be if he'd bought mine. As far as my ideal director and actor for my book, and this is now all Monday morning quarterbacking, no one but Cameron could've done that job. His other deep-sea diving film, *The Abyss*, was a comparative failure at the box office, but was one hell of a movie. I don't think any director could've done better. I couldn't even begin to guess about actors. It's the kind of movie where you don't even need stars. The ship, the story, the tragedy... the mistakes, they're all so overpowering that you could take any collection of half-way good actors and made a great movie. I thought his casting was superb. I'd venture to say that if you interviewed 1,000 people who'd seen the movie, and asked them to name who played Captain Smith, you'd be lucky to get five correct answers. That's exactly what I mean. He didn't use any big name stars.

BB: The resurgence of interest in Titanic has led to the reissue of your novel once again. What led to the original three-year delay between the St. Martin's hardcover and mass-market paperback release?

SERLING: They don't promote anymore. Here's an example: when the movie *Titanic* came out, and it started to fill the theaters and it was getting rave reviews, I wrote the publisher, St. Martin's, and said, "For God's sake, reissue the paperback." On which incidentally I still owe them money, since it never made back the advance. They were going to send me on a promotion tour when the paperback first came out in '92 and I never heard from them... no tour, no advertising. Then, after I wrote them and asked them to re-release the book, they still didn't answer my letter. My agent kept prodding them and it wasn't until the movie won the Academy Award that they decided to reissue the paperback, which was too late. I've seen it around in drugstores and such but I'm not sure how it's doing. The sales are disappointing and yet it's probably the second favorite book that I've written.

BB: What's the attraction to ghost themes present in several of you novels?

SERLING: I never really got interested in the whole subject of psychic phenomenon until I got the idea of putting Franklin D. Roosevelt's ghost on Air Force One. That's when I did a little research on psychic phenomenon. That's when I transferred that research to the Titanic story. I wrote a complete outline of another novel called **The Hindenburg Haunting,** which so far has been rejected by everyone. My agent's never been able to sell it but I think it's a hell of a story because it's the other great disaster that still lives in people's minds. It's about the Germans, Americans and British building a brand new Zeppelin after the Year 2000... a commercial dirigible that's twice the size of the Hindenburg. The second officer's grandfather was an officer on the Hindenburg who, according to the grandson, was probably the one who sabotaged the Hindenburg. So when he gets on the maiden voyage of this new Zeppelin, he starts seeing his grandfather's ghost. At this point, no one has liked the story and it's harder than hell to sell fiction these days.

BB: Did you ever work on any projects with your brother?

SERLING: Yeah, a couple of times. I helped him with one of the *Twilight Zone* plots. It was the one about the 707 flying over the Atlantic, and it hit a freak tailwind and broke through a time barrier, and when it came in to what they thought was New York, they were back in prehistoric times. It was called "The Odyssey of Flight 33." I gave him the cockpit dialogue for that story. Then he did a Playhouse 90 called "Panic Button." I gave him the plot for that one. Those are the two we really worked on together.

BB: Would you say that you and your brother were similar or different?

SERLING: Similar in some ways, different in many others. He was handsomer, younger... wealthier. We were alike in our sense of humor, and literary taste. We were both World War II buffs because we had both served in World War II. We were both science fiction nuts from way back. I think between the two of us, we saw *King Kong* at least 150 times, and it still ranks as my favorite movie.

BB: You both turned into successful writers, you in fiction and non-fiction, he primarily in television. Did you ever have an interest in working in film or television?

SERLING: Yeah, I did the screenplay for *The President's Plane is Missing*. That was the only book of mine that was filmed into a movie. I did the screenplay for it but then the studio went bankrupt and sold all their properties to ABC, and ABC didn't like my script so they had someone write another one. That was the last I saw of it.

BB: Was it ever finally made into a movie?

SERLING: Yeah, it was shown as an ABC television movie. It stunk. The character in the book who actually was made as the aviation editor for the fictitious wire service,

when I knew that it was gonna be a movie, I kept saying "Boy, who's gonna play him, Mickey Rooney or John Wayne?" It turned out that they changed the character to a woman. God, sometimes I can't figure out Hollywood.

BB: Whereas most writers are known only by their works, your brother eventually became a celebrity. Was this a difficult transition for him, and was it hard to develop a writing career as the brother of Rod Serling?

SERLING: His personality and mine were different. He loved the limelight. He loved adulation and attention. He was much more articulate and extroverted than I am. He fit in well into the TV and radio mold. He was a remarkable phenomenon in that he was probably the only writer in history who became visually famous because he was emceeing *Twilight Zone*, so everyone recognized him. That kind of fame and public recognition... I don't know any other writer, television, literary or anything else who would be so easily recognized. We used to go to restaurants together and it was hard to eat because people kept coming up to ask for his autograph, and he loved it. It drove his wife nuts, but he loved it.

It wasn't hard to be a writer because we took different paths. He took the radio and then television. He was a playwright. He never wrote a novel though he wrote short stories based on *Twilight Zone* plots. I went the other way. Before the war, I was a reporter. After, I went back to being a newspaperman with the wire service. My background, my newspaper years, were really years of research for what I eventually wound up doing, writing books, whereas Rod just stayed in the medium of motion pictures and television. Our careers really took different paths though we both wound up writing for the public.

BB: What work of your own are you most proud of?

RS: In non-fiction, my airline histories. Three standout... the one I did on TWA, the one on American and the one on Western. The TWA one, maybe more than the others because it was the only book I've ever seen that I thought treated Howard Hughes objectively instead of some wild-eyed nut. If they ever do a movie on his life, which I've heard Warren Beatty has in the works, I hope to God they read that book first. That book was the real Howard Hughes. He was a nut, but he was a genius. For fiction, my favorite book is one that didn't sell that well and yet I'm prouder of that than anything I've ever written. It was called **She'll Never Get off the Ground**. It was about a woman airline pilot. As I told you earlier, there were no such things when I wrote it. To do research for the novel, I went through Western's 737 school and actually entered a pilot's class. I went through the training so that my training scenes would be authentic. It was also the first book I ever wrote where my chief character was a woman and I had to put myself into position of a woman entering a man's world. That was difficult. After it was published, years after, airlines started to hire their first women pilot's and I started to get letters from new women pilots saying the only reason they had the guts to apply is because they had read **She'll Never Get off the Ground**. That made me prouder than anything else I've ever done. I also think it was a hell of a book.

BB: What have you been doing since the release of **Something's Alive on the Titanic**? Are there any more books in Robert Serling looking to get out?

SERLING: I wrote a Boeing history and then I had a dry spell where I couldn't sell anything, I mean nothing. I tried with **The Hindenburg Haunting**, I have a non-fiction called **What If?**, which was what if certain things in history had happened differently, like if Custer had won at Little Big Horn, if the Titanic instead of reversing engines, it kept full steam, that got turned down by everyone. I've always wanted to do a book on the history of the airlines in World War II. That got turned down by every major publisher in New York. The title is **When the Airlines Went to War**, and it's not only a story of the airlines in WWII, but also in Vietnam, Korea and the Gulf War. They ran literally half of the military airlifts. I finally got it sold

due to a good friend of mine underwrote the publishing costs and a fairly obscure publisher, Kensington, agreed to publish it since my friend guaranteed the sale of 10,000 books, which many have been donated. It's a chunk of World War history that's never been done before though it hasn't sold very well. It's gotten little to no reviews or press in the mainstream so no wonder it's not selling. I begged Kensington to spend some money advertising but they didn't want to spend any money. They thought it could be sold by word of mouth and reviews, but if they don't advertise, how's anyone going to spread the word if they don't know it's there?

I'm working in a collaboration now on the history of the air-rail service. This was in 1929 when there was no transcontinental air service, where they concocted an idea to go partway by air, partway by train... revolutionary for its time. Lindbergh planned the air service part of it because he was a technical advisor with T.A.T. It's called **Steel Rails and Silver Wings** and I'm doing the text and my partner is doing the research for photographs because it's going to come out more as a coffee table book. There is no publisher right now, and my partner is talking about self-publishing, though it will mean we won't make any money on it since there's no way to distribute a self-published book. But it keeps me busy and at 80 years old. I don't want to retire. I want to be buried with a Mac computer strapped on my chest, still running.

I still want to get my agent to sell the Hindenburg novel, and I sent in an outline for a book called **Prehistoric**, which is the story of a pilot who discovers that Arthur Conan Doyle's **Lost World** wasn't really fiction. That's still making rounds.

BB: Thanks very much for taking the time to speak with us.

SERLING: I enjoyed it.

I have never met anyone more in love with writing about writing than Stefan Dziemianowicz. Stefan has, seemingly, an unending supply of excitement when it comes to paper, the older and moldier the better. I first met Stef at the 1990 World Fantasy Con in Chicago. Bob Weinberg had asked if I would like to sit on a panel with Stef and a couple other uber-fans to give our feelings about 'the future of horror" (or something similar to that). Stef had contacted me a month or so beforehand to run a few things by me, and we hit it off immediately. This guy could tell you which issue of Amazing *Clark Ashton Smith debuted in, but he wasn't some nerd who slept in his basement with headless dolls; this guy was funny and warm and giving. Still is. Though we haven't seen each other in decades, I can lay money down that he's still the same guy he was back then. So when I called him and told him I had a goofy idea about covering all three phases of the* Saturn *Web saga but couldn't face reading serious science fiction (as opposed to* Super *Science Fiction), Stef volunteered on the spot. I think our collaboration came out nicely.* -Peter

BY ANY OTHER NAME: UNLOCKING THE MYSTERIES OF *SATURN SCIENCE FICTION / WEB DETECTIVE / WEB TERROR*
Part One: The Annotated Index to *Saturn Science Fiction*

by Stefan Dziemianowicz

If it looks like a duck, and it quacks like a duck, it's gotta be a duck—right? A leopard can't change its spots—right? If you answered yes to either of the questions above, do not pass "Go." Instead, go back to the 1950s science fiction market, where things were not always what they seemed, and what master anthologist Groff Conklin might have called "science fiction adventures in mutation" were an everyday part of genre magazine publishing. This was the era in which *The Avon Fantasy Reader*, an irregularly published, saddle-stapled digest, and its offshoots *The Avon Science Fiction Reader* and *The Avon Science Fiction and Fantasy Reader*, featured interchangeable contents (despite their different titles) and were promoted by editor and publisher alike as paperback books. The era in which the entertaining fiction magazine *Other Worlds* morphed into the goofy non-fiction embarrassment *Flying Saucers*. And, most interestingly, the era in which *Saturn*, a magazine with a respectable editor and increasingly respectable contents, began life as a science fiction digest and ended as a shudder pulp mystery rag.

The story of *Saturn* is a strange one, but in some ways it describes the many gyrations and weird tangents science fiction took in the post-pulp years. What little is known about the magazine has come to us through the efforts of Mike "Bring 'em Back Alive" Ashley, who interviewed a number of the magazine's principal players when compiling his entry for *Science Fiction, Fantasy, and Weird Fiction Magazines* (Greenwood, 1985). *Saturn* came into existence in 1957, near the end of the short-lived postwar science fiction boom jump-started by the dawn of the Nuclear Age. This was a period where opportunism dovetailed with prosperity, and publishers who didn't have a clue as to what science fiction was all about spawned a vast brood of "sci-fi" magazines, most of them blatant attempts to cash in on the fad of the moment. One of these publishers was Robert Sproul, son of the news company that distributed the burgeoning Ace Books paperback line.

When Sproul got it into his head to beef up his Candar Publishing Company line-up with a science fiction magazine, it made perfect sense that he would tap Ace's science fiction editor, Donald A. Wollheim, for editorial input. Despite the well-connected Wollheim's years of experience editing *Stirring Science Stories*, *Cosmic Stories* and the aforementioned Avon digests, he would never merit a title more distinctive than "Editorial Consultant" on the masthead. Wollheim, as Ashley reports, chose the full contents for each issue, but he was paid only on a flat-fee basis. And as readers of science fiction and fantasy know, all too often you get what you don't pay for.

The first issue of *Saturn the Magazine of Science Fiction* was dated March 1957. It sold for 35 cents and featured a cryptic Leo Summers cover of an astronaut in full spacesuit regalia recoiling from a large, scantily-clad, Finlayesque maiden ascending from the planetary landscape. (Virtually all of the magazine's covers were in this mode.) If the audience to whom the cover was supposed to appeal was a puzzle, so was the editorial reprinted on the inside cover. "Saturn seeks the unique in science fiction, the stories which encompass the greatest thrills which have built upon the [Jules] Verne heritage a whole new literary cosmos of science-fantasy." Indeed, the centerpiece of the first issue was Verne's "Eternal Adam," a "thrilling full-length novel" (actually, at 14,000 words, barely a novella) of the far future reportedly receiving its first translation into English by Willis T. Bradley (who had just translated Verne's **A Journey to the Center of the Earth** for the Ace science fiction line). The five other stories in the first issue were all modern tales by modern writers, not one of whom could be said to be writing in the tradition of Verne: Robert Silverberg contributed a story that reflected his nascent interest in anthropological and psychological themes, and Noel Loomis and Allan Barclay both muscular space operas full of typical human heroes and breast-beating patriotic platitudes. Stories by Barclay and John Brunner were both reprints from the UK's *New Worlds Science Fiction*. The first issue of *Saturn* was probably no worse than any other magazine at the newsstands, and its contents were a reflection of its editorial consultant's taste for old-fashioned science-fantasy as much as contemporary coin-of-the-realm science fiction. This diversity made for an interesting mix, but in hindsight it suggests a lack of vision and direction that may have had much to do with *Saturn's* failure to find an audience.

For its first three issues, *Saturn* kept to its projected bi-monthly schedule. However, changes at a number of levels were already apparent with the second issue. William Clark replaced John Giunta as the magazine's art director, although what this portended is not clear, as Giunta, a seasoned science fiction and fantasy illustrator since his debut in *Weird Tales* in 1942, supplied nearly all of the interior illustrations for the first five issues. There was no editorial in the second issue, nor would there ever be again. Neither was there a letters column despite the debut issue's editorial assurance that "your letters and comments will be welcomed." However, this was not inconsistent with the policy of most science fiction digests, which had less space than the pulps to publish text and usually greater ambitions to pass themselves off as a more distinguished literary product free of the fannish taint of pulp letter columns. The biggest change, however, was the subtitle, which now read "Magazine of Fantasy & Science Fiction" (and which would change again with the third issue to "Science Fiction and Fantasy"). No doubt, this change was made to justify the selection of "The Murky Glass," one of the so-called posthumous collaborations between H. P. Lovecraft and August Derleth that was keeping Lovecraft's horror-based Cthulhu Mythos on life support following the death of *Weird Tales* in 1954. Fantasy fiction would become a staple of the magazine from that point on, and some of the best stories to appear in *Saturn*—Verne's "The Ordeal of Doctor Trifulgas," Clark Ashton Smith's "The Powder of Hyperborea," Robert A. Heinlein's "The Elephant Circuit"—would have no science fiction element at all.

Even more interesting in the May 1957 issue was the lighter tone of the selections. James H. Schmitz (whose novella

"The Big Terrarium" comprised more than a quarter of the issue), Evelyn E. Smith, and Lloyd Biggle, Jr. all contributed humorous stories in which ordinary people wrestled with the awkward incongruities of science fictional possibilities. In subsequent issues, they would be joined by Manly Banister, Charles E. Fritch, and August Derleth, whose stories showed a wittiness and sophistication that elevated them above the more dramatic, but often teen-oriented fare. One can only speculate whether the magazine would have gained a longer lease on life had Wollheim been able to make it a showcase for this type of whimsical science fiction. It was clear, however, that simply trying to match or outdo competing magazines on their own terms did little to advance *Saturn*'s cause or sales.

Over the next three issues, *Saturn* boasted coups that any other magazine would have gladly claimed, including a rare new story from Clark Ashton Smith, the last published story of early science fiction titan Ray Cummings, and an all-star fourth issue line-up that included Heinlein, Harlan Ellison, Jack Vance, Frank Belknap Long, Robert F. Young, and Wollheim himself (under his Martin Pearson pseudonym).

But though the quality of the fiction published was somewhat above average, there was little to distinguish *Saturn* from the dozens of other science fiction magazines at the newsstand. With the third issue, financial realities began to set in, and *Saturn* cut its pages from 128 to 112. (The magazine gave the illusion of adding another two pages with the fifth issue, but this was only because it counted the front and back of its cover as pages one and two).

The fourth issue was dated October 1957, a full month behind schedule, and the fifth issue did not appear until March of the following year. That issue led off with "Red Flag Over the Moon," Romney Boyd's jingoistic essay on Russia's launching of Sputnik, and featured a provocative cover - the only one that ever had anything to do with the magazine's contents - showing cosmonauts staking their claim to the lunar surface. This blatant stab at topicality proved too little too late. The next issue of the magazine did not appear for another five months, and when it surfaced it bore the confused title *Saturn Web Detective Stories*. Gone were Donald Wollheim's editorial input and all vestiges of science fiction and fantasy.

Thenceforth, the magazine specialized in hard-boiled crime fare, of an even cruder type than could be found in *Manhunt*, *Suspense*, and similar mens' mystery digests which were beginning to supplant science fiction publications. All that remained to remind readers of the magazine's former legacy was the word "Saturn" (which, Ashley reveals, Sproul retained solely to hang onto his postal registration), and even that was gone by the next year.

As *Web Detective Stories*, Sproul's magazine published sporadically until 1962, at which point it became *Web Terror Stories*, a feeble pretender to the throne of the shudder pulp and weird menace magazines. In all, it lasted for a total of 27 issues, and a longer period than most of the science fiction digests that failed to evolve - or devolve - along the same path.

The best that can be said of *Saturn* is that it comprised another interesting chapter in Donald A. Wollheim's colorful publishing history. What made it unique was not the science fiction it published, but the strange pathway that took it out of the science fiction field altogether.

Vol. 1 / #1, March 1957

"The Chaos Salient" by Noel Loomis   *
(9,000 wds)

Space opera set in Earth-year 324,972 in the Second Metagalaxy. Frank Rockman, Captain, Earth Contingent, Combat Engineers, finds his efforts to locate the Terebellum Stone and learn its secret of navigating the interstellar Void hindered by the nosy Major Fisher and treasonous Alphirkian Snakes, who have infiltrated the Metagalaxy's Intelligence division. He is helped by an elusive stowaway whose identity is intimately tied to the stone and linked to its discovery by Rockman's forebear 60,000 years before.

"Father Image" by Robert Silverberg ** (5,500 wds)

With a visit by suspected delegates pending, Swift, Earth's Resident Administrator on Malok IV, reluctantly turns confrontational toward the natives he has befriended and educated over the past five years. The outraged Malokians turn upon him thus fulfilling the plan that an alien culture establish independence from its paternalistic teachers in order to achieve true maturity. A deceptively complex tale that likens Earth's relationship to backwards extraterrestrial cultures to a Freudian father-child relationship.

"A Jacko for McCoy" by Alan Barclay * (6,100 wds)

Interplanetary battle adventure, first in Barclay's series about the 20-year war between Earthmen and the Jackos, an extraterrestrial race whose ships have invaded our solar system "from the direction of Aries." McCoy, a scout pilot, engages a Jacko ship in a game of cat-and-mouse until both run out of fuel and are forced down on an asteroid where the battle continues hand to hand. McCoy's efforts to bring the Jacko and its ship back alive for study are thwarted when both Earth and the Jackos send war parties out to rescue their stranded soldiers. Reprinted from the April 1955 New Worlds.

"The Bridey Murphy Way" by Paul Brandts * (5,700 wds)

A study of cultural differences between aliens and humans. A misunderstanding of language leads Old Pop Winder to believe that Venusians have mastered the secret of immortality. When he visits the House of Second Life, he discovers that the Venusian form of life everlasting is transmigration of the soul in to another life form.

"Eternal Adam" by Jules Verne (trans. by Willis T. Bradley) *** (14,000 wds)

Set on Earth approximately 170,000 years in the future when most of the planet's land mass has fused to form a single continent known as Hars-Iten-Schu, or Empire of the Four Seas. Zartog Sofr-Ai-Sr ("the learned Doctor Sofr") ponders puzzling evidence in the fossil record which suggests that while plants and animals have evolved linearly from simple to complex forms, a sophisticated human civilization paradoxically pre-existed his own. An excavation near his house turns up a sealed manuscript from the early 20th century recounting a cataclysmic inundation of the world from which only a handful of human beings survived to start civilization again. These peoples' discussions of the biblical Adam and Eve, Zartog realizes, are analogous to his own culture's discussions of Hedem and Hiva, and thus confirm humanity's habit of immortalizing "the endless ordeal of regeneration" in popular mythology. Purportedly one of the last stories written by Verne, unpublished in his lifetime and possibly edited by his son Michel. One of Verne's better speculative fantasies.

"Visitor's Book" by John Brunner *** (6,000 wds)

Future extraterrestrial invasion story. When the solar system is penetrated by alien vessels with faster-than-light drives, humanity deploys a secret warship of apparently awesome capabilities that frightens the aliens away. The ship is a fake meant to fool invaders. Reprinted from the April 1953 New Worlds.

Vol. 1 / #2, May 1957

"The Big Terrarium" by James H. Schmitz *** (14,300 wds)

Fred Nieheim, his wife Wilma, bum Howard Cooney, and a friendly snake-like alien of the Cobrisol species are trapped in "the Little Place," a plot of land with an Earth-like environment surrounded by a strange impenetrable mist. Fred and the Cobrisol defend Wilma against Cooney's advances, protect themselves from a ray-like alien of the Icien species who is also transported into the environment, and endure dangerous changes of temperature and climate before discovering that they have been collected for the terrarium of some incomprehensible alien child. One of Schmitz's semi-comic tales of strange alien monsters.

"The Earthman" by Milton Lesser * (4,800 wds)

Against his parents' wishes, Augie Haller plans to get "fashioned," or physically transformed, in order to blend in with the fashioned human beings who superseded nonfashioned families on Tollier's planets. He changes his mind, though, when he finds a normal human physique better equipped to handle a potential tragedy.

"Tunnel 1971" by Charles Einstein * (1,000 wds)

A series of diary dispatches about America's discovery of brontium, a substance that will allow mankind to travel through the Earth, and the comic turn of events when it is revealed that Russia has discovered it at the same time.

"The Night Express" by Damon Knight ** (2,500 wds)

Impressionistic science-fantasy. Duveen boards a special train only to discover, en route, that its course is out of this world, and possibly out of life itself.

"Mark XI" by Cordwainer Smith ** (5,200 wds)

Thirteen thousand years after she was put in suspended animation and sent on a missile into space, Carlotta vom Acht, daughter of a Nazi scientist, returns to earth. Though the war is long over, True Men, Morons, and sentient bears continue to engage in the same power struggles that fueled it. Droll science fiction satire.

"Mr. Frightful" by Charles A. Stearns ** (4,300 wds)

Mr. Gaup, the local mortician, boards and buries the indigent, after relieving them of their earthly possessions. Mr. Frightful, the town loony, is unable to convince anyone that the mysterious Mr. Zee, Gaup's newest border, is an extraterrestrial Porglie, preparing to give birth to others of his kind. Guess what?

"The 4D Bargain" by Evelyn E. Smith *** (4,400 wds)

A handbag that opens into the fourth dimension solves the problems women have of finding enough space for all their accessories. But it upsets the social fabric of the fourth dimension, when the items that materialize from the third dimension become status symbols for four-dimensional civilization.

"The Murky Glass" by H. P. Lovecraft and August Derleth ** (7,000 wds)

The narrator moves into the home of his antiquarian cousin Wilbur Akeley upon Wilbur's death and discovers a strange window in an upstairs room that Wilbur constructed his household around. The window proves a gateway to other dimensions that allows their horrors to cross the threshold into our own. The fifth "posthumous" collaboration in which Derleth fleshed out the germ of a story idea from H. P. Lovecraft, filled with Derleth's controversial reconceptions of set pieces from the Cthulhu Mythos. Retitled "The Gable Window" when collected later that year in the **The Survivor and Others**.

"Male Refuge" by Lloyd Biggle, Jr. ** (4,000 wds)

Henpecked Harry Jennings befriends Garn, an extraterrestrial, and offers him a room in his house when he discovers that Garn can coin perfect replicas of Earth money. The relationship sours, however, when it is revealed that Garn has completely misunderstood the nature of the relationship between Harry and his wife, Christine. A comic take on the battle of the sexes as perceived from an alien POV.

Vol. 1/#3, July 1957

"MX Knows Best" by Gordon R. Dickson **** (8,200 wds)

In the near future, everyone on Earth is beholden unto the predictions of MX, a Big Brother type mechanical brain whose database was created through "a joining of the census records with the economic integration computer and... psychologic computation methods." When a potential love interest turns him down because MX predicts a failed romance, Alan

Morg joins a rebel group determined to sabotage the machine and force it to make inaccurate predictions that will destroy its credibility. But Alan proves incapable of overcoming the human frailties necessary to defeat the machine.

"The Ordeal of Doctor Trifulgas" by Jules Verne (trans. By Willis T. Bradley) *** (2,500 wds)

Another Verne fantasy never before translated into English. Greedy Doctor Trifulgas refuses to make a house call to attend a dying man in the middle of the night until the townspeople promise him an extraordinary sum of money. When he finds out who the man is, he wishes he'd been more compassionate.

"The Single Ship" by Alan Barclay * (7,700 wds)

Second tale of Barclay's Jacko war series (after "A Jacko for McCoy" in the March 1957 issue). Lieutenant Jason agrees to pilot an Earth-built decoy Jacko ship back to the Jacko home base in order to learn where the Jacko command is based. His exploits are complicated by a run-in with an Earth patrol that isn't aware he's not one of the enemy, and a defense system that doses him with potentially fatal radiation every time he triggers it. Reprinted from the September 1955 *New Worlds*.

"The Martian Artifact" by August Derleth ** (3,800 wds)

Eccentric bibliophiles Samuel Millerand and Herman Schliemann are high bidders for a strange lute-like instrument from the collection of Gregory Saunders, an equally eccentric collector who claimed to be in contact with Mars. Skeptical reporter Tex Harrigan writes their acquisition up for his newspaper, and several days later it disappears from their house with a trail of inhuman footprints leading from the upstairs room where it was kept the only clue to its fate. One of more than a dozen tales of Tex Harrigan that Derleth published in a variety of magazines in the 1950s and '60s, and eventually collected in **Harrigan's File**.

"Purple with Rage" by Irving Cox, Jr. *** (5,700 wds)

Distressed at the number of transfers from his classes, jealous Mr. Stratten sits in on the classes of Miss Venter, and finds her teaching highly unorthodox subjects to her impressionable students. Miss Venter informs Stratten that she is an alien attempting to develop the full intellectual potential of Earth children before they become stunted by the logic of adulthood. Of course no logical adult believes Stratten when he tells this story.

"Bright Sentinels" by Charles A. Stearns ** (4,500 wds)

The comic trials and tribulations of Ruthie May, a gold-digger whose fifth husband proves to be an alien Limquat, who is thus impervious to her usual methods of murdering men for their money.

"Psi for Survival" by Manly Bannister ** (7,700 wds)

Seranimu, a hapless citizen of the overpopulated planet Zingu, attempts to improve his status by enrolling in a course advertised on a matchbook cover that promises to boost his psychic power. No one takes him seriously, even when the program works, and his frustratingly comic efforts to demonstrate his powers of telepathy and teleportation prove to have an unanticipated commercial use.

Vol. 1/#4, October 1957

"The Golden Calf" by Frank Belknap Long ** (5300 wds)

On the planet Kull, colonists from Earth discover that their robots may not be the slaves they were made to be. And what's with those seemingly stupid bovines known as the Kull? Does anyone care?

"California will Fall Into the Sea" by William F. Drummond, Ph. D. * (3700 wds)

Dr. Drummond hypothesizes that earthquakes and thermonuclear devices will render the Golden State useless to anyone not equipped with scuba gear. Some bibliographies categorize this as an article and some as fiction. Ostensibly the cover story because the inappropriate cover art features a burst that reads, "California Is Doomed!"

"Observation Platform" by Martin Pearson *** (4000 wds)

Three scientists are convinced that somewhere amid New York's skyscrapers, an alien being keeps watch over mankind, reporting all of our misdeeds to his home planet. Good slice of Cold War paranoia.

"The Elephant Circuit" by Robert A. Heinlein *** (6,000 wds)

Afterlife fantasy. John Watts is a man who "travels in elephants," i.e. specializes in knowledge of them and their habits. This is one of several imagined scenarios John and his wife Martha concocted to explain their need to travel around the country. On a bus trip after Martha's death, John finds himself conducted to a mysterious fair where all of their whimsical fantasies prove real, and where John's meeting with his beloved wife is inevitable. An uncommonly poignant fantasy from Heinlein, usually reprinted as "The Man Who Traveled in Elephants."

"A Time of Peace" by John Christopher *** (2550 wds)

In a future world ruled by television, little Seba just wants to read a good book. This annoys his parents, who want the lad to assimilate himself into society. Reprinted from Christopher's 1954 collection **Twenty-Second Century**.

"The Hot Potato" by Alan Barclay **** (8800 wds)

Enjoyable space comedy about a research team on Mars given the assignment of guarding an abandoned booby-trapped spaceship. Growing bored with the mission, Captain Nicholls and his boy howdy, radioman Joe, both radio-controlled model fanatics, rig up a contraption (cannibalized from other electronic devices around the base) to enter the big ship. When the big boys down at Mission Control get wind of this wonderful invention, they, naturally, decide to take credit for everything and intercede in the defusing. Of course, everything goes blooey. Reading almost like a two-character

comedic play, "The Hot Potato" is filled with wonderful dialog and a couple of well-developed brilliant goofs. Reprinted from the January 1956 *New Worlds*.

"The House Lords" by Jack Vance ** (5300 wds)

Spaceship commander Richard Emerson and his band of merry space travelers land on "Planet Two of Star BGD 1169 in Argo Navis Four" (and you thought only *Super Science Fiction* was responsible for this kind of nonsense) and discover the humanoid nasties known as the House Lords.

"Tiny Ally" by Harlan Ellison *** (1,600 wds)

Eighteen thousand feet up the slopes of Annapurna, a mountain-climbing expedition stumbles upon a three-inch tall astronaut with a knife stuck in his back. The dying astronaut is trying to warn them of a danger that stretches all credibility.

"Structural Defect" by Robert F. Young * (3400 wds)

In the future, everyone has the same house, the same life, the same existence. Happiness is a commandment and real live bluebirds are hard to find.

Vol. 1/#5, March 1958

"Red Flag Over the Moon" by Romney Boyd * (3,000 wds)

Inflammatory essay that warns of Russia's intention to parlay the successful launching of Sputnik into a space program that will culminate in their turning the moon into a weapons base targeting America. Although brief, it pushes all the buttons of Cold War paranoia, promotes G. Harry Stine's **Earth Satellites and the Race for Space Superiority** (published by Ace, naturally), and slaps science fiction fans on the back for having the foresight to have anticipated the threat.

"The Orzu Problem" by Lloyd Biggle, Jr. **** (5,000 wds)

A civil servant's amusing account of the events leading up to his recent demotion. He is given the responsibility of bringing back a pair of live Orzus for the Galaxia Zoological Gardens, but his trip to the uninhabitable planet of Arnicus, home of the Orzu, is a comedy of miscommunication, ignorance, and (it turns out) misunderstanding of Orzu life.

"The Skitz and the Unskitz" by Jefferson Highe * (5,000 wds)
> Dystopia of a future earth society that runs on mindless consumerism and the problems that arise for Jill when a rebellious boyfriend attempts to introduce her to an old-fashioned, value-filled lifestyle.

"Sputnik Shoes" by Charles A. Stearns ** (5,000 wds)
> Brainy Phelps, a young man of average appetites and substandard intelligence, acquires the shoes of an electrocuted convict that have been transformed into powerful magnets. Placing them in close proximity with one another permits astonishing feats of travel and inevitably a comic encounter with extraterrestrials when they take Brainy on a trip of unusually long distance.

"The Powder of Hyperborea" by Clark Ashton Smith ** (4,200 wds)
> Mischievous master thief Satampra Zeiros, who lives in the prehistoric realm of Hyperborea, engineers the theft of chastity belts from the virgins in the temple of Uzuldaroum with the help of his lady love, Vixeela, and the dishonest magician, Veezi Phenquor. A comic sequel to Smith's "Tale of Satampra Zeiros," better known by its title "The Theft of Thirty-Nine Girdles."

"Never Marry a Venerian" by Charles L. Fontenay * (1,000 wds)
> Comic science fiction short. Lassa Virdo marries Tobi, a Venusian, before studying the Venerian law that makes all wives slaves to their husbands, or anticipating Tobi unusual demands.

"Requiem for a Small Planet" by Ray Cummings ** (6,600 wds)
> The last short story story of Cummings, who died shortly before its publication, evokes both H. G. Wells' **The Time Machine** and Cummings' own tale of a microcosmic universe, **The Girl in the Golden Atom**. Jan and Mara are Marans, who live peacefully among the ruins of the once dominant Hittag culture. Mama Megan, custodian of the Maran secret, is murdered by Hido, a descendant of the Hittags, and Jan and Mara's pursuit of Hido eventually brings them an understanding of the limits of their world and the vast universe beyond.

"The Stars Are Waiting" by Marion Zimmer Bradley ** (4,000 wds)
> Secret agent David Rohrer must find out from comatose field operative Flanders why India has shut its borders and cut itself off from communications with other countries. Is it because India is developing weapons of awesome destructive potential or is there a more benign explanation?

"Alaree" by Robert Silverberg **** (5,200 wds)
> Forced down on a planet to repair their ship, a crew of earthmen make contact with Alaree, a member of an alien group mind. The earthmen teach Alaree the meaning of individuality with disastrous results.

"Shaggy Dog" by Charles E. Fritch ** (2200 wds)
> The problem with robots made in the image of men and animals, the story's resident barfly explains, is that robots outlast their mortal models, and persist at habits - like eating, drinking, and scratching fleas - that serve no purpose for them.

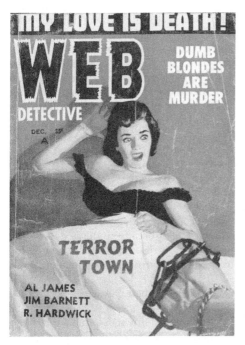

MY LOVE IS DEATH!

WEB D

DETECTIVE

DEC. 35¢
A

DUMB
BLONDES
ARE
MURDER

TERROR
TOWN

AL JAMES
JIM BARNETT
R. HARDWICK

JUST KILL HIM, DARLING!

SATURN

WEB A

DETECTIVE
STORIES

APRIL
35¢

LADY
FROM
HELL

Don Unatin—Al James—Zack Steele

SATURN MAGAZINE OF

WEB
A

SEPT.
15¢

DETECTIVE STORIES

DAUGHTERS
OF HELL

SCREAM
BLOODY
MURDER

Jim Allen. Tony Phillips. Don Unatin.

BLOOD BARGAIN BY HENRY SLESAR

WEB

DETECTIVE STORIES A
SEPT. 35¢

A CORPSE
CAN HATE
BY HARLAN ELLISON

REQUIEM FOR
A JUNKIE
BY JAMES STEVENS

ANGEL
OF EVIL
BY ROBERT ROSSNER

As we were assembling this volume, I asked Peter which one of his annotated indexes he felt was the best example to include. He suggested this, paired with Stefan's preceding Part I. I also asked if in the last twenty years, he had ever completed the article series with an "Annotated Index to Web Terror,*" and he confirmed that he had not. I suggested that since we were bringing these two parts back into print, maybe it was time to finally put this series to bed. I'm pleased to report that the pressure worked, and he is currently at work on a* Web Terror *article. Watch for that in a forthcoming issue of the new and improved bare•*bones. *-John*

A TANGLED WEB: UNLOCKING THE MYSTERIES OF *SATURN SCIENCE FICTION / WEB DETECTIVE / WEB TERROR* Part Two: The Annotated Index to *Web Detective Stories*

by Peter Enfantino

Of all the crime digests I've collected, the one title that gave me the most trouble was *Web Detective* (*WD*). It's not just that *WD* suffered from lousy distribution and rack placement (as did most of the lesser crime digests of the early 60s), but it also has the distinction of being one of the most confusing digests of all time.

WD was born *Saturn, The Magazine of Science Fiction* (Candar Publishing) in March 1957. The editor was the respected Donald A. Wollheim, editor of Ace Books (later to found DAW Books), and the contents varied from non-fiction to reprints to fiction by such genre mainstays as Harlan Ellison and Robert Silverberg. Not able to distinguish itself from the dozens of other sf digests of the late 1950s, *Saturn* soon found itself facing extinction. For some unknown reason, the publisher[1] chose to simply change its title to *Saturn Web Detective Stories* after only five issues, rather than kill *Saturn SF* and start up a crime digest (I'm assuming that the publisher, in his infinite wisdom, decided that the crime waters weren't as crowded as the SF sea). This contributes to some of the mass confusion surrounding *WD*. If it weren't for scholars and historians like Bill Pronzini and Mike Ashley, youngsters such as myself would still be searching the internet for those illusive first five issues of *Web Detective*. Add to the confusion the fact that there are actually two issues labeled Volume Two/Number Three, and that some issues are dated differently on their covers and contents page (presenting the dealer with a dilemma: which date do I list in my catalog?), and you understand why this run is such a collecting nightmare.

So what constitutes *WD*, and is it worth plunking down from 20 to 30 bucks an issue? I think so, but then I'm a crazed crime digest collector. Obviously not many others side with my opinion since I've yet to see a *WD* story anthologized[2], even though there are at least two dozen (out of 148 stories) that are worthy of a second look.

Much of the time, the titles of the *Web Detective* stories made little, if any, sense, and related to the story even less. For instance, "A Skeleton For Her Bed" from Volume 3/#1 not only omits the skeleton, but also the bed. The story could have and should have been titled "Woman in Chains." The formula for a *Web* title might just have been something resembling a "Mad Lib," a substitute word game:

"The (*place noun here*) Was a (*place noun here*) for the Mob!" or "She (*place adjective here*) Me For My (*place noun here*)!"

Try it, it'll work.

After 14 issues, Candar decided that maybe the money wasn't in crime stories, so they folded *WD* and jumped into the profitable waters of bondage horror stories. In our third (and final) installment of "The Tangled Web" next issue, we'll see just how profitable those waters really were.

Saturn Web Detective Stories
Vol. 1/#6, August 1958

"Night of Discovery!" by Art Serra ** (4100 wds)
Two juvenile delinquents break into the house of fiftyish Hugh Davy and his (much) younger wife Nan and threaten the woman with assault. Much to the husband's surprise, Nan seems up to the occasion. In fact, she welcomes becoming the object of molten desire after "being the good little wife for eight months." Seething with rage, Hugh manages to get the two youths stone drunk, off his adulterating bitch of a wife, and successfully pin her murder on the two boys.

"Blood Bath For the General!" by Bill Ryder **1/2 (4600 wds)
The narrator owns a cover bar (lots of illegal activities flourish in the back rooms) frequented by "the general," a big bruiser who's usually bombed and spouting stories about women he bedded during WW II. Enter Cora, an enterprising young dame who decides to cut herself in on the bar's action through blackmail. This doesn't sit well with our storyteller, so he rapes and murders Cora and attempts to frame the General. After murdering the General, he strips the body in anticipation of the arrival of the police. Our amazed, but not amused, protagonist then discovers why the General never bragged about his conquests *after* World War II!

"Too Hot to Handle!" by Art Crockett *1/2 (3800 wds)
Barry does some dumb gambling and ends up owing a bundle to big-time shark Matteo Fink. Fink gives Barry two days to cough up the dough, but on the way to pay, Barry gets rolled by luscious Leslie. The beautiful redhead, however, cops a tude, insisting she had nothing to do with the rip-off. Enraged, Barry brings Leslie to Fink (aka "The Mad Dog Lover") as "collateral" until the green shows up. After the mad Dog begins pawing Leslie's ripe vitals, Barry develops a sudden fondness for Leslie and stomps the big man. He flees with the nubile nymph and begins a life of love (albeit on the run).

"Jealous Husband!" by Leslie G. Sabo * (2100 wds)
Matt and Lila don't have what you'd call an ideal marriage: he drinks and she's an adulteress. When Matt swears to kill all of Lila's lovers, Lila pulls a fast one and cons her dopey husband into killing his own brother in a fit of jealous rage. She plans to hold this over Matt's head: she'll go to the cops if he won't let her play the field. Matt agrees, but as the phone rings once again for his wife, the lush, we see the thought balloon rise over Matt's head, warning us he'll kill again.

"Rumble Bait" by Jimmy L. Carroll *** (2950 wds)
Cal Johnson's life has never been the same since he turned squealer on his partner. Now he's opened himself up for beatings from everyone on the street, including our man of the moment, Slim. Our story opens with Slim doing the squealer stomp on poor Cal on his way to meet up with partner-in-crime, Fats (not to be confused with Abbott and Costello). The two are caught by a shotgun-toting farmer while lifting watermelons. Fats gets away but Slim goes right to jail without passing **GO**. To avoid severe beatings from the sheriff and his sadistic deputy, Slim gives up Fats on the condition that no one on

the street is to find out exactly who gave up Fats. But the sheriff isn't known for his honesty and Slim becomes "open game" on the streets just like his old friend Cal. Not Harlan Ellison, but still an enjoyable j.d. tale.

"Terror Has Many Faces!" by Don Unatin ** (3350 wds)

Aggie decides to turn in her vicious mob boss, Big Mike, after she witnesses the brutal murder of her friend, Jerry. The DA promises protection for Aggie if she'll testify against the Big Man, and she's whisked away to a remote cabin. There to greet her is Big Mike, who we learn has bought the services of the DA.

"Daughters of Hell!" by Jim Allen * (4000 wds)

PI Calvin Dugan has been hired by Mrs. Lloyd Harrison to keep watch over her daughter Carol, who's joined a female gang dubbed the Brazen Beauties. Having dabbled in the horrors of cigarettes, alcohol, and dope, the BBs turn their attention to hot sex. Carol is to be initiated, by losing her virginity, when Dugan breaks up the gang and saves the day. Turns out that Carol is the mastermind behind the gang and had plotted to blackmail her socialite mother to keep the details quiet.

"Alley of the Damned!" by Tony Phillips * (2750 wds)

Francine, a teasing alley cat, is found murdered and the suspect list includes many former lovers.

"Murder a Dead Man!" by Al James *** (2500 wds)

Pete Brennan is conned by a lush into killing her rich old man, a stock investor. Every night the old man goes for a walk across San Francisco's Bay Bridge, so Pete plans the attack on the span. After shooting the man and watching the body hit the water far below, Pete is confronted by the police, who patrol the bridge for potential suicides. While fleeing, Brennan is shot and hangs from the bridge, awaiting death. He overhears the cops discuss how ironic the case is after they find a suicide

"Sorry," I said. "I'm not your type."

"I'm everybody's type." She answered, moving closer through the mist.

"Know any place where I can get a little action?"

"My apartment."

"Different kind. Cards, dice, that action."

"You a queer?" she asked, watching me more closely.

"I hope not."

-from "The Night People"

note in the old man's coat pocket. He had just lost his fortune on the stock market and, rather than face his wife with the failure, decided to cash in his chips.

"Come Die With Me!" by Les Samlie *** (1900 wds)

Nasty short-short about a bank robber who kidnaps and rapes a passing motorist. The girl is so humiliated and shamed she ends up offing both of them by wrecking her car. "Come Die With Me" is one of the best illustrations of just how violent, dark, and downright vile some of these late 1950s crime stories could be.

"Scream Bloody Murder!" by Jim Barnett *1/2 (2750 wds)

The musings of a sexually-driven serial killer. Below average chiller does have a neat twist ending to elevate it above total sludge.

"Journey to Murder!" by Jim Allway * (6500 wds)

Harvey Muller exits the slammer with only two objectives: find his remarried ex-wife and get back the fifty thousand in stolen loot she's got stashed for him. His plans quickly fall apart when he's followed by cops right up to the ex's doorstep. "Journey"'s climax is proof that even nasty *Web* villains can have a "happily ever after."

"The Lady Was No Angel!" by Al James * (3400 wds)

Ex-con Mike Brent loses his job and wife and is contemplating re-entering the safe-cracking business when he has an afternoon fling with Mrs. Kessler, a neighbor down the hall. Mrs. Kessler confides in Brent that Mr. Kessler hasn't exactly been raising the pole lately. That same night, Brent returns to his apartment to find the police. Mr. Kessler has been murdered and the Mrs. is claiming Mike raped her and offed her hubby.

"Life is Worth Dying!" by Marvin Gray *1/2 (3400 wds)

Steve McGann rescues Marcy from drowning, an attempted suicide. In a bizarre twist, McGann had come to murder the girl to avenge the death of his brother, who had fallen in love with Marcy and turned to crime to maintain a rich lifestyle. McGann nurses Marcy back to health (she has TB) and happiness, only to reveal that his intention is to carry out her murder once she attains that happiness.

"For Sale - Death!" by Pete McCann *1/2 (4600 wds)

A drug pusher named Fang enjoys the immense power he holds over his customers. After a bad beating from a cokehead, Fang decides to restrict his clientele to women. At the same time, he decides that money isn't everything and puts the moves on a new druggie named Sylvia. Fang gets his just desserts in the end when it turns out that Sylvia is actually the wife of a former customer who was killed in a liquor store holdup, trying to get bucks for his drugs.

He hit the girl so hard in the gut the sound was enough to make you sick. Squishy, like when you squeeze a sponge. I thought she'd upchuck everything she'd ate for a week.
-from "As Hot as Ginger"

"Murder's Icy Finger!" by Bill Ryder * (4250 wds)

Dan and Sylvia plot to steal an old woman's jewels by torturing her, but the cops show up in the middle of their fun. Cynthia escapes with the jewels and Dan is thrown in the big house for seven long years. When he's released, you guessed it, he tracks Cynthia down and threatens to kill her if she doesn't fork over the jewels. But Cynthia has a contingency plan all worked out for the thug and, before long, Dan is no longer a problem.

"Lust Without Pity!" by Art Crockett *** (3600 wds)

Johnny Santos is hired by adulteress Grace Brandon to off a blackmailer. Santos does the hit and then finds he's been suckered into murdering Mr. Brandon. Grace stands to inherit a mountain of green, and makes the mistake of attempting a stiff on Johnny. Not a wise move.

"The Lady Was Furious!" by Hal Crosby ** (3000 wds)

Flash Floran and his assistant Mona take dirty pictures of married men and then sell them to the wives to use in divorce cases. Flash becomes infatuated with one of his wealthy clients and reels her in. Mona, in a jealous rage, uses some of Flash's own tricks on him to bring him back to earth.

"Bloody Holiday!" by G. G. Revelle *** (5300 wds)

Tracey, attending a real estate convention, decides to hire some female companionship and reels in the voluptuous Marcia. Fearing that one of the other agents might tip-off his wife, Tracey suggests that he and Marcia should head off to a different spot. Marcia steers him towards a park bench, where the two are accosted by thugs who snap photos of Tracey in unpuritan poses with Marcia. The crooks threaten to send the photos home to the little lady. The joke's on the crooks though, as Tracey reveals that it's they who have been set up. Seems one of his buddies fell prey in the past to Marcia and her camera-boys and committed suicide. Now Tracey and a batch of buddies, who soon arrive on the scene, exact a nasty revenge.

"A Touch of Evil!" by Jim Allen *** (3350 wds)

Card shark Johnny Morgan rolls into town and joins in a game with the respectable, and quite wealthy, Lou Shero. Morgan takes Shero for every penny he's worth, which doesn't sit well with the big man. Morgan is set up as fall guy for a rape charge by one of Shero's "girls" and is hauled away. Last line is a hoot.

"Short Cut to Hell!" by John Thorn * (3200 wds)

Unintentionally (I assume) hilarious story of Larry Fenton, whose only goal in life, it would seem, is to continually top his worst crime. In the course of this story, he smokes marijuana, drinks to excess, beats the whores he pimps for, and, oh yes, kills women and fondles the stockings he removes from their corpses. Fenton leads the good life until he picks up a hooker who turns out to be a serial killer as well.

"You're Already Dead!" by James Albert *1/2 (2100 wds)

Pete Strand is the only man on a jury panel who votes to hang a transient accused of murdering a well-known local named Quincy in Strand's barn. The other men are curious about Pete's behavior since it's widely known that Quincy had an affair with Strand's wife. Wouldn't Strand be happy to let loose the man who killed his wife's lover? Pete makes a convincing argument that, revenge be damned, there is just too much physical evidence to let the guy go (Quincy's body was never found but the barn was splattered with his blood). Strand finally gets his way and a guilty verdict is handed down. He drives home and takes a badly wounded Quincy out of a closet and puts a bullet in him, musing that a jury couldn't convict him of the murder now because Quincy has been ruled dead. A very average story that raises a couple amusing red flags. How could Strand serve on a jury at a trial that so obviously affects him and his judgment? Most importantly, how the heck did Strand manage to keep the mortally wounded Quincy alive all during the judicial process?

"A Long, Violent Night!" by Tony Phillips * (5500 wds)

Undercover cop Don Cassidy's new hush-hush assignment is to roust prostitutes. This isn't sitting well with Don's conscience nor, it turns out, with his wife. Seems Don is so ashamed of busting call girls that he avoids notifying his wife, who, noticing the lipstick on Don's collars, follows him to one of his busts. She spills his guts before he can. "A Long, Violent Night" is a wildly bad story, one of those "so bad it's good" tales that usually populates the Mike Avallone universe. With priceless prose like:

"Somebody put another slug in the jukebox and the scratchy record came to life again. A girl's plaintive, whining voice told of wax heartbreak. Cassidy hated the song. He hated the cheap bar. He detested being there in the first place. But most of all he bathed (sic) himself tonight."
and:

"He saw the weazened man's yellow teeth glaring nakedly and obscenely from behind the leering smirk which creased the death's head skull."

Vol. 2/#2, February 1959 (inside cover incorrectly states V.2/#1)

"Scream the Night Through!" by Don Unatin ** (3050 wds)

MaryLou is savagely raped in an alleyway but doesn't report it to the police because her husband wouldn't emotionally be able to handle the violation. What author Unatin lets us in on towards the climax is that hubby Charlie is "too much of a gentleman" and MaryLou could no longer "deny her instincts schooled through the ages - of wanting to be over-powered and mastered." Something that Charlie could never give her. Misogynist, yes, but a curio that tells a lot about the climate in the 1950s. MaryLou dresses up sexily and gets what she deserves, but judging from the last line, it's also what she wants.

> **"But Captain, how long does a gink stay with a hustler? Marchione could've pulled out at any minute."**
> **-from "Comfort Her Corpse"**

"Hell's Deadly Lover!" by Al James * (4200 wds)

Steve Donovan, sadistic cop from hell, plays every angle he can to make extra dough, including muscling business owners. He happens onto a woman in a bar, goes to her place, beds hers, and then finds out she's a bank robber by stumbling onto her money sacks. "Hell's Deadly Lover" is a dopey read, filled to the brim with wild and unbelievable coincidences. This kind of story (bad cop on the take) was done to death in the 1950s by writers much more esteemed than Al James.

"Terror Has No Face!" by Jim Arthur *** (3200 wds)

The Daggers are sick and tired of patrolman Dan Vinton busting up their action, so they take their complaint to his wife. They string her up, torture her, and warn her that, if hubby don't lay off, next time's fer keeps! The cop disappears and the Daggers are convinced that their troubles are over until their members start showing up dead; the Dagger has become *the* Dagger. Vinton and the Mrs. have returned.

"You'll Die Laughing!" by Arnold Sherry * (2100 wds)

Marvin, a decorated war hero, and his wife Donna are closing up the diner they own for the night when two thugs enter. The men beat Marvin and rape Donna repeatedly, all in the name of chuckles. A pointless, nasty exercise in torture and degradation. Brian De Palma would probably want to take out an option on this one.

"Stakeout of the Damned!" by Doug Flanders ** (4250 wds)

A typically no-brains bad-luck *Web* crook flees from a botched supermarket heist and kidnaps a woman and her child. Well, the dimwit *assumes* it's the woman's kid until he's captured and the police inform him that they were actually after the woman, who had kidnapped the kid!

"Twist the Knife Slowly!" by Jay Folb * (3150 wds)

After a bad real estate deal, Al Draper owes Tony Tibbett five big ones, and Tony, understandably, wants his money right now. Al doesn't have the moola but it turns out that Dot Draper, Al's vixen wife, has found a way to pay in full. No *Web* mystery or detective in this one, just plain boring adultery.

"I'll Blast You Yet!" by Pete McCann *** (4250 wds)

The horrors perpetrated by the killer known only as Doug are seen through the eyes of our narrator, who is forced to participate in Doug's reign of terror. Doug robs and murders women with obvious glee and our tour guide describes each and every painful detail. A fairly routine *Web*ber, but the obvious question (who is the narrator?), is averted by our storyteller, who avoids any personal details until the all-important last paragraph. Hey, McCann fooled me.

"Cross Me and Die!" by Art Crockett *1/2 (2950 wds)

Jack Hogan makes a jailbreak and heads right for Terry Martin, a beautiful dame (with a nice set of headlights, of course!) who's been hiding Jack's stolen booty of 50gs in her fireplace for him. Little does Hogan know that Terry has married a cop while he's been in the big house and now the cop wants to keep Terry and the green, but erase Hogan from the picture.

"Lust Sets the Scene!" by Luke Hogan ** (3350 wds)

Successful Broadway producer Matt Landers knows he owes 100% of his good luck to his secretary (and play reader) Ann Small. Landers can have any of the young chippies who try out for his productions, but still he lusts for the older, yet still vivacious, Ann, who, until recently, has spurned all of Landers' advances. Together the two mine gold on Broadway and they hope to continue that streak by producing a play by a young eccentric unknown playwright/dwarf hunchback named Oswald Upham. What is the startling secret from Ann's past that ties her to the misshapen Oswald? Why is the dwarf hunchback having such a hard time completing Act 3 of the smashing play? Will Matt finally get to lay his hands on Ann's hooters? These questions and more are answered in the story's startling climax. A wildly goofy story, "Lust" harkens back to the Spicy pulp days and is an indicator of the direction that *Web* would follow soon. A guilty pleasure.

"Death Bait!" by Leslie G. Sabo * (2150 wds)

Brad Sterne strikes up a deal with Lydia Winthrop: he'll steal her skinflint hubby's millions in diamonds from their wall safe, off the old dude, and split the loot with Lydia. All she has to do is revel in the pleasures of the flesh with Brad. But alas, like most of the *Web* Black Widows, Lydia doesn't like to share in the end.

"Don't Run From Evil!" by Hal Pierce * (3250 wds)

It's David and Goliath time as mousy alcoholic Marc Taylor takes on his new garbage collector, the sadistic youth known only as "Chin" (but better known to Marc's wife as "Big Chin"). Marc stumbles onto an attempted rape by the big man on one of Marc's lovely, nubile neighbors (who gets stripped down to her pink panties) and does the Thunderbird Two-Step on Chin's cranium, becoming a hero in the process.

"Sure Bet on Death!" by Buck Grimes *** (6100 wds)

Boxing manager Sandy Michaels spots the surest thing he's ever laid eyes on: Mugsy Thomas. With no money, Michaels has to go to bone-breaking loan shark Whitie Malone for the bucks to train Mugsy. In the meantime, the big lug falls for Greta, a (hold the phones) busty, curvy knockout. The bimbo lures the fighter away from Sandy with promises of lust-filled nights and diamond-studded dog collars. All the walls seem to be coming down on Sandy Michaels at the same time and the nice guy is definitely finishing last. A really good

sports/mob thriller that's about as close to a short Gold Medal novel as you're going to get in *Web*. It's no secret that Sylvester Stallone devoured every issue of *Web* when he was a little pug, and the influence of "Sure Bet on Death!" (in particular, in his screenplay for **Rocky V**) is evident in his fine body of work.

Vol. 2/#3, April 1959

"Look Death in the Eye!" by Lawrence Block * (2700 wds)

A beautiful nameless woman frequents bars, picks up "hungry" men, and murders them. A very early story from the author who would later go on to author the highly-acclaimed "Matt Scudder" novels. The only worthwhile passage is its final paragraph (reprinted elsewhere in this article).

"I'd Die For Her!" by Art Crockett **1/2 (3450 wds)

Pete is being held in the rape/murder of his girlfriend, Angela. He asks the sheriff if he can attend her funeral, where things get out of hand and Pete's strung up with a noose. He's saved at the last minute though when he averts the crowd's attention to Angela's boyfriend, whom Pete claims is the real murderer. The frenzied mob strings up the ex, while Pete (the actual killer, by the way) looks on in amusement. The prose equivalent of one of those great EC Comics *ShockSuspenstories* (the rapist is really the sheriff, the murdering bigot learns that he's half-Jewish, etc.).

"Lady From Hell!" by Don Unatin *1/2 (4625 wds)

The wife of a prominent attorney (who longs to be on the school board!) is being blackmailed by a scummy little man known as "Old Gardiner." Seems the lady used to be a dominatrix at the local cathouse before becoming a wealthy socialite. Joke's on Gardiner though, when he finds out that not only does the attorney know about his wife's vixenish past, he helps her keep in practice.

"The Lonely Doom!" by Al James ** (2950 wds)

A mafia hitman wipes out a former gofer who ran off with a hundred grand, then beds the dead man's wife. After he kills her, he finds out she was a leper and now he's infected. Seriously sick, goofy little fable. Here's one you can read out loud at a dinner party.

"Murder Wins the Jackpot!" by Zack Steele *1/2 (4625 wds)

Taxi driver Charlie has the worst luck in the world until he wins an English cruise and meets a beautiful French babe onboard. As usual though, the odds are against him when Charlie finds out that the woman is a smuggler and has been using him. Outrageous climax has Charlie narrating his own death a la those creaky old horror stories wherein the writer ends his journal with "...it's breaking down the door...it's strangling me...aaaaahhhh...!"

"Just Kill Him, Darling!" by Jay Richards *1/2 (5450 wds)

Danny Russo, "rehabilitated jd," comes into the employ of kindly Mr. Milner. But, of course, as with most Web jd stories, there's the bad dame just itching to off her wealthy old husband. Danny falls for beautiful Stella Milner and helps Mr. Milner descend his basement steps at an accelerated rate. All kinds of sexual innuendo only leads to a one-plus-one-equals-three finish.

"Mark Him For Me!" by Jim Barnett *** (4200 wds)

A violent gang with the moniker of The Pythons moves into town and immediately starts to shake everything up and everyone down. A rival gang, newly crowned The Mongooses, decides to do something about it. Decent JD tale with a nice surprise climax.

"Death Muscles In!" by Luke Hogan ** (4200 wds)

Big mean casino owner Steve Peck has a way with the ladies, including his secretary, Kate. For reasons known only to the writers and editors, beautiful Kate falls madly in love with the big lardass despite the fact that he continuously uses her as a punching bag. Convinced that she's actually a plant from the D.A., he murders her and eventually offs himself in a spectacular gore-soaked finale.

"The Lusting Ones!" by Jim Arthur * (3050 wds)

"Gunther had that fearful ache. The girl could ease it. It all added up to murder."

Goofball Gunther stalks tantalizing Toni, all the while musing about all the violence he'll do to her when he gets her alone. Could Gunther be the Tyler City Strangler? Will Toni be the next victim? Well, no. In an unconvincing and (hopefully intentionally) hilarious twist finale, it's revealed that, surprise, Toni is actually an escaped mental patient aka The Tyler City Strangler. So who is Gunther? Don't ask me.

"Fright Prowls the Night!" by Gil Grayson * (7350 wds)

God's gift to the serial killer novelist, the abused child, grows up to be an abusing psychopath who stalks a lovers' lane, torturing couples for kicks. Bottom of the barrel, this could possibly be the worst story to appear in WD.

•

Web Detective Stories
Vol. 2/#3, June 1959
(this was the second issue to be labeled Vol.2/#3)

"Satan Thumbs a Ride!" by Al James **1/2 (2800 wds)

Dopey thief steals a car, kills its owner. On the run, he picks up a babe, who turns out to be on the run as well. She steals the car and is later picked up by the cops, who suspect her of killing the car's original owner. Nice ironic twist.

"Murder's Lovely Stand-in!" by Art Crockett ** (2700 wds)

While enduring a third degree from some tough bulls, Harry Ross dishes all the dirt he knows on his boss Raymond, and now the mobster is understandably peeved. Being the scumbag that he is, Harry heads to his girlfriend's pad and uses her as a decoy to ensure his escape.

"Tide of Evil!" by Richard Hardwick ** (4700 wds)

After serving a few years in the stir, Gus Leach runs into his old partner Marta one day and discovers she's in the middle of a big con. Marta's about to become Mrs. Walter Telfair and Gus wants a piece of the action or he'll let ol' Walter know what his fiancé was up to before he gave her a ring.

"One Foot in Hell!" by Bill Ryder ** (3400 wds)

Roger Townshend intends to take the big dive off a 22nd story ledge unless his estranged girlfriend is brought to him. The woman turns out to be the wife of the cop who's trying to talk Roger down. Ryder (showing unusual restraint in his writing here) cheats all the way from the beginning of the story to mask the identity of the woman until the big 'surprise' climax. This has been done before, and better.

"Crash Out to Doom!" by Micky Fairbanks *1/2 (4200 wds)

Burger and Jim bust out of prison by kidnapping the warden's wife and stealing her car. They head off into the swamps where they run into some nasty swamp critters, but all's well that ends well for the captive woman because it turns out that the real reason Jim broke out was to get away from the bullying Burger. Once Burger is dispatched, Jim gives himself up and goes back to peace in the prison.

"Hate Goes Courting!" by Lawrence Block **** (3200 wds)

Very short and very stark, "Hate Goes Courting" (yet another stupid title) tells the story of two brothers, John and Brad, and John's fiancé Margie, a girl with a questionable past. Brad knows about that past and continually taunts his brother until the man finally bursts out in rage:

When you're up close a shotgun makes a big messy hole, big as a man's fist, but when I squeezed that trigger the shell went through him like a sword through a piece of silk, like the wind blowing outside. He let out a moan and sat down slowly. His eyes were staring like he couldn't believe it happened.

Much more indicative of Block's future work than the previous issue's "Look Death in the Eye!"

"The Hunger of Death!" by Buck Grimes **1/2 (4200 wds)

Sandy's a starving artist and now he's hooked on junk. Once he runs out of daddy's dough he turns to a life of crime to get his daily fix. Not a bad story, but a bit uninspiring in its delivery.

"Terror's Sultry Sister!" by Sam Holt * (3400 wds)

Try to follow me closely: Don is keeping time with Lila, whose brother Archie is a j.d. thug. When Archie plays like Lila's pimp and demands bucks for her time, Don puts the kid on the ground. Later, driving home from work, Don thinks he hits a man in the street. Turns out Archie has just pulled a robbery and been shot. He's the man Don has run over! Archie dies naming Don as his accomplice and Don heads for a nice cell. The king of Ripley's Believe It Or Nots. If I gave out zeroes, "Sultry Sister" would earn one.

"Company for a Corpse!" by Bruce White *1/2 (2000 wds)

Monk Donzeg is mad as hell after being a fall guy and goes after the cop who framed him.

"Hot Slug - Cold Dame!" by Jim Allen * (3200 wds)

Frank, not at all pleased about spending ten years in the pen for a job he did with Claude Sanders (who got away), goes looking for the fifty grand that was to be his cut. When he finally finds Claude, his former partner has been given a third eye by his wife, who quickly frames Frank. Entry two in this issue's Ripley's sweepstakes.

> **He walked off down the street, jamming the stockings into his pocket as he went. In his pocket, his fingers released the stockings and fastened on something else—something as hard and male as the stockings had been female.**
> **- from "Short Cut to Hell"**

The man at the door was expressionless. The gun in his hand belched six times. Ben's body twisted grotesquely and fell to the floor.

The phone still clung to his hand.

But it was dead.

And so was Ben...

-from "Gang Girl's Revenge"

"Lust's Lone Witness!" by Don Unatin * (5900 wds)

Mousy Henry Wiggins blurts out to the police that he witnessed the murder of his lovely neighbor, the latest victim of a serial lust killer, and gives a false description of the fiend. Problem is, Harry saw nothing because he was busy cowering in his apartment at the time of the murder. Obsessed with his new found fame and morose over the soon-fleeting aforementioned fame, Wiggins decides the best way to stay on top is to become a lust killer himself. Of course, the woman he stalks turns out to be the latest target of the real killer and Ripley see three strikes and he's out.

Vol. 2/#4, September 1959

"Murders Flashes Dark Eye!" by Grover Brinkman ***1/2 (4600 wds)

(Note: Title given is the one on the actual title page. The contents page reads: "Murder Flashes Dark Eyes," which makes a little more sense.) Ollie and Clint pull off a bank heist but it gets messy and two end up dead. They hightail it over the river into Mexico, only to find themselves wanted by scavengers more deadly than the police. Excellent tale ends dark when Ollie's back is to the wall and there's only one way out.

"Love Nest in Hell!" by Flip Lyons * (3950 wds)

Escaped con takes honeymooners hostage in snowbound cabin. A complete and total snoozer, right up to its laughable expository climax.

"Her Knife Carved "Love"!" by Jay Folb * (5200 wds)

Dreamboat Ernie Scorr decides that Shirley Diamond must die. To accomplish this he enlists Maria, who's madly in love with him and will do anything he says. Or so he thinks.

"Slaughter Will Find You!" by Luke Hogan *** (3900 wds)

With that title, you're probably expecting something like one of those 70s blaxploitation flicks, but what you get is a real good gripper. Syl Myers has been dreading the inevitable day when his brother Pete would come calling, after spending fifteen years in prison. Pete wants Syl to be the driver in another stickup, but Syl just wants to be left alone to his good life and home. Unfortunately, Pete is well-versed in the art of coercion.

"No Guts to Die!" by Jim Arthur * (3350 wds)

Ex-stripper Tina Bondi hasn't gotten over being dumped by mobman Lennie Rogers and spends her waking hours in the bottom of a glass of booze. She's decided that before she drinks herself to death, she'll tell the world all about the dirty life of Lennie Rogers.

"Fear Finds a Mate!" by Pete McCann * (3950 wds)

Because of Carol's strict upbringing, sex has always been something evil to her. No man ever gets to second base with Carol until the serial-rapist "The Cat" comes knocking on her door and Carol finds out what it's like to be a fulfilled woman. Another in the *Web* sub-genre of stories where the female protagonist "had it coming to her and when she finally got it... she liked it!"

"A Slob Can Hate!" by Robert Silverberg *** (3950 wds)

Poor Theodore Reese is tortured by the other boys in his cabin at summer camp. They make up derogatory nicknames, dump buckets of water on his head, pants him, and generally make life for him a living hell. Then comes the night of the dance, when one of the most beautiful girls in camp asks Theodore to accompany her. The unwitting boy doesn't know it's a set-up and, when he finds out, he explodes in a fit of violence. An above-average revenge saga. I'd make a joke about Stephen King reading *Web* in his early days, but he has a lot of lawyers.

"Beautiful Bait for Benny!" by Al James ** (2950 wds)

Pickpocket Benny runs into fellow hoodlum Angie at the track one day. Benny's just served ten years for a job he pulled with Angie. Now Angie's got a great pickpocket scheme all worked out and, in the end, suspicion will fall on Benny. The joke's on Angie though when, after the cops converge on the two men, it's learned that Benny couldn't be the culprit because his hands have become gnarled from arthritis.

"The Added Mourner!" by Donald Honig *1/2 (3800 wds)

Joe Barton might be the world's stupidest murderer. Barton and his wife Janet despise each other but, for some reason, stay together. Joe's spineless ways irk Janet, and he just can't stand her nagging. Joe finally decides to off her but can't come up with a plan 'til one day in a bar when an old man stumbles in, claiming he watched his family drown in a ferry accident. The light bulb goes on over Joe's head. He races home, offs the ol' ball and chain, and dumps her body in the bay. Only later does he find out that the old man had lost his family years before.

"Reserve My Hot Seat!" by James Allen *** (3250 wds)

Nick Norris believes he's committed the perfect crime while he sits on death row, hours away from execution. He kills his boss, robs him of half a million bucks, and pays another crook to use Nick's gun in a similar crime while he's rotting in a cell. This way, Norris is convinced the cops will listen to his pleas of innocence. The hired crook gets ideas of his own though in a neat twist.

"I.O.U. - Lust!" by Bill Ryder *1/2 (4300 wds)

Racy S&M/bondage fairy tale about Hilda Queen, little girl lost, who must turn to the kinkier side of prostitution to pay off gambling debts, only to find out that the ringleader of the bondage gang (and her prospective lover) is none other than her dear old dad, a wealthy, influential man of the community. Real sleazy material, bordering on softcore porn (though very tame compared to today's stuff).

Vol. 2/#5, December 1959

"Come Home to Hell!" by Al James * (3900 wds)

Prison life is rough on Phil, but parole finally comes and his loving wife Mira (celibate for five years, Phil thinks in awe) is there to help him pick up the pieces. One of those pieces is the box of embezzled loot Phil has hidden on their property. Problem is, Mira hasn't been as faithful as Phil had hoped. Out of left field wrap-up expository doesn't help at all.

"Dumb Blondes are Murder!" by Don Unatin **1/2 (5200 wds)

Tony and his number-one hooker, Nikki, have been running con games on married business executives. Tony plays the murderous husband who walks in on his wife in the act of adultery and, hopefully, the John pays in spades. Unfortunately for the goofy couple, this particular John doesn't act as he should and ends up with a big black smoking hole in his head compliments of Tony's rifle. Things get real wild when the two fugitives make their escape into the woods. After beating the hell out of Nikki, Tony manages to get himself caught in a bear trap and then eaten by the trap's intended victim! A gruesome (but nevertheless funny) climax makes up for a ho-hum build-up. Probably the best short-story in history with "Dumb Blondes" in the title.

"My Love is Death!" by G. G. Revelle * (4800 wds)

Author tires of the couple upstairs exchanging blows. When he falls in love with the unfortunate female, he realizes the only out is... boredom.

"Fear Casts a Long Shadow!" by Hal Ellson * (1900 wds)

Tod is a mugger who keeps several women company throughout the city. A weak tale devoid of anything resembling suspense or logic.

"Terror Town!" by Art Crockett *** (3200 wds)

After a steamy rendezvous, Rod Baxter learns to his chagrin that the town vixen is actually an "innocent teen." To add to his troubles, the townsfolk don't cotton to their innocents being deflowered by total strangers, and drag Rod out to the woods to string him up. Good twist at the conclusion as we learn that the town might just suspect the truth after all.

"Evil's Executioner!" by Jim Barnett ** (4000 wds)

William Leighton seems to be a bit of a split personality: by day, dapper, well-to-do war hero; by night, rapist and murderer. So-so story builds to a peak of nastiness and gore, wildly so. Entertaining, but the first-person narrative loses its surprise by the second page. You'll know who's really telling Leighton's story.

"Gang Girl's Revenge!" by Hal Crosby **1/2 (3400 wds)

Detective Ben Sommers has a security problem since bringing down mob boss Maxie Grant. Every shadow could be an armed mobster. Every move could be his last. When he's approached by Grant's moll, Carrie Powell, he naturally suspects the worst of her. Turns out though that Powell has been running a double cross on her beau and wants nothing more than to see him burn. As with most of the really effective Web stories, "Gang Girl's Revenge" has a nice twist ending.

"Lust Tells Big Lies!" by Richard Hardwick * (3300 wds)

Yearning for the good life that his prosperous brother leads, Howie Potter borrows his brother's caddy and drives down to Florida for a little vaca. Along the way, he picks up a dame, stacked to the nines, who falls for Howie's line that he's an oil magnate. Of course, the woman has set up Howie for a shakedown (in a scene that screams "quite illogical") and finds himself regretting his new fantasy life.

"Woo Her With Slugs!" by Flip Lyons * (2700 wds)

Myra Nolan loves living high on the hog, thanks to her husband, the hit man, but she just hates to hear him brag about his job.

"Passion Must Die!" by Leslie G. Sabo * (2000 wds)

Ray Miller plans to off his mistress before his rich wife finds out about his adulterous ways and cuts him out of her fortune.

"A Skeleton for Her Bed!" by Bill Ryder * (5700 wds)

Connie Sorrel thinks she's finally found happiness after years spent in a woman's prison manned by sadistic guards. Her happiness comes in the form of her parole officer, who she falls in love with. In a twist that comes as a surprise only to the dim-witted Connie, her new found love also happens to be involved in the same S&M racket as the guards. "Women in Chains" done Web-style. Misogynistic and vile, with not a trace of the goofball charm found in the "Women Prisoner" movies of the 1970s.

Vol. 2/#6, March 1960

"The Framing Frail!" by Al James *1/2 (4300 wds)

Cynthia thinks she's found the perfect dweeb to pin her husband's murder on in Albert Franklin. Little does she know that Franklin is the notorious Albert Franklin, the sex killer who's just murdered his wife. Coincidence? You be the judge.

"Gang Job!" by Zack Steele **** (3050 wds)

No, that's not a typo--4 stars! A beat cop has to bring in a retarded boy who has been tricked into murdering his own brother by a street gang. Not the usual j.d.

story, "Gang Job" focuses on the damage the gang leaves in its wake rather than the sensationalistic aspects inherent in a j.d. story. In fact, the gang itself is never actually featured in the story. Powerful, almost too powerful for *Web*, "Gang Job" brings to mind the best 1950s youth crime fiction of Ed McBain.

"Terror Springs the Trap!" by Bill Ryder *** (4050 wds)

Another dumb title for a fairly good story, the narrative of Dirk, aka Mr. Death, a gallows hangman, whose latest execution is a bit different than those in the past: two vicious teens accused of sexual molestation and murder. You can tell there's a twist in the offing all the way from the beginning of the story, but when the payload is delivered, it's pretty effective and quite original.

"Don't Cheat on Passion!" by Art Crockett ** (5050 wds)

Officer Paul Harkness walks in on his wife while she's playing hide-the-salami with her side dish. Harkness plugs her with lead (in a delightfully graphic description of bullets-meet-arteries damage) and quickly turns himself in. The twist here, which is pretty far-fetched even for a *Web* story, is that the escaped lover turns out to be the D.A. who'll prosecute Harkness.

"Show Her His Blood!" by Leslie G. Sabo * (1800 wds)

Meek Andy helps young thug Bart drag nubile Rita Kemper into the woods and rape her. After Andy gets a case of the guilts, he lets Rita talk him into murdering Bart.

"Hot Dames Spell Trouble!" by Jack Kavanaugh **1/2 (3700 wds)

There's a new kid in Sammy's organization and everyone loves him. Everyone, that is, except Sammy's right hand man Butchie. Seems "the kid" is seeing Butchie's moll on the side and Butchie's bound and determined to put the youngster six feet under. Decent mob story with a good twist.

"Bodies Won't Sink!" by Grover Brinkman **1/2 (4450 wds)

Sheriff Milt Brady investigates the disappearance of one of his deputies, Pete Wiley. Seems Wiley was a nasty fella, beating on his girlfriend and generally raising hell with the local populace. Evidence leads the sheriff right to the patch of quicksand just outside town. Is Wiley down there or in the lake? "Bodies Won't Sink" is just the kind of story you'd find in *Ellery Queen's Mystery Magazine* in the 1950s, with a long expository at its climax just in case we can't connect the dots ourselves.

"Mark Her for Murder!" by Jay Richards *** (1600 wds)

Johnny and Frankie, two likable hitmen (yeah, just like Travolta and Jackson) are given a tough assignment from the syndicate: rub out Anne Carpenter. Right off the bat, the reader knows that Carpenter is no stranger to these gentlemen and this won't be one of their usual hits, but the darkly humorous double whammy in the final line is still effective.

"Tease Me and Die!" by Jim Barnett ***1/2 (5000 wds)

A psycho with delusions of grandeur and a mousy physique chronicles his stalking of a co-worker who has spurned him. Some genuinely creepy writing elevates what might have otherwise have been just another madman saga. For example:

"No matter what I do to you tonight, you'll never feel the agony I've suffered at your hands. In a way it's poetic justice that I'll follow you into the freezing night. You've already killed my soul with your cruelty. All that is left is my body and my lust for vengeance. I will have that revenge. You can't deny it to me."

"Take My Slug, Killer!" by Hal Crosby * (2500 wds)

And then you get dopey clichés like this: Author writes short story about a

From a distance he heard a woman laughing wildly, then a second explosion and the world fell on his head.
-from "Hell's Deadly Lover"

cop killer, but keeps cop's name secret all through narrative. Only problem is: only a dolt would be surprised when the identity is revealed.

"Penny Cost Plenty!" by Don Unatin ** (4500 wds)

Arnie and Penny have a great racket going. Penny seduces middle-aged millionaires and Arnie gets it on film for blackmail money. Unfortunately for Arnie, Penny gets ambitious about her stage career and decides to do away with her cameraman.

Vol. 3/#1, May 1960

"Sisters of Slaughter!" by Edward D. Hoch *1/2 (5050 wds)

Steve Bradburg has a way with the ladies. Most of them, that is. His way doesn't work with Myra Nolan and he delivers her a good beating. Naturally, when Myra's corpse pops up, Steve is the prime suspect.

"The Devil is a Darling!" by Hal Crosby ** (5350 wds)

Mob priestess Tandy Morgan and her notorious prostitution ring have the town literally eating from her hand (and other parts of her body, I'm sure), until revenge-starved Cal Henderson attempts to bring her evil empire crashing down around her.

"Madness Claims a Mate!" by Bill Ryder *** (5575 wds)

A maniac stalks the city and beautiful barfly bimbos are at risk of losing their lovely limbs. Turns out that goofball professor Roger Sylvester has a woody for torture devices and puts them to good use at any given opportunity. Another s&m wacko tale that would hint at the things to come for Web, "Madness" is so bad, it's almost good. The three stars awarded are not for quality, obviously, but for entertainment value, and this one packs a lot of guffaws into its 5575 words. Searching for a standout proquote, I realized that none would do it justice. We'd have to reprint the whole damn thing! Well, okay, just one line: "A fiend stalked the streets and kissed Sherry. Was it a dream out of a horrible past? Hideous death did not claim its victims in this manner any longer!"

"You Can't Escape!" by Bob Shields * (2950 wds)

PI is stuck with one very jealous girlfriend who ends up using the guy's own investigative tricks on him. The opening quote: "She stood over me stark naked with a gun in her hand..." must have eluded the artist, since his illo depicts the woman in a nightie.

"The Glory Kids!" by John Block *1/2 (1650 wds)

There's nothing much to this short-short about teenage cop killers who eventually get theirs in a nasty shootout.

"Die Hard, Lovely Cheat!" by Greg Burns * (4100 wds)

James Harlan is arrested for the murder of one beautiful red-headed babe and grilled by Homicide detective Johnny Daniels. The detective himself is telling the story in first person, filling in details he couldn't possibly know, or so you think until, about half way through, the pieces start falling into place. The redhead was married to... surprise, surprise, surprise!

"Passion Fears No Peril!" by Frank Cannon **1/2 (5050 wds)

When Jed Gage is labeled a stoolie, he must escape or die at the hands of a crooked warden.

"Mask of Hate by Jay Richards ** (2625 wds)

The cops need a little help when the local mobster ends up in the river minus his head and hands, so they question a shopkeeper whose specialty is shrunken heads.

"Lust Steals the Scene!" by Art Crockett * (4625 wds)

Marcia Henry comes to the Big Apple to become a star. The parts just don't come up for her, but her disgustingly obese agent has a swell idea: Marcia puts out and her agent will work double-time for her career. The would-be Monroe doesn't cotton to his advances and puts a bullet in him, or does she? A loser from the word go, "Lust Steals" at least can lay claim to one of the just plain stupidest twist endings in crime story history.

"You'll Die Laughing!" by Jack Kavanagh *** (2625 wds)

Artie has a falling out with his mob boss Christy over, what else, a dame, and becomes target practice for the mobster's gang. Wounded both mentally and physically, Artie decides to confront and mow down the big man before he himself becomes part of the sidewalk. Strictly average crime short until the closing paragraphs which find the crazed Artie at last face to face with the boss man.

"Terror Trail!" by Grover Brinkman * (2950 wds)

John Daly's been messing with a tiff-miner's girl (please don't ask), a big no-no in the backwoods. When he forces himself on the girl, he lives in fear that a knife will find its way into his back.

Vol. 3/#2, August 1960

"A Grave Matter!" by Frank Kane *1/2 (8200 wds)

Ace PI (and chauvinist pig) Johnny Liddell investigates the murder of a beautiful young client ("*A loosely-tied dressing gown gave ample evidence that the magnificence of her facade had needed no artificial assist*") . What he turns up leads him to a ring of arsonists. Overlong (21 pages actually feels more like 2100) relic of the early 1960s, a time when the paperbacks teemed with well-hung PIs like Mike Shayne and Shell Scott. Liddell appeared in over two dozen novels and several short stories in magazines such as *Manhunt* and *Pursuit*. Many of the stories were collected in the paperbacks **Johnny Liddell's Morgue** and **Frank Kane's Stacked Deck** (the latter reprinted "A Grave Matter").

"And Sin No More!" by Jack Kavanaugh **1/2 (2300 wds)

Frankie falls for a hooker and murders her pimp so he can have her for his own.

> **Here was a girl who knew what her sisters had forgotten! - from "Life is Worth Dying"**

"Blood Bargain!" by Pete McCann **1/2 (4400 wds)

When a young lawyer is blackmailed by his sexy mistress, he turns to the only man who can help him: an aging hit man. The real identity of the hit man is a nice touch, albeit one that should be guessed at fairly quickly.

"Murder is Eternal!" by Edward D. Hoch *** (5475 wds)

Our unnamed narrator accepts the job of assassinating "The Eternal Brother," a cult leader who's amassed a fortune for himself from a legion of gullible believers. The job goes awry and the gunman finds himself on the run. Frustrating or fascinating. Either adjective applies to "Murder is Eternal!" Frustrating in that Hoch leaves us high and dry on a few details (why is the Brother assassinated in the first place? Why is the Brother armed when he's gunned down?). Fascinating for just that reason. So many of these stories spend their last eight to ten paragraphs in boring expository that it almost becomes a given that Hoch will finish with: "You see, Bobby, the Eternal Brother was murdered because he had an affair with my Aunt Gertie and..." Thankfully, that never comes. Instead you get a fairly suspenseful narrative and neat prose such as: "*Oh God, we live so many days, so many terrifying days, and then without warning, we always die.*" or "*The bullets took him in the chest and face and he just stopped living all at once.*" Hoch is well-known for such mystery series characters as: Simon Ark, a supernatural sleuth; Ben Snow, a nineteenth-century gunman who wanders into impossible situations; super thief Nick Velvet; and Dr. Sam Hawthorne, a country doctor who solves miracle problems. Hoch also has the distinction of appearing in every issue of *Ellery Queen Mystery Magazine* since 1973.

"The Loving Corpse!" by Leslie G. Sabo ** (2775 wds)

Larry Kendall, who's often fantasized about killing his shrewish wife, comes home to find someone's granted his wish. Unfortunately for Larry, the killer has left evidence pointing to Kendall as the murderer. Nice double twist ending elevates mediocre story.

"Burn in Hell, Darling!" by Bill Ryder * (5100 wds)

Completely predictable tale of a mobster's scorned moll, who's ready to testify against her ex, but the mobster's got other ideas. The police put her under protection. Do I have to tell you about the big twist at the end?

"Punks Don't Kill!" by Cliff Garner *1/2 (4500 wds)

Murdering punk Jackie lies dying in a gutter with a cop standing over him. The one thing Jackie's always longed to do is murder a cop. A 12-page story built around a delivery that could have been wrapped up on the second page.

"Death Wears Black Lace!" by Art Crockett ** (4450 wds)

Larry Striker makes off with $50,000 in mob money. Everyone knows that you can't get away with that kind of behavior, but Larry gives it the old college try. He holes up at an old girlfriend's place, only to be betrayed by the woman.

"Hot Rod Honey!" by Frank Hueppner ** (5050 wds)
(note: contents page lists this story as "Hot Red Honey!")

War vet Joe Wood sets out to

> I told her who I was and what I wanted. I also gave her a smile, half power. What I could see above the typewriter looked usable. It couldn't be all hers. But, what the hell, I've got padded shoulders in my jacket, so we're even.
> - from "Just Kill Him, Darling"

avenge an old girlfriend's son, who's been savagely beaten by a gang of thugs. Joe Wood's an interesting character trapped in a humdrum story. "Hot Rod Honey!" feels like a piece in a bigger story but, as far as I can tell, it's the only story to feature Wood.

Vol. 3/#3, October 1960

"The Triple Cross by Richard Deming ***1/2 (5700 wds)

PI Manville Moon is hired by wealthy socialite Henry Sheffield, who's convinced he's being stalked by mobster Eddie Dallas. A solid PI mystery with a compelling character in Manville Moon, who's a card-carrying member of the so-called "Defective Detectives," sleuths who suffer from some form of handicap but who still save the day. Moon maintains a sense of humor despite the absence of a right leg--at one point in the story, his client "checks his credentials" while gazing at Moon's artificial leg. Manville Moon was also the star of three novels by Deming: **The Gallows in My Garden** (1953), **Tweak the Devil's Nose** (1953), and **Whistle Past the Graveyard** (1954). Deming is perhaps best known by crime fans and pb collectors as the author of several *Dragnet* and *The Mod Squad* TV tie-ins.

"Model of Murder by Christopher Mace * (4000 wds)

George Carlton, a frustrated artist, decides once and for all that he must kill his grossly overweight wife Bernice. It's not just that she's obese, but also because she's loaded and George's girlfriend is getting a bit impatient waiting for Bernice to have that hoped-for heart attack. A dopey story with the most outlandish wife-killing scheme ever devised in the history of mankind: to evoke the heart attack, George sculpts a severed arm, dips it in chocolate (to simulate blood--remember this is the black and white era) and hangs it in his wife's closet. Not the most reasonable method, but hey, it works.

"Daughter of Darkness by O. W. Reynolds ** (2400 wds)

Sick of being a kid stuck in a one horse town, working at a drive-in with old pervs grabbing at her tooties nightly, seventeen year-old Margaret hooks up with the stranger in town, who loves young lasses almost as much as he loves holding up filling stations. Margaret quickly shows the hood how much she hates men.

"Comfort Her Corpse" by Jim Barnett * (4000 wds)

Cain and Abel - *Web* style. Author Barnett can't even keep the two brothers' names straight. Hands down the most ludicrous expository dialogue in, maybe, the whole issue.

"Dumb Bull" by Flip Lyons *1/2 (3200 wds)

Rosie Hauer, hooker, is with Jose Marchione, mobster, when Teddy Landon (our titular hero) breaks in to haul the crook away. In all the confusion, Teddy forgets to bring in Rosie (which is why he's a dumb bull) and she becomes a target of the rest of the Marchione brothers, who fear she'll rat them out to the cops.

"You Can't Cheat Death" by Earle Smith * (6000 wds)

George Smathers is blackmailed after he commits a hit and run.

"The Smell of Fear" by Buck Grimes ** (4100 wds)

No, not a *Naked Gun* story. Frank Cooney, prison guard, is taken hostage by Cass Rawn, bad dude, and a handful of other inmates. If the cons don't get their every wish, they'll start plugging Frank and the other guards. When Frank is given a message to deliver personally to the warden outside the prison, he must fight his urge to run to safety rather than save the other guards, even if one of those guards is his son.

"Lust Isn't Funny" by Fletcher Flora *** (2500 wds)

Mrs. Baldwin lives a life of hell with her philandering husband, a successful comedian who loves to booze and womanize. The pressure gets to be too much and the woman cracks under the strain. A nicely- written just desserts story by the author of such well-respected crime

novels as **The Hot Shot** (1956), **The Brass Bed** (1956), and **Wake Up With a Stranger** (1959), as well as over a hundred short stories published in the crime digests.

"Mistress of Evil" by Bill Ryder * (3800 wds)

Margery Coleman has a big time hang-up: she can't do the nasty with her husband unless he promises to beat and degrade her. Something's wrong with her husband's brain because instead of doing the sensible thing (beating and degrading her), he goes the sensitive '90s husband route and sends her to a psychiatrist. Once she gets there though, Margery seduces her shrink. Unfortunately (or fortunately, for Margery) her doctor turns out to be none other than Gustave Himmelman, aka Gerheardt Heinrich, medical officer of Dachau (still holding a torch for Adolf after all these years). Margery's offer of naked, blistered, whipped, and sweaty flesh triggers some long dormant desires in Little Hitler's brain and he shows her how to really have a good time. From beginning to end, "Mistress of Evil" is one long laugh-fest, enjoyable for its soft-corn and sado-masochist debauchery. When Himmelman asks Margery what makes her believe that she is a wanton hussy given to forbidden fruit, Margery whips a riding crop from her purse and dangles the weapon of love before the headshrinker:

Margery Coleman's shoulders heaved with the force of her sobbing. Her breasts rose and fell swiftly under the tight confines of her silk dress. Himmelman thought how like a sinner she looked on the final Judgement Day.
"Why can't I be normal like other women? Why must I have such horrible desires?" she wailed.

Back in the early '60s, publishers with names like Nightstand, Greenleaf, and Bee-Line served up tons of novel-length trash along the lines of "Mistress," usually introduced by some phony sex therapist attesting to the importance of the story to follow. Bill Ryder sold 26 stories to the Holyoke group, including 10 that were published in *Web*.

"As Hot as Ginger" by Art Crockett ** (5200 wds)

Petey and his buddy Big Sal Cherry burglarize the apartment of Ginger Lansing, unaware that she is a policewoman. After she gets the upper hand on the two, Ginger ventilates Cherry and turns her attention to Petey. The thug manages to escape but becomes the subject of a massive manhunt. The real challenge for Petey then is to get the hell out of Dodge, which he attempts by changing his physical appearance. Routine crimer is highlighted by the humorous passages of Petey's transformation.

Vol. 3/#4, January 1961

"Hang by the Neck!" by Stephen Marlowe ** (5725 wds)

PI Chester Drum is hired by Senator Hartsell to protect his son Blair from a hit man. If I didn't know otherwise, I'd swear that "Hang by the Neck!" was written by Michael Avallone. The dialog is peppered with such Avos as "*I rolled over on my Labonza for him. Afterward Tony did some more bullskating.*" There's also a fairly risqué (for the day) exchange between Drum and a hooker:

"How do you like it?" she asked.
"With your mouth open," I said.
Her eyes got hard. "Now listen, mister," she said. "Maybe Rose should have told you I don't do anything like that." The hard look faded. "Unless," she said, rubbing her thumb on her extended fingers, "you can tempt me."
"I meant with your mouth open so you can talk."
"You mean just talk?"

Stephen Marlowe's Chester Drum was the star of 19 novels , with titles like **Danger Is My Line**, **Death is My Comrade**, and **Double in Trouble** (the latter written with Richard Prather). The novels, as opposed to "Hang by the Neck," have more of an espionage slant to them.[3] Marlowe was actually a pseudonym for Milton Lesser, who wrote tons of science fiction for the sf digests in the 1950s (see the *Super Science Fiction* index back in *b*b* #1).

"Evil is a Redhead!" by Hal Ellson * 1/2 (3875 wds)

A beautiful redhead is running a unique scam: she works her way from boat to boat, first bedding then robbing each ship captain. Told with all the excitement of a police report.

"Love Her to Death!" by Gil Grayson ** (4300 wds)

Wally and Maria murder a Vegas high roller and make off with his loot. When Wally decides that he'd rather not halve the 200 big ones, Maria takes matters in her own hands.

"Ghost Beat!" by Ed Lacy *** (1600 wds)

Harry's a retired cop who's having a hard time just hanging around the house. Good little character study with no *Web* violence whatsoever. Respected writer Ed Lacy wrote over 100 short stories for the crime digests and such well-respected novels as **Sin In Their Blood** (1952), **Be Careful How You Live** (1959), and **Room To Swing** (1957). Marcia Muller wrote of **Room to Swing**'s PI Toussaint Moore: "he is the first convincing black detective in crime fiction."

"Portrait in Passion!" by Grover Brinkman ** (3900 wds)

Up in hillbilly country, cheesecake photographer Mort Murray stumbles onto one of the most beautiful chunks of flesh he's ever laid hands on. Faster than you can say "Ellie May Clampett," Mort's got the girl consenting to nudes and on the way to hot porno action. Then her brother comes home. A fairly amusing finale, but with one or two too many twists.

"As Silent as Doom!" by Arnold English **1/2 (3675 wds)

Manson is an inmate of a maximum security prison. The facility's warden allows no speaking, so most of the communication comes through sign language. When Manson secretly circulates a petition to the warden to abolish the silence rule, he's sold out by a fellow prisoner. Unique tale ends with a big "OUCH!!"

"Lust Claims a Bride!" by Bill Ryder * (3950 wds)

Due to some major mental scars, Babs doesn't want to make love to her husband. He's getting fed up and takes to stepping out. Enter the crazed sex maniac who has been roaming the neighborhood raping and beating beautiful women. Babs is next on his list. I won't be ruining anything for you by giving away the nasty twist at the climax: Hubby comes home to find Babs twirling from the ceiling, getting flogged by the maniac. Being a karate expert, he kills the rapist, but then is taken aback by how lovely his wife looks spinning like meat on a hook:

"I'm going to be a caveman. I'm going to beat the hell out of you. Then I'm going to take you. I've decided that's a better treatment for a frigid bitch like you than all the crap (Bab's psychiatrist) *Palmer can conjure up to waste money"*

More incredible than hubby's transformation from pent-up but understanding mate to masochistic animal is Babs' resignation to her fate:

"It might work," she told herself. "It's worth a try."

"The Soft Arms of Murder!" by Al James * (3200 wds)

Celeste tires of her millionaire husband and cooks up a scheme to off him, but in the usual dumb *Web* broad style, she screws up big time.

"Harness Bull!" by Don Unatin ***1/2 (5925 wds)

Officer John Stewart reflects on his life as an honest cop and how that honesty has kept him at odds with the other cops in his precinct, all graft-takers. "Harness Bull" is almost like two short stories: one, the main plot, deals with Stewart's endeavors to put away a mob boss who has gotten away with murder. The more interesting piece of the story though is its question of whether Stewart should have gone along with his fellow bulls in their crimes (and live the good life overflowing with money, women, and friends) or stay the straight course and

What happened next to Marc is something that has defied understanding ever since man left the caves.
-from "Don't Run From Evil"

keep a clean soul (and suffer the scorn of colleagues, wife, and worse, his own self doubts). In the end, Stewart contemplates just that after he stumbles across a dead man with a load of cash. The author wisely ends his narrative right there before filling in the blanks and, instead, puts the question to the reader - *"what would you do?"*

Vol. 3/#5, May 1961

"Deadly Error" by Frank Kane ** (6600 wds)

Johnny Liddell and his Girl Friday Muggsy Kiedel (Frank Kane's version of Lois Lane) run into the usual trouble when Liddell investigates the suspicious fires that have claimed five expensive homes covered in articles written by ace reporter Kiedel. A couple of antiques thieves are making off with priceless paintings and furniture and selling them for the big payday.

"Death Watch" by J. Simmons Scheb **1/2 (2100 wds)

Ever since his mother left him when he was four and screwed up his life completely, Frankie's wanted to kill a tall blonde. So when the opportunity presents itself, he springs into action.

"So Young to Die" by Ed Lacy *** (3900 wds)

15 year-old Joe Lancaster is duped into the boxing arena by a shyster fight manager, only to find that he has a natural punch, one that can level anyone it's aimed at. But with more punches, Joe becomes more punchy until he's pert near brain dead. The "boxer who's supposed to throw the fight but doesn't" storyline has been done to death in the movies, but Lacy manages to throw a sly twist into this one.

"Requiem for a Heel" by Jim Arthur *** (2800 wds)

Phil and Helen Mandler have been waiting ages for Uncle Jerry to croak

133

and leave them his pot of gold. The couple has slaved years for the old man and they're owed that much. But the old goat is cantankerous and finally Phil loses patience and puts a bullet between Uncle Jerry's peepers. The only problem is that the sheriff doesn't believe Phil's "hunting accident" line and demands to be cut in on the booty. Then there's the funeral parlor director who's suspicious, and the mortician... Funny story would have made a great episode of *Alfred Hitchcock Presents*.

"The Night People" by Edward D. Hoch **** (2900 wds)

A reporter is given an assignment: find a story, any big story to fill a front page. He sets out to find sensation and finds a prostitute resigned to life in the street. What the hell is this wonderful character study doing in the pages of *Web*? This is the type of story you would have found in *Collier's* or *Saturday Evening Post*.

"Murder's No Bargain" by James Holding **** (4200 wds)

Assassin Manuel Andradas, aka The Photographer, is hired by the Italian mafia to take out Giovanni Corelli, a well-known and wealthy building contractor who has been using faulty materials for his structures. Believing he has been underpaid for his services, The Photographer approaches Corelli with a deal: Corelli pays the hitman and he'll smuggle him out of the country. When the contractor ponies up, the assassin kills him anyway (in a particularly nasty way too). James Holding wrote hundreds of short stories for the crime digests, including several more adventures of The Photographer for *Ellery Queen Mystery Magazine*. A humorous aspect of the stories is that the hitman always haggles over the price his bosses are willing to pay him, feeling he's always worth more.

Afterwards, back in her own apartment, she put his eyes in the box with the others.
- from "Look Death in the Eye"

"Woe is For Wednesday" by Hal Ellson ***1/2 (3800 wds)

Wild and wacky tale of an inmate named Flint, who begins his tour of his new home (an asylum) and meets all kinds of goofy occupants. "Woe is For Wednesday" almost defies description with its many twists and turns, some relevant, some not.

"Dumb Rookie" by Art Crockett **1/2 (2400 wds)

Johnny Grogan, rookie cop, falls into the clutches of Tom and Sandra, who need Johnny's uniform to pull off their warehouse heist. Peppered with very funny passages:

"The crazy gal stood on a ledge ten stories up and Joe had been assigned to get out on the ledge and drag her in. But she'd grabbed Joe's tie and told him that if he touched her she'd jump and take him with her. So he opened his pocketknife inside his pocket and then told her that her slip was showing. The crazy dame looked and Joe cut the tie."

"Track of Fear" by H. A. DeRosso *** (3900 wds)

Johnny returns from a day of hunting to find his dad murdered. The man responsible is looking for the jewelry he and Johnny's dad had stolen many years ago. But Johnny's a smart kid and soon he's got the killer in a trap. H. A. DeRosso wrote several dozen crime stories for such respected digests as *Manhunt, Hunted, Pursuit*, and *Mike Shayne*, but is best remembered for his gritty western novels, including **End of the Gun** and **.44** (Bill Pronzini called the latter "a stark and suspenseful portrait of a professional gunfighter"). My first encounter with DeRosso was the story "Vigilante," which first appeared in the old pulp magazine, *New Western*, back in 1948, and was reprinted by Ed Gorman in his anthology of westerns by crime writers, **The Fatal Frontier**. DeRosso had a gift for showing the dark side of his characters, even those identifiable as "heroes."

"Talk Me to Death" by Seymour Shubin ** (1700 wds)

Mrs. Brown is an inconsiderate

clod on the party line and Mr. Hammond, after exhausting his patience, decides it's time to clean her clock.

"No Passion to Kill" by C. B. Gilford **1/2 (5200 wds)

Clare Kusick has fallen in love with her supervisor, James Dysart. Problem is, Dysart doesn't love her, so Clare threatens to tell a tall tale of sexual harassment on the work room floor. No other avenue is available so Dysart kills her and mutilates the body to make it appear as if a maniac has struck. Fairly interesting story serves up something of a taboo at its conclusion (a taboo, at least, for its time): the reason Dysart murders Clare is not because of a fear of losing his job, but because he's a latent homosexual and therefore hates all women. When the truth becomes clear to him, he commits suicide. Probably wouldn't appear in any of today's mystery magazines.

Vol. 3/#6, September 1961

"Blood Bargain" by Henry Slesar ** (5200 wds)

Hitman William Derry is hired by mob kingpin Rupert Harney to kill embezzler Eddie Breech. Derry shows up for the kill but then discovers he has a heart when it turns out that Breech's wife is in a wheelchair. He concocts an elaborate plan to enable Breech and his wife to escape. Derry soon learns that being a nice guy ain't all it's cracked up to be. Not one of Slesar's best.

"Angel of Evil" by Robert Rossner **** (6600 wds)

Sandy, Mitch, David, and Kevin are staunch members of the He-Man-Women-Haters Club, living together, partying together, vacationing together, until Mitch falls for the lovely Leora. At first the other three men find her charming, but eventually the false charm erodes away and what stands before them is the angel of emasculation. The three men decide the best thing for Mitch is to kill Leora. So they do. Rossner does a good job of showing both dark and bright sides to each character. These three men only want what's best for their fallen comrade and that justifies any

actions they may take. The matter-of-fact conversation wherein the trio plans Loera's death evokes memories of the famous (and very similar) scene in Paddy Chayefsky's *Network*. The narrative also conjures up a well-told EC comic story (right down to the *Shock SuspenStories* ending), with the cherry on top being an art job by Jack Kamen. A highpoint in *Web* history.

"Requiem for a Junkie" by James Stevens ***1/2 (4200 wds)

Max is a recovered junkie, only wanting to put his woes behind him when part of his past, in the form of his old junkie pal Herb, comes knocking at his door. Herb begs Max to put him up and help him kick his morphine addiction. Now married and a father, Max sees Herb as a mission, hoping to save the poor guy and save himself at the same time:

The lost ones. They call for the God they've never known. There are no atheists in foxholes. Outside the world the day they're born, frightened, they sell out for a ride to cloudland. Their God is a thirty five pound monkey perched lovingly between the shoulder blades. Heaven is a dirty room and a vein charged full of hope.

Unfortunately, Herb doesn't take well to rehab and grabs Max's daughter by the throat, threatening death if he goes without a fix. Max must think quickly. The final paragraphs are a little too much Happy Hollow, but the message of the story, though told a thousand times before, is told starkly, pulling no punches.

(Max) shed his tears for the weed-heads and the short-time-one dollar fix who would soon be taking the C train or the H train or the M express for the trip to oblivion. For the bug house, the big house, the death house.

And the tears won't help.

"The Dumb Die Hard" by Henry H. Guild * (4200 wds)

Danny Bolton was once bug man of The Ramblers gang until Bill Harper muscled his way in. Danny's got a plan to wrest away control and it involves the delicious (but brain-dead) Connie Rondel. A shortened title of "Dumb" might have been more appropriate.

"To Serve the Dead" by Edward D. Hoch ** (5600 wds)

Ben Ferrel goes to Puerto Rico with Senator Eaton as companion/bodyguard. When the Senator is brutally gunned down, it's up to Ben to find the killer. Though it's written well, "To Serve" just doesn't have much excitement. It's a short story that seems mighty long.

"A Corpse Can Hate" by Harlan Ellison *** (4800 wds)

Piddy Sandoz is only doing a Good Sam for a blind guy at a Salvation Army food kitchen when he recognizes the old man as the once-great prize fighter Kid Walders, now reduced to living on the street. Walders promises to pay Piddy the princely sum of five dollars if he'll help him find his old manager, Primo, who pushed the Kid into the ring one too many times, thereby rendering him damaged goods. A very funny road trip, so unlike the usual *Web* fare, "Corpse" is a breath of fresh air amidst the misogyny, sado-masochism, two-timing dames, and sadistic wardens (not to mention the horrors that were to beheld starting with the next issue). Once the Kid finds Primo, a fight breaks out and the manager is forced to kill the man who was once his property. This means nothing to Piddy, who just wants his five bucks. Amazingly, Primo is outraged at the sight of the man rummaging through the dead fighter's pockets:

"Why you lousy little grave-robber, get your effing hands off that guy, you ain't fit to wear his dirty underwear, that was Kid Walders and he could of been a contender..."

But my favorite line comes from Piddy in a moment of fright and self-doubt:

I was frankly dropping my load.

"Trail of Doom" by Bill Engeler ** (2100 wds)

Carl Steadman is obsessed with the West but his money-loving wife sure isn't. When they visit an old ghost town, Carl finally hears one too many shriek-fest from his lovely wife and exacts some good old-fashioned Western justice on her.

You Don't Have to Kill by Grover Brinkman ** (2600 wds)

Silas Greentree has big bucks stashed on his ranch and three conmen are up to killing him and taking possession of the loot. Brinkman's best writing attribute was his way with a title. He wrote dozens of stories for *Offbeat, Pursuit, Two-Fisted,* and *Hunted* with such wonderful titles as: "Smooth Siren of Death," "Soft Arms-Bloody Hands," "Her Corpse Needs Loving," "Death's Errand Boy," and my favorite of Brinkman's: "Hell's Lovely Gravedigger."

"Fear Stacks the Deck" by William H. Duhart ***1/2 (5600 wds)

Good cardtable yarn about two pre-teens who take on an old card shark and teach him some of his own tricks. No violence, two thrusting breasts, lots of early 60s vulgar lingo. Should have been included in a one-shot called *Web Gambling Stories.*

Notes:
[1] Our good friends in Holyoke; see previous indexes for publisher history.
[2] Though I will continue to berate Stefan Dziemianowicz until he picks some of these stories for his "100 Stories" series for Barnes and Noble.
[3] In fact, as the series entered the mid-sixties, the titles became more uniform: **Drum-Beat Berlin**, **Drum-Beat Dominique**, **Drum-Beat Erica**, etc. Very much like Edward Aarons' seemingly never-ending Sam Durrell **Assignment-**(*insert country here*).

References:
Clute, John and Peter Nicholls. **The Encyclopedia of Science Fiction**. St. Martin's, 1993.
Cook, Michael L. **Monthly Murders**. Greenwood, 1982.
Cook, Michael L. **Mystery, Detective, and Espionage Magazines**. Greenwood, 1983.
Hubin, Allen J. **The Bibliography of Crime Fiction 1749-1975**. Publisher's Inc., 1979.
Pronzini, Bill and Marcia Muller. **1001 Midnights**. Arbor House, 1986.
Tymn, Marshall and Mike Ashley. **Science Fiction, Fantasy, and Weird Fiction Magazines**. Greenwood, 1985.

Her eyes took in my clothes, looking for a bulge.
-from "The Devil is a Darling"

NEW JOHNNY LIDDELL MYSTERY BY FRANK KANE

WEB DETECTIVE STO...

35¢ AUG.

A HOT ROD HONEY

AND SIN NO MORE

TEASE ME AND DIE!

WEB DETEC...TORIES

35¢ MAR

A GANG JOB!

SHOW HER HIS BLOOD

JETS

Al James-Bill Ryder-Don Unatin

FEAR FINDS A MATE

WEB DETECTIVE STORI...

SEPT. 25¢ A

NO GUTS TO DIE!

LOVE NEST IN HELL

· Luke Hogan
· Al James
· Pete McCann

SISTERS OF SLAUGHTER!

WEB DETECTIV... ...RIES

35¢

A JUNE

LUST STEALS THE SCENE

YOU'LL DIE LAUGHING

MURDERER WANTED

Frank Cannon · Hal Crosby · Art Crockett

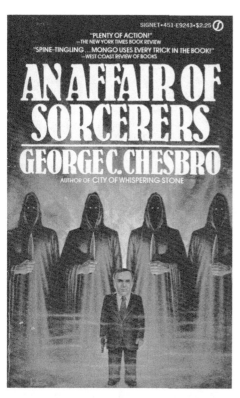

SIGNET • 451-E9243 • $2.25

"PLENTY OF ACTION!"
—THE NEW YORK TIMES BOOK REVIEW

"SPINE-TINGLING ... MONGO USES EVERY TRICK IN THE BOOK!"
—WEST COAST REVIEW OF BOOKS

AN AFFAIR OF SORCERERS

GEORGE C. CHESBRO

AUTHOR OF CITY OF WHISPERING STONE

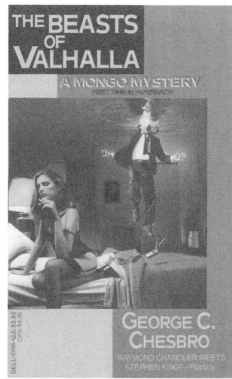

THE BEASTS OF VALHALLA

A MONGO MYSTERY

FIRST TIME IN PAPERBACK

GEORGE C. CHESBRO

"RAYMOND CHANDLER MEETS STEPHEN KING!" —Playboy

TWO SONGS THIS ARCHANGEL SINGS

"RAYMOND CHANDLER MEETS STEPHEN KING!" —Playboy

A MONGO MYSTERY

GEORGE C. CHESBRO

DELL • 20105-5 • U.S. $3.95
CAN. $4.95

CITY OF WHISPERING STONE

"RAYMOND CHANDLER MEETS STEPHEN KING!" —Playboy

A MONGO MYSTERY

GEORGE C. CHESBRO

DELL • 20035-0 • U.S. $3.50 CAN. $4.25

I'm fairly certain that it was Tom Deja's idea to tackle the screwy career of George C. Chesbro's dwarf detective, Mongo, but it obviously fit right in with what John and I were doing with bare•bones. As was typical with all of the subjects discussed in bb, I immediately ran out and picked up all the Mongo paperbacks (back in the day when there were several used paperback stores in every city), but just couldn't get into them. Too… unique. Unique would be an adjective I'd apply to the overview's author as well. Though we never met in person, Tom and I shared a few raucous phone calls back in the day, discussing bad comics, bad horror novels and, undoubtedly, bad horror movies. His is a unique voice amidst a lot of yadda-yadda-yadda on the internet. -Peter

THE PROFANE SCENT OF FORBIDDEN KNOWLEDGE
George C. Chesbro's Mongo
by Thomas Deja

It was the advertising poster that drew me in: a lingerie-clad femme fatale who bore a resemblance to Mimi Rogers sat on a bed in a lonely hotel room, smoking, oblivious to the man in a business suit trying to keep his head above the now-liquid ceiling. On a blue and purple frame surrounding the painting was the legend **The Beasts of Valhalla**: A Mongo Mystery.

I *had* to have that book.

The Mongo series of mysteries is one of the most insanely wild detective series you'll *ever* encounter. In twelve books (eleven novels and a short story collection), East-Coast native George C. Chesbro grabbed heaping handfuls of espionage, science fiction, and horror, and tied them inextricably to a mystery framework in a grand epic continuity. When it was finished, with **Incident at Blood Tide**, Chesbro had created an elaborate worldscape of characters and incidents that used as its center one Robert Fredrickson, aka Mongo, a criminologist and part-time private eye— not to mention former circus acrobat and dwarf.

The first novel in the series was **Shadow of a Broken Man** (although it *wasn't* the first novel released by Dell when they reprinted the novels in 1987, something I learned to hate them for once I realized how tight the series' continuity was). Published in 1977, **Shadow** began with Mongo being hired by one Mike Foster, a contractor, to determine if famed architect Victor Rafferty is still alive. Foster is married to Rafferty's widow, and she has become disturbed by the work of another architect which mirrors that of Rafferty's unrealized work. As Mongo digs into the curious circumstances around Rafferty's death, he disturbs certain branches of the government both here and in Moscow (this *is* 1977, after all) that he may wish he hadn't. He learns that Rafferty was prepared to defect to Moscow—an unusual prospect for an architect who cared nothing for politics. Mongo soon learns that Rafferty wasn't being pursued for what he knew, but what he could do.

I won't give away the solution to the mystery (one of the reasons I was upset with Dell's releasing the books out of order was because the solution to this novel is discussed matter-of-factly in **Beasts of Valhalla**). Needless to say, Rafferty's accident left him with certain valuable powers. One of Chesbro's strengths in this book is that he sets the groundwork for this revelation early, injecting subtle hints that Mongo's quarry is somewhat superhuman. When the solution does come, you're surprised, but you don't feel gypped the way certain other novels like this make you feel. My only real complaint is that, after two hundred and thirty deliberately paced pages, the final confrontation between Mongo, Lippet and Rafferty seems rushed.

However, in **Shadow**, all the hallmarks are in place: a supernatural or science-fictional bent to the mystery, a espionage/world political angle, an obsession with the questions of identity, strange adversaries (in this case a giant of a Russian interrogation expert), and brutal, nasty violence—a scene in the last half involving a crossbeam and a telephone is practically guaranteed to put the average reader in a cold sweat. It's a loose formula that will serve Chesbro well over the next fifteen years.

The next book in the series, **City of Whispering Stone**, may seem atypical. After all, there's no supernatural gimmick involved and the mystery seems generic. However, when you realize that Chesbro is married to an Iranian national, it makes a lot more sense. In this novel, Mongo is hired by his old employer, Phil Statler. Statler is still running a 'mud show' that's barely breaking even thanks to an Iranian strongman named Khordad. Khordad turns up missing after telling Statler he's going to New York to see a friend. Statler asks Mongo to find out what's happened to the Iranian. In doing so, the detective finds out that Khordad was a member of SAVAK, the Shah's secret police, and that the true reason for his disappearance involves the search for the head man of the revolutionary army, GEM. Unfortunately, in discovering this, Mongo endangers his brother, compelling the detective to travel to Iran.

City of Whispering Stone is very densely packed for its two hundred and seventeen pages; the last half, taking place in Iran, could have taken up the whole book and not seem stretched out. It's the cultural aspect of that last half that makes the book. Unfortunately, it's also the aspect that dates the book horribly. As with **Shadow of a Broken Man**, **City of Whispering Stone** is very much a book of its time—in this case, Iran just before the fall of the Shah. So much has gone on in that corner of the world since the book's publication that the goings-on seem almost...quaint, especially considering the book lacks the sheer ruthlessness of its predecessor. It's telling that this is the last book that Chesbro will set firmly in one time frame.

That's not to say it's thoroughly bad, just slightly below average. There are some great portraits drawn in **City**, including an absolutely stunning one of the Shah himself, who tries to bribe Mongo in the middle of the vault containing the Iranian Crown Jewels. It's just that there's very little in this one that lifts it out of the morass of other detective/espionage novels. **City of Whispering Stone** just sits there, and that's too bad.

The last book of this initial trilogy, **An Affair of Sorcerers**, is a bit of a cheat for hard-core Mongo fans, as it's been restructured from three of the novellas that appeared in *Alfred Hitchcock's Mystery Magazine* (and reprinted in **In The House of Secret Enemies**). It also seems to have been intended as the last book in the series. The book not only reveals that Mongo is dying from a degenerative disease that's never mentioned again in the books, it ends with an ambiguous scene that implies our hero is killed by his opposition! Indeed, it looked like **An Affair of Sorcerers** was it for five years, since the first book of what Chesbro refers to as 'The Valhalla Trilogy' didn't see light of day until 1985.

Affair takes place a year after the events of **City of Whispering Stone**, (although the actual date is never mentioned; one suspects Chesbro realized the peril of anchoring books in specific time periods at this point). Mongo is given, in rapid succession, three cases. His administrator at NYU wants him to look into the background of a fellow academic who may be misappropriating college funds, a nun asks him to spring a faith healer accused of murder, and his neighbor's daughter gives him her milk money to locate her daddy's 'Book of Shadows.' When his neighbor ends up dead and the child in a mysterious coma, Mongo delves into the occult underground of New York and finds a secret 'super-coven' of ceremonial magicians run by a mythical figure named Esobus. Fredrickson must find out Esobus' identity before a prophecy comes to pass that will endanger not only the girl, but the girl's mother, who our hero is beginning to have feelings for.

Considering that **An Affair of Sorcerers** started out as three novellas,

The Mongo Bibliography

Shadow of a Broken Man (Simon and Schuster hc, 1977. Signet pb, 1978)
City of Whispering Stone (Simon and Schuster hc, 1978. Signet pb, 1979)
An Affair of Sorcerers (Simon and Schuster hc, 1979. Signet pb, 1979)
The Beasts of Valhalla (Atheneum hc, 1985. Dell pb, 1987)
Two Songs This Archangel Sings (Atheneum hc, 1986. Dell pb, 1988)
The Cold Smell of Sacred Stone (Atheneum hc, 1988. Dell pb, 1989)
Second Horseman Out of Eden (Atheneum hc 1989. Mysterious Press pb, 1990)
The Language of Cannibals (Mysterious Press hc, 1990. Mysterious Press pb, 1991)
In the House of Secret Enemies (short novels reprinted from *Alfred Hitchcock's Mystery Magazine*) (Mysterious Press hc, 1990. Mysterious Press pb, 1992)
The Fear in Yesterday's Rings (Mysterious Press hc, 1991. Mysterious Press pb, 1992)
Dark Chant in a Crimson Key (Mysterious Press hc, 1992. Mysterious Press pb, 1993)
Incident at Bloodtide (Mysterious Press hc, 1993. Mysterious Press pb, 1993)

Short Chesbro: Mongo and Beyond

"Book of Shadows" *Mike Shayne Mystery Magazine* (June 1975)
"Broken Patterns" *Alfred Hitchcock Mystery Magazine* (May 1972)
"The Club of Venice" *Mike Shayne Mystery Magazine* (March 1974)
"Country for Sale" *Mike Shayne Mystery Magazine* (June 1973)
"Dark Hole on a Silent Planet" *Alfred Hitchcock Mystery Magazine* (Nov. 1973)
"The Dragon Variation" *Alfred Hitchcock Mystery Magazine* (Aug. 1975)
"Dreams" *Mike Shayne Mystery Magazine* (April 1975)
"The Drop" *Mike Shayne Mystery Magazine* (Oct. 1971)
"Falling Star" *Alfred Hitchcock Mystery Magazine* (Nov. 1974)
"The Finest of Families" *Mike Shayne Mystery Magazine* (July 1977)
"Firefight on the Mind" *Alfred Hitchcock Mystery Magazine* (Nov. 1970)
"First Strike" *Ellery Queen Mystery Magazine* (Dec. 1991)
"Forced Moves" *Ellery Queen Mystery Magazine* (Mid-Dec. 1993)
"Four Knight's Game" *Alfred Hitchcock Mystery Magazine* (Sept. 1974)
"Haunts" *Ellery Queen Mystery Magazine* (Oct. 1993)
"The Healer" *Alfred Hitchcock Mystery Magazine* (Aug. 1974)
"High Wire" *Alfred Hitchcock Mystery Magazine* (March 1972)
"House of Rain" *Mystery Monthly* (Nov 1976)
"King's Indian Defense" *Alfred Hitchcock Mystery Magazine* (Dec. 1974)
"The Lazarus Gate" *Ellery Queen Mystery Magazine* (Sept.-Oct. 1996)
"Lone Wolf" *Ellery Queen Mystery Magazine* (July 1993)
"Night Flight" *Alfred Hitchcock Mystery Magazine* (June 1974)
"The Paper War" *Alfred Hitchcock Mystery Magazine* (Jan. 1971)
"Priests" *Alfred Hitchcock Mystery Magazine* (Sept. 1991)
"The Problem With the Pigs" *Ellery Queen Mystery Magazine* (June 1997)
"Rage" *Alfred Hitchcock Mystery Magazine* (Feb. 1973)
"The Shadow in the Mirror" *Alfred Hitchcock Mystery Magazine* (March 1971)
"Short Circuit" *Alfred Hitchcock Mystery Magazine* (Oct. 1971)
"Snake in the Tower" *Alfred Hitchcock Mystery Magazine* (March 1969)
"Strange Prey" *Alfred Hitchcock Mystery Magazine* (Aug. 1970)
"Tiger in the Snow" *Mike Shayne Mystery Magazine* (March 1976)
"Tomb" *Alfred Hitchcock Mystery Magazine* (Oct. 1993)
"Tourist Trap" *Alfred Hitchcock Mystery Magazine* (Oct. 1970)
"Unmarked Graves" *Ellery Queen Mystery Magazine* (Sept.-Oct. 1997)
"The White Bear" *Ellery Queen Mystery Magazine* (May 1992)

it's not a surprise that the book comes off disjointed; one of the plot lines is alltogether abandoned early on, and isn't brought back until the last act, when Chesbro seems to need another gruesome torture for our hero. The romantic angle is another thorn in the book's narrative flow, but that's not surprising. For some reason, Chesbro has never really been comfortable with romantic subplots, and this is the last time Mongo will have a serious relationship with a woman until **The Fear in Yesterday's Rings** many years later.

But **Affair** is also one of the roughest of the Mongo books — people die frequently, awfully and at great length, including a few characters you wouldn't expect to turn up staked in the middle of Central Park. It also plays the ambiguity game most successfully—Chesbro never comes out on one side or another on whether supernatural powers are at play, but manages to give us a few situations where you're *sure* something's going on. **Affair** is also the most successful of the three up to that point at creating a sense of otherness. The bulk of detective fiction is about the detective as obtrusive 'other,' Chesbro's conscious decision to make Mongo into a dwarf emphasizes this theme, and he manages to make our hero more normal than his adversaries here effortlessly. This entry ends up being a bit more successful than the one preceding it, but still not up to the high standards set by **Shadow of a Broken Man**.

As mentioned, the last chapter of **Affair** implies that Mongo is accidentally electrocuted when his ultimate quarry attracts a lightning bolt with her gun. And it did look like Mongo was a dead issue to Chesbro until 1985, when he produced his thickest novel in the series, and the beginning of his magnum opus.

The Beasts of Valhalla.

Beasts opens with Mongo back in his hometown of Peru, Nebraska, attending the funeral of his teenage nephew. The local sheriff, a former tormentor of Robert, claims that the boy died as part of a homosexual suicide pact with the brother of another bully, Coop Lugmoor. Mongo finds out that both boys were participating in a game called Sorscience, in which players gain points for discovering real life parallels to **The Lord of the Rings**. Another player was Obie Loge, the son of the owner of the Volsung Corporation, a mysterious company that has apparently paid the residents of Peru to grow 'special crops.' Just as Mongo begins to uncover some darker truths about the Loges, they are injected with something that has an unusual side effect, as he finds out in a discussion with Lippet:

Mercifully, Lippet stopped when I held up my hand. "Are...we going to end up like...that?"
"I have no idea. By rights the two of you should have been dead and looking something like that within an hour after Bolesh gave you the first injection. The stuff...just tears apart the cellular structure and reforms it, virtually before your eyes. It seems to act by magnifying the genetic information of the evolutionary past, throwing all the biological controls out of whack and commanding the cells to try everything at once. Naturally, the organism quickly dies as a result of the...molecular insult."

And so Mongo, who is displaying disturbing reptilian characteristics, and Garth, who is reverting back to his primate ancestry, end up searching for Obie Loge's grandfather, a geneticist turned cult leader, in the hopes that they can find the information needed to turn them back before he releases 'Loge's Treasure,' a legacy sure to change the world.

What makes **The Beasts of Valhalla** so brilliant is its seamless creation of a fantasy quest novel in a modern day, hard-boiled setting. The book is rife with parallels to standard fantasy elements—Mongo and Garth could be considered `cursed'; Mongo finds a sword made out of Damascus steel called 'whisper'; one of Loge's creations, a mentally enhanced gorilla named Gollum, becomes Mongo's ally—and Chesbro makes them all sound absolutely plausible. He also manages to twist some conventions; when Lippet calls on a 'Genera Baggins' for aid, he turns out to be not a heroic figure, but another high-placed figure in the thrall of the Loges.

And, needless to say, Chesbro's fascination with 'otherness' gets a workout.

As Mongo becomes more and more of a freak (needing first smoked glasses, then a parka and finally a battery-powered heater), he's bounced from one bizarre subculture to another. The Loges have set up communes all over the country promising different things to different cultures—the Fredricksons meet a group of right-wing white supremacists and a colony of former circus freaks hoping to be `cured,' and mention is made of Muslim fanatics hoping for the destruction of Israel, and South Africans believing Seigmund Loge is designing a virus that will make all colored people docile. Of course, none of these subgroups are getting what they want—it's actually the most massive shell game of all; the fate of the world literally hanging in the balance.

The Beasts of Valhalla is a magnificent book that works on many levels; science fiction and fantasy fans should enjoy it as much as mystery fans. And yet it was just the first book in a trilogy that would see Chesbro transform his characters, while also begin to tie together the various threads of his writing career into a coherent universe.

The second book in the Valhalla trilogy, **Two Songs This Archangel Sings**, ties the Mongo books in with another series Chesbro had started featuring former CIA operative and 'lucid dreamer' turned artist Veil Kendry. **Two Songs** begins two years after the fall of the Loges, with Mongo discovering that Kendry, his friend and martial arts sparring partner, has disappeared. The only clues he finds are a painting of an angel hovering over a group of Asians, a bullet hole, and an envelope of money addressed to him. Convinced that this is Veil's way of hiring him, Mongo starts looking into his friend's mysterious past and uncovers a conspiracy reaching back to the days of Vietnam—and an enemy who may be in a position of power too great for Mongo to reach.

Now keep in mind that after **Beasts**, any book would be a bit of a disappointment. But even taking that into account, **Two Songs** is a mess. Chesbro is trying to say something about the dangers of power, tying it specifically into the Vietnam war (one of the climactic scenes

actually takes place at the War Memorial), but in exploring these themes the author loses sight of the story he's telling. One of Chesbro's strengths is his ability to balance action with the philosophical musings of his characters, but in **Two Songs** the philosophy *so* overwhelms the action that he gets sloppy. Characters disappear midway through, an entire society is introduced only to be given short shrift and summarily written out in the next chapter, the character of Lippet is given a *deus ex machina* appearance in the last third of the book, and one massive plot point—the plot point that leads into the next book—is so badly set up that it might as well have come out of nowhere. There are certain elements in this book, such as the Hmong villagers and the polite assassin-for-hire, Henry Kitten, that seem to be crammed in just because Chesbro thinks we expect them to be there. Unfortunately, they're pretty much abandoned the next time Chesbro rants about war and diplomacy.

The simple fact is **Two Songs This Archangel Sings** tries to accomplish too much. Maybe Chesbro felt he had to up the stakes after **Beasts**; maybe he really wanted to start building the Chesbro universe by introducing Veil Kendry to Mongo readers. But in doing so, he wrote what is pretty much the weakest Mongo book until **Dark Chant in a Crimson Key** surfaces, a book that, not coincidentally, tries to introduce another Chesbro series character into the Mongo continuity.

Two Songs This Archangel Sings ends with Garth, poisoned by industrial saboteurs, being committed to a psychiatric facility by Lippet and Mongo. The final book of the Valhalla trilogy, **The Cold Smell of Sacred Stone** takes up that plot thread and focuses on the other Fredrickson, giving us further ruminations on responsibility, activism and diplomacy.

It's very obvious where Chesbro's head is at with his prologue—a rambling monologue by Mongo and his brother and `Garth's credo,' a civics code of some selfishness:

"...the only help for his own affliction was to attempt to alienate the suffering of others, in whatever way he could. He was never quite

certain what others meant when they talked about salvation, and he was certainly not seeking it for himself. He simply needed to nurse the fever of the world so that he can be at peace and sleep without the night terrors of his own fever dreams."

From there, we take a quick side trip to clumsily wrap up the loose end that is Henry Kitten, and join Mongo at a government run institution, where Garth is being treated for his NPPD poisoning. Despairing at his brother's comatose state, Mongo utilizes Wagner music to hopefully revive his brother. It works, but with mixed results; Garth emerges from his coma speaking in the third person, devoid of any emotional attachment to his brother and with an overwhelming empathy for others—an empathy that is utilized by those around him to create the above-mentioned religious movement. Unfortunately, Mongo learns that the true powers behind `Garth's People' are preparing for a big move that will prove fatal to both Fredrickson brothers.

Like **Two Songs This Archangel Sings**, **The Cold Smell of Sacred Stone** is disjointed and all over the place. Chesbro tends to switch gears a bit too abruptly, going from 'saving Garth' to 'dealing with the pain' to `Garth's People' without really letting us get used to things. Once again, the `viper in our midst' concept is brought forth, with a red herring to cover it up that's wholly unconvincing. One interesting thing is the character of Marl Braxton; meant to be the strongarm of the opposition, Chesbro creates a character whose intelligence and admiration for Mongo gives him a special dimension. Not so the other opposition characters, such as the dwarf-hating Ma Baker and Dr. Slykce, who are cardboard. In all, **The Cold Smell of Sacred Stone** is a disappointing ending to the Valhalla trilogy.

In the final chapter of **The Cold Smell**, Chesbro gives us another coda. Wisely, however, it is not a final `Mongo is dead' coda like in **An Affair of Sorcerers**. The next book in the series, **Second Horseman Out of Eden**, found Chesbro with a new publisher, Mysterious Press, and a new cover scheme. His heroes were comfortably ensconced in a new situation

and ready for action.

Second Horseman takes place two years after **The Cold Smell**, and finds Mongo and Garth in business for themselves as private detectives. It's coming up on Christmas, and the brothers find amongst the letters to Santa at the New York Post Office (it is a tradition of the Post Office to set out letters to Santa for New Yorkers to inspect and maybe send a gift to an underprivileged child) a plea from Vicky Brown. Vicky is being sexually molested by a 'reverend Billy,' and her letter comes covered in a peculiar sort of dirt. Trying to locate the girl by tracing the source of the dirt leads the Fredrickson brothers to a televangelist known for his extreme views, a reclusive billionaire a la Howard Hughes, a mysterious company devoted to developing biospheres, and the nagging feeling that the Rapture some of these people are anticipating is coming a lot sooner.

Second Horseman is the only Mongo since the earliest ones with a very precise time-frame—it takes place in the weeks before the Millennium, and with good reason. Chesbro's topic is belief here, and how religious faith can be used to justify anything even, in the case of this book, murder, genocide, and suicide. There is quite a bit of symbolism here, with the biosphere the Fredricksons find, code named Eden, turning out to be a cesspool of rotting vegetation. Unfortunately, Chesbro seems to take too much time in getting to his point; the first half of the book is too slow, making the climax seem rushed.

But this book ultimately pays off. **Second Horseman** re-engineers some of the elements of Chesbro's older books and in many cases improves on them. Eden is in many cases Valhalla redux, but there is a power to its decay, as if it reflects the misguided beliefs of its inhabitants. And the main thug, a former football star with a homicidal bent named Tanker Thompson, is a truly terrifying creation, popping up like a slasher movie monster at regular intervals, yet still retaining elements of humanity (much like **Cold Smell**'s Marl Braxton).

Second Horseman Out of Eden may sometimes stray far too close to rewriting, especially when one of the villains is found tortured and killed in Central Park a la Daniel in **An Affair of Sorcerers**, but it's still a good kick-off to the next phase of the series.

Having beaten religious faith into the ground with **Second Horseman**, Chesbro decides to go after political thought in **The Language of Cannibals** a year later. The book takes place in an upstate 'artist's colony' named Cairn, where Mongo's friend Michael Burana died in an apparent boating accident. Mongo comes up to Cairn to tell the police chief that Dan couldn't possibly have died accidentally. Encounters with some of Cairn's other residents, like the Rush Limbaugh-esque Elysius Culhane and his aide Jay Acton, folk singer Mary Tree, and especially the sadistic Gregory Trex, keep him in Cairn. He learns from Tree of a death squad operating in the town, but begins to suspect the cause of his friend's death was learning that a major right-wing figure was actually a KGB mole, sent to corrupt the conservative movement from the inside.

Just as **Second Horseman** seems to be a rewriting of **An Affair of Sorcerers** and **The Beasts of Valhalla**, **The Language of Cannibals** seems to be a reworking of **City of Whispering Stone** and **Two Songs This Archangel Sings**, with the focus turned way inward. However, Chesbro doesn't even bother disguising his opinions here—characters go on for literally pages about communism, the far right, and the corruption of symbolism, and these speeches that can be deadly. And because it's so weighed down with Chesbro's convictions, there are times when it is impossible to keep track of the plot threads (In fact, when one character shows up after disappearing for the bulk of the book to kill another character who's suddenly revealed to be a KGB assassin, it destroys what little sense of momentum the book has).

The Language of Cannibals reads like a short story idea infused with so much of Chesbro's rhetoric that it bloats out of control. Sadly, it's indicative of the way the books were going. Obviously, Chesbro was chafing at being obligated to turn out Mongo after Mongo—at this time he was trying to write another series based on Veil

Kendry, and an interesting stand-alone thriller featuring a homeless protagonist. Unfortunately, none of these other books caught the public's imagination as well as Mongo, and Chesbro ended up having to go back to the well three more times before he was done.

Thank God the first of these last three is one of the best in the series.

The Fear in Yesterday's Rings starts with Mongo visiting his old boss Phil Statler. Statler, who figured in **City of Whispering Stone** is a mess. Having lived on the streets for who knows how long, riddled with parasitic infections and missing digits on his hands and feet, Statler tells Mongo how his circus fell into ruin and was bought by something called 'The World Circus.' Deciding to buy back the circus with the support of other freak show performers and old flame Harper Rhys-Whitney, a herpetologist, Mongo goes off in search of the new owners. However, there are problems: a rash of vicious mutilations in a pattern matching that of the circus leads a cryptozoologist to believe Mongo is investigating the matter. And he's not the only one—the owner of the World Circus is actually a mastermind arms dealer, who, through 'reverse breeding,' has created a creature that could be mankind's only natural predator, and he is convinced that Mongo is after him.

Evidence that Chesbro's restlessness with Mongo was increasing could be found throughout the last two novels, and in **The Fear in Yesterday's Rings** it's on the surface. Many elements that were strong threads throughout previous books, like Mongo's relationship with Garth, are glossed over in favor of the plot, and a major subplot about his attraction to Harper is given such a perfunctory arc that one suspects Chesbro *thought* we'd expect it to develop this way (up to and including very passing references to April Marlowe, whose name hadn't been mentioned since **An Affair of Sorcerers**). There are points in reading this book where you might even wonder why Chesbro was continuing. My guess involves a television development deal for the character that was being bandied about at the time.

That being said, **The Fear in Yesterday's Rings** is the best book in the series since **The Beasts of Valhalla**. Chesbro hits upon the one aspect of Mongo's background that's never really been delved into—the circus—and runs with it. Mongo's ambivalence to and eventual acceptance of his past as a performer creates a strong through line for a plausible, but wild as get out, story. Maybe because it is territory that had been alluded to but never explored, it energizes Chesbro, and makes for a much more interesting story.

On top of that, the plot of **The Fear in Yesterday's Rings** is a definite return to the bizarre territory of the first couple of books. Utilizing as its base the idea of 'reverse breeding'—reviving extinct species by breeding existing ancestors for recessive traits—Chesbro tosses in a dollop of espionage to create an exciting little goose chase, run by the most vividly sketched villain of the series. Arlen Zelezian and his son Luthor are biological arms dealers, utilizing the circus as a cover for their operation. Both Zelezians are overly polite, genteel, and are experts in animal behavior. The father just happens to look like Abraham Lincoln.

Sure, things get goofy; a climax featuring Mongo, Garth, Harper and an African elephant trying to stave off Zelezian's weaponry in a grain silo just borders on ridiculous. But overall, there are enough thrills and scary set pieces to make **The Fear in Yesterday's Rings** a wonderful coda to the last trilogy.

That doesn't mean it was the last book (even though, yet again, Chesbro's final chapter shows Mongo making a commitment to Harper in what can be construed as a happy ending for the series). Mysterious Press asked Chesbro to go back to the well one more time for another set of books. This time, however, it would be composed of two novels and a collection of short stories. At this point, the bloom was certainly off the rose for Chesbro; unhappy writing about his diminutive protagonist, he proceeded to produce the worst book in the series.

Dark Chant in a Crimson Key begins on the eve of the capture of "the man universally considered to be the world's most wanted criminal, an individual who specialized in what might be described as terror-driven confidence scams and extortion." John 'Chant' Sinclair is caught in Switzerland after having stolen money from a charitable foundation, and the foundation's owner hires Mongo to go witness his capture. Seeing a free vacation for him and Harper, Mongo grudgingly goes. The second he sets down in Switzerland, however, he finds himself caught in a maelstrom of death and violence that forces Mongo to do the one thing he really didn't want to do: locate Chant Sinclair.

Dark Chant in a Crimson Key is a miserable book, mainly because it's not a Mongo book. The character of Chant Sinclair was actually the subject of three novels Chesbro wrote under the pen name of David Cross, and he is allowed to push our protagonist to the side. Literally half of this book is taken up by a frighteningly meticulous summary of the three Chant novels, as Mongo encounters various characters from those stories. And all Mongo does is go from character to character, getting the skinny on what Garth sneeringly refers to as `ninja bullshit stories.' Mongo literally becomes a cardboard cut-out of himself; even more so than in **The Fear in Yesterday's Rings** (which at least benefited from a wild, well-paced plot), the psychological underpinnings of Mongo are given lip service. You have to wonder when reading this mess of second-hand stories just who the hell this was supposed to interest—Mongo readers would certainly be left in the dark.

One interesting element, though, is how Chesbro deals with the obvious similarities between Chant and Veil Kendry. Maybe because he never expected the connection would be made between David Cross and George Chesbro, many elements in the two characters' backstories are identical. Chesbro sort of hems and haws his best to create a tenuous connection between the two (in fact, Veil not only becomes the device by which one of the novels is summarized, he also gets to discuss the MacGuffin of the book—a botched CIA operation called 'Cooked Goose'). It's fascinating, in an almost perverse way.

Dark Chant in a Crimson Key is simply a bald-faced 'contractual obligation' book, something Chesbro seemed to throw together half-assed to make his commitment. And it definitely heralded his disinterest in the character that had ridden on his back for so long.

But, fortunately, there was still one more dance with Mongo to come. In 1993, Chesbro finished his final book-length adventure of Robert Fredrickson to date, **An Incident at Bloodtide**.

It's approximately a year after **Dark Chant**. Mongo is staying with Garth, his wife Mary (from **The Language of Cannibals**), and their foster child Vicky (the little girl from **Second Horseman**), when they are visited by a bizarre character named Scara Silver. Silver claims that he has come back for Mary, and spouts a lot of ceremonial magic mumbo-jumbo. Of course, Silver—who actually drives Garth out of Mary's house—didn't count on meeting someone who really knows a thing or two about sorcery, and is sent packing. But when the local river keeper shows up in the Hudson hacked to death, and Mongo finds a connection between what the dead man was investigating and Silver, he plunges into a case of environmental abuse.

Thankfully, **An Incident at Bloodtide** is a great final novel. While reading it, I suspected Chesbro realized the series had become unmanageable, because so much of the detritus that made later entries so insanely implausible is gone (most importantly, Mr. Lippet and Mongo's ties to the President, both of which had become annoying *deux ex machina* machines in later books are only mentioned in passing). The story here is well-designed and mightily streamlined, which is so refreshing after the complex, Byzantine plots of **The Language of Cannibals** and **Dark Chant in a Crimson Key**. In fact, as with **The Fear in Yesterday's Rings**, Chesbro manages to take a plot that has far-reaching implications and, by tying it to the character of Sacra Silver, who has this unhealthy hold on Mary, makes it very personal.

An Incident at Bloodtide also works because Chesbro comes up with fascinating opposition to Mongo. In Sacra Silver, he creates a strange mix of sadism and child-like rage, a character that can easily stand beside the Loges of **The Beasts of Valhalla** and the Zelezians of **The Fear in Yesterday's Rings**. Silver is sinister, clever and vicious while also being surprisingly juvenile, a larger than life character that becomes more realistic the more his life closes in on him. And even though he disappears for a large chunk of the book, he does have a presence in what is arguably the most blackly comedic scenes in the series' history: a hypothermic Mongo sneaks aboard a tanker and not only gets a surprise confession, but is chased around the ship by the drunken, gun-wielding captain.

Unlike the other 'last books' in the series, Chesbro leaves the ending of **An Incident at Bloodtide** open. Which is why it's puzzling that this ends up being the last book in the series. With this last novel, one gets the impression Chesbro's interest in the series had been revitalized, and that his enthusiasm for the Fredrickson brothers was back. Why there has only been a single short story in *Ellery Queen's Mystery Magazine* since is a mystery in and of itself.

It's easy to see where the Mongo books strayed beyond a certain point, the stories just became too insanely large-scale to be plausible. But at their best, the adventures of Mongo slipped between so many genres—first mystery, then horror, then science fiction, then espionage—that they were unique unto themselves. And I guarantee you that this is as odd a series as you are ever going to read.

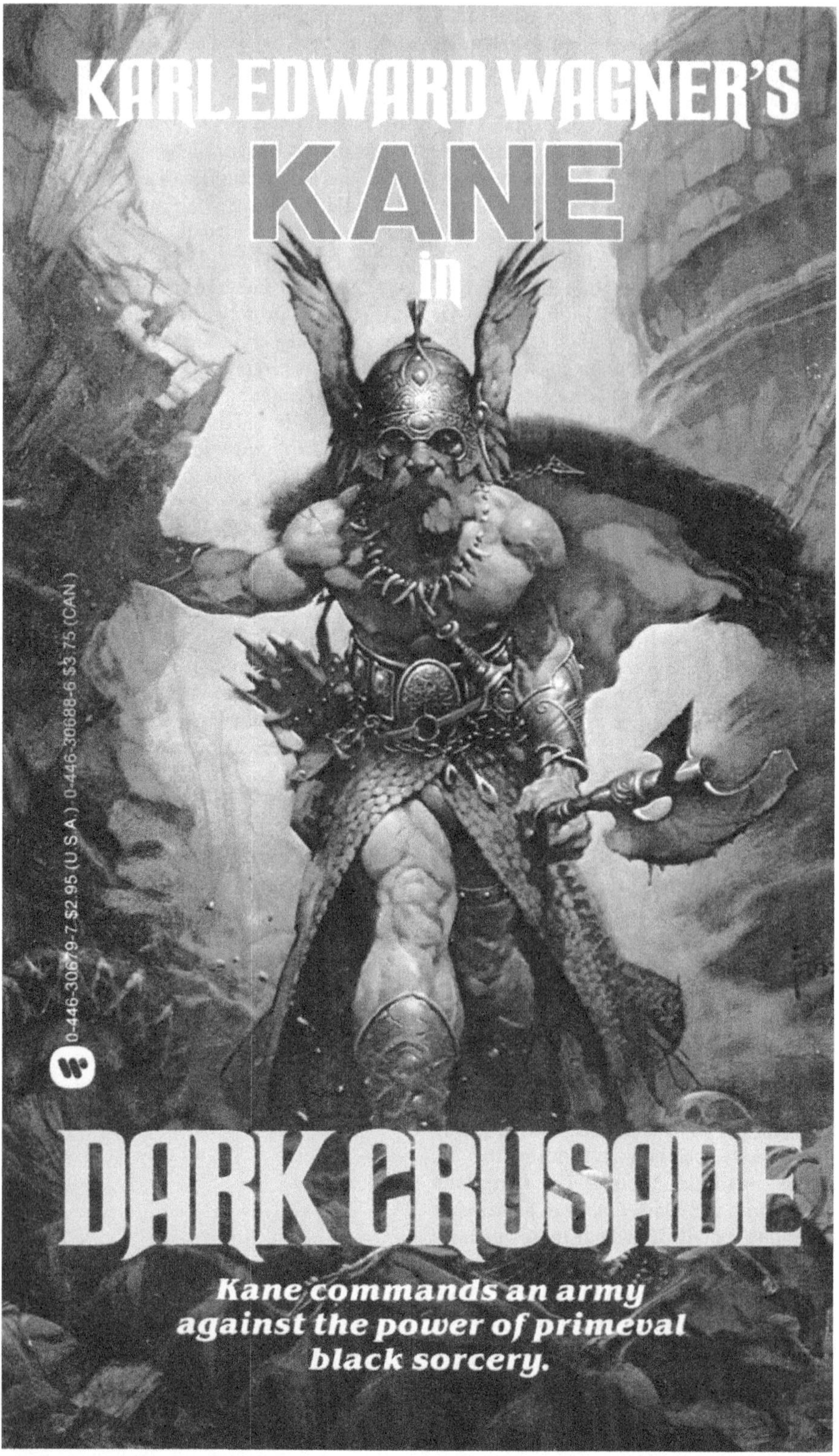

KARL EDWARD WAGNER'S
KANE
in
DARK CRUSADE
Kane commands an army against the power of primeval black sorcery.
0-446-30679-7 $2.95 (U.S.A.) 0-446-30688-6 $3.75 (CAN)

In the Scream Factory *days, the three of us were nothing if not completists. If I saw some cool looking series paperback at the flea market and picked up #5, I had to have the first four and however many other installments came afterwards. Admit it—you're the same, aren't you? Or else you probably wouldn't be reading this book. Anyway, I bought a copy of one of Karl Edward Wagner's Kane paperbacks, read a few of the stories, and was immediately taken by the character and the sophisticated plots. From there, it was only a hop, skip, and a jump to Derek Hill. Howard's Conan is obviously the most popular barbarian of all-time (thanks mostly to Lancer and Marvel) but sophisticated writing isn't usually a term associated with the ol' Cimmerian. Kane is a thinking man's savage.* -Peter

STARING INTO THE WOLF'S LAIR ABYSS:
A Look at Karl Edward Wagner's Kane, the Mystic Swordsman
by Derek Hill

The late Karl Edward Wagner should need no introduction; in a better world he'd be a household name.

He is probably best remembered for his great horror fiction ("Sticks," "In the Pines," "More Sinned Against," "The River of Night's Dreaming"), and his 15 years spent as editor of DAW's **The Years Best Horror** anthologies (VIII-XXII), in which he brought to the attention of horror aficionados plenty of young, ambitious, and energetic talents who would have otherwise been hard to find amidst the sea of small press magazines, anthologies, and journals. Wagner, along with David Drake and Jim Groce, was also responsible for founding Carcosa, which published such fine eldritch tomes as Hugh B. Cave's **Murgunstrumm and Others** (winner of the 1978 World Fantasy Award for Best Collection), and Manly Wade Wellman's **Worse Things Waiting**, possibly the coolest horror title of all time. Both handsome books were also chock full of wonderful black and white illustrations by legendary *Weird Tales* artist Lee Brown Coye.

Most of Wagner's horror stories (which more than deserve their own critical analysis) are set in the modern world. And though they may be steeped in the cosmic dread and otherworldly traditions of the *Weird Tales* masters, his short horror fiction never loses sight of the very real contemporary madness crashing down at all times; the characters in his horror stories are transfixed by their loneliness, alienation, and anger at having to watch the world plunge into nothingness all around them.

His sword and sorcery fiction is the same deal. Featuring the immortal satanic hero Kane the Mystic Swordsman, these stories are set in a world where the primal urge for survival is not masked by modern-day concessions toward civility and altruism. They are tough. Mean. Vicious. Unforgiving. Brilliant.

Kane is part of a long line of legendary creations, many of them brought to life through Robert E. Howard's savage pen (Conan, Bran Mac Morn, Kull). And then there are, of course, the stories and novels by Michael Moorcock (Elric), Fritz Leiber (Fafhrd and Gray Mouser), Jack Vance (**The Dying Earth**, **The Eyes of the Overworld**), C.L. Moore (**Jirel of Joiry**), and the countless others who have tried to keep the heroic fantasy flame burning bright. Not an easy task considering how moribund and restrictive the genre can be.

But Kane has more in common with the Gothic tale and the horror genre than he does with the above esteemed creations. The world that Kane struggles through is one mean, dirty, ugly place. Creatures from the outer reaches of the universe press ever closer into our world; elder races rise from the ocean depths; giants war with humans; a lamia lures men to early graves; a nation of savage men, women, and children plunder across the land murdering all who resist the New World Order; a little girl joyfully plays with her mother's severed head.

Horror. The world of beasts and men. Kane's world. He knows it well.

Now, Wagner had a great affinity for Howard's heroes, and he eventually penned his own robust takes on Conan (**The Road of Kings**) and Bran Mac Morn (**Legion from the Shadows** and **Queen of the Night**, which is still unpublished). Wagner reedited the definitive collection of Conan tales back in 1977 for Berkley as well. He also worked on the screenplay of what would have been the third installment in the Conan saga. Robert E. Howard's Conan is probably the closest to Wagner's Kane in lineage. But that's where the family resemblances end.

The juvenile romanticism of the Conan tales seem a far cry from what Wagner wrought. Kane is not chivalrous, valiant, or trying to make things 'right.' Nor is he a lovable lug fancying himself as some free spirit. Kane is a prisoner of Time, which sets him closer to the likes of Melmoth the Wanderer, or the vampire (though without the whiny pretensions), than to his sword and sorcery pedigree. Kane knows the game's been fixed from the start. If anything, he's trying to speed things up towards the final boom. The guy is seething with hate. If he helps someone out, it's more than likely he's got an ulterior motive. A friend of mankind, he is not.

But Kane does have his own code of honor, ethics, and morality. It's just not always apparent. And despite our initial trepidation, we can't help but read on. Throughout these novels and stories we are exhilarated by his actions and exploits; we can't help but admire, and perhaps even envy, his hunger for autonomy within the cosmos. The game may be fixed, but Kane refuses to be a slave to anyone or anything. And Kane will do whatever it takes to survive and maintain his sense of freedom. Murder means nothing to him. It's just another experience, just another notch.

Kane is brooding, self-destructive, indulgent, and more than a bit mad. But he's also cultured and extremely well read, with a real thirst for knowledge. This alone would separate Kane from the rest of the heroic fantasy horde. And Kane knows that to be the most efficient killer, leader, warrior, he must strive for excellence in all areas of life. A warrior-poet if there ever was one.

This article is in no way meant to be a comprehensive examination of the Kane saga. There's just not enough space. It's just a beginning. Just a taste. Something that will hopefully spur you on to your local used bookstore or specialty shop so you can take the journey yourself.

Though they're not as easy to find as they once were, the Kane novels and short story collections are still out there (emblazoned with those fabulous Frank Frazetta covers), waiting to be rediscovered.

So on that note, let us take a swim into the killing tide.

Darkness Weaves

This review is based upon the Warner Books edition from 1978, and not the earlier abridgment known as **Darkness Weaves With Many Shades** published by Powell Publications in 1970, which Wagner disavowed. **Darkness Weaves** was subsequently the first Kane novel published, though chronologically it is the last of the novels.

Darkness Weaves, which sets the tone for all subsequent tales in the series, is a big, brooding, bloody, bad ass of a book. Incorporating everything from a vengeful witch to swashbuckling seafaring adventure to court intrigue to unearthly horror on an epic scale, **Darkness Weaves** exudes a power and an open-eyed willingness to steamroll into macabre territory few fantasy novels would dare. So beware ye lovers of valiant incorruptible heroes and downey virginal maidens with hearts o' gold, Kane is not a character to be relegated to the safety-zone of fantasy escapism.

Darkness Weaves wastes no time getting started. Kane, who has been hiding out in a crypt among the treacherous mountains outside of the seaport Nostoblet, is found by a mysterious man by the name of Imel, who offers Kane a chance to obtain great wealth and power. All Kane has to do is journey with Imel back to the kingdom of Pellin, the northernmost island of the mighty Thovnosian Empire, and meet with Efrel the strange, disfigured, and vengeful Queen to the House of Pellin. Imel weaves for Kane a sad and horrible story of how the once beautiful Efrel fell from grace not long after she married the present emperor to the Thovnosian Empire, Netisten Maril. He chose Efrel as his new bride in a hope that she would bear him a son. Netisten already had a daughter, M'Cori, from his first marriage. But he desperately needed an heir to the throne.

Unfortunately, things failed to materialize quite as planned. Like Netisten's first wife, Efrel couldn't bear children, which in turn put a great strain on their marriage. And upon Efrel's ambition to rule the Thovnosian Empire herself. Efrel, who was educated in the ways of the black arts, harbored a fiery ambition to reclaim glory to the House of Pellin. But as her marriage slowly turned to dust, she found her ambition harder and harder to realize through normal channels. So she confided and plotted with Leyan, Netisten's bastard brother, to take the crown by force (Leyan as king, she as queen). This too failed to come to fruition. Netisten uncovered their betrayal and killed his half-brother when Leyan was caught by surprise in Efrel's bed. But the worse punishment was waiting for poor, poor Efrel. After being forced to watch the slow execution of the six lords who'd sworn allegiance to Leyan, as well as their entire households—men, women, and children—Efrel was then strapped to the bottom of a mighty oxen. She was dragged through the streets until dead. Or so everyone believed.

Kane accepts Efrel's invitation to lead her navy against that of the Thovnossian Empire, and to help her wreak vengeance upon Netisten Maril.

But things are never that simple for Kane. Ever. So by the time the 288 page novel is over, all hell has broken loose more than a few times. Doomed lovers; cyclopean biomechanical monsters from the deep; strange cults; and much much more, all crammed into a novel which has enough plots within plots within plots for a couple of books. It's amazing that Wagner never loses focus nor steam.

Wagner's tale is a perfect melange of terror, the gothic tale, and high fantasy, all set to the brisk beat of a suspense novel. Wagner has no patience for dry philosophical tangents or endless paragraphs of masturbatory world building. The writing is muscular and clean, for the most part, though it occasionally falls into that serpentine indulgent purple prison of word error that so many pulp-era *Weird Tales* stories also fell victim to. But it comes with the territory. And it's a credit to Wagner's genuine story-telling expertise that he rises above those minor infractions and kicks the series off to an energetic start.

Death Angel's Shadow

The next book in the Kane series was originally published by Warner Paperback Library in 1973, with austere cover art by John F. Mayer. Warner Books then reprinted it in 1978, using Frazetta's more appropriate artwork. **Death Angel's Shadow** is a collection of three novellas, any of which is a perfect introduction to the Kane saga.

"Reflections for the Winter of My Soul"

One of the best of the Kane tales. The story, which takes place after the strange and other-worldly events in the novel **The Dark Crusade**, finds Kane lost and fatigued from days of being chased through the woods in subzero temperatures by soldiers. Kane gets away, and discovers a dark and foreboding castle amidst the forest. Soon, it is apparent to Kane that he has stumbled into a far more dangerous plot than him being chased by vengeful soldiers.

A werewolf is thought to be loose in the area, and with Kane's mysterious arrival,

From the werewolf's lair...
to the vampire's nest...
Kane wields his
bloody sword

KARL
EDWARD
WAGNER

WARNER BOOKS 90-001 $1.95

he is fingered by the court astrologer/ physician as the most likely suspect. Throw in a deranged prince (who eats raw meat and is kept locked in his room most of the time), an albino minstrel who sings of the legend of the killer Kane, and what you end up with is a classic whodunit in the **Ten Little Indians** vein, which culminates in a satisfying finale, surprising yet inevitable. Great.

"Cold Light"

A crazed megalomanical moral crusader (sort of a cross between Matthew Hopkins AKA the Witch-finder General and Kenneth Starr), with the help of his band of mercenaries, butchers a tribe of pirating ogres called the Red Three and all the humans who were forced to serve under the hideous beasts. The crusader, named Gaethaa, then sets his hate-filled eyes on Kane.

Kane, who is severely depressed and despondent (a frequent ailment for him), is holed up in the almost ghost land known as Demornte — Dead Demornte. The area, which at one time had been an oasis of people and trade, is now virtually devoid

of all life, and is appropriately sandwiched between two huge deserts. Plague has laid waste to the population. Now only a few hundred people roam the capitol Sebbei's streets, including Kane. But Gaethaa the Avenger and his men also end up there, bent on instructing Kane (and anyone who stands in their way) in the lessons of the cold light.

The story is a western, plain and simple. And a damn good one at that. Tight, action-packed, and fascinating since it puts Kane on the defensive; the hunted instead of the hunter. We also get a chance to see Kane interact with a strong female (who is not half-human, or a warrior). One of the best stories in the bunch.

"Mirage"

Kane, who aided Prince Talyvion in a failed coup-d'etat against Talyvion's brother King Jasseartion, is now fleeing with his life (and a small motley band of mercenaries) through the mountains. But Kane and his men are ambushed, and Kane is seriously injured and knocked out. When he awakes, Kane scrambles into the woods, just avoiding detection by a hungry mob of ghouls who have come to feast upon Kane and his men. He then discovers some gigantic caves and the fabulous ruins of an ancient city. Then more ghouls, though this time the creatures are accompanied by a beautiful girl who has the power to command the ghouls to do what she wills. And before the reader can shout, Don't trust her, Kane! Kane and the girl are doing the nasty, and more.

The story is Wagner's take on the vampire tale. Interesting since we get to see Kane weak, feeble, and subservient to the wiles of an enchantress. Not a pretty sight. Mirage is a melancholic tale which, though not a great addition to the series, nevertheless captures superbly the pain and loneliness which forever haunts Kane.

Bloodstone

The next book in the series was the novel **Bloodstone**, published by Warner Books in 1975. Baen Books later reprinted it in 1991, retaining the Frazetta art.

The novel, which takes place

a little over a thousand years before the events of **The Dark Crusade**, primarily focuses on Kane's discovery of a strange ring of bloodstone and the immense power it bestows upon the one strong enough to harness it. **Bloodstone** is the best of the Kane novels. From its opening prologue, in which a hunter portentously kills a doe with fawn, then happens upon the strange ring, to the novel's breathtaking fantastical conclusion, **Bloodstone** more than delivers the horror show goods.

As in **Darkness Weaves**, there is enough plot in **Bloodstone** for a number of fantasy novels. Kane (as in many of the stories) hires himself out to a warring kingdom, this time to the services of Lord Dribeck, ruler of Selonari. Dribeck is gearing up for an invasion from Lord Malchion of the neighboring kingdom of Breimen. Dribeck's power is weak, his hold on his kingdom unstable, Kane wisely surmises. Not exactly the ingredients needed to stave off an invasion. But Kane enjoys a good fight, especially when the odds are against him. Kane tells Dribeck of the bloodstone, and of the great power which resides somewhere among the ruins of Arellarti, a pre-human city once built by an elder race of beings known as the Krelran. Kane promises Dribeck that, if given the chance and the proper group of soldiers, he would be able to obtain whatever power awaited in Arellarti and hand it over to Dribeck. But, of course, there are some drawbacks. Namely, that Arellarti is located in the center of a large expanse of swampland called Kranor-Rill, and that the city is guarded by monstrous man-like amphibian creatures who worship the power residing there like a god.

Bloodstone contains so many plots, so many beautifully executed set-pieces (the battle sequences alone could make this novel a classic), that it is difficult to hit the highlights. The whole novel is a highlight! Majestic, thrilling, and ultimately sorrowful, as Kane encounters a power bigger and badder than even him.

One of the most interesting characters in the novel, and in the series as a whole, is Lord Malchion's heir, his daughter Teres. Since all of Malchion's sons have died in numerous fashions, there is only Teres to

KANE UNEARTHS A DREADFUL RELIC OF AN ANCIENT CIVILIZATION THAT WILL GIVE HIM DOMINION OVER THE WORLD

lay claim to his crown. Which only seems right since Teres can out-fight, ride, drink, and curse, any man around her. And she's attractive to boot, which makes her even more desirable to Kane once he sets his predatory eyes upon her. Their relationship thickens as the plot does. Kane has tasted and experienced plenty of women in his time, but Teres promises to be one of the most memorable, and not just for the obvious reasons.

And though **Bloodstone** is probably the most fantastical of the Kane novels, it is also the grimmest. As Kane plays the two kingdoms off of one another (like Yojimbo or The Man with No Name), he shows no compunction or remorse about watching them destroy each other, all the while trying to keep his own bloody hands from being cut off.

Magic, blood, war, sacrifice. These are the primal elements which feed the power of the bloodstone. And the elements which make it difficult for the reader to put the book down. A classic.

Dark Crusade

Dark Crusade was published in 1976 by Warner Books, though the final chapter 'In the Lair of Yslsl' had originally seen daylight as a short story published in *Midnight Sun 1* in 1974.

If **Bloodstone** is the best novel in the series, **Dark Crusade** comes in a close second. With its self-assured prose (the finest and cleanest of the novels) and its locomotive pacing, Wagner wastes no time throwing the reader headfirst into the novel's deceptively simple storyline.

When we rejoin our intrepid anti-hero, Kane is currently a general in the Sandotnery calvery. The kingdom of Sandotnery, ruled by an aging and heirless King Owrinos, is on the verge of a civil war between the Reds (the status quo) and the Blues (the rebel faction) who are led by the menacing Jarvo, a distant relative to the king. Jarvo and Kane are at odds for a number of reasons, though the one that gets things rolling is over which one of them is strong enough, mean enough, to take control of the nation.

Now, while all this is going on, something far more malevolent is brewing: The Dark Crusade, a cult of thousands led by an insane Prophet (who had been a bandit) named Orted Ak-Ceddi. Orted, who was lured into the dark sanctuary of the Lair of Yslsl by a Sataki priest, and who is now a vessel for the otherworldly power nestled in the lair, unleashes a jihad across the land the likes of which the world has never known. The Crusade is comprised of men, women, children; young, old, smart, stupid; anyone may join. All you need is a taste for blood, a hunger for death, an appetite for chaos. Orted, and the masses who give strength to the Crusade, roll like a mighty killing machine across the land, converting to its cause anyone foolish or stupid enough to be caught in its wake. They are seemingly unstoppable.

Until the Crusade meets up with Jarvo and the Sandotnery army. Jarvo cuts the Crusade down, in one of the novel's best chapters, exposing that Orted's fanatics are not as powerful as they believed themselves to be.

Then arrives Kane (complicating matters as usual), who would like nothing more than to take Jarvo down for good. So Kane offers his military expertise and services to the Prophet. Kane will give order to the Crusade's chaos; help shape the mob into a disciplined army. Then the world will know the deathcrush of the Dark Crusade. Then the world will know true horror.

The battle sequences between the Crusade (also referred to as the Sword of Sataki) and Jarvo's Sandotneri army is the finest war sequence Wagner ever wrote for this series. The prose is precise; just the right details magnified and given life.

Kane has seldom been as supremely satanic as he is in this novel. His thirst for revenge against Jarvo is convincing and scary. But Jarvo's strength and hunger for vengeance is just as compelling, if not more so. And as these two characters (after plenty of plot twists and near-deaths) converge within the Lair of Yslsl, where things that should not be dwell in forever darkness, Wagner pulls out all the stops, delivering the wildest most crazed ending in the series. Wagner takes a lot of chances with the **Dark Crusade** (especially the ending), and it pays off. The novel is his most focused and most challenging. It perhaps lacks the inspired lunacy of **Bloodstone**, but Wagner has crafted a superb novel of fantasy and vengeance, nevertheless.

Night Winds

Published by Warner Books in 1978, **Night Winds** is an outstanding and haunting collection of six stories, all of which had been previously published in various magazines or collections (*Whispers, Fantastic, Midnight Sun, Chacal*). Perhaps the best of the Kane short story collections.

"Undertow"

An undead woman, sweet mad Dyssylen, attempts to flee from the stranglehold of power which her lover holds over her. `How many times, Dyssylen? How many times will you play that game?' A strange tale of tainted love, and one that can only involve the mystic swordsman, Kane.

"Two Suns Setting"

After almost a century of residing in the great city of Carsultyal, wielding the power and prestige as that city's greatest sorcerer, Kane abandons his post to roam the desolate and dangerous regions to the south. And it is there that he encounters the giant, Dwassllir, who offers Kane the chance to join him in the search for King Brotemllain's legendary burial ground and the treasures that await within it. Suspenseful, brutal, and ultimately melancholic, "Two Suns Setting" (as in the best of the Kane stories) reminds us of a past which can never be, because it never existed in the first place.

"Dark Muse"

Kane and a mad, sensation-hungry poet named Opyros, grapple and do battle with the tumultuous Gods of Poetry.

Opyros, who holds more notoriety than respect within the literary circles (due to his macabre subject matter), is finding it harder and harder to complete his newest masterpiece, "Night Winds." Kane, whose passion for art and culture is just as strong as his passion for violence, helps the young poet out by conjuring up the darkest, deadliest muse of all, the Dark Muse. Tread softly all ye poets of the darkside. Disappointment and death await!

"Raven's Eyrie"

Kane (along with two of his bandit colleagues), seriously wounded from a skirmish with men from the Combine's calvary, finds refuge in a mountaintop inn called Raven's Eyrie. But Pleddis (leader of the calvary) and his men are in hot pursuit, and soon Raven's Eyrie becomes anything but a sanctuary. And if that isn't enough to screw up Kane's day, he must also confront the ghosts of his past, present, and future; one of which concerns an illegitimate daughter he may have. Oh, and then there's the little problem of the horrible Demonlord who aims to take Kane down to Hell. Just another day for ol' Kane. Excellent stuff indeed.

"Lynortis Reprise"

The once majestic fortress city of Lynortis, is now in ruins. The once bountiful land surrounding it, now littered with the bones and bloody memories of a war which should never have been. For two interminable years Lynortis was under siege by the army from Wesvetin, led by the power hungry Masale.

Kane comes across a young woman being hunted down by a mob of bandits. He helps her evade the bandits, then escorts her back to her home, Lynortis. But when Kane and the girl, named Sesi, arrive back to the dilapidated fortress, they receive anything but a warm welcome. The place has been overtaken by a gang of Masale's mercenaries, who have come to obtain the whereabouts of some vast hidden treasures which supposedly Sesi's mother (the daughter of Lynortis' last ruler) had confided to the girl before her death. Soon, Masale and his troops return to Lynortis, bent on plundering and destroying it all over again—this time for good.

A sad, bitter story. The best of this impressive collection.

"Sing a Last Song of Valdese"

A priest, traveling alone along a dark country pass, encounters a strangely exotic young woman who steps out from the deep dark woods. She propositions the priest. He declines. You see, he's on his way to Carrasahl for business. And besides, the girl might rob him. The priest may very well enjoy losing his seed, but God forbid losing his gold. The woman lunges at him, and steals his horse. The priest follows her on foot. He comes to an inn and pleads with the owner to allow him to stay the night. The owner begrudgingly lets him in. But there's no sight of the woman.

Once inside, the priest is quickly engaged in a round of friendly talk and drink. Tales abound about the strange folk tales from the region, and about the mysterious swordsman named Kane, who's legacy of brutality within the region knows no bounds. Talk also centers upon Valdese, the lamia who haunts the dark forests and the men who dwell there, leading them to their deaths.

A splendid fable of revenge.

Book of Kane

A Kane short story collection published by Donald M. Grant in 1985. Available as either a limited edition or a trade edition. Both versions include Jeff Jones' wonderful chiaroscuro-like artwork. All five stories previously published.

"Reflections For the Winter of My Soul" See **Death Angel's Shadow**.

"Misericorde"

Another fine tale of revenge. Tamaslei, a beautiful woman who hungers to reinstate her family to the power and prestige it once held, hires Kane to retrieve the ducal crown of Harnsterm from a rival clan. Easy enough. But there's a catch, of course. Proud, vengeful Tamaslei also wants the blood of the four leaders of the clan. It seems that the four men murdered Tamaslei's lover, as well as stole the ducal crown. Kane must now set things right and collect on old debts.

"The Other One"

A story within a story within a story. Kane rises to prominence as general to a floundering kingdom's army. He gains the king's confidence, rises higher in the court (a typical Kane machination), then causes great turmoil when he uncovers a plot to kill the king. He beds the king's youngest wife (also a typical Kane move), and plays everyone off of one another, thus ensuring his own power. The king dies, and everything should now fall into Kane's hands, right? Wrong.

A chilling, though nevertheless, blackly comedic fable.

"Sing A Last Song of Valdese" See **Night Wind**.

"Raven's Eyrie" See **Night Wind**.

Miscellanea

The following is a list of Kane stories which saw publication elsewhere.

"In the Wake of the Night: An Excerpt"

Originally published in *A Fantasy Reader: The Seventh World Fantasy Convention Book* in 1981, and then in the posthumously published collection **Exorcisms and Ecstasies** in 1997, it was intended to be an actual Kane novel. All that was actually completed of the novel was this prologue.

A colossal ship forged of black metal, the Yholsal-Monyr (mentioned in **Bloodstone**), beached upon the shore for over a thousand years, awaits the day of its resurrection. Kethrid, a man who dreamed of the ancient vessel, aims to be the one to sail the ship into glory.

"The Treasure of Lynortis"

Written in 1961 when Wagner was sixteen years old. It is the first Kane story he ever wrote. It first saw publication in *Kadath* 6/7 in 1984, and then in **Exorcisms and Ecstasies**. "The Treasure of Lynortis" is an earlier version of the far superior "Lynortis Reprise."

As in the latter story, Kane happens upon Sesi, who is being hunted by a group of bandits; another group of bandits, led by an old acquaintance of Kane's, enters the picture in search of the lost treasure of Lynortis; and Masale, the man who first laid siege upon Lynortis, returns to claim the fabled riches supposedly hidden underneath the city.

But many characters and plot points are drastically different from the latter story: Sesi is the daughter of Masale (he took her mother as booty after destroying the city); the bandits in search of the treasure are not working for Masale; and most importantly, Kane's character is quite different than his later incarnation. In this story, Kane is softer of heart and more sentimental, though not that much more sentimental. He's still a lone wolf. It's just that compared to Wagner's conception of him in the later stories, he is not nearly as menacing and threatening here.

The story is really for completists only. Interesting to see how it metamorphosed into the masterful story it later became. It's poorly written and clumsy in spots, and contains some of the unintentionally funniest dialogue Wagner ever wrote. But that's a bit of a cheap shot since, as Wagner points out in his afterword to the story, "Reader, be gentle, and remember that this was written in 1961 by a very earnest teenager. We all must begin somewhere and at sometime…"

"Lacunae"

Originally published in the Dennis Etchison edited anthology **Cutting Edge** in 1986, and then in Wagner's own short story collection **Why Not You and I?** in 1987.

"Lacunae" is a hard hitting tale of an artist pushing herself to finish a series of paintings — long overdue — before her next big show. And if that isn't stressful enough, she's also got some serious gender issues to come to terms with. And then, of course, there's Kane and his new sidekick Blacklight to contend with.

Set in the present, Kane is now a designer drug manufacturer. Blacklight, a zonked-out Vietnam vet with a taste for the kinky, works as his courier. What at first seems strange and disconcerting following the earlier Kane stories, eventually falls into place and kicks the last batch of Kane stories into high gear.

"At First Just Ghostly"

Originally published in *Weird Tales* No. 294 in 1989, then later in **Exorcisms and Ecstasies**.

Best selling horror novelist Cody Lennox—born to lose and as of late, more adept at downing shots of whiskey than success with the written word—travels to London for the World Science Fiction Convention during the Harmonic Convergence. Still deeply disturbed from the loss of his wife, Cody numbs himself with booze, booze, and more booze. Kane, who has recently acquired a British publishing house, requests to meet with Cody so that they can talk business, which concerns Cody's reclaiming his life.

A wild story to say the least. "At First Just Ghostly" is the best of the later Kane stories. Self-referential (Kent Allard, a character who has appeared in several Wagner stories shows up, as well as Klesst, Kane's daughter from "Raven's Eyrie"), though not in an indulgent manner, and with many other winks and nods to pop culture movies and television programs

(Fu Manchu, *Citizen Kane*, *Harvey*, and *The Avengers*, among others), "At First Just Ghostly" works wonderfully. Especially the Mexican stand-off at the end involving the forces of evil, and more forces of evil. London burning was never so much fun. Touché.

"Deep in the Depths of the Acme Warehouse"

Originally published in **The King is Dead** anthology in 1994, later in **Exorcisms and Ecstasies**. Chronologically the last Kane story.

Kane, Blacklight, two women named Lucy and Mina, and Elvis' cock. What else do you want to know?

"The Gothic Touch"

Originally published in **Tales of the White Wolf** in 1994, an anthology in tribute to Michael Moorcock's Elric character. It later saw publication in **Exorcisms and Ecstasies**.

In what is chronologically the first of the modern Kane stories, the legendary albino Prince Elric (with his trusty sword Stormbringer) and his compatriot Moonglum happen upon the ruins of a desolate castle. They run into the equally legendary Kane, who has just dispatched the duke and his soldiers who had been hounding Elric. It seems that Kane has conjured Elric and Moonglum to the castle by magic, in order that Kane could use Elric's runesword against a treasure-guarding radiation-emitting demon. Ghouls, mutants, secret passageways, time slips, parallel universes, and an ending that is literally out of this world. What more could someone want?

Interesting to see Kane and the albino prince hurl verbal barbs like so many daggers, compare sword size, and otherwise try to one-up each other. Excellent fun.

References:

Clute, John and Peter Nichols. **The Encyclopedia of Science Fiction**. New York: St. Martin's, 1995.

"Obituaries." Locus November 1994: 70-72.

LE TOMBE DEI RESUSCITATI CIECHI

CON **JOHN BURNER** · **HELEN HARP**
BRIGITTE FLEMING · **GRAY THELMAN**

REGIA: **JOSEPH HARVEST**   EASTMANCOLOR

I love the Blind Dead films. Blinded Templar Knights, returning as bearded skeletons terrorizing people? It doesn't get much cooler than that (until you see the crazy **Revenge From Planet Ape** *intro added when a distributor tried to take advantage of the 70s* **Planet of the Apes**-*mania). While Derek had written articles for us on several book series (including those represented in this volume), this piece gave him a chance to write about a cool series of horror films. Even reading his comments on the worst of them has me itching to revisit them all. And that has always been an unstated goal of ours with bare•bones—to get you to add things to your must-read/must-watch lists.* -John

THE BLIND DEAD RIDE!
The Blind Dead Films of Amando de Ossorio
by Derek Hill

In the early 1970s, European cinema—especially from Italy and Spain—was churning out some of the finest, grossest, silliest, and most terrifying horror films in ages. It was a heady time indeed for horror film lovers, a time that valued the stripping away of Old World morality and censorship while welcoming in the New with a firm and bloody embrace. It was a perfect time to bury old ghosts.

It was a time for the Blind Dead to ride again. And ride they did.

This period of openness regarding sex and violence in films did not leave Spain untainted. If anything, the screams of *show me more! more! more!* were heard loudest from her. The years Spain spent under the oppressive iron fist of Franco were coming to an end, and there was a fevered interest by the filmgoing public for provocative and risqué subject matter. Filmgoers wanted sex; they wanted violence. And if they could get the two together, even better.

Horror films splashed across Spanish screens like never before. Paul Naschy, Jess Franco, and Amando de Ossorio were all committing their fair share of the mayhem, too, with their tales of blood, madness, and gothic depravity. Unfortunately, though, all good things must come to an end, or as in the case of horror films, become victim to the censors, or even worse, a bored and jaded public.

But during their time, the Blind Dead films added quite a punch to that nasty and totally cool subgenre known as the zombie film. Though not as viscerally repellent or grandiose as their Italian brothers, the Blind Dead films were nevertheless uniquely gothic and hallucinatory. The Old and New Worlds collided within the films, reconfiguring the shape of the European horror tradition forever.

The Blind Dead mythos, throughout all four films, is also ripe with a strong Freudian, reactionary sexual subtext, as are most horror films. The Blind Dead represented a twisted Old World morality. But they also perfectly realized the public's utter horror and revulsion toward the new age of freedom chiming in.

Amando de Ossorio, one of Spain's most prolific directors during this time, created all four of the Blind Dead films and with them, will forever be remembered for his unique contribution to the horror genre. And it's a credit to him that, despite sometimes laughably bad scripts and acting, he managed to keep things lively, interesting, and frequently awe-inspiring. When the Blind Dead ride, it is impossible for you not to feel the creepy-crawl taking over.

Tombs of the Blind Dead aka *La Noche del Terror Ciego/Crypt of the Blind Dead* (1971).

The film begins in the 13th century with a group of Templar Knights riding with a young peasant girl in tow, back to their decrepit castle. The knights drag the terrified girl to a large procession hall and strap her to cross, which has been placed in the middle of the spacious room. The Templars, who are positioned around the perimeter of the room, watch on as two of their brethren on horses gallop past the girl and slice at her with their long, steely swords. The screams of the girl visibly excite the other Templars. Great open wounds cover her now bare chest, and blood flows, pours, splashes, upon the dirty ground. One of the knights, possibly the leader, signals for the horsemen to refrain from their torture—not because he feels any remorse for the girl, but because the other knights deserve a taste of her blood, too. At this point, the other knights lunge at the dazed and confused girl. Like rats they feed upon her flesh, sucking the blood from the gaping wounds that adorn her breasts.

This prologue has been routinely cut from most prints of the film, though Elite's recent digitally remastered collector's edition of the film on laserdisc and videotape has restored the scene. Strangely enough, though, it's been stuck about halfway into the film.

From the 13th century, we fast-forward to the present day (circa 1970). Two old girlfriends, Betty and Virginia, run into one another at a busy, overcrowded public pool. Briefly, they reminisce about their school days when they used to share a room together. Betty, the older and more worldly of the two, has come to Lisbon to set up a dress making shop (which is, we are told throughout the film in capitol letters, located right NEXT TO THE MORGUE!). Shy and demure Virginia is about to take a trip with her simian-looking boyfriend Roger, who is every inch your typical early-70s Euro-stud. Roger takes a liking to Betty, and insists that she accompany Virginia and him. Betty refuses at first, but at the last moment agrees to join them.

The next day the three of them hop on a train and head out into the country. But things get hairy when the square-jawed Roger won't cease hitting on Betty. Virginia is not amused. Obviously upset at having to watch her boorish boyfriend man-handle her old school friend, Virginia goes to the caboose to get some fresh air. Betty immediately runs to her aid. The two women talk and look at each other with a secret longing, remembering the nights they used to spend with one another.

True to the times, and to the public's fascination with the *unnatural*, de Ossorio flashbacks to a silly lesbian scene involving Betty and Virginia—bellowing fog included.

Them were the days. Unfortunately for Virginia, though, not good enough. Tired of watching Roger paw at Betty, Virginia bails out and jumps off the train. Betty and Roger yell after her, but she ignores them and instead heads for an old village perched atop a hill not too far away. Betty and Roger urge the young conductor (who will return during the finale of the film) to stop the train. Of course, the conductor is unable to. Don't Roger and Virginia realize that the old village on the hill is haunted?!

Virginia, much to her disappointment, discovers that the village is deserted. But she's resourceful and makes the best of the situation. She finds a suitable place to bed down; she lights a fire; smokes, strips down to panties and bra, listens to some bad jazz, and reads before finally succumbing to sleep.

It doesn't take long for the Blind Dead to rise. Gravestones shift and smolder as the living dead Templars crawl out of their tombs, and de Ossorio's camera lingers upon every excruciating creak and shudder the Blind Dead make. And the use of slow-motion works beautifully. Dirty, maggoty, and exuding a centuries old putrefaction that only Europe can attain, the Blind Dead are a veritable gothic nightmare come to life. Upon their ghostly stallions they glide through the cavernous ruins of the cathedral, bent on tasting the hot blood of the living once again.

These scenes are without a doubt some of the creepiest, coolest, and most atmospheric zombies-rising-from-the-grave sequences ever put on film. With the exception of Romero's original *Night of the Living Dead*, zombies have never looked so . . . well, creepy-crawly.

It cannot be stressed enough that one of the major reasons these sequences of the Blind Dead work so effectively is due to the chilling music of Anton Garcia Abril, who scored all four movies. His music is highly reminiscent of the modern Polish classical composer, Krzysztof Penderecki, whose sharp dissonant style was used to great effect in William Friedkin's *The Exorcist*, and in Stanley Kubrick's *The Shining*. The makeup for the Templars, by Jose Luis Campos, is also brilliantly done. There is hardly a moment when the Blind Dead are on screen, in any of the four films, that the illusion is broken.

The Blind Dead storm the dilapidated building where Virginia is camping. She makes her escape by hopping atop one of the spectral horses and rides off. But the Blind Dead are right behind her, and as Virginia makes it out into the middle of a large open field, the Templars pounce on her and savagely kill her. The next morning, her brutally mutilated corpse is spotted by the engineer and his conductor/son from the same train Virginia had jumped from the day before.

While Virgina's corpse is throwing a party for the maggots, Betty and Roger are living it up in a swank hotel. But the next morning they go back to the village and discover the horrible truth of what happened, not to mention running into two detectives who are working the case, and who strangely enough, just happen to be hiding out in the ruins of one of the buildings, as if they were hoping the *killer* would return to the scene of the crime.

Betty and Roger return to Lisbon to identify Virginia's corpse. And in what is undoubtedly the strangest scene in the film, we are introduced to the very peculiar, totally off his rocker mortician, who giggles maniacally and loves to torture his menagerie of small animals. Later that night, as our lovable mad mortician puts in some overtime, Virginia awakens from her *nap* and kills him. She then sets out to punish her old friend Betty, apparently

remembering that Betty's dress shop is RIGHT NEXT DOOR TO THE MORGUE! Unfortunately for Virginia, there's no one next door except for one of Betty's workers, who ends up dead, dead, dead. Guess working overtime just doesn't pay in Spain.

Virginia's resurrection is completely unconnected with the rest of the film, as if de Ossorio realized that he didn't have enough story to fill up two hours. The Virginia sub-plot is never developed outside of her killing the mortician and Betty's co-worker. And once she kills them, the sub-plot is dropped. There's also the little matter that no one else who is killed by the Blind Dead turns into a zombie, nor is this particular affliction developed in any of the other films.

Meanwhile, Betty and Roger meet with an old medieval history professor who tells them about the sordid, bloody, violent tales of the Templar Knights. And it is here that Elite has chosen to insert the scenes of the Templars torturing the young peasant girl, in what was originally the film's prologue. Interestingly enough, the scene actually works better this way. But one wonders why Elite Entertainment chose to make such an artistic decision, presumably without Amando de Ossorio's guidance, considering that he died in 1996.

The film then abruptly and awkwardly turns into a catch-the-killer plot, as Betty and Roger enlist the help of the professor's wayward son, who just happens to be a smuggler and is quite familiar with the region where Virginia was killed. So Betty, Roger, the smuggler and his chick return to the ruins to await the Blind Dead.

And it doesn't take long before things get nasty. The smuggler rapes Betty out by the graves, which in turn awakens the Blind Dead. They don't waste any time in dishing out some poetic justice upon the smuggler. They then attack the others. Roger's hand gets hacked off; Betty and the chick get into a laughable cat fight. And the Templars raise hell.

In an inspired bit of filmmaking, which would in turn become one of the Blind Dead's chilling trademarks (not to mention a major selling point), the ghastly knights seek out Betty by the pounding of her heart. Since the knights are blind, sound becomes their manner of stalking their prey.

But Betty escapes and flees to the same field where Virginia was killed. This time, though, the train happens to be chugging by and Betty manages to get the attention of the young conductor (the same one from earlier in the film). The train stops and the young conductor jumps down to help Betty, despite his father's protestations. As he drags a hysterical Betty aboard the train, the mighty Templars rip him apart and hop aboard, too.

The following scenes of the Blind Dead butchering everyone aboard the train are some of the most nightmarish sequences a horror film ever delivered. And though de Ossorio never really wallows in the carnage, as he did in the later films, don't be fooled into thinking this finale doesn't pack a punch worthy of a few sleepless nights.

The train then pulls into the next station, where a group of unsuspecting passengers are eager to board. One of the station attendants discovers a white-haired Betty hiding. She screams out—a scene which is also used at the beginning of the film, as well, following the title sequence—and the Blind Dead descend and kill everyone at the station. Betty, through her promiscuity and worldly ways, has brought the curse (ie. plague) upon herself and that of civilization.

Return of the Blind Dead aka El Ataque de los Muertos Sin Ojos / The Return of the Evil Dead (1972).

After the huge success of *Tombs of the Blind Dead* (in Europe, at least), de Ossorio resurrected his lovable ghouls for a sequel. Though not as chilling or nihilistic as the first film, *Return of the Blind Dead* nevertheless packs a mighty punch, and gives the viewer plenty of opportunity to ogle at the shambling, zombified Templars.

It begins again in the 13th century, with the Templars torturing yet another beautiful peasant girl. But this time around a mob of crazed villagers (is there any other kind?) attack and torture the Templars. The leader of the Templars hurls a curse at the angry mob, that he and his mighty knights will return and kill everyone in the village. This of course doesn't sit well with the mob, and one of the villagers responds by shouting that the Templars will have a pretty hard time coming back from the dead with no eyes. He then burns out the eyes of the Templar leader, and orders that the rest of the knights get the same treatment.

It is here that de Ossorio changes the original mythos concerning the blinding of the Templars. In the first film, when Betty and Roger are meeting with the medieval history professor, they are told by the old man that the Templars were hung from trees by the angry villagers and that crows plucked out their eyes while they were still alive.

From this we fast-forward to modern day, just as the descendants of those same angry villagers are about to celebrate the massacre of the Templars. A huge festival is expected—food, drink, dancing, and fireworks. The village idiot (who looks strikingly like Stephen King from his role in *Creepshow*) watches the villagers prepare for the big shindig, but he's spotted by a group of kids who just don't care for his looks, and they subsequently beat the hell out of him. Luckily, a pretty young blonde comes to his rescue, and with the help of her Euro-stud boyfriend, they chase off the brats. Seems this village really knows how to make people feel comfortable.

Things get even worse when the fireworks engineer, Jack Marlow (the token square-jawed *American*), arrives into town. Jack is introduced to the piggish Mayor Duncan, the mayor's *assistants*, who are nothing but hired thugs, and the mayor's *private secretary*, Vivian. Jack and Vivian make eyes and talk as if they've met each other before. This, of course, infuriates Mayor Duncan, but he keeps his anger in check. The mayor likes fireworks and doesn't want to spoil the show by beating the hell out of Jack just yet. The group make a toast to the evening's festivities, and Jack promises that the fireworks will be the best anyone has ever seen.

After the drinks, Jack and Vivian take a walk through the nearby graveyard. It seems that the two of them had had quite a steamy thing going a few years earlier. Before you know it Jack and Vivian try to conjure up some of that old demon passion. As they do, the village idiot creeps around in the bushes, spying on them. But Jack and Vivian see him and stop fooling around, much to the disappointment of our lovable loon, who pleads with them not to stop. But the passion is gone. Jack and Vivian get up off the dirt and start to head back to the village. Possibly in retaliation for quitting their lovemaking, the village idiot warns them that tonight is the night when the evil Templars will return and destroy the village. Our hero and his girl laugh off his warning and return to the village to party down, leaving the village idiot alone in the cemetery.

It doesn't take long before the gravestones start to smolder and shift, much to the delight of the village idiot.

Soon, the Blind Dead rise. Unfortunately, de Ossorio chooses to use footage from the first film's resurrection scenes, instead of filming anew. Regardless, it's good to see the Blind Dead do their unique creepy-crawl again.

Meanwhile, on the other side of the village, the pretty young blonde Monica, who rescued the village idiot from the beginning of the film, and her boyfriend (yet another Euro-stud), decide to get it on in her father's house. But obviously ignorant of the heavy Freudian sub-texts which fuel the Blind Dead, the two become perfect victims for the shambling, lust-filled knights. The Blind Dead surround the house and eventually break in, killing the foolish boyfriend. Monica, who escapes from the house by way of a window, hops atop one of the Templar horses and rides off towards the train station. Once there, she tries to convince the drunken station attendant that she is being followed by the legendary Templar Knights. He doesn't believe her, so the girl runs off towards the village. But soon the attendant sees that she's telling the truth just as a few of the Blind Dead come to pay him a visit. He then makes a frantic call to the village for help.

Back in the village, Jack is having his own problems. Tired of watching this stranger making the moves on his *private secretary*, Mayor Duncan orders his boys to kick some sense into Jack. Jack performs well, but not well enough. Luckily, the fight is called off when Mayor Duncan orders his boys to go see what's going on down at the train station. Jack and Vivian decide to flee the village. But as they're driving out through the countryside, they happen upon the petrified Monica. They decide to whisk her back to the village for some medical attention. At the same time, the mayor's boys return from the station and warn Mayor Duncan that the Templars have indeed risen and are about to attack the village. The Mayor makes a call to the governor for help, but his plea goes unheeded. The governor is convinced that Mayor Duncan is drunk and is pulling his leg.

The pacing of the film during this whole time is speedy. No time for character development or even much suspense. De Ossorio knows what we want and he has no qualms about giving it to us. From this point on the film becomes a roller coaster ride straight to hell.

One of the mayor's thugs tries to escape the village with his wife and daughter by motorcycle. But the Blind Dead have already surrounded the perimeter of the town. The family head for an old church and lock themselves within it.

Back in the village square, where the festivities are still going on, the Blind Dead descend upon the oblivious partygoers, dishing out some more Old World retribution. Jack, Vivian, Mayor Duncan, and Howard (his *personal assistant*) watch on from a balcony overlooking the square, helpless to do much of anything. But Jack, being the man that he is, can't stand to not fight, despite the mayor's pleas to the contrary. Jack, with the mayor's thuggish assistant by his side, arm some of the villagers with farming implements, and the newly formed mob start to fight back. But the battle is ugly and bloody. Eventually, though, Jack gets ahold of some of his fireworks and starts blasting the Blind Dead to kingdom come. Enough of the Blind Dead go up in flames for the surviving villagers to make it out into the maze of streets. Jack, Vivian, Howard, Mayor Duncan, and Monica, jump into a jeep and try to make it out, too.

But they don't get far. The Blind

Dead have surrounded all the exits from the village, and the group is forced to hole up inside the same church the where the family is. The Blind Dead soon surround the church. *Return of the Blind Dead* now becomes a siege movie, with the survivors forced to play a waiting game with the zombies.

Monica discovers the village idiot hiding behind some curtains inside the church, and he convinces her that he knows a way to safety. She saved his life, and now he wants to repay her kindness. Monica wants him to warn the others, but he doesn't care for them. When did they ever care about him? The two of them make their way through an underground tunnel which will lead them to safety.

As they make their escape, Mayor Duncan tries to convince Howard to flee with him. But Mayor Duncan's influence over the man is not as powerful as it once was. So the mayor tries to convince his other thug, Burt, to join him. Burt agrees. He's got a family to think about. But since Burt isn't exactly a smart guy, he botches things up when the mayor sends him outside— alone!—to fend off the Blind Dead with nothing more than a torch. The Templars cut him down like a rag doll, in what is one of the film's more horrible deaths.

Bastard that he is, Mayor Duncan then forces Burt's little girl to go outside and holler for her papa, distracting the Blind Dead long enough for the piggish mayor to make his escape in the jeep. But the jeep won't start, so he heads off into one of the side streets. Of course, the Blind Dead catch up with him, and Mayor Duncan cries, pleads, and whimpers for his life to be spared, though knowing full well that it won't. A cathartic horror movie moment indeed, as the Blind Dead penetrate the mayor with their long, rusty swords.

One of the film's more frightening scenes occurs a little later when Jack must slip out of the church to rescue the dead Burt's little girl, who is still outside surrounded by the Blind Dead. Silently the horde of undead knights surround the two of them, and it is only after the child's mother runs out to distract them, that Jack and the child manage to get to safety. But despite her heroism, the child's mother isn't so lucky.

While all of this is going on, we cut back to Monica and the village idiot, who are still trying to find their way to safety. Eventually, the two make it to the end of the tunnel, but their fates are surely not what they expected.

Back in the church, Howard tries to rape Vivian. But he ends up dying for this little act, when valiant Jack shoves back against a spear. Don't let it ever be said that de Ossorio didn't understand poetic justice.

The film ends with Jack, Vivian, and the little girl, slipping out of the church just as dawn comes. Like vampires, the Blind Dead's enemy seems to be that of the sun. This last sequence, as the survivors weave between the still, motionless Templars, is one of the most powerful scenes from any of the films. It recalls the uneasy truce finale in Hitchcock's *The Birds*.

As Jack, Vivian, and the little girl literally walk off into the new day dawning, the evil Blind Dead collapse and crumble to the ground.

Return of the Blind Dead is a worthy sequel to the first film, with its non-stop action, eerie set pieces, and relatively top-notch production. De Ossorio knows that we want to see more of the Blind Dead this time around and he doesn't disappoint. Remarkably, giving the Blind Dead so much screen time doesn't dilute their fear appeal. The only real problem with the film is the same problem that plagues all of them, actually—its uninvolving narrative and stock characterizations.

The music, cinematography, and makeup effects are still up to par this time around. But be warned that the recently released collector's edition videotape claims that it is subtitled in Spanish. It isn't. It's dubbed, and rather poorly at that. Also note that during the opening titles, the film is known as *Return of the Evil Dead*.

Horror of the Zombies aka *El Burque Maldito/The Ghost Galleon* (1974).

The third entry in the series, which came sailing into theaters two years later, is without a doubt the worst of the four films. Sandwiched somewhere between an

Ed Wood film (though completely lacking his earnest charm) and your Aunt Martha's home movies of her trip to Branson, Missouri, awaits this dreck.

Stilted, horribly acted (and that's saying something considering the acting *talents* in the other entries), and lacking a narrative drive of any sorts, *Horror of the Zombies* must go down as one of the more excruciatingly boring film experiences. If it weren't for the still somewhat chilling shots of the Blind Dead roaming about the deck of the ghostly galleon, this film would've been long forgotten.

Bypassing a prologue, the film starts with the disappearance of two fashion models aboard their tiny boat. It seems that the models were to be a part of some kind of publicity stunt, but their getting lost in a thick, tropical fog ruins that plan pretty quickly. But before you can holler *Flying Dutchman*, things get strange when a 13th century Spanish galleon runs into the models' boat. Before long, one of the women boards the strange ship and subsequently is never seen again. The next morning, the other model follows suit and also ends up meat for the creepy Blind Dead, though only after she wanders about the seemingly deserted ship for a while. The only excuse for the endless shots of her roaming about the ship seems to be that de Ossorio had to fill up some time.

The girlfriend of one of the models threatens to inform the police about the disappearances, but she is kidnapped by a sporting magnet (the brain behind the publicity stunt), his thuggish right-hand man, and a fashion photographer. The dashing, not-so-smart-as-he-thinks-he-is sporting magnet decides that the best thing to do is to go out and find the lost models themselves, without having to bother the police. So with the help of a cartographer, who also happens to be very knowledgeable about Templar history and all of their devilish deeds, the five of them set out to rescue the two models.

Eventually the rescue team arrives and figures out that the galleon actually exists in some kind of alternate dimension (which is supposed to help explain why so many scenes are shot with no continuity concerning night and day?), a plot device which not given credence in any of the other films.

To be fair, when the Blind Dead do show up, the film does pick up and generates a modicum of chills. But in following the earlier films the Templars fail to be that threatening. They're on a ship, for crying out loud! How scary is that? No more slow-motion, spectral horses, or fog-shrouded cemeteries at night. There's just a bunch of shambling corpses in robes milling about. Sigh.

Pretty soon all hell breaks loose when the cartographer figures out that the Blind Dead on board need a good exorcising (de Ossorio's attempt to generate some post-*The Exorcist* dollars?).

The film ends with the galleon burning into the sea (in what has to be one of the phoniest, most hilarious non-special effects ever) and only the sporting magnet and fashion photographer making it to shore alive. All is well for our survivors... until the dead Templar Knights rise out of the dark waters around them, in what is undoubtedly the finest, scariest, scene in the film. With this darker than dark finale, de Ossorio seems to have awoken from whatever catatonia he was in, and the film delivers a nihilistic ending worthy of the series.

Horror of the Zombies' lack of production values is apparent throughout, most notably in the ineptly filmed sequences of the Spanish galleon floating in what looks to be a tiny swimming pool. But the footage of the Blind Dead shuffling about are nicely done. There is also plenty of graphic violence—a dismemberment among other cruelties—which had been somewhat downplayed in the previous films. But there's no tension, no thrills in this one, since you care absolutely nothing for any of the characters. Now, the first two films weren't exactly filled with stellar performances, either. But the characters were at least a little more likable, and some care was given as to what motivated them, however ridiculous those motivations were. When the Blind Dead attacked, you wanted the characters to survive.

Not so with *Horror of the Zombies*.

Das Blutgericht der reitenden Leichen

Half-way through it, you're just about screaming for the Blind Dead to take out de Ossorio.

Night of the Seagulls aka La Noche de las Gaviotas (1975).

After the ludicrous mess that was *Horror of the Zombies*, the series looked as if it had reached the end of its life. But in 1975, de Ossorio returned for one more tango with the Blind Dead, and dished up a savory, if ultimately disappointing end to the Blind Dead mythos.

But the film does have its moments, from its eerie cinematography and locale by the sea, to the fact that the Blind Dead are back on solid ground where they belong.

Night of the Seagulls begins sometime in the 13th century, with a young couple losing their way on the outskirts of a small seaside village. They unfortunately also meet up with the evil, diabolic Templars. The knights kill the man and abduct the woman, taking her back to their lair. Once there, the mysterious knights serve her up as a sacrifice to their amphibian-looking Lovecraftian elder god. A knight plunges his hefty knife deep into the woman's chest and rips out her still beating heart. He then places it into the statue's mouth. Then, in what is one of the series' strangest and most ridiculous moments, a battalion of carnivorous crabs creep towards the dead

woman and start to chomp, pinch, and rip her to shreds. Absurd, but nevertheless weird and somewhat disturbing.

Following the structure of the first two films, we're spirited away to the present day (in what, we are told, is based on a *true story*), and introduced to a young doctor named Henry and his wife Joan, who are moving to the same seaside village where the earlier couple met their fates. Henry has plans to set up his general practice in the village. But unbeknownst to the two of them, the quaint little village was once the sanctuary to the Templar Knights, and to this day the superstitious villagers (with good reason mind you) still offer up sacrifices to their ghostly oppressors. For seven successive nights, seven young virgins must be strapped to a rock out on the beach as a gift to appease the wrath of the Blind Dead.

The previous doctor, an old man who wants to get the hell out, warns Henry and Joan that the villagers don't want any of *them* around, but he neglects to elaborate.

Henry and Joan start to uncover the sordid truth and subsequently become hated and feared by the villagers. It also doesn't help that Henry is always referring to the villagers as *primitive* and *backwards*, and reminding us that the village is depressing, evil, and utterly horrible. All of these things are true, but there are more tactful ways to express oneself.

Luckily a virginal local girl takes pity on the couple, when she witnesses the doctor's wife being refused service in one of the little village stores. Joan then offers the girl a job as their maid, and the girl accepts. The village idiot (yes, yet another one) pays the couple a visit, after spying on Joan, and rambles on to Henry and Joan about the black deeds the villagers are up to. Immediately, Henry demands to know about the strange, eerie tolling of the bell he and his wife heard the night before, the sounds of seagulls in the night (which we are told never come out at night), and about the procession of black-clad villagers somberly shuffling out along the beach.

Eventually things get very bad, when the villagers take it upon themselves to get rid of Henry and Joan. Some of the village men beat the hell out of the village idiot and throw him off a cliff, leaving him for dead. And the parents of the young girl take her back home, only to be sent out as that night's sacrifice.

But Henry rushes to save the girl, just as the horseback-riding Blind Dead arrive to have their way with her. As you may well imagine, this doesn't sit well with our carrion knights and they retaliate by riding through the village, attacking everything that moves (or makes a sound, as the case may be).

Henry and Joan end up trapped in the cavernous lair of the Templar Knights. Henry then destroys the hideous stone idol, just as a group of Blind Dead are about to serve them up to the crabs. Foiled once again, the undead knights crumble to the floor.

Night of the Seagulls is not a great film by any stretch of the imagination. But coming on the heels of the last installment, it's not a piece of garbage either. The film lacks any tension and suspense whatsoever, though it does regain, for the most part, the strangely gothic atmosphere which permeated both *Tombs of the Blind Dead* and *Return of the Blind Dead*. The scenes of the villagers escorting the virgin sacrifices out to the beach are suitably morose and chilling.

It most be noted, though, that much (if not all) of the footage showing the Blind Dead rising from their graves, is lifted from the first film.

•

The Blind Dead films were never perfect examples of what constitutes great horror films, though they definitely had their fair share of amazing moments. There was obvious care and attention taken by de Ossorio for the first two films in regards to the special-effects makeup, the music, and photography. But de Ossorio's disregard for even the slightest attention to character development, narrative drive, or logic(!), keeps these films from achieving true horror film glory—though *Tombs of the Blind Dead* comes damn close. The ending of that film is no less a horror film masterpiece. Without a doubt one of the single, most horrifying endings any film ever produced.

Horror films have rarely come equipped with logic, character development, etc. And they don't always need it in order to scare, disturb, revolt, or enchant us. Just look at the work of Italian maestro Dario Argento, who has given us some of the greatest horror films ever made, all in defiance of external logic, or even memorable characters. And John Carpenter's *Halloween* is chock full of characters doing incredibly stupid things. But Argento's films, and Carpenter's *Halloween* still retain great power in what they know how to do . . .

Scare us.

So Amando de Ossorio's contributions should not be devalued. He's in good company. The Blind Dead films may appear a bit bruised and worse for the wear, but there's no denying their strength and vitality in giving us nightmares. And thanks to Elite Entertainment, the first two installments have been given a new lease on life. No serious horror fan should do without them.

Tombs of the Blind Dead (1971) ***1/2
Return of the Blind Dead (1972) ***
Horror of the Zombies (1974) *
Night of the Seagulls (1975) **1/2

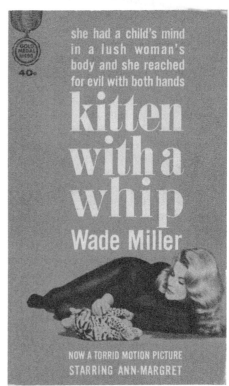

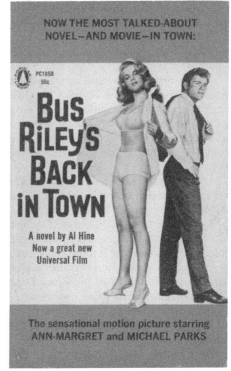

Our double issue (#3/4) was the only one offset printed rather than xeroxed, so it looked the best out of all of our issues, particularly when it comes to book cover reproductions. Don't tell Peter, but I took advantage of the opportunity to upgrade this piece, covering twice as many titles as I did in the original version. Because let's face it—you can never have too much Ann-Margret. -John

KITTEN ON THE COVER
Ann-Margret Movie Tie-Ins (1962-1966)
by John Scoleri

Ann-Margret Olsson made her motion picture debut in *A Pocketful of Miracles* (United Artists, 1961). She would follow that up in a remake of Rodgers & Hammerstein's *State Fair* (Fox, 1962). These early portrayals as an innocent young girl would peak with the release of *Bye Bye Birdie* (Columbia, 1962) the first of her films to be supported by a novelization featuring her on the cover.

Though there was no similar tie-in for *Viva Las Vegas* (MGM, 1964), that film continued her migration from ingenue to sex kitten, if not outright bad girl. This transition was solidified with the release of *Kitten With A Whip* (Universal, 1964). Gold Medal re-released the Wade Miller paperback original with an Ann-Margret photo cover (albeit one from a rather playful photo-shoot pairing her with a real leopard cub, and not a still from the back and white film).

While even Annie *(right)* appears to be upset there was no novelization for *The Pleasure Seekers* (Fox, 1964), she soon found herself on the cover of the novelization of her next film, *Bus Riley's Back in Town* (Universal, 1965).

She also made an appearance on the *Once a Thief* (MGM, 1965) tie-in (a reissue of Zekial Marko's **Scratch a Thief**), though she's nowhere to be found on the movie tie-in to *The Cincinati Kid* (MGM, 1965). Her film *Made in Paris* (MGM, 1966) did not warrant a novelization, nor did the remake of *Stagecoach* (Fox, 1966). Her next film, *The Swinger* (Paramount, 1966) received a novelization with a great cover. Surprisingly the domestic tie-in to Donald Hamilton's Matt Helm adaptation, *Murderers' Row* (Columbia, 1966), also failed to feature the actress; a situation rectified across the pond on the Coronet UK tie-in in 1967!

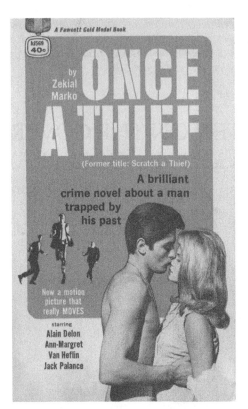

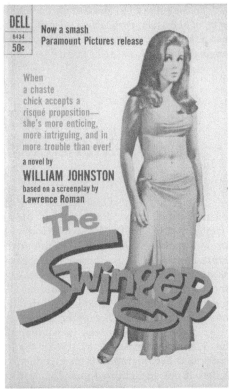

Ann-Margret's golden age ended in 1966, before she closed out the decade starring in a number of Italian productions/co-productions: *The Tiger and the Pussycat* (1967), *The Prophet* (1968), *Criminal Affair* (1968), and *Rebus* (1969). Her marriage to Roger Smith in 1967, and his taking over as her manager, seemed to coincide with (if not drive) the domestication of her sixties sex-kitten image. But we'll always have these movie tie-ins to remind us!

Bye Bye Birdie by Ruth Ives
Macfadden 50-178, 1963

Kitten With A Whip by Wade Miller (Robert Allison Wade and H. Bill Miller)
Gold Medal k1490, 1964 (copyright page retains the original publication date of 1959)

Bus Riley's Back in Town by Al Hine
Popular Library PC1050, 1965

Once a Thief (Former title: **Scratch a Thief**) by Zekial Marko
Gold Medal k1569, 1965 (copyright page retains the original publication date of 1961)

The Swinger by William Johnston
Dell 8434, October, 1966

Murderers' Row by Donald Hamilton
Coronet (UK), 1967

bare•bones $5

UNEARTHING VINTAGE AND FORGOTTEN
HORROR/MYSTERY/SCI-FI/WESTERN
FILM-PAPERBACKS-PULP FICTION-VIDEO

An epic drama of adventure and exploration

Space Station One, your first step in an Odyssey that will take you to the Moon, the planets and the distant stars.

MGM PRESENTS A STANLEY KUBRICK PRODUCTION

2001: a space odyssey

SUPER PANAVISION® AND METROCOLOR

STARRING KEIR DULLEA · GARY LOCKWOOD · SCREENPLAY BY STANLEY KUBRICK AND ARTHUR C. CLARKE
PRODUCED AND DIRECTED BY STANLEY KUBRICK

MGM

Everybody likes a top ten list... even, it would seem, the guy who hates them the most: David J. Schow. You know the name: screenplays, novels, comic books, short stories, TV; David's been everywhere. He's also one of the nicest guys I know and kinda took John and I under his wing a couple decades ago. Our annual trek to L.A. wouldn't be complete without a visit with David, his girlfriend Kerry, and their (canine) son, Muggsy. Anyway, John and I were putting together a compendium of the top films and fiction of the 1990s, with input from all of our regular contributors. Schow's contribution went in a different direction. Which was all the better. Or Bestest. -Peter

MOSTEST BESTEST
by David J. Schow

Unfortunately for all of us, the popularity of the Top Ten list has no symptoms of losing steam any time soon. Under normal circumstances, the end of the year freights in a number of requests for lists of every-damned-thing, year-end wrap-ups, picks and pans, thumbs up and down and four stars to no stars—all of it, thickheaded, populist horseshit designed to render down, oversimplify, make palatable for mass consumption and otherwise navigate the clueless toward a statistically satisfying consumer experience.

But in 1999, *Star Wars* mania can be outclassed by only one thing—millennial fever, which has the benefit of centuries of advance PR. Most of its ominous portents are based on our entirely arbitrary Julian calendar and contain as much raw truth as a newspaper horoscope.

It's the Millennium! It's Y2K! And you can be sure that most of the panic attendant to New Year's 1999 will be caused not by a nationwide digital crash, but by jumpy dimwits cleaning out your local foodmart, stockpiling way too much ammo, yanking their cash out of banks, and causing freeway gridlock in their bovine-brained rush to escape the cataclysms they've fantasized and are damned sure going to help implement. The only funny Y2K joke I saw on the internet was the one pointing out that the Dark Ages were a result of "that Y1K bug." We also have to conveniently forget that the first year of the new century doesn't roll around until 2001, a year which, let's face it, should be re-dubbed Year Kubrick. But it won't, because idiots, fanatics, Armageddonists, Apocalypsoids and religious loons all over the globe will waste most of 2000 in a fight-or-flight panic about the very *next* year.

So with all this torment in mind, we get not only end of the year lists, but end of the decade, end of the century, end of the world lists.

All pop lists attempt to hierarchize art; in this context we may interpret everything from movies to soft drinks to athletes as products, executed better or worse than other products. "Most popular" quickly translates as "most units sold," and sales are no basis upon which to judge art, but literally nobody gives a damn. This is, after all, a mercantile society.

List-making attempts to throw artforms like movies, books or music into an elimination derby, with, ideally, one survivor in each category. It is *not* a meritocracy. Imagine your favorite recording artists all pitched into some Thunderdome and forced to kill tooth and nail until one remains standing, and you have a pretty good model of the bottom line in corporate showbiz. America loves a winner, we are told, this being the land of bigger-is-better-and-biggest-is-best (how else to explain the popularity of SUVs among feckless Boomer losers?). But America also loves a good dinner spread, which is why it manufactures fast-track stars almost as fast as it can eat them alive. The biggest and best turkeys always get eaten during our way-too-many national holidays.

On the next rung down from the "#1 Syndrome," we find our culture awash in Top Ten lists. But once asked for your ten favorites in any category, you'll then be asked to cull it down to a Top Five, then a Top Three, as the very fundament of our list-making capacities as homo sapiens are tidally magnetized back toward the only True North that matters—Numero Uno, #1.

Many entertainment outlets like to poll what they call "experts" in selected fields for their own Top Tens. Very often, all the Top Ten lists are published or presented together … at which point conclusions are drawn as to which stars or books or films or songs were mentioned the most often, leading inevitably toward … well, you're getting the pattern by now.

Top Tens desperately need to be made fun again.

I've noticed a number of requests made for Top Tens—usually movies, in my own case—fail to account for criteria or timeframe. Experts asked to list their ten "best" science fiction movies in 1960 had fewer movies to sort out than their modern counterparts, who naturally are required to specify the ten best "of all time" without any decent definition of just what qualifies. As the decades just keep on piling up, the cap stays at ten. Therefore, any film replaced on a given list by the march of time and new movies automatically, I guess, becomes "less good" than it was the previous year, when it qualified. And is *Alien* a science fiction film or a horror film? Is *Silence of the Lambs* a horror film, or does supernatural stuff have to occur? Should we care one damn about such nerdland nitpickery?

The natural solution would be to compile a Top Ten for each decade in each category. But that means you'd have to choose only one film per year to represent your tastes. And even if you started from 1950, and even if you could pinpoint ten good genre films from the last couple of dismal decades, the floor would be fifty films, minimum, per genre—too tedious for a Lite audience to wade through. Can't you just name—wait for it—your *all-time favorite*? And we're back to #1, again.

"Best" is a word with far too many operative definitions in this arena. Your own Top Ten might comprise the movies you thought were the best as movies, or the best in terms of their genre, or the most groundbreaking and influential, or the basic coursework everyone needs before they could be considered qualified enough to judge more sophisticated stuff. Or you might just pick ten of your favorites. To me, "favorite" indicates a movie which, while not necessary good or bad, you can watch over and over and never tire of.

Shit! That's five different categories—another fifty films again. Already. Another fifty you'll probably have to winnow down to ten, and that's not counting all the Guilty Pleasures you'll have to justify in yet another list at the end.

The most recent time I was boxed into this corner was by *The Astounding B-Monster* (www.bmonster.com), probably the best and most useful website devoted to sci-fi, horror, fantasy, and cult flicks. While other genre 'zines kill millions of trees with crap content that most film fans already know or would rather skip, the B Monster always has another unique interview or profile up its digital sleeve, especially if the subject is someone you thought had already been thoroughly profiled. Its editor/creator, Marty Baumann, asked for my lists, and it's tough to say no to someone who credits you as an expert. Simple, right? Easy, right? I started by firing off what I thought were my Top Ten science fictioners, in no order, as:

1. *Miracle Mile* (1989)

The best movie ever made where the world blows up at the end (*Strangelove* included), and the only one that made me shed a tear for the characters, who are absolutely nothing like me. That's important.

2. *Lifeforce* (1985)

A much-reviled film with a surprising overage of cool stuff, including a breakneck pace, dead serious, fanatical performances, Mathilda May's two biggest talents, and a scene where Steve Railsback has to kiss Patrick Stewart and like it. It's also an invasion film in which the whole goddamned Earth *loses*—the vampiric aliens top off their tanks and leave.

3. *It Conquered the World* (1956)

Corman, Beverly Garland, the teepee monster, "umbrella bats," Bronson Cave, and Jonathan Haze as a Mexican. Every character in this film has at least one lush, fruity, declamatory speech. Plus, this movie made for one of the best *Mystery Science Theatre 3000s* ever.

4. *Planet of the Apes* (1968)

I watched it twice in a row (at a drive-in) when it came out, then went back and saw it again, and could probably watch it twice right now. A movie whose groundbreaking qualities were much-overshadowed by *2001: A Space Odyssey* ... a film not on this list only because it's on so many others.

5. *The Thing (From Another World)* (1951)

I like the Bill Lancaster/John Carpenter remake, too, but ultimately this is the film that has spawned so many ripoffs and retellings that you couldn't count them all. It's also one of the few monster movies that is (unlike its remake) as exciting to *listen* to as to see. You don't realize it, but that's important too.

6. *World Without End* (1956)

Hunky Americans with lots of firepower meet horny subterranean babes in tight clothing actually designed for the film by Alberto Vargas in a plot inversion of *The Time Machine* that combines space travel, time travel, post-Apocalypse, giant spiders, and homicidal mutant cave guys with faces like goulash. A favorite of my misspent youth.

7. *The Andromeda Strain* (1970)

I read the book as soon as it came out in paperback and hungered to see the movie. I was not disappointed. How often do you get to honestly say that?

8. *Accion Mutante* (1993)

The only fresh twist I've seen in years on the usual pile of sci-fi clichés. And when it's all done, like a Monty Python sketch, it wraps up with a song!

9. *Singin' in the Rain* (1952)

Mostly because it's about people learning to cope with a brand-new technology; an unexpected form of sci-fi, if you will. Watch it again if you don't believe me, and pay attention this time.

10. *Videodrome* (1982)

I like virtually Cronenberg's entire canon (the jury's still out on *M. Butterfly*), but this is the one that sticks with me. When I saw all the missing footage broadcast by A&E, I thought someone was scanning an alternate universe version of *Videodrome* into my soon-to-explode head.

Special vote for most overlooked *prophetic* sci fi movie: *Looker* (1981).

Of all the movies that try to predict the future, *Looker* (directed by—surprise—Michael Crichton) comes closer than anybody with its scenario of digitally-created actors. The same technology, today, enables advertisers to indulge in post-facto product placement in any movie that doesn't ballyhoo enough commercial goods (it also permits wrong-headed correctness fanatics to omit cigarettes and their smoke from old movies, too). Is this movie important? Yes,

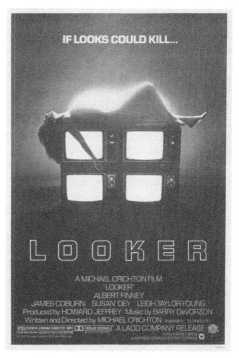

considering that every know-nothing ever interviewed about science fiction brays on about how he read H.G. Wells as a child, and how prophetic it's all supposed to be. Is it a good movie? It depends on your tolerance ceiling for the fashion catastrophes of two decades past, or your gag reflex for watching Albert Finney trying to woo Susan Dey. It'll be a joyride if, like me, you relish bearing witness to the savage destruction of a gang of cameo-ing *Playboy* Playmates (by extension, a negation of the whole *Playboy* conception of mass-consumer beauty). See it with the cut scenes if you can (a network broadcast of *Looker* about ten years ago reinstated two sequences vital to the plot. One is an escape, and in the other, James Coburn explains why the bad guys are doing what they're doing. Neither scene will confer greatness upon *Looker*, anymore than all the laserdisc supplements in the world can make *The Abyss* into a good movie ... but it deserves a historical note.)

•

With the ten films cited in the main list above, problems are already obvious, namely that for every film on the list there's another that should be there, too. *Solaris*. *Day the Earth Stood Still*. *Forbidden Planet*. *Invasion of the Body Snatchers*. *Quatermass and the Pit*. *Them!* Or the films that were undeniably influential, like *Blade Runner* (which I dislike, but which changed the whole visual aesthetic of sci-fi) or *The Road Warrior* (which I did like, and ditto). Don't get me started; just know they're out there, like the film which is probably the apex of 20th Century science fiction, *2001*.

Moving on to the "horror" list presented even more difficulties.

1. *The Creature from the Black Lagoon* (1954)

Like *Alien*, like *The Thing*, a horror film masquerading as a sci-fi film. But *this* one (and the two sequels) features the greatest monster ever to emerge from the 1950s, period, Godzilla included.

2. *Alien* (only the 1979 original)

A movie that drew from a bunch of movies before it, stirred in a wild club of diverse talents, and subsequently affected every genre film made after it. Probably the first techno-Gothic horror film.

3. *Repulsion* (1965)

This near-flawless portrait in close-up of a mental crash-and-burn remains a skin-crawler; the perfect definition of a "disturbing" horror film, as opposed to one that just throws scares into your face or viscera into your lap.

4. *Psycho* (the 1960 original, dammit!)

But only if you see it in a theatre.

5. *La Casa Dalle Finestre Che Ridono* (1976)

Eerie atmosphere reigns in a nightmare tone of isolation in Pupi Avati's best horror film ever.

6. *Tras El Cristal* (aka *In a Glass Cage*, 1982)

Think *Schindler's List* was wrenching, upsetting, traumatic? Then this film is definitely not for you. Think it was pap, like I did? Then treat yourself to something *genuinely* upsetting. Writer/director Augustin Villaronga crafted an unrelentingly bleak scenario based on the vengeance structure of a horror film, yet which doesn't pander to the easy emotional push-buttons—it only gets *more* horrifying until you feel like you're on some sort of hallucinogen. Sort of a cross-clone of *I Spit On Your Grave* with *Henry, Portrait of a Serial Killer*, with a Nazi child molester tossed in. You will not forget this movie.

7. *La Maschera Del Demonio* (aka *Black Sunday*, 1960)

Despite the (now-) hokey Satanistics, still a wonderfully upsetting and remote movie to watch late at night with all the lights out. The crypt in this film still looks to me as though it is at the literal ends of the earth.

8. *Abbott and Costello Meet Frankenstein* (1948)

Not a scary movie, but, I've found, the movie upon which more people base their memories of the Universal monsters of the 1930s and 40s than any film you'd expect.

9. *The Mummy's Tomb* (1942)

The first horror movie I can remember watching front-to-finish, on a local version of TV's *Shock Theatre*. It's actually two movies in one since it incorporates so much flashback footage from the previous film, *The Mummy's Hand* (1940), which introduces us to Kharis, the slightly, eh, *weight-challenged* Egyptian priest who reanimates for love. The two sequels, *The Mummy's Ghost* and *The Mummy's Curse* (both 1944), tip the whole saga into the surreal via an interesting separation gambit: Each sequel is stated to take place some 20-30 years following the events of the previous film, which means that *Curse* wraps up, minimum, in a theoretical post-1995 during which World War Two is still going on!

10. *Dawn of the Dead* (1979)

A reverse on the theme mentioned in (1): Here's a flick that is technically sci-fi (if you pay attention to the plot) masquerading as horror. I *lived* with this goddamned film—literally, I lived in the theatre in which it was playing, for a time—and watched people stagger out of it as though bashed in the head by a rubber mallet. You all think you're way too cool, now. Too bad you couldn't have tasted it when it was fresh.

As you might be able to tell, "genres" are already breaking down like crazy and the lists would be next to meaningless without the added copy to describe *why* certain films are on the list. Do we separate out "supernatural" from "non-supernatural" horror films, and if so, on which list does *Les Yeux Sans Visage* go? As far as "influential" horror films go, it's pretty easy to trace the generational links back to the likes of *Nosferatu* (which begat *Dracula* and that whole family), *Cabinet of Dr. Caligari*, the 1932 *Dr. Jekyll and Mr. Hyde* (the first horror movie to win an Academy Award), *The Uninvited* (which, in an odd way, begat the classic line incorporating *The Innocents* and *The Haunting*), *Night of the Living Dead*, *Rosemary's Baby*, or *The Exorcist*...

...unless we create a separate listing for what are quaintly called "psychological horror" films, in which case the bloodline must be declared for everything from Fritz Lang's *M* to *Les Diaboliques*, *Freaks*, *The Body Snatcher*, *The Texas Chainsaw Massacre*, *Last House on the Left*, and *Targets*.

And that's not counting *A Clockwork Orange*, which fits into *every* category I can think of, including comedy.

The only solution was to foment a third list, of titles unexpected by the jaded, or cocksure, or hair-splitty. Hence:

HORROR FILMS NOT THOUGHT OF AS HORROR FILMS ... (But They Are!)

1. *Heavenly Creatures* (1994)

The story of one of New Zealand's most infamous matricides. When Peter Jackson did *Meet the Feebles* (1989—or, *Sesame Street* reimagined by way of *Barfly*, *Panic in Needle Park*, *Sid & Nancy*, *Dawn of the Dead* and *All That Jazz*), his rep was cemented as "low-budget gross-out king." *Heavenly Creatures* altered that assessment to "Academy Award nominee."

2. *Spirits (of the Air, Gremlins of the Clouds)* (1987)

Alex Proyas' first feature, a post-apocalyptic fable shot in Broken Hill (*Road Warrior* territory) using minimal sets and three actors...and almost none of it takes place at night, or in the rain.

3. *Red Dawn* (1984)

A fantasy film in almost every particular. The moment when the schoolteacher glances out the window and sees the impossible—Russian parachutes—has seldom been matched for sheer, off-down-the-rabbit-hole giddiness in other so-called "fantastic" films.

4. *The Warriors* (1979)

1979's hippest gang movie looks dated today, but never mind. It's an ancient tale—Xenophon's **Anabasis**—retold from the urban gutter point of view, and wearing the kind of colors you only see in the movies.

5. *The Road to Wellville* (1994)

If you don't believe this is a horror film, consider the scene in which Matthew Broderick is compelled to shit in a pan before an audience, then have his "formless, mushy and foul-smelling" excreta critiqued by the guy who invented Corn Flakes.

6. *Kingpin* (1996)

A film that gleefully subverts almost every movie cliché about down and out champions rallying one final time, and if that doesn't getcha, then Randy Quaid's nipples will. And if *those* don't freak you out, wait for the sex-starved landlady. You, too, will sink to your knees murmuring, "Terror, thy name is *Kingpin*."

7. *Never Take Sweets From a Stranger* (1960)

An overlooked classic about a genuinely shuddersome child molester, from Hammer Films, a studio that really should have made more movies like this and fewer piss-poor **Frankenstein** and **Dracula** sequels.

8. *Salon Kitty* (1975)

Fuck *Cabaret*, bring on the Fatherland's most superior women! Some of the stuff they have to do will freeze your blood, though.

9. *Crash* (1997)

Cronenberg, again, inevitably. A film so thoughtful in its architecture that it demands to be seen in a theatre, for its framing, compositions, and color palette alone. If not a bonafide art film, damned close.

10. *Welcome to the Dollhouse* (1996)

Sold as satire but forged in the crucible of humiliation that is grade school. This film made several of my friends weep, and not with laughter, as it snapped the sheer torture of childhood into a most-unwelcome flashback focus. Being a kid flat-out sucks, and this movie is a document of that, even if it is wincingly funny. Letting this movie in also opens the floodgate for a new tide of horrors the likes of *Gummo* (1997), which has to be seen to be believed.

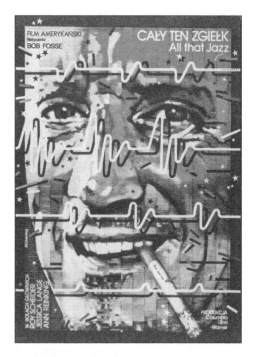

All That Jazz reminds us that there are movies that apply to no category or genre unless you want to make up new ones, like "death musicals." Then there's stuff made strictly for TV—enough to justify a bonus list that would include the *Night Stalker* telefilms, the BBC's two-and-a-half hour version of *Day of the Triffids* (superior in every way to the 1964 film), along with an unnerving little exercise called *A Cold Night's Death* (aka *The Chill Factor*, 1973). You'll also notice the cunning trick of listing other films in the copy for the one-of-ten numerical choice, a good way to sneak in extra titles the next time someone asks you to generate one of these goofy lists. All tolled, we've cited about sixty to seventy movies here; not bad for a Top Ten.

As John M. Ford once said, "I reserve the right to change this list every five minutes, if necessary." The *B-Monster* listings are presented here at such length (and with two minor changes) on the theory that if you haven't heard of or seen at least one of these movies, perhaps you'll be in for a pleasant surprise, or at least consider a reappraisal … and if you do that, then all this frivolous list-making will have had a point, as we kiss the 1900s goodbye.

I truly believe that Donald Westlake's Parker series is the greatest set of continuing adventures ever written. Those who haven't read them will thumb their noses and pelt me with fruit and remind me about Ian Fleming's Bond or Donald Hamilton's Matt Helm or some other series that might have started out on fire and withered after time. The Parker books only got better! And that goes for Westlake's return to the character in the 1990s. Bill covers the series up through the second book in the reboot, but there would be six more novels before Westlake's death in 2008. Each one of those books is immensely more readable than most of what passes as "crime fiction" these days. Reading each new novel as it came out was like being magically swept away to the late 1950s. Bill's piece is the longest article we ever ran in BB. Savor every word. -Peter

RICHARD STARK:
DONALD WESTLAKE'S DARK HALF
(The Parker Novels at a Glance)
by W.D. Gagliani

"You told me no more favors," Parker reminded him. "You should have meant it." He grabbed Stegman by the hair and rammed his face into the steering wheel. Then he rabbit-punched again, the side of his hand slicing up, jolting into the underpart of Stegman's nose, snapping his head back. Hard enough, that meant blinding pain. A little harder, it meant death. This wasn't quite hard enough to kill.

Stegman moaned, spittle bubbling at the corners of his mouth. Parker was suddenly disgusted. He didn't want any more of this, only to get it over. He picked up the gun by the barrel, swung four times, and Stegman was dead.

—from **The Hunter**

INTRODUCTION

There is no way to improve on the above passage. Each word carries more than its face-value weight. Each sentence wastes no breath and no time. Each thought wastes no meaning, and each meaning requires little thought because it is so self-evident. Yet the implications loom large and mysterious—who? what? why? Even out of context, the terse language draws you in. The staccato burst of words hits its target like a particularly tight group of slugs. The violence in the passage is mirrored by that burst of .38-caliber words.

I read my first Donald Westlake novel over a quarter of a century ago. I'm certain it was **The Hot Rock**, though I can't remember whether I read it in response to seeing the movie, or whether I read the novel first and was later delighted to learn it had been filmed. It didn't matter—in those days of youth, with time stretching forever before me, I kept a list culled from the beginning credits of every movie I saw. "Based on the book by…" If I thought there was even a glimmer of a possibility I would like the movie, I jotted down the book's author for later transfer to the master list. This was how I came to read the Raymond Chandler and Ian Fleming canons, and such diverse novels as **King Rat, Planet of the Apes, The Poseidon Adventure, Escape from Colditz, Bridge on the River Kwai**, and (yes) **Love Story**. I had varied tastes. I was a true reading junky, and I loved how my reading led to movies and movies led to more reading.

Donald Westlake's **The Hot Rock** was a hilarious caper in which a likable but luckless bunch of professional thieves led by John Dortmunder are forced to keep stealing the same diamond from location after location, each more outrageous than the last. Indeed, Westlake almost single-handedly invented the comic caper, which survives to this day as a subgenre of mystery and crime fiction. But a decade before giving a life of comic crime to the burglar named after a German beer, Westlake brought another thief to life. And this thief, too, like Dortmunder, has survived to this day.

Parker.

No first name.

Just Parker.

THIS IS PARKER

He was tall and lean with corded veins and hard, tanned flesh. His torso was creased by old scars. His legs had a bony angularity to them; the muscles were etched against the bones. His hands were big, thick, knotted with veins; they were made for gripping an axe, or a rock. When he picked up the .32 again, his hand made it look like a toy.

—from **The Outfit**

THE LURE OF CRIME

Though hard-boiled fiction traditionally portrays the detective ("good") side, Westlake clearly enjoyed bringing to the fore the other ("evil") side, the criminal's side. As Magill's **Critical Survey of Mystery and Detective Fiction** points out, "these novels draw the reader into sympathy with, or least suspended judgment toward, Parker and Alan Grofield." Why does this tactic work? Perhaps we all want to "walk on the wild side," and be a little bad. Actors often acknowledge the fact that it's more fun to play an antagonist than a protagonist, unless the two are blurred together for increased complexity. Movie villains are celebrated as much as they are reviled—see the Batman universe, for instance. But Westlake taps into something more equivocal with Parker and the rest of the heist experts in the series, for instead of making them colorful he has chosen to make them normal, almost

bland. They are skilled in various aspects of the science of robbery, but otherwise they might as well be technicians working in foundries or factories. The darkness perhaps comes from the matter-of-fact way in which they approach their work. Indeed, the organizational aspect of each operation is as important here as in any Frederick Forsyth novel, leading toward a major thematic coup. Magill again: "Engaged by the detailed planning and execution of the caper, a reader temporarily suspends the disapproval that such an immoral enterprise would normally elicit. Thus, the reader experiences the release of vicarious participation in antisocial behavior."

Or it's just fun to be the bad guy. Parker is, having the chance to "stick it to the Man." Parker will remain one of crime fiction's most vivid refusals to play by the rules, retaining his puzzling charisma despite his lack of colorful characteristics and a clever first name.

Parker.

No first name.

Just Parker.

WESTLAKE'S STARK STYLE

It's interesting to note the linear and nonlinear approach to the patented Westlake simple plot, in which each individual timeline also folds back over the others and is explored at length. Rather than spend a little time with each POV character and keeping all action simultaneous, Westlake chooses to simply go back over a specific time period from another POV, employing a much less colorful narrative voice to summarize the character's history, actions, and motivations. In essence, Westlake takes a cinematic approach to the action, describing it almost in terms of the establishing shot. His voice remains aloof, almost a parody of how Parker himself might describe the events.

While perhaps this version of noir has come and gone as a style, it is amazingly effective—economic, concise almost to a fault, and emotionless (much like Parker). This stylistic quirk explains how Westlake managed to keep his novels—certainly Stark's—so clean and crisp...and so compulsively readable.

About one of his most successful pseudonyms, Westlake himself writes: "The name was Richard Stark—'Richard' from Richard Widmark, whose Tommy Udo in 'Kiss of Death' defined a generation of villains, and 'Stark' because that's what I wanted the writing to be."

Parker was supposed to be caught at the end of **The Hunter**, but an editor at Pocket Books wanted him to escape so that Westlake could write more Parker novels. This Westlake did, until he couldn't do it any more. "I don't know why Richard Stark retired. In 1974, and subsequently, I tried several times to put him back to work, but he was tired and leaden. His imagination was gone, the simplicity of his prose was gone, the coldness of his view was gone. It never worked. (On the other hand, I've learned from embarrassing experience never to make absolute statements about the future.)" Indeed, possibly due to the popular demand about which Westlake seems astonished, Stark and Parker returned in 1997. Though some of Stark's new flaws, as Westlake complained, would be visible in **Comeback** and later in **Backflash**, he managed to resurrect an anti-hero of ambiguous age and outdated mentality who could still exist on the periphery of our rapid-transit, rapid-communicating electronic world.

PLAYING THE NAME GAME

Westlake chose the name Richard Stark to write about Parker, signaling the starkness of the prose as he has said, but possibly also the hero's moral underpinnings. One certainty is that Westlake's choice of character names, and sometimes place names, is always important, even if the reference in the name is not so obvious.

Referring to Burke Devore, the protagonist in the Westlake novel, **The Ax**, Westlake explains in an on-line interview the intended significance: "Many of the names in the book have to do with death one way or another. For 'Burke,' one of the meanings is to strangle. And 'Devore' is to devour. Another example in the book

is 'Longholme,' in Massachusetts, and in old slang 'the long home' is the grave." It's true that one could enjoy the novel (about a downsized middle-manager who decides to whack not only a poor schlub who holds the job he covets, but also the likeliest replacement candidates) without catching all the death references, but knowing they're there gives the whole enterprise a backhanded literary depth and therefore the kind of legitimacy not usually available to the standard "crime novel." In a *Booklist* interview, Westlake adds: "I thought the book couldn't have enough death in it, so I used town names that referred to death, like Lichgate, which is Scottish for cemetery gate. I just larded it on."

Turning back to Parker, one can see Westlake's preoccupation with names even in the very first Parker novel, **The Hunter**. In it, Parker's nemesis—the man who forces the double-cross which leads to Parker's troubles and eventual revenge—is named Mal Resnick. "Mal" is a French word which means both "evil" and "pain," thus characterizing the scumbag nicely. (Note that in the movie *Payback*, also based on **The Hunter**, the name was changed to "Val"— inexplicably feminizing the character since the first name one might think of would be Valerie, whereas Mal doesn't lead to any obvious male or female names.)

Some of Parker's associates bear symbolic names, either reiterating their jobs (the driver Carlow), their personalities (Grofield the actor has grown beyond the field of professional crime), their ethnicity (Salsa is Hispanic and a bit of a firecracker— and written long before every American understood "salsa" as both food and music), or their personal value to Parker (Handy McKay is "always there," or "handy" for his friend). Buffonish characters have names such as "Tiftus," "Stubbs," "Skimm," or "Fusco."

It would be pointless to search through every book and seek out every name's reference for the purpose of character analysis. Some are too subtle for such an exercise, and others too obvious. Suffice to say that many, if not most, of Westlake's name choices are not random in the least.

When planning each "job," Parker or whoever runs it puts together a "string," the group of men (and more rarely, women) who will pull it off. Sometimes he is pulled into someone else's string, through a common acquaintance. Westlake built up a varied pool of skilled heisters for Parker's strings—drivers, juggers (safe men), lock men, and so on. Several recur quite often, unless they turn out to be double-crossers like George Uhl or George Liss (Westlake must have a feud with a George, since Georges seem to be less than trustworthy). Many of the previous heisters reappear in **Butcher's Moon**, the original end to the Parker series, as part of Parker's army in his war against the mob in Tyler, Ohio. Though Parker sometimes has doubts about someone in a string, he still accepts the job because he either needs the money or it's too sweet a job to pass up. Often, trouble does not come from where it's expected, but trouble always comes and Parker does not always stay ahead of it. There is an ironic, almost deterministic streak running through many of the novels.

STRINGS AND FATE

Each job has someone in charge, running things. Whoever proposed it, whoever bought the plan from someone else (often an inside man or a straight man), or whoever is financing it. Sometimes the money man also runs it, unless another's skill is acknowledged to be better. Parker is often asked to run a job because of his no-nonsense style, and because he is a pro everyone knows will do right by the others. Parker often shops for weapons from illegal dealers in the network, who either know him or accept him once he drops a name they recognize. In the same way, cars and trucks are purchased for each job from not quite legal dealers, who may provide falsified papers to cover a car's history. Parker and his cronies are also known to steal cars for a few hours' use, only to dump them when finished, or to steal a series of cars to leave a trail which turns back onto itself without fingering a new location.

Sometimes a heist goes through a dry run, so that everyone knows what they're supposed to do, but Westlake loves to throw obstacles in Parker's path. A strong realistic streak runs through the novels, as unplanned problems or actions on the part of a fellow heister, or hostage, or security guard, cause a portion of the plan to fall apart and force Parker to improvise on the fly. These sections are generally intense and provide the needed suspense, while still using a deadpan delivery built on simple sentence structure and words rather than sensationalistic descriptions of exaggerated action.

Westlake's use of random events, which Parker accepts as possible in any job, successfully integrates fate (or Fate, if you will) into the equation, and thereby again adds a degree of realism. Parker's personality is perfectly suited to this rather entropic quality—the tendency toward chaos would drive any of us out of the heist business, but unspoken is Parker's enjoyment of such elements. While he would never admit to enjoyment, it's clear that the rush of a well-planned job is self-sustaining. And Parker's aversion to small-talk indicates the focus with which he approaches his work—indeed, Westlake's Parker is nearly incapable of small-talk, though he has trained himself to grunt an answer in all the right places because he is aware that others must tell stories their own way. Parker is a machine, designed for and perfectly suited to a life of crime that parallels a normal person's career. In Parker's universe, he is fated to be an outlaw, or "bent" as Westlake sometimes describes it, perhaps because normal boundaries and rules could never contain him.

PARKER THE ANTI-HERO

On Killing

Parker lowered the gun. There wasn't enough reason to kill these three. It was dangerous to kill when there wasn't enough reason, because after a while killing became the solution to everything, and when you got to thinking that way you were only one step from the chair.

He'd wanted to kill her, to even things, but when he'd seen her he'd known he couldn't.

She was the only one he'd ever met that he didn't feel simply about. With everybody else in the world, the situation was simple. They were in and he worked with them or they were trouble and he took care of them.

—from **The Man with the Getaway Face**

Parker is at heart a pragmatist. Killing is messy, and he'd rather avoid it if possible. On the job, Parker almost never kills unless in self-defense, and he is disgusted by any members of his string who might. But in **The Man with the Getaway Face**, he has no trouble sawing off a head to bring back and prove that the problem is taken care of. It's crude, not quite as neat as a photograph, but it has an appealingly gruesome humorous quality. It's also telling that the character never stoops to such unnecessary violence again, though his mellowing does not keep him from murdering two particularly damaging enemies in the very last book, **Backflash**. But Westlake seems to have realized that our sympathy must lie with Parker, even if uncomfortably, and removing heads goes just too far beyond the occasional shooting to allow that. The series is noteworthy because of its skewed sensibility—"Prepare to root for the bad guy!" was the slogan for the movie *Payback*—and, while not unheard of in the annals of crime fiction by far, it is unusual enough to require some careful thinking. Parker's brutality has to be aimed at people demonstrably worse than he is, or the reader's sympathy will slip. If Parker brutalized bank tellers and innocent bystanders, the house of cards would collapse and with it our ability to "root for the bad guy."

It should be noted that one of Parker's best characteristics is the use of psychology during heists. He speaks in a calm voice, asks people their names (and uses appropriate nicknames: "They call you Bob?"), and agrees with people who inform him they will be happy to identify him and send him to prison. Westlake repeatedly makes the point that Parker's style and demeanor both go a long way to making his heists a success, leaving room only for Fate to enter the picture and mess it up. Parker's awareness of the random possibilities

makes his tendency to avoid agonizing over spilt milk, so to speak, a great part of his charm. Emotion is a waste of time, and regret is the worst emotion a heister can harbor, according to Westlake. Revenge, on the other hand, is just fine as a motivator.

Sex

Every anti-hero needs some quirks, and here's Parker's best: before a heist he doesn't care about women at all and lives like a monk. But after a successful heist… well, that's different.

During the planning of a job, the build-up and the waiting, he'd never been any good with a woman, not even Lynn. But as soon as the job was done and turned out right he was always as randy as a stallion with the stud fee paid.

—from **The Man with the Getaway Face**

… immediately after a job, he was always insatiable, satyric, like a groom on a honeymoon after a long and honorable engagement.

—from **The Outfit**

Some of Parker's brutality is strangely channeled toward women, a fact which may not pass in today's PC world, but which seems to make sense in the noir tradition. An anti-hero must hurt some around him in order to make his character acceptably ambiguous, and Parker's tendency to be overly physical with women is a way to achieve this state.

Jacksonville was twenty miles away, so that's where he went for a whore. She was the same as the Richmond whore and the Columbia whore, disinterested till he hurt her a little. He didn't get his kicks from hurting whores, it was just the only way he knew to get them interested.

—from **The Man with the Getaway Face**

It should be noted that, like all series characters, Parker does mellow somewhat as he (and his creator) ages. The above examples are taken from the second book, but by the last book, Parker is almost sentimental about Noelle, the woman needed in the string. And by then he has also nearly settled down with his own woman, Claire, who makes a home for him when he is not working. Westlake doesn't waste words describing their love, settling for: "…now he and Claire were together most of the time, warming themselves at each other's fire, liking the calm." (**Backflash**)

In **Murder Off the Rack**, Westlake says of Peter Rabe, an obvious Fifties influence on his own work, "It is never entirely right or entirely wrong to identify a writer with his or her heroes. The people who carry our stories may be us, or our fears about ourselves, or our dreams about ourselves." These are revealing words indeed, from the creator of Parker.

No first name.

Just Parker.

BOOK BY BOOK

The Hunter (1963)

Parker returns from the dead—and a prison farm, from which he's escaped after killing a guard—itching for revenge. It's obvious from the way he gets himself on his feet that he's not a nice guy, but his drive for payback is understandable in a primal, gut-wrenching sort of way. First he visits his wife, Lynn, who shot him on behalf of Mal Resnick, a double-crossing partner. Lynn is somewhat of a tragic figure in that she did not want to kill her husband, and the guilt has rendered her almost useless as a human being. Resnick pays her a monthly fee to live and keep quiet, but he has long since given up trying to own her sexually. Parker's anger is subdued, but leads to Lynn's pill overdose suicide, which leaves him out in the cold regarding tracing Resnick. Parker waits until the first of the month brings a delivery boy with a new monthly payment, and extracts enough information to climb one rung of the ladder that leads to Resnick.

The story's onward rush is halted by a long flashback detailing the crime—how it was set up, and how Mal Resnick double-crossed everyone involved and why. Desperate to repay the Outfit money he cost them in a botched job and thereby resurrect his career in the mob world, Mal Resnick recruits Parker and Lynn for a scheme set up by an acquaintance. The job is a hijack of money being paid by South American revolutionaries for a load of arms and munitions, an event that is to take place on an old island airbase. The idea is simple—kill all the participants and make off with the cash. No doubt is left about Parker's willingness to kill, as he and his string murder a dozen gunrunners and their clients pretty much in cold blood. But then Mal plants seeds of doubt into the mind of one accomplice, convincing him that Parker is going to double-cross and they have to act first. Mal then forces Lynn to take part—Parker's life for hers—and they leave Parker for dead, after Mal divests himself of even the last partner. The problem is, no one checks to make sure Parker's dead. Parker escapes the fire and manages to mostly recover from his wounds, but he's picked up for vagrancy and sent to the prison farm.

As Parker tracks Resnick, it's obvious that he will stop at nothing to have his revenge. He traces the messenger to a taxi service run by Stegman and then threatens Stegman with death unless he helps lead Parker to Resnick. Stegman gives Parker a tidbit, but also flags Resnick's attention, and for this he will indeed die. As Parker tracks Resnick, the cowardly Resnick is warned and his first move is to ask the Outfit for help. Put in his place by Mr. Carter, an Outfit executive, Resnick is left out to hang—if he can take care of his problem, it will look better for him in the underworld. But it's his problem. And, by the way, can he please move out of the Outfit's swanky hotel until this is all taken care of? Wouldn't want a mess to clean up and blow the Outfit's cover.

So Resnick and Parker begin the dance, circling ever closer to each other as each attempts to outthink the other. Parker looks up a hooker he used to chauffeur, and it's obvious there might have been a thing, so she helps him—only a little, though, because her paychecks come by way of the Outfit, too. Still, she puts Parker onto the Outfit hotel, but he breaks in only to find that Mal has flown the coop. Parker takes this sad fact out on Wanda, now Rose, physically abusing her until she makes a phone call that garners the information he wants—Mal's new address, given up by the escort service even now sending him a girl for the night.

In the meantime, from Mal's point of view we have seen him deal with the Outfit, get booted out of the safe hotel, and eventually decide to spread word on the street that if Parker asks about him he should be told where Mal now lives—and Mal would hole up with a couple freelance gunmen (no regular Outfit guys allowed, said Mr. Carter) and lie in wait. Then he arrogantly orders up the classy blonde whore who is in bed with him when Parker comes through the window.

Parker really only wants revenge, and the $45 grand Mal took from him doesn't really become an issue until this point, when he's about to kill his nemesis. This is the payback he really wanted. But now it seems only right that the Outfit refund him the money—after all, it was his money to begin with, not Mal's to give. Parker forces Carter's name and location out of a slightly hopeful Mal, then Westlake proves his Starkness by having Parker kill Mal with his bare hands—all in less than four pages.

Parker knows the Outfit won't just hand it over, but he visits Carter and asks about as nicely as he can. When Carter refuses, Parker gets him to call one of the two men whose word is law in New York, Bronson. Parker says, pay me or I kill Carter. Carter lunges for a gun in a drawer, and Parker shoots him, reinforcing his claim. Next, he promises to visit Bronson. But first he visits Carter's counterpart, Fairfax and holds him up until he calls Bronson. Faced with another loss of a top underling, Bronson caves and promises the money, calling Parker a mosquito that can be swatted anytime. Parker sets up a meeting at the end of a subway line. Of course Bronson sends an army of innocuous-looking gunsels to do in Parker, but Parker is just too good— he spots them all and sends them back or holds them up, getting the best of them all and ending up with a suitcase full of money, more than enough to buy him a new face and to replenish all the stashes his wife had depleted after "killing" him.

In a typical Westlake move, though,

Parker is picked up by two cops who paid attention to him earlier in the book and suspected him of running narcotics or other contraband. Sheer luck doesn't usually run with Westlake protagonists, and Parker is no exception. Managing to bull his way out of custody, Parker grabs one of his two identical suitcases and flees—only to find that he has grabbed the wrong suitcase, the one with his clothes.

At this point, a normal reader grits his teeth and screams in frustration. After all, this kind of scene is more likely to be found in the funny capers of Westlake's Dortmunder novels. But Parker is not burdened with emotion, as Westlake has said, so the last chapter finds him and three accomplices robbing an Outfit operation—a St. Louis collection center for bookie joints. Parker's split, twenty-three thousand, seems to make up for all his bad luck just fine. Now, time for that plastic surgery.

The Man with the Getaway Face (1963)

Parker inaugurates his new face, courtesy of Dr. Adler, a safe doctor who uses a private sanitarium as a front for his discreet plastic surgery by request business. Then Parker is pulled into a job, an armored-car heist fingered by an old heister's girlfriend, a diner waitress with a bad attitude and bigger plans for the take than even her boyfriend Skimm knows. Parker needs the job so badly to refill his coffers that he secretly bankrolls it himself with three grand of his own dwindling stash. In a good scene, though improbable, Parker leaves five grand in a typewriter case with a motel owner for a $500 fee. "I don't like banks," Parker explains.

When Dr. Adler is murdered, his "staff," a punch-drunk former Communist Party agitator and a cook who's a former whore, figure one of the last three patients did it to keep his new face a secret. So they begin the process of trying to trace them by sending the dull-brained Stubbs after each of the three, while May, the cook, waits for one month. If she doesn't hear from Stubbs, she'll blow the whistle on all three suspects.

Unfortunately, Parker is in the middle of planning the heist when all this

continued on page 188

The Hunter Resurfaces as *Payback*
(A few comments on the film)

The first striking fact to register is that Brian Helgeland's direction and camera work both seem appropriate for the bleakness of both Parker's world and his soul. Blues and greys and concrete and metal, bleached of almost all color, permeate the early establishing shots. Parker's world is a cold, grey hell. Not coincidentally, no modern buildings are even to be glimpsed in this metropolitan wasteland. The occasional Eighties car may be identified in that fraction of a second before the picture blurs and it is gone. The phones all sport dials— including car phones. A security guard seems to be wearing a Secret Service-like wire and ear-bud, but there's not a cell phone anywhere. In fact, if one were to try to peg the time frame, one would have to settle on the early Seventies—if disco and funk never existed.

By contrast, John Boorman's vision for *Point Blank*, the first film based on **The Hunter**, is a surreal blend of late-Sixties California hip and more traditional noir elements which come crashing together like runaway locomotives. The Los Angeles setting just doesn't fit the story, and the mobsters are too cool in their shades and light-colored suits.

Evident early on in *Payback* is Helgeland's surprisingly loyal vision of Parker, here tritely called "Porter" due to a contractual clause designed by Donald Westlake to avoid being saddled with a poor choice of lead actor. The character's the same, so let's call him Parker anyway. Parker's an asshole through and through who doesn't take guff, or "no" for an answer. He's still after his former partner, who double-crossed him, and he still wants his cut from the job, here bumped to $70 grand from the original $45, and nearly the amount for which Parker started a mob war in **Butcher's Moon**. Gibson's Parker manages to portray this pit-bull quality, which is why there's no reason at all for the hokey voice-over, especially if it's used to spout clichés like "Nice guys finish last." Which it is. The real Parker, that two-dimensional Parker who still seems pretty rounded to me, doesn't rationalize his behavior this way. He doesn't have to. If Richard Stark allowed Donald Westlake to attempt explaining it, the mystique would slide right off. If Westlake chose to blame it all on a strict father and weak mother, say, the character would collapse under the weight of analysis...suddenly you'd have to compare his actions with those of real people. By making his instincts mysterious, Stark has forced Parker to work harder for our sympathy, thereby creating a more memorable character.

For a while, it seems Gibson understood all this. Except for the voice-over, his version of Parker has the right world-weary quality—he's seen too much and done too much, been to the edge and back, and now he's pissed. He wants revenge, and he wants his money back. He doesn't care who he gets it from, or how. This is Parker, exactly as Westlake intended him. Still, in Boorman's *Point Blank* Lee Marvin makes a better Parker (Walker) than Mel Gibson by virtue of his stony, faraway look. He's truer to the author's image, but Gibson's Parker is perhaps more believable. Gibson loses his take on Parker when he allows the performance to slide into the typical crazy-eyed Mel. Too many plot element changes take *Point Blank* away from its source material, while *Payback* sticks closer to the milieu we expect from reading the novel. In a head-to-head, *Payback* wins by a half-star, though Lee Marvin made an awesomely wooden Parker.

But the *Payback* vision goes bad when (apparently) Gibson didn't like the relentlessly dark tone of both the film and the role. It was okay to play tough with bad guys, but women and dogs? Gibson apparently reshot the last third of the film, most likely with himself as director, watching over his own image. In Gibson's reshaping hands, the film takes a strange turn—it continues to beat relentlessly at your temples, like the mobster's sledge-hammer (a particularly gruesome addition), but it diverges from its truthful inner core by seeming to say: "But look! See, Porter/

Parker isn't as bad a guy as you thought! He has a soft spot for the girl and her dog!" The real Parker, Richard Stark's Parker, would never allow that digression. Test audiences are the movie studios' worst invention—who ever thought you could select one of several endings for *Taxi Driver*, or God help us, *The Godfather*? Who ever thought movies and films should please audiences by fulfilling their expectations? Since when did surprise and exploration drop off the film-maker's job description? Apparently Gibson thought he should end up with our sympathy—not just because Porter/Parker is a good guy compared to the bad guys, but because deep down inside he's a good guy period. Maybe a good guy with bad breaks. Maybe a good guy with a crappy childhood. In any case, Gibson wants us to like Porter/Parker—despite the fact that the uniqueness of the character is our sympathy when none would normally be given. Gibson saves his image in the last third of the film, but he derails the vision.

Helgeland (either fired or a walk-out) tried—God knows he did. Entire runs of dialogue are lifted damn near verbatim from the novel. But the film is pierced through the heart by Gibson's egotistical, last-minute remorse and turned into a lie if you've read the novel—in which Parker roughs up his old hooker girlfriend even after she's helped him. He threatens to kill her if she lied to him. That Parker'd never share the swag with her, or save her dog. *Payback*'s Parker is a lie because when Gibson says "Just drive, baby," at the end, you know the real Parker would have driven himself no matter what his toes had been through. This Parker is a lie because he must have seen every Tarantino flick in which some gunman looks stylish firing double sideways semi-autos when there's no earthly reason to mess with the recoil of two bucking handguns in this manner. Not if you want to survive the shoot-out. By contrast, Marvin's Parker shoots his revolver with conviction and displays an economy of words that Westlake must have admired—Marvin's lines must have fit six pages out of the 120. And Marvin's physical violence, coiled within during quiet scenes,

but allowed to rampage without facial expression during fights, seems just a touch more like the Parker we know from the novels.

As a stand-alone film, *Payback* works well enough on an action level, even with its tacked-on Asian-thug sideshow lifted apparently from John Woo. Lucy Alexis Liu damn near steals her scenes as a beautiful dominatrix really turned on by violence, though she has no equivalent in the novel. Greg Henry makes a palpably sleazy Val (inexplicably changed from the original meaningful name, Mal), though John Vernon's Mal in *Point Blank* appears more dangerous and conniving without sniveling in his scenes. William Devane's unctuous Mr. Carter hits the mark better than Lloyd Bochner's performance in *Point Blank*. Other casting comparisons with *Point Blank* can't be made because Boorman's film takes a different path, while *Payback* wants to follow Westlake's map. Strangely, James Coburn fits the Fairfax role quite well, especially his concern for the costly suits he has collected. Kris Kristofferson has been fine in many an asshole role, but here he is just too darn cowboyish and not enough the head of the Outfit. He seems way too lost for words in dealing with Porter/Parker and his threats. And the tacked-on kidnapping merely plays like the plot device it is. Maria Bello is just too fresh-looking to have lived a long hooker's life, and her heart of gold routine just doesn't fit in the Parker milieu. In Parker's world, everybody has an angle. In **The Hunter**, the character wearily packs her bags after telling Parker what he needs to know, and thanks him for at least giving her a head-start—the Outfit will be after her for having helped Parker, and they won't care that he threatened her. In *Payback*, she somehow sees Porter/Parker as her way out of this life—never mind the fact that Porter/Parker knows no other life. The lie rears its ugly head again.

*** (if you haven't read the novel)
** (if you have)

continued from page 185

comes up and bites him. Stubbs blunders into the set-up and Parker, who claims he doesn't relish killing unless there's a reason, sees the danger immediately. If he lets Stubbs go, one of the other suspects—the guilty one, perhaps—is just as likely as Parker to get the drop on the old guy and kill him, and May would blow the whistle on Parker, too. So, Parker puts Stubbs on ice at the deserted farm that was to be their hideout, and they rotate letting him out of the cellar once a day like a dog.

A bigger problem for Parker is that he and Handy McKay know that Alma, the waitress, plans to double-cross them and most likely Skimm, too. The job involves two trucks and a car boxing in the armored car as it sits in the diner's parking lot during its regular Monday stop, but Parker and Handy have also scouted on their own and know where and how the cross will take place. In essence, Parker is running two simultaneous jobs and trying to keep Stubbs alive but out of his hair for two weeks.

When it's time for the robbery, it goes off like clockwork. Unfortunately, its anti-climactic quality makes it a weak center for the novel. Even the double-cross is taken care of offstage. By the time Handy gets to Parker, "the job was finished and Parker was putting the Sauer away again under his shirt. Alma had run only three steps from the car." Alma had already stabbed Skimm, so Parker and Handy split the take and head their separate ways as they had planned. Parker goes to release Stubbs, but the old man has escaped—on the very day he would have ceased to be a problem. Now Parker has to find him before Stubbs tracks down the second suspect.

Here the novel takes a bizarre (but characteristic) digression when it follows Stubbs through his confinement at the farm, and his eventual escape. The POV shift is jarring because it's so different from Parker's and, realistically, it's rather dull. Stubbs finds his car and collapses at a third rate hotel, where his money pays for a house doctor and nurse to get him back on his feet again after malnutrition and fatigue. Stubbs has almost forgotten his ordeal by now, and he's back on the hunt for Dr. Adler's killer. First stop, Charles F. Wells of New York. A

digression within the digression takes us briefly through how Charles Wells made his illegal money in postwar Florida land swindles, how he fled the country only to hope for a safe return many years later, and how Dr. Adler's work had provided him the new identity he needed—but only after Adler's death had sealed the secret. His killing of Adler initiates the chain of events that brings Stubbs to the point of almost ruining Parker's armored-car heist.

Parker returns to Dr. Adler's place to find it run-down and managed by May the cook and two Neanderthal boyfriends. He has to beat heads to make them understand that he didn't kill the doctor. He doesn't want to kill all three, so he again makes a bargain. He'll find the next patient on the list and determine if he is guilty, then he and Stubbs will return to the sanitarium and Stubbs will vouch for Parker.

Stubbs finally locates Wells and pays a visit, only to find that someone called him beforehand and put him on his guard. As Stubbs dies, killed by Wells, he sees that Wells has another visitor—Parker, whose call came just before Stubbs arrived. This sort of coincidence is true to life and infuriating, and typical of Westlake. Parker now shoots Wells in the ankle and tortures him, making him write a confession that Parker can bring to Adler's staff. Then a single bullet to the heart silences Charles Wells forever, perhaps an appropriate payback for the grief he has caused Parker.

Westlake's humorous side takes over in a grim last chapter, in which Parker returns yet again to Adler's sanitarium and presents May and her henchmen not only with the confession of Charles Wells, but also his head—probably Parker's most grotesque act, of the kind never repeated in the entire series. Westlake clearly realized that he'd taken Parker too far.

The Man with the Getaway Face is one of the weakest of the Parker novels—it has all the elements, but seems to stitch them together in the wrong order, deriving very little suspense from events that should have been suspenseful. There is hardly any suspense at all in the robbery set-up, and even the attempted double-cross plot is resolved almost as an afterthought, offstage.

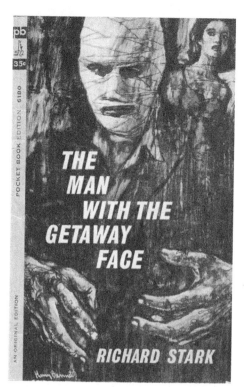

POCKET BOOK EDITION 6180

AN ORIGINAL EDITION

**THE
MAN
WITH THE
GETAWAY
FACE**

RICHARD STARK

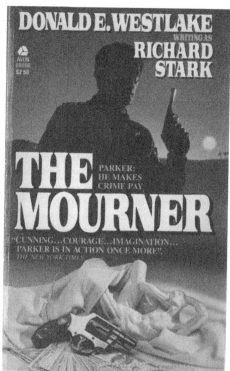

DONALD E. WESTLAKE
WRITING AS
**RICHARD
STARK**

AVON
88868
$2.50

**THE
MOURNER**

PARKER:
HE MAKES
CRIME PAY

"CUNNING...COURAGE...IMAGINATION...
PARKER IS IN ACTION ONCE MORE!"
THE NEW YORK TIMES

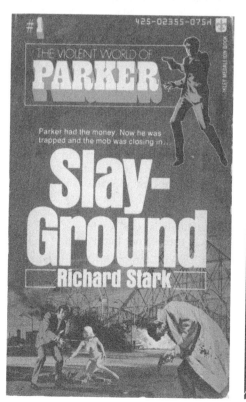

#1

425-02355-075H

THE VIOLENT WORLD OF
PARKER

Parker had the money. Now he was
trapped and the mob was closing in...

**Slay-
Ground**

Richard Stark

DONALD E. WESTLAKE
WRITING AS
**RICHARD
STARK**

**BUTCHER'S
MOON** PARKER:
HE HITS HARD,
FAST, AND DEADLY

"CUNNING...COURAGE...IMAGINATION...
PARKER IS IN ACTION ONCE MORE."
THE NEW YORK TIMES

The Outfit (1963)

Parker barely escapes a murder attempt in the first few pages—a real attention-grabber of an opening. The attempt fails and Parker's date gets all excited at the prospect of torturing the prisoner to find out who sent him. Parker is impressed with Bett Harrow, not only rich and beautiful, but nonplussed to learn about his other life. But when she disappears with his gun, after displaying her new-found talent in the amateur art of persuasion, he wonders about blackmail. Especially since the hitman, Stern, may not have survived (one of Westlake's very few ambiguities). Also, Parker knows that the Outfit is indeed after him, as had been promised—and they know about his new face. It's now time to fulfill his promise as well, so he sets about writing letters to every professional thief he knows or has worked with. The letter, somewhat coarse and perhaps a bit too uneducated, making Parker seem strangely semi-illiterate, explains that the Syndicate has wronged him and, if the recipient has ever cased a mob job before, just for fun, then now would be a good time to hit it, ripping off the Syndicate in Parker's name and keeping the take.

In fulfillment of the promise Parker had made Bronson in **The Hunter**, his letter leads to twelve robberies on Parker's behalf, totaling one million in 1963 dollars—a real blow to the Outfit.

Parker gets Fairfax at gunpoint again, wanting to know who would take over from Bronson. The answer is Karns, so Parker talks to him by phone and makes a deal—Parker will go after Bronson with the understanding that Karns will call off the contract when he succeeds to the leadership of the Outfit. Several of the robberies hitting the Outfit are shown in great detail, even though Parker is not personally involved. Each is clever and professional, as one would expect from Parker's friends.

Meanwhile, Parker and Handy McKay track Bronson to his lair in Buffalo, where they bide their time learning his schedule before invading his house and, in a wild room-to-room shoot-out, kill him and his bodyguards. By this point in the book,

Parker seems fated to beat Bronson, who has grown as complacent as his underlings—his bodyguards indulge in a nightly Monopoly game for money—and who has just learned of the complacency from an underling specifically called in to "investigate" the robberies. This underling represents the new Outfit, the corporate mob, because he acts as investigator, accountant, consultant, and corporate hatchetman—he carries a briefcase, not a gun, and when Bronson has met his fate he is pragmatic enough to know that Parker has won and that business will no longer be conducted as it was. Parker and McKay let him live so he can bring a message to Karns—that Parker will begin contacting his friends and calling off the robbery spree, so the terms of their deal will be honored soon, if not immediately. The name of this corporate employee? Quill. Westlake's penchant for names again, reminding us that this guy does his killing with a pen instead of a gun.

In the end, McKay agrees to postpone his retirement to a tiny diner he wants to buy in Maine, and instead travel with Parker to Florida, where they'll meet Bett Harrow and figure out what she wants for the assassin's pistol—the one with Parker's fingerprints all over it.

The Mourner (1963)

Parker's partner, Handy, is late. Two down-and-out assassins make an attempt on Parker's life in his hotel room. Parker's too good for them and they fail, and he is led to a girl and a fat man, who also shoots at him and runs. Then, in a bit guaranteed to keep Parker as unlikable as possible, he tortures the girl to find out where Handy is being kept.

It turns out that Parker is looking for a statue—The Mourner—that Ralph Harrow (Bett's businessman father) badly wants for his collection (he's a romantic, apparently). The fat man is Auguste Menlo, a sort of secret policeman from one of the Communist countries whose mission is to apprehend Kapor, a diplomat who has been stashing money to defect—and who owns The Mourner. But Menlo sees his opportunity, and now he wants Kapor's money for himself. Parker and Handy and Menlo decide to work together, knowing full well there will be double-crosses. During the job at Kapor's fancy house, Menlo shoots both Handy and Parker and leaves them for dead, taking Kapor's hundred grand and the statue. He is able to bed Bett Harrow, too, who likes his "power" now that he has "killed" Parker. But Parker returns from the dead once again to make a deal with Kapor—he'll watch out for a wounded Handy, and Parker will manage to recover half his money.

Then there's a strange POV shift to Menlo, as he reaches Miami to enjoy his new-found wealth and girl. Menlo is about to sell the Mourner to Ralph Harrow when he sees Parker, who has in the meantime reached Harrow, and Menlo unexpectedly commits suicide by biting down on his poison tooth!

It's disappointing to snatch the confrontation from Parker's hands at the last second.

Strange ending to a strange book. Parker takes Bett to Bed. And why not?

The Score (1964)

Parker is bored, so when he's offered a job that sounds crazy, he's more interested than he ought to be… He's pulled in by Paulus, a jugger—a safe-cracker—who has a friend, Edgars, who has set up a bigger job than usual. Indeed, the target is a whole copper mining town, complete with two banks, jewelry stores, police department, and so on, with a projected take of at least $250 grand. Parker rather matter-of-factly kills a tail put on him by Edgars, Paulus's friend, who seems not quite right. Parker doesn't like the job set-up, but…he's bored. So he does what he does best and looks at the plan, whittling down a projected 25-man team to twelve, thereby increasing everybody's take.

The job goes smoothly enough. Parker's gang takes over the police station, the firehouse, the telephone company, and wrecks the radio station. But Edgars has a grudge, all right—he was the town's police chief, dismissed after a grand jury couldn't indict him on numerous charges.

His revenge comes late in the job, when he machine-guns the cops and the firemen, then uses hand grenades to start fires and destroy the town. One grenade explosion kills him, but not before he has killed one of the team. Meanwhile, Grofield has picked up a girlfriend—one of the ladies at the telephone company office—which is typical for the actor whose charm can't be turned off, not even during a robbery. With the unplanned murders, the job's gone sour though, and this streak continues after the gang heads for their hideout, a group of abandoned sheds near a river polluted by an abandoned copper strip-mine. After three days in the hideout, Paulus gets itchy and decides to pull out. He is accidentally killed during the face-off with Parker and two others. But the money is split among less players, and eventually Parker ends up with Edgars' blonde squeeze, in a nice—if familiar—noir scene.

The Jugger (1965)

Parker comes to Sagamore, Nebraska, to decide whether he has to kill Joe Sheer, his "mailman" contact for a few years. Joe has passed on messages sent by acquaintances attempting to recruit Parker for jobs, and occasionally put Parker in touch with other heisters when more manpower was needed on a job of Parker's. Now Joe has sent Parker a note about being in trouble, and Parker knows that if the old man gives him up, Parker's Charles Willis cover will be compromised. But Joe is already dead, and Parker is immediately beset by people looking for "it," Joe's supposed stash from his life of crime. There's a penny-ante heister named Tiftus and his chick, and then the chief of police, and Joe's neighbor kid—all looking with one eye toward a hidden fortune in cash. But Tiftus is mysteriously killed, Chief Younger pulls Parker in for the murder, and a Fed named Regan takes an interest. Parker pretends to work with Younger to find the stash, which he doesn't believe exists.

In a sort of Lawrence Block move, Parker arranges things so it looks as though Younger killed the boy and Tiftus, then heads out of town with the chick and his Willis cover intact—he thinks. But in Miami it all falls apart. The Feds are looking for Charles Willis, so Parker has to run—abandoning his cover identity and at least sixty grand in various stashes now too dangerous to recover. The ending is about as bleak as a Parker novel can get, and about as noir.

The Seventh (1966) Also as **The Split**

A superb noir opening starts this novel—Parker goes out for cigarettes and beer and returns ten minutes later to find that someone has murdered his nude female companion—with a sword off the wall. And taken the suitcase filled with $140 grand he was baby-sitting after a successful heist. When two cops arrive—way too quickly—Parker tells them *he* called the police and the ploy almost works, until they look in the closet and find the guns (including submachine guns). Parker manages to elude them and heads for the abode of one Dan Kifka—the guy who set up the job, a college stadium game-day knockover—when a guy gloms onto him and Parker shakes him off, but then the tail is killed when Parker's shot at by a mysterious assailant outside of Kifka's building. Kifka seems legitimately sick, in bed and with a cute brainless co-ed taking care of him, and Parker has to own up to the other five heisters about the robbery...which goes down like the proverbial lead airship. In the meantime, someone is still gunning for Parker. Most of the string believe him, but one half of a gay team (Feccio and Negli) doesn't. Parker's plan is simple—they need to locate and interrogate the shooter to get their loot back, and Parker *needs* his split because of his cover being blown in **The Jugger**.

Parker is always willing to take chances. He goes right to the cop in charge—Dougherty—and manages to obtain a list of guys who knew the woman with whom he'd shacked up to lie low. Dougherty knows what's going on, but he's intrigued, and he wants to play it so that he catches all those involved. Meanwhile, Parker and his string start taking a "survey" while eventually leading up to the cops'

list. When they start visiting names on the police list, all hell breaks loose because the cops put people *inside* at each place, a nice and tricky move courtesy of Dougherty. Everybody gets killed or caught, Negli goes gunning for Parker because Feccio died, and Parker has to kill the dead woman's old boyfriend—the mystery shooter—who has enough cash on him to make up Parker's "split" ($16 grand). It's a very ironic end, a sort of "even-Stephen" denouement that Westlake would have given Dortmunder if Stark hadn't appropriated it for Parker.

The novel is also noteworthy for the big point of view shift to the boyfriend, who is basically an unknown character—in a mystery, that would be cheating, but this is a crime novel, and it's okay to spring a shooter out of a hat, because that's the way one would pop up in real life. Fate once again.

The Handle (1966)

Yancy and another thug take Parker out to Cockaigne, an island in the Gulf of Mexico 47 miles from Galveston. The island belongs legally to Cuba, but Wolfgang Baron (Baron von Altstein) operates a high-priced casino/whorehouse there, complete with private shuttle service. Parker is here, in the middle of planning a heist, because Karns—head of the Outfit—has offered him the job of robbing the island and destroying it, because Baron won't split profits with the Outfit and they hate the competition which is siphoning off the mainland's big spenders.

Parker brings in Grofield and Salsa, two he trusts, and Heenan—a boatman—whom he doesn't quite trust. Heenan's a stoolie sprung from jail by the Feds, who want Parker to do the job and bring them Baron von Altstein in trade for Parker's own getaway. Parker's mistrust of Heenan boils over, so a new boatman is brought in, and the string is now complete.

Then the POV switches and we see Baron relaxing—faking out Cubans and Russians with his fake spy "network," a nice scam in order to keep his elite hands-off status on the island, all while raking in gambling profits. Then Heenan—the spurned boatman—shows up to warn him; after all, Heenan had been a part of the string long enough to get the gist of what was up, and now he figures he can turn a profit by selling out Parker's game. Thus warned, Baron prepares for the eventual attack, knowing it'll come because of the Outfit. Meanwhile, Parker's string keeps the Feds guessing as to when the job will go down, spending eight eventless nights on the island as gamblers while casing the operation. The Feds are shadowing Parker and his men, and have to be taken care of as well.

When the deal goes down, Grofield is able to get rid of his pet Feds, but Salsa is captured and tortured by Baron's tame Nazi. In the melee, Grofield is shot four times, but he is still able to help Parker with the goods. The fires and explosions turn the island into an inferno. A cowardly Baron manages to shoot both Parker and Grofield, leaving Parker for dead and taking a seriously wounded Grofield with him in a boat headed for Mexico, where things don't turn out quite as he expected. Meanwhile, Parker plays the Feds his way and soon he's on a helicopter tracking Baron and Grofield and the suitcase full of cash they managed to take off the island. While Parker is surely after the money, reading between the lines here suggests a certain loyalty to Grofield— as long as the actor-thief might be alive, Parker finds an excuse to look for him. And the search pays off, for Parker manages to come up with both the suitcase and a barely breathing Grofield.

This novel is difficult to judge. On the one hand, it's a more complex plot than Westlake has allowed Stark to try. On the other hand, it has an unreal feel to it, taking place as it does on an island casino—more of a James Bond feel, especially when the place goes up at the end in a typical Bondian orgy of death and destruction. Then the ending takes the book in yet another direction, winding up the story in a most surreal fashion. Successful at what it attempts, this chapter in the life of Parker nevertheless shoots a bit wide of the mark.

The Rare Coin Score (1967)

Parker is bored—again. He's thinking of women all the time. He moves a few times, hoping a change of scenery will help. But finally he's relieved when Handy McKay calls with a possible job in Indianapolis.

Parker's contact is Claire, who set up the caper with her sort-of lover Billy Lebatard (yet another prophetic name!), a coin dealer whose puppy love for her amuses Parker even as he takes Claire from him. Claire is contemptuous of Billy, and so are the others in the string: Lempke, an old guy just out of prison who may have lost his nerve, Carlow to drive the tricked-up truck, and Otto Mainzer to set a fire and mule the coins. Bill French is another heister who attends the first meeting, but wants out when he sees the set-up. Billy's role as the inside man is to map out which dealers' tables to hit, while Lempke will pack the coins. The mark is a dealers' convention in a hotel ballroom, and they figure to go in through a hole in the wall between the hotel and a travel agency in the building next door.

It's a big, bold and brassy caper, and it's doomed from the start. The immature Billy, who likes to pretend he's one of the cool bad guys and carries heat, is very jealous of Parker. Parker is warming up to Claire behind Billy's back. Lempke really has lost his nerve. Otto is a mean-spirited Nazi type. And Carlow seems to have become some sort of thorn in Otto's side.

Westlake follows his own formula and switches POV to that of a coin dealer who spots Billy during the casing, and a suspicious Pinkerton guard. These POV switches would seem to break the rules— their occurrence is isolated and without repetition. Sometimes they seem frustrating, placed right where you'd like to see more detail on Parker and his string. Perhaps therein lies their charm.

During the operation, everything goes well until they are suddenly hijacked by a returning Bill French, who has cased *them*. French strong-arms Carlow and Otto, and Billy pulls the gun Parker forbade him

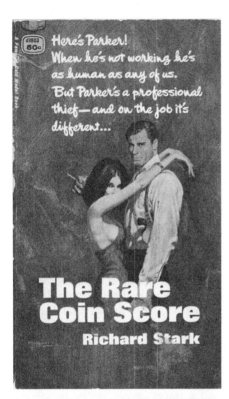

Here's Parker! When he's not working he's as human as any of us. But Parker's a professional thief—and on the job it's different...

The Rare Coin Score

Richard Stark

Here's Parker! swinging at the wildest curve ever thrown a professional thief...

The Green Eagle Score

Richard Stark

Here's Parker! Teaching a class in advanced jewel theft, with post-graduate work in kidnaping, mayhem, and applied terror...

THE BLACK ICE SCORE

By Richard Stark

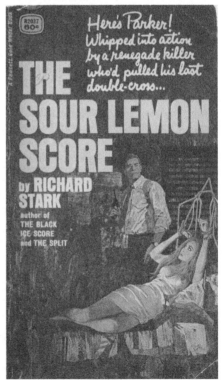

Here's Parker! Whipped into action by a renegade killer who'd pulled his last double-cross...

THE SOUR LEMON SCORE

by RICHARD STARK

author of
THE BLACK
ICE SCORE
and THE SPLIT

to carry, and French kills him. Suddenly Parker is faced with a traumatized Claire and a partner he doesn't want. French has a fence ready, though, and with Billy dead Parker makes a deal, knowing he and French will cross each other anyway. They shoot it out with the guards, then steal into a parking ramp where Parker switches the loot from the hot truck to a Minibus. They hole up at the apartment of Claire's friend, Mavis, who takes a shine to Parker and does something about it before and after being tied up—almost uncharacteristic sexual activity, except that it's immediately after a caper, and Parker's randy. Then they arrange for Claire, who had been spotted during the shoot-out, to go to the authorities and act like a hostage who has been released, telling her bogus story for a full two months. When it's time to split the loot, Parker and French are forced to play the cat and mouse game for the whole pie (Lempke died in the shoot-out, and Otto and Carlow were caught). Parker overpowers French, deals with the fence and turns the $750 grand loot into $200 grand cash to be collected in 60 days, allows Mavis to thank him again, then kills French when his hand is forced. Two months later, Parker and Claire meet as planned—and stay together.

An interesting sidelight is Westlake's depiction of Parker's honor—he earmarks a quarter of the pie for each heister arrested, and would let French go if the other wasn't so set on murder. Westlake's naming game continues beyond Lebatard—see also Carlow the driver—and Parker is uncharacteristically smitten by a woman, the traumatized Claire, who wants to stay with him but only if he promises never to involve her in his other life again. All in all, **The Rare Coin Score** is a pivotal novel in the series, while still exhibiting the typical Stark formula, which includes Parker doing well even though the caper technically went to hell.

The Green Eagle Score (1967)

Parker and Claire are in Puerto Rico, enjoying the fruits of his labors, when Marty Fusco comes to visit. His ex-wife's shacked up with an Air Force guy, Stan Devers, who may have a caper in upstate New York—a $400 grand cash payroll from the base at which he works in the finance office.

Parker considers the heist once on location. He's not too sure of the Devers kid, but the job looks doable. Three more heisters are brought in for a total of six. They work out a plan involving a blue bus decked out for a band (complete with prop instruments) with which to get on base. Then they would hide out at an abandoned, burned-out lodge near the Canadian border.

Ellen Fusco is shacked up with Devers and Marty is staying with them—a tense, weird situation that has Parker rightly worried. Yet, the job looks promising if everyone can keep it together. Still, problems stack up. Devers has been pulling a dodge at work, embezzling cash over time and spending more than he makes, which could well shine the light of suspicion on him after the heist is over. Ellen Fusco is messed up because she believes Devers will end up in jail like Marty did. She *hates* Parker for that. The hitch—and there is one—is that she has been telling all this to her analyst, Dr. Godden, who has been very supportive... and very interested. So interested that he has recruited two weirdo patients to help him heist the score from Parker's gang.

Meanwhile, the job goes off as planned with only minor hassles. As usual, Westlake excels at describing the pace of a robbery with his matter-of-fact tone and no-nonsense descriptions.

The real trouble begins afterwards, when one of Godden's unstable henchmen goes nuts and kills three of Parker's men and his partner. Parker and his two surviving men take Godden prisoner and hide out at his place, while the good doctor is called into the hostage situation caused by his henchman, who kills his father and gives up about two thirds of the loot. But there's a third suitcase, and Parker and his guys get something—$42 grand each. Ellen kills Godden, runs, and Stan Devers can never go back because of the mess, which seems to lay at Godden's door...for the moment. Parker gives Devers Handy Mckay's address, and the world of professional thievery gets another recruit.

This novel is a perfect example of Westlake's tendency to allow Parker to plan and carry out a beautiful caper, only to have it ruined by some outside force Parker isn't even aware of (Fate). There's the requisite POV shift to Godden and his plans, but not until late in the novel. I like to think Dr. Godden is named because of how he plays God with his patients and, finally, rains ruin upon Parker and his string from afar. Though he pays for it in a most un-Godly way.

The Black Ice Score (1968)

In a novel which seems to parallel Westlake's own **The Hot Rock** in general terms, Parker is hired to plan a museum heist. But first, Parker and Claire are accosted by several law-like thugs while on a shopping trip to New York. The thugs are convinced Parker is involved in planning a heist and warn him off. The irony is, Parker hasn't yet been approached by the "other side," but now he's approached by a solo adventurer, Hoskins, and four representatives of Dhaba, a small South African nation whose leader is about to abdicate with his stolen treasury. Karns, head of the Outfit, recommended Parker to UN representative Gonor and his men, who want to hire him to plan a robbery to recover the country's treasury, which the crooked president has converted to diamonds and smuggled to New York by his sister and brother-in-law and three brothers for protection.

With Claire's blessing, due to the conviction that it's a just cause, Parker accepts the offer of $25 grand to plan the heist out of Dhaba's New York museum, where the diamonds and their protectors are secretly holed up. A further $25 grand is offered if Parker decides he must participate in the robbery, otherwise he is merely to plan and train. Besides Gonor, his string consists of the US-educated Formutesca and the young Manado, all of whom have never participated in a robbery. Major Indindu, groomed to take over the Dhaba presidency, is a presence behind the scenes.

After casing the outside of the museum and lining up a plan which involves maintenance disguises and a night trip into the neighboring building, along with weapons and knockout gas officially ordered by military attaché Formutesca, Parker has to fend off a drunken Hoskins—who wants in at any cost, especially since his plan and, he assumes, Parker's, is to rip off Gonor after the caper is done. Parker speaks to him forcefully while holding him partially out a window, attempting to communicate the fact that Hoskins is not wanted. Unfortunately, Parker creates an even more bitter enemy.

Parker and Formutesca dress as city water utility employees and visit the office building next to the museum at two in the morning, fooling the superintendent and "working" on a fifth-floor men's room. Parker is then able to case the museum's roof, a mere four feet away from the washroom window and easily reachable by ladder. The crooked president's sister and brother-in-law (and brothers) are suspected to be hiding with the diamonds in the apartment above the museum, so they will have to be neutralized before the heist can take place. Since Gonor is certain the Kasempas would kill any intruders and bury them in the museum cellar, there's no incentive to pussyfoot around during the heist—just avoid capture. Gonor takes Parker to the museum, which is by appointment with Gonor only, and they plant time bombs during the fake official visit. Then Parker's out, richer a quick $25 grand—leaving the hard work to his protégés. This is a Westlake novel, though, so nothing is that simple. In the meantime, Claire has been snatched by the other side (whites now out of power in Dhaba, Rhodesian-style, who want to fund a rebel leader's guerrilla war).

Parker has quietly evolved. Early in the series, he cares for no one—not even himself—but by this time he has become strangely responsible for Claire, as if she were a delicate ceramic flower he has glued back together and which he must protect. He never shows or voices his devotion, yet time and again he defers to her wishes or places himself in jeopardy for her sake. It almost seems as though Parker chose to evolve on his own, despite Westlake's best efforts. It's difficult to imagine Westlake planning to "soften" his tough-guy character, but it seems a natural enough path for Parker to take. Perhaps Westlake's subliminal message is that even a guy with payback constantly on his mind can spare a few tender moments, though with Parker they must all be located between the lines.

Using a series of differing POVs, Westlake gives us a look at Claire's relatively comfortable confinement, takes us through the robbery, and allows us to watch as Hoskins almost screws everything by ignoring Parker's warning and killing Gonor, who is waiting in a car on the street. During the robbery, Formutesca and Manado must kill all five Kasempas holed up in the museum and make their bodies disappear. After a harrowing—for Westlake—throat-slitting, the two exit the museum and walk right into Hoskins's gunfire. But Parker has also arrived and he kills Hoskins, then helps Formutesca bring a wounded Manado into the museum. You see, when faced with Claire's abduction, Parker told the white Dhabans that the robbers would be *taking* the diamonds to the museum about an hour later, so he could be there to meet them and finish it.

Setting a trap for the three opponents, Parker and Formutesca learn the whereabouts of the farmhouse where Claire has been stashed, but the leader escapes, presumably heading there to kill Claire or ambush Parker. There's a long car ride, and then a brief shootout on a deserted road over the hill from the house. Parker wounds Marten with a shotgun blast, then offstage "finishes" him with a single pistol shot. The novel ends as he puts his hand on Claire's cheek, which is the most tender gesture he has ever made. He's so romantic, when referring to her, he routinely calls her "my woman."

While Parker generally ignores race altogether, in this novel Westlake makes some points within the narrative and even more frequently in the POV of Formutesca or Manado: "It was America's ambivalence toward him that first made him consciously a patriot about his homeland. He saw that Dhaba with idealistic men at her helm could eventually offer everything America offers, and without the left-handed taking away."

The Sour Lemon Score (1969)

Parker's string for the bank robbery is Andrews, Weiss, and a nervous driver named George Uhl. Parker almost calls it off because Uhl seems like the kind of driver who might panic and take off, stranding the inside guys. But Weiss vouches for Uhl and they go for the bank, which is in the process of being serviced by an armored car. Smoke grenades and brandished weapons, and the string is out of there with a strongbox. At the hideout, a lonely farmhouse, they are disappointed to find a very low $33 grand in the box when they expected twice that. Suddenly, Uhl blows away Weiss and Andrews, and Parker leaps out the window, losing his handgun and leading to a nicely described tense hunt in the woods. Uhl gives up the hunt and burns down the farmhouse, making the huge mistake of leaving Parker alive to carry the kind of grudge that will rule his life until he can resolve it.

This superb opening sequence then slows into a methodical search, as Parker makes the most of the one name he has—Matt Rosenstein, one heister who has worked with Uhl before. Parker's usual connections show up again: Madge, the old hooker who runs a "safe" motel, and Handy McKay, who still keeps his feet wet from his diner in Maine. All this leads Parker to a Greenwich Village used record shop owned by a guy named Brock, who takes messages for Rosenstein. After some amusing tough-guy runaround, Parker meets with Brock, who slips him a mickey and interrogates him about his need to locate Rosenstein and Uhl.

After recovering, Parker breaks into Brock's swanky apartment and tears it apart, learning that a second man lives there as well—his interrogator, Rosenstein? But what use is Parker's information to Brock and his pal? Parker visits Weiss's widow and learns two addresses—Uhl's girlfriend the previous year, and Pearson, a fellow heister whom Parker visits first. In the middle of the visit, while Pearson is telling Parker that he didn't much trust Uhl, shots are fired and Pearson is killed. Parker barely escapes and heads for Uhl's old girlfriend's place. Joyce Langer is a bit of a loser whose interest in helping Parker is solely because she still carries a grudge against Uhl. She gives Parker three names—Howie, Barry, and Officer Dumek.

Westlake then jumps POV, first to George Uhl who takes us through his side of the events prior. It becomes obvious that the guy Joyce knew as Barry is actually Barri, a woman with whom Uhl was two-timing Joyce. Now Uhl is staying with Ed, a high school buddy and his family, who have come to realize Uhl's leeching ways and the fact that he might be dangerous. In the meantime, and in another POV shift, George's dance instructor and ex-stripper girlfriend gets beaten up by Rosenstein, who is now also looking for Uhl. Rosenstein has sex with Brock "for business advantages," and because he's no good with women (maybe not beating them up first would help in that department), but he still considers Brock "the faggot" and himself as straight. In the midst of this series of POV shifts, Brock and Rosenstein manage to track Uhl to Ed's house, thereby immediately endangering the lives of an innocent family whose only mistake is letting dad relive his high school hero-worship of slime-ball Uhl. Ed's also stashed Uhl's suitcase, after Uhl's call to warn him some "others" might come around. Then Uhl ends up at Joyce's, where they renew their sexual relationship and reawaken her hatred of him enough for her to call Parker's hotel, breaking out of the superbly constructed round-robin POV shifts.

Meanwhile, Parker has entered the Uhl circle by questioning Howie, who leads him to Barri, who's been beaten by Rosenstein. And then Joyce's message leads him back to her, and to a sleeping Uhl, who's rudely awakened by the poking barrel of Parker's gun. Parker uses the same drug used to interrogate him, and learns that Ed has hidden the money—and that Rosenstein has more than a day on Parker. Now Parker must head for Ed's house blindly, not knowing what the Rosenstein situation might be. A call determines that Brock and Rosenstein are at the house, so they don't have the money yet. Parker could kill Uhl now—in fact, he almost pulls the trigger. But in an uncharacteristic (and therefore

terrifically effective) switch, Parker can't kill a docile, drugged Uhl no matter what Uhl put him through. So Parker breaks three "fairly important" bones and leaves him in the middle of a field. Then he's off to Ed's house. The gears mesh and tighten, and the game enters the last period.

Parker can't approach the house because it has lawn all around it, so he calls Rosenstein and Brock and makes a deal. Ed hasn't told them where the money is, so Parker bluffs by saying he has Uhl, and he's the only other way to get the money, which they can then split. They set up a way for Parker to enter the house by driving into the open connected garage. But it's a trap, as Parker well understands, and he has all the luck. The shoot-out is quick and brutal, and everything you'd want it to be in a noir thriller with very few happy ending possibilities. Family man Ed is dead, for instance, and there's no one left who knows where the money is. Sour lemon indeed. Parker wins, but the prize is nothing.

This one could make a swell little movie, if they could keep it personal and didn't decide to blow up everything in sight. In fact, most Parker novels would make great movies if unenhanced.

Deadly Edge (1971)

Parker, Keegan, Briley, and Morris break through the roof of the Civic Auditorium during the last rock concert to be held there before demolition. Westlake provides a detailed account of the robbery, step by step, as they take guards prisoner and deal with the Auditorium employees, all while being able to see the concert from a window overlooking the stage. (From Westlake's less-than-flattering description of the band and its sound, I'd say he's describing either Black Sabbath or Deep Purple.) The operation goes off with military precision, thirty-odd pages of tense detail and psychology as they deal with their captives in a way which will resurface in **Comeback**. When they reach their safe house, there's a corpse inside—Berridge, an older heister who had pulled out of the job earlier.

Days later, Parker pulls into a

driveway in rural New Jersey. Claire has bought a house on Colliver's Pond, an area mostly populated by summer folks. She is adamant that she wants both Parker and a house she can call her own, where she can be Mrs. Charles Willis. In the summer, when Parker and she live in resort hotels on the proceeds of his "jobs," the house can be closed, thereby avoiding scrutiny from the locals. In some ways, it's the perfect set-up, and Parker is visiting it for the first time. Claire is thrilled to show him the house his money bought, with its boathouse and woods, and faraway neighbors gone for the winter, their homes closed up. This home is almost mystical to Claire, who has connected with Parker on a level neither of them really comprehends.

Parker's cut of the job was $17 grand, five of which he has stashed. Four days later, Handy McKay calls and tells him that a day ago Keegan wanted to contact Parker, so Handy had innocently given him the new phone number—Claire's house. Since Keegan has not contacted Parker, there's something wrong. Parker heads out to see Keegan in Minneapolis, after attempting to convince Claire to leave the house for a few days. But Claire stubbornly refuses to leave her house, perhaps the only grounding she has ever had. When Parker finds Keegan, he's been nailed to a wall and tortured. Parker is able to determine that there may be two gunmen, but he doesn't know how they connect to the concert robbery. He calls Claire, but again she refuses to leave. To be driven from her house. In a show of patience very unlike Parker, he convinces her to hide all his belongings in a neighbor's house and tell any visitors that she barely knows Parker and merely takes his messages. Parker heads to Detroit to find and warn Briley, and arrives in the aftermath of what appears to have been a shoot-out, and Briley dying. When he is able to call Claire, she calls him Mr. Parker—and he knows that she has company.

A Westlake POV shift follows, as Claire watches Parker leave her brand-new house. A good long section follows in which her attachment to Parker is explored. When Parker calls to warn her the first time, she buys a rifle. But all too soon,

she's startled to find that her house—her home, her sanctuary—has been invaded by two vaguely hippyish, long-haired thugs, the drugged-out Manny and the cunning Jessup. From there the novel turns into a superb cat-and-mouse psychological game (reminiscent of **Wait Until Dark** without the blindness angle) in which Claire must keep the two thugs from raping or otherwise hurting her as they wait for Parker to call for his "messages." She spins a yarn about having the clap, which chills the rape possibilities for a while. Mostly she has to keep them happy, especially Manny—drugged-out and eventually proven to be the real sadist of the two. Five hours after Parker's call, during a dinner in which the suspense is drawn out deliciously to a near breaking point, the fourth hold-up man, Morris, arrives to consult with Parker about the Berridge and Keegan killings, stumbling into a true nest of vipers. Ironically, Morris has most of the story straight—Berridge had a grandson who wanted a piece of the old man's action, which evaporated when Berridge did not participate in the job. So they killed the old man, and then the grandson and his buddy began to track down each heister, one by one, to take their stashes. Morris realizes too late that Manny the grandson and Manny the guy in Claire's kitchen are one and the same, and he joins the list of the deceased. Claire manages to lock herself in her bedroom and retrieve her rifle, but the two thugs manage to outwit her. However, the stalling helps Parker arrive just in time to shoot it out with Manny and Jessup, chasing them off.

From that point, Parker is in clean-up mode. He has to dump the body of poor Morris, who almost managed to rescue Claire. Then he chases down Manny and Jessup, who haven't got far at all on the tires Parker shot out. He finds them barricaded in a closed-up home, and finishes it.

Noir? You bet. Psychological? Uh-uh. Suspenseful? And how. A masterpiece of crime fiction, albeit one which works best if you already know Parker and Claire.

Slayground (1969, 1971)

One of the best all-around starts is **Slayground**. In the first several paragraphs Parker and Grofield break into an armored car they've just flipped over with a land mine, then they pop the door with another explosive device and remove $73 grand. Unfortunately, Laufman is a second-rate driver who flips their getaway car negotiating a nearby curve. Both Grofield and Laufman are injured and unconscious (and Laufman will die of his injuries), so Parker grabs the money and heads off on foot, sirens getting closer. The location of the armored car heist is a long, lonely road with nothing nearby except Fun Island, an amusement park closed for the winter. Parker has no choice, so he hops the fence. But he realizes he is being watched by two men from a black Lincoln and two uniform cops from a patrol car, both parked out of sight on a side road. In the process of exchanging an envelope, the four men watch Parker carry the money into the park.

The crooked cops turn in a report that one of the gunmen drove off in a second waiting car, chase was given, but he lost them. Meanwhile, armed guards appear in the amusement park office, to keep Parker from escaping from the only gate he can climb. The park is split into eight sections, each representative of a type of island— Desert Island, Voodoo Island, New York Island, Treasure Island, Alcatraz Island, Island of Hawaii, Pleasure Island, and Island Earth—and each with its associated type of rides and funhouses. Face it, the setting is a natural for the cat-and-mouse game that ensues as Joe Caliato, a local mob lieutenant and his two tame cops slowly involve more and more gunsels to chase Parker down. Unfortunately, circumstances give Parker a whole night to plan and prepare—and try to warm up—and not only does he stash the loot in a water ride backdrop, but he also sets ingenious booby-traps and makes weapons out of various found materials. When Caliato and the cops and their thugs finally come into the park, Parker leads them to a hall of mirrors, where he manages to kill Caliato himself in a shoot-out complicated by the various mirror images (the later-

produced Bond-Scaramanga confrontation in *The Man with the Golden Gun* could almost have been based on this scene, as it was the first I thought of). In a hand-to-hand with one of the cops immediately afterwards, Parker lands in the cold water of the Buccaneer! ride and, though he eludes his pursuers again, he now nearly freezes to death without dry winter clothes.

Caliato's death leads to more complications for Parker. The man was like a son to the local mob boss, Adolf Lozini, who now takes an intense personal interest in ending the life of Parker—and who brings an army of thirty thugs with him to hunt down Parker. Through several more confrontations, Parker gets the drop on them and reduces their number one by one. Westlake as usual presents short sections in various POVs, usually those of thugs who are about to find Parker. Each scene is violent and spine-tingling (the cliché works here!). Using knives and whatever else he can lay his hands on and, eventually, a handgun taken from a thug, Parker whittles down their number and actually begins to frighten Lozini's minions as the avenging angel he's become.

In what might be a bit of a stretch for a climax, Parker gets the two cops at gunpoint and uses them to escape from Lozini—it's clever, but a mite too "Hollywood" to be truly convincing. Still, it comes after a minor masterpiece in suspense, and you can hardly fault Westlake for that. Lozini knows he's beaten at the end, and this is important because we haven't seen the last of him. **Slayground** is a superb thriller, and one which nicely shows off Westlake's narrative style, since there is relatively little dialogue.

A note regarding the cover painting on the Berkley Medallion paperback edition—there's a blonde in a bikini stuck in a crossfire, with the dark amusement park and an explosion in the background. Which would be great, except that there's not a single woman in the book, let alone a blonde in a bikini! It must have sold a few more copies though.

Plunder Squad (1972)

Somebody opens fire on Parker as he sits down to meet with Ducasse, Kirwan, Stokes, and Ashby. Turns out the sixth guy was George Uhl, the same guy Parker should have killed in **The Sour Lemon Score**. Ashby is wounded in the attack, so they have to abandon both him and the scheme—a sweet department store Mother's Day heist—and move on. Fate rears an ugly head again. Parker is in desperate need of a score, because the last couple have gone sour, including the armored car heist after which he was forced to stash the loot in the amusement park. A call from Handy sends him to San Francisco and another set-up meeting, this time at the home of a driver named Beaghler. Present also are Ducasse, George Walheim, and Beaghler's wife Sharon, whom Parker immediately pegs as "almost a parody of a suburban slut," and therefore trouble. Beaghler's caper is an art heist, in which some precious statues on loan from the Hearst mansion, San Simeon, would travel the coast highway by armored car. Beaghler plans an ambush, then an escape over the mountains in a all-terrain vehicle (ATV), but he needs someone to set up a buyer. But then Sharon comes to visit Parker's motel at 2:30 AM, followed by a steamed Beaghler Parker has to punch out (Parker hasn't fooled with Sharon, but he's so cool he doesn't even try to explain—he just walks away from the caper).

Parker breaks into a house—a tip has led him to George Uhl's new digs, where he's shacked up with some woman. Nobody's home except the Doberman, and Parker shows what he really thinks of dogs (see *Payback* review). When the couple returns, Parker's play is ruined by the woman and Uhl gets away—again. Parker then ransacks Uhl's own apartment and takes four grand salted away in a corn-flakes box. But it's still not enough. Then Ducasse passes on the news that Ed Mackey is looking to put together an art heist himself. Mackey and "his woman" Brenda have scoped out a traveling exhibit of 21 pop art paintings which a guy named Griffith wants heisted for a flat fee of $130 grand split however many ways. Parker insists on meeting the nervous Griffith, and talks him up to $160 grand Parker-style—standing on a non-negotiable $40 grand fee for himself in a private deal. Parker doesn't know that Griffith is in turn being bankrolled by another art lover type, who won't go the extra money.

Parker and Mackey push for a payment plan, not realizing they are squeezing Griffith into a very tight place. In the meantime, Beaghler contacts Parker with information on Uhl—and there's some money in it. Beaghler's well-equipped (and strangely well-prepared) ATV gets them to Uhl's secluded farmhouse in the mountains. But Parker's been reading the signs, and he knows Beaghler and Uhl cooked up a little trap. He springs it instead on an unsuspecting Uhl, finishing his nemesis almost in too detached a manner. A cowed Beaghler says Parker has nothing to worry about—"You don't have to do anything about me." "That's the mistake I made with Uhl," says Parker. Next scene, he's driving the ATV. Westlake's decision to leave out the scene of Beaghler's execution is an interesting one, and probably well-advised, given the time period. Ironically, not showing it makes the act more chilling—its matter-of-factness—and without leaching away any sympathy readers have for Parker.

Free of Uhl at last, Parker enters into Mackey's art heist, bringing in Stan Devers (**The Green Eagle Score**). Mackey also brings in VW-Microbus-driving Tommy Carpenter, a young hippie-type, and his girlfriend Noelle. They are joined by Lou Sternberg—he of sour-disposition—who lives in London and "works" in the US only when he absolutely has to.

In the meantime, Griffith has no luck getting any money from his buyer, Renard, who insists his client only wants six paintings of the 21. Griffith planned to sell the remainder for his own profit, but he's so broke that he can't meet the robbers' need of up-front cash. And he can't pay them the rest of the money either, until he can sell the paintings. Between the contemptuous Renard and his fear of Parker and the rest, Griffith has no choice but to take out an $80 grand loan from an associate of Renard's—at 2 percent interest with a six-month minimum in advance. Of course, this pushes Griffith further down the spiral.

The requisite Westlake POV shifts show each member of the string arriving for the big meet and, as usual, most of those POVs are never revisited. When the heist goes off, Westlake has chosen an omniscient narrator's POV, following the packing of the paintings in Indianapolis and their subsequent road trip to where bogus state police troopers Mackey and Devers pick up the convoy and lead it astray. The scene in which Parker and his men take out the two real state troopers is noteworthy because sex is used for the first time—the troopers are amazed (and distracted) when they come up on a couple doing the deed right on the median. It's Tommy and Noelle, of course, and the whole thing's an ambush. While it goes off like a military maneuver, a little extra something happens between one of the troopers and Tommy which later comes back to haunt both him and Noelle. The second part of the ambush is sprung when the convoy arrives upon an "accident," a second distraction which leads to the armed robbery itself. Another military maneuver, and the gang splits up. Sternberg takes an REO truck with the paintings to Chicago, Parker with Devers and Mackey head for Griffith's for the rest of their payment, and the young couple drive right into the arms of the law, which the rest of the gang learn about while in a motel. Tommy's run-in with the trooper has led to a positive ID, making everyone nervous. Parker's group reaches Griffith only to find a bloodless corpse in a cold tub of rose water—just too unstable, the news of the gang's imminent capture drove him to the edge. Finally locating a letter from Renard and figuring him as the buyer, the three frustrated thieves travel to New York and pay Renard a visit. After an amusing song and dance, Renard agrees to pay $60 grand for the six original paintings, a puny $12 grand for all their work and risk. The other paintings they decide to dump, as finding a buyer would be too difficult. In the meantime, Tommy and Noelle are released despite the cops' ID—anti-brutality and hippie organizations lobby successfully for their release.

With one of the most downbeat endings of the series, **Plunder Squad** gives Parker not a single break. He and Mackey deliver the six paintings, but it's an ambush. Renard has given up the thieves to the loansharks who lost a lot of money on Griffith (who did manage to take it with him, sort of). Parker's ingenuity gets him out, but Mackey is killed in the shoot-out. Parker takes a cab. You win some, you lose some. This caper's a big loss all the way. Westlake takes the unpredictable nature of real life (Fate) and uses it to great effect. Parker won't pout—he'll line up another score. Anger is a wasted emotion. Parker's outlook is refreshing in its own way—pragmatic and therefore realistic.

If there's any flaw here, it might be that Parker's tracking down of George Uhl and evening the score happens so quickly, and has almost no bearing on the main climax. It's true that both failed heists are somewhat connected, but most writers would have saved Parker's confrontation with Uhl until the end, where it could impact the new heist. Placing it early in the book and detaching it from the Mackey heist makes for a twinge more realism, but also hurts the book's dramatic thrust. Still, even a slightly flawed Parker novel rates as a noir masterpiece.

By the way, Westlake spent a lot of time vacationing in Wisconsin—catch the name of my hometown (and Orson Welles') painted on the door of the REO truck!

Butcher's Moon (1974)

In another quick start that turns out to be Westlake's style of red herring, Parker, with Hurley, Briggs, Michaelson, and Dalesia are retreating through a tunnel they've dug from one basement to another. Cops are hot on their trail. Michaelson is shot, and they blow up the mouth of the tunnel, making good their escape through the other building. Empty-handed. The perils of buying a ready-made plan from someone who may not know about the new silent alarm in the jewelry store.

Parker's not kidding when he says he's running a streak of bad luck. He decides to return to the Fun Island amusement park in Tyler, Ohio, to get his stash from the botched armored car robbery a couple years before. He calls Grofield, and they agree to meet and locate the loot. But of course, the loot's not there. Parker knows just who to call, and he's not taking no for an answer.

Butcher's Moon is an atypical Parker novel—almost three times the normal length, more complex, and containing numerous POV shifts. For instance, Grofield has become a character almost as important as Parker. He's shown at his failing Indiana summer theater—a converted barn—taking Parker's call while attempting to explain his lack of income to an IRS man. A good number of his adventures apart from Parker's are also shown in detail, such as his trysts with an attractive young librarian in Tyler.

Adolf Lozini can't believe the nerve of the heister. He kills a number of Lozini's men, including Caliato who was like a son to him, and now he's calling to request his money back. Lozini doesn't have it, and he'll be damned if he's going to take this kind of crap from someone like Parker. Parker says, call Karns—the national head of the outfit—but Lozini brushes him off. So Parker and Grofield make good use of the information Grofield gathered from the library and overnight hit several Lozini operations: a nightclub, a brewery, and a parking garage. They even remove checks and credit card receipts, which are no good to them, but which hurt Lozini plenty, as they must be either replaced or forgiven. By night's end, both Lozini's thugs and tame cops are on the streets looking for Parker.

Lozini meets with his lieutenants, each of whom runs a portion of his operation, and Calesian, a top cop on the force's organized crime squad (nice irony there, and Westlake uses it well). All's not well in Lozini's organization, as he begins to see. Also, there's a mayoral election in a few days which his pet incumbent mayor is likely to lose (to his opposition's pet candidate). Lozini confirms what kind of a problem Parker can be by talking with Karns, whose amusement has just the right tone. Lozini then agrees to meet with Parker and Grofield—he doesn't have the money and never did, so it's obvious that someone in his organization kept it. Or worse, is using

it to fund a campaign against him. With Parker and Grofield's help, Lozini starts to make some connections and realizes that some of his associates have been stacking the deck against him, leading up to his "retirement," and that only Parker's stirring of the pot has led to these conspiracies rising to the top. Reluctantly, Lozini agrees to help Parker get his money, if Parker can help flush the enemy. There's nothing for Parker to lose, and only his money to gain. A strange alliance is struck.

In the meantime, Lozini's enemy attempts to have Parker and Grofield hit. Also, O'Hara, the cop from the amusement park is assassinated because of what he knows. In a separate hit, his former partner, now not even a cop, is also assassinated. Westlake takes a few well-aimed potshots at modern politics—the photo-op and sound-bite style goes back a bit further than we sometimes think—following the corrupt mayoral candidate briefly as Parker and Grofield "approach" him, too, about the identity of his boss. Westlake handles the first half of this novel more as a traditional mystery, because no one knows exactly who is involved in the killings. But it's no real surprise when Lozini faces down Calesian, the tame cop, only to be killed halfway through the novel. With Lozini dead, and his death momentarily blamed on Parker, the main conspirators' identities begin to jell. Parker and Grofield meet with Lozini's opponent and, just as he's about to make a deal and pay them (and take a business write-off) Calesian breaks in and shoots Grofield, almost killing him—Grofield should stop working with Parker since it always ends badly for him when he does. Parker thinks his partner dead and escapes. Then Calesian, who has taken over from a suddenly weakened prospective boss, sends Parker one of Grofield's fingers as a message: come for your partner and your money or we take a finger a day. Parker knows what this means, so he sends a message of his own—he kills the messenger then heads for a meet with the rest of Lozini's henchmen, a couple more of which he exposes as enemies. But when he asks Lozini's henchmen for men to take Grofield away from Calesian, he's rebuffed. What do they care, now that Lozini's dead? The king is dead, long live the king. Parker doesn't take no for an answer, as everyone who's dealt with him should know by now. If they want a war, he'll give them one.

After a series of phone calls, Parker has eleven men on their way to Tyler. Handy McKay, out of retirement because his diner's failing, and a few more names from the past. Stan Devers, Dan Wycza, Ducasse, Hurley, Dalesia, Mackey, Carlow, Elkins, Wiss, and Webb all want in. Westlake's typical POV shifts jump from man to man, as each comes into Parker's operation for his own reasons. (As an aside, Westlake makes a tiny mistake by including Ed Mackey, who was killed in the garage shoot-out after the screwed art heist in **Plunder Squad**.) Meanwhile, Parker has kidnapped one of Lozini's lower-rung men and put him on ice, grilling him for every detail to just about every mob operation in town. Parker offers his men all the job plans in which they can have equal cuts of the overall take. Parker wants no money, just their help on his own job after all the others are done: rescue Grofield from Lozini's opponent's house guarded by several dozen men now run by the rogue cop, Calesian, who sees himself as a rising mobster after having really gotten his hands dirty. Parker's loyalty—never played up with a fanfare—is proven by the lengths he's willing to go to save Grofield, a partner who is about as different from him as can be. When Handy and the others question his altruistic streak, "what happens to him (Grofield) is up to him," Parker responds: "Not when they send him to me piece by piece. If they kill him, that's one thing. If they turn him over to the law, get him sent up, that's his lookout. But the bastards rang *me* in on it."

What follows is an orgy of heists and robberies throughout the night, a larger-scope version of what Parker and Grofield did at the beginning of the novel. A gambling operation, a crooked stockbroker, a loan-shark operation, and even a private alarm company, hit so as to avoid a certain alarm when hitting a safe. Within hours, the happy heisters are back. Their take, over a quarter million dollars in cash. Westlake's POV shifts have shown each heist in detail,

and now he switches to the house where Calesian and a couple other mob bosses and forty armed men are holed up, receiving the news of each heist and blustering about how things will be when they locate and kill Parker. Feeling safe. That's when the lights go out, and the attack is on.

With continuous POV shifts, Westlake visits every angle of the attack—from the six cars pulled up to the front of the house, headlights burning, to those covering the back, and to Parker, moving through the house like an avenging angel, executing anyone in his way. Any organized resistance dies before it can start, as the armed thugs are rendered leaderless and more thoroughly confused by the hardened platoon Parker has put together. A couple of men are slightly wounded, Ducasse is killed, and then the stolen ambulance arrives for Grofield. Parker takes the $54 grand from the blown safe—it's not $73 grand, but he'll settle. The whole operation has taken a half hour, and the police haven't even shown up yet. When Grofield wakes up, he's in the ambulance with Devers, and Parker's driving.

And so ends the last of the original series of Parker novels, literally with a bang. It's the *Magnificent Seven* of the bunch, a worthy end to the series and a good way to say goodbye to Parker, whether planned or not. It would be nearly a quarter of a century before Parker's comeback.

Comeback (1997)

Parker and his string—the resurrected Mackey and his woman, Brenda, and a rather unreliable George Liss—have an inside man in William Archibald's Christian Crusade. Archibald is a not quite on the up and up Billy Graham-style evangelist, and Tom Carmody is a disgruntled "angel" and parole counselor on his staff who's fed up with how the money is (or isn't) spent. The novel begins fast, as Parker novels usually do, with Parker and his men brazenly going behind the scenes at an arena hosting twenty thousand cash-paying celebrants in the revival crusade and grabbing the take—while the event is going on! Reminiscent of the earlier rock concert score, except much easier. But at the last second Carmody wants to back out, confessing that he told his girlfriend about the heist and now she's disappeared. Parker is not one to be trifled with, and the heist goes down as planned.

A flashback tells how Liss approached Parker with the needed score, and Parker's acceptance despite his better judgment about Liss—he and Claire need the money, and Mackey's involvement is solid. In the present, the heist goes down as planned, and Parker's gang lies low in a stolen construction trailer parked at the far end of the stadium parking lot! Carmody takes a nasty bump on the head to throw off police suspicion, but Dwayne Thorsen—ex-Marine and highly capable head of Archibald's security—spots Carmody's guilt immediately. Meanwhile, Carmody's girlfriend is found murdered, but no one realizes that she was killed accidentally while being interrogated by two idiotic thug friends of her brother, Ralph, who decided they could slip in and grab the loot after the heisters had stolen it. The problem is, they don't know the entire plan—for instance, about the trailer hideaway. To complicate matters even further, while at the trailer, Liss has made an attempt on Parker and Mackey, scheming to get all the loot to himself. Only Parker's foresight in unloading the shotguns keeps him from being blasted awake and into the next life. They blow up the trailer as planned—no clues—but have to improvise now that Liss has spoiled the party. The next hideout is an all-night gas station on the freeway, but Liss hasn't given up—he's on their trail, and dressed as a cop, no less. Liss almost foils the plan yet again, this time managing to separate Parker from Mackey and the money.

Meanwhile, the cops move in on the three wanna-be heisters because they fit the description of the robbers—and, of course, they *are* connected because of Ralph's dead sister. Semi-sadistic Detective Calavecci is on the trail and he's no fool, and Thorsen runs into an insurance investigator named Jack Orr. But wait, Orr is none other than Parker, who assumes one of his false identities and gets himself inside the investigation by convincing Thorsen he's been after Liss for a long time on an unrelated matter. There's no better way to keep his nose to the ground for the money, all the while hoping a message left for Mackey and Brenda will reunite him with the good guys and the loot. Posing as Jack Orr places Parker in the hospital when Liss kills Carmody and takes Ralph hostage. While on the inside, Parker also meets Archibald, the evangelist whose portrait is an interesting study in contradictions—he lives well and regularly bangs the sultry choir director, Christine Mackenzie, but he does also sponsor counseling and other programs benefiting the poor. Archibald immediately bribes Parker to help recover the loot for a cash retainer and a percentage finder's fee. With all he's worth, he still really misses that $400 grand they grabbed. The wild finish takes place in the string's original post-heist hideaway for the loot—a deserted, decrepit Frank Lloyd Wright-style house in which Parker, George Liss and Ralph all end up. It's not just a shoot-out, as they talk and maneuver around each other—who needs whom? Who has the guns? It's a strange three-way stand-off, and it only gets worse after dark... when Ralph becomes an unfortunate human shield caught between the two gladiators who will fight to the death. It's not much of a surprise that Parker wins, but the novel ends with the most delicious understatement of the series (all right, I could find one or two more...): when Mackey and Brenda pick up Parker, Mackey asks, "You see George?" and Parker answers, "Yes." And that's an end you savor, bitterly, like a mouthful of spoiled milk. It's a beauty to behold.

Also of note in **Comeback** are Westlake POV shifts with a twist—actually several within the same scene, something Westlake almost never did in the earlier books. Mackey's continued return from the dead strikes me as one of Westlake's few actual mistakes, as he probably forgot to note the reliable Mackey had been killed at the end of **Plunder Squad**. Finally, take note of the name "Liss." It's a hiss, like that of a snake.

Backflash (1998)

His "comeback" must have felt right indeed. **Backflash** follows the tradition of fast openings, as Parker's car crashes into a ravine and pins Howell in the driver's seat. Pursuit is near, so Parker takes the $140 grand and considers using his Glock to make sure Howell won't rat him out. But he doesn't, and later this decision will come back to haunt him.

Later, at home with Claire, Parker is contacted by Hilliard Cathman, an ex-bureaucrat and now consultant with a strong anti-gambling obsession. He wants Parker to pull a job for him. The target: a casino cruise ship on a four-month, cash-only, politically-charged trial run. To prove the reality of the dangers of legalized river gambling in the state of New York, Cathman wants Parker and his string to pull off a daring robbery of the *Spirit of the Hudson*, thereby bursting the balloon of total security sent up by everyone involved. "I don't like boats," Parker says. "I don't like anything where there's one entrance, one exit. I don't like a cell. A boat on the water is a cell, you can't just get up and go away." But Cathman provides plans and blueprints, and Parker knows the score can be done. With a string of Carlow, Wycza, Sternberg (from London), and Noelle (Tommy's old hippie ex-girlfriend), Parker starts to set it up, even while continuing to dig for a reason to ditch Cathman. A boatman with shady connections is hired to take care of the getaway boat driving, while a plan slowly takes shape. Sternberg will impersonate a little-known NYC assemblyman known to be an anti-gambling jerk, and Wycza and Parker will impersonate his escort of state troopers on a "fact-finding" junket. Making as much anti-gambling noise as possible, Sternberg will take them on a company-sponsored kid-gloves tour of the ship, a tour which will include the money room even though it's supposed to be off-limits. In the meantime, Noelle—in a rigged wheelchair—will continue playing a role she'll have perfected for a couple of weeks, that of a rich young invalid who takes a liking to the ship's brief Hudson cruises. With Carlow as her chauffeur-

escort, and a set pattern of visibility, she will trade on everyone's willingness to please a handicapped person—and remove the money quietly in the wheelchair. The actual thieves are to escape a different way, hence the need for Hanzen.

It's a bold and daring plan which comes together both as it's being set up and then as it is put into practice. Of course, Westlake throws in the usual difficulties including a nosy reporter who just happens to know the assemblyman Sternberg is impersonating, and some last-minute traitorous action by Hanzen and some biker buddies. As if that weren't enough, a desperate and about to be former rogue cop who was on the trail of Parker's original $140 grand is now hot on their heels, looking to take the loot away from them at any cost. Though the heist goes pretty much as planned, even with unexpected obstacles, Parker still ends up in the hands of the rogue cop along with a suicidal Cathman, who had planned to turn in the heisters and take credit for foiling a robbery which proved his point about gambling attracting the wrong kind of criminal element—creating his own crime wave in order to decry the increase in crime, so to speak. When it's just Parker and the cop, Parker plays a tight game and maneuvers him to where he can get the upper hand and rub him out. This time, too, Westlake gives Parker a break.

Prone to just a bit more humor than usual (a little Westlake influence on an aging Stark), and working off a much more elegant plan than usual—in fact almost a *Mission Impossible* scenario (the TV show, not the movie)—this novel reads more like a Westlake caper than a Stark noir. But the author can't be faulted for imposing bits of one persona on the other; after all, both are his to do with as he wishes. The same brief, limited Westlake POV shifts are there, as is the noir ending that ties it all together neatly. In **Backflash**, Parker seems to have mellowed noticeably, even allowing himself the odd bit of smalltalk while still hating it. Westlake has fleshed out his descriptions, too, and the truly stark rhythms of **The Hunter**-era Stark are now replaced by the more genteel tones of Westlake. But then Parker should be in his sixties by now, and he is certainly not described that way. Suspended in time like, say, James Bond or the Saint, Parker seems to have aged not at all even if his creator has. And in this paradoxical situation we are left with a Parker who clearly has one or two more capers in him, difficult ones, even if he is destined to have better luck now than when he was "younger." Claire still waits for him at Colliver's Pond, seventy miles from New York, and I assume that is the place to which he'll always return.

The Hunter ****
The Man with the Getaway Face **1/2
The Outfit ***1/2
The Mourner **1/2
The Score **1/2
The Jugger ***1/2
The Split (The Seventh) ****
The Handle **1/2
The Rare Coin Score ***
The Green Eagle Score ***1/2
The Black Ice Score **1/2
The Sour Lemon Score ****
Deadly Edge ****
Slayground ****
Plunder Squad ***
Butcher's Moon ****
Comeback ***1/2
Backflash ***1/2

Works Cited and/or Consulted

Donald Westlake—Author Chat Transcripts; Monday, August 11, 1997; http://www.barnesandnoble.com

Donald E. Westlake—The BookList Interview; _BookList_ April 15, 1997 pp.1408-1409.

"Me," by Donald E. Westlake, in **Contemporary Authors** (Autobiography Series), v. 13, edited by Joyce Nakamura; Gale Research, Inc. (Detroit, 1991)

Contemporary Authors, v. 17-20, edited by Clare D. Kinsman; Gale Research, Inc. (Detroit, 1976)

Contemporary Authors (New Revision Series), v. 16, edited by Linda Metzger and Deborah A. Straub; Gale Research, Inc. (Detroit, 1986)

Contemporary Authors (New Revision Series), v. 44, edited by Susan M. Trosky; Gale Research, Inc. (Detroit, 1994)

Critical Survey of Mystery and Detective Fiction, edited by Frank N. Magill; Salem Press (Pasadena, 1988)

Encyclopedia Mysteriosa: A Comprehensive Guide to the Art of Detection in Print, Film, Radio, and Television, by William L. DeAndrea; Prentice Hall (NY, 1994)

Murder Off the Rack: Critical Studies of Ten Paperback Masters, edited by Jon L. Breen and Martin H. Greenberg; Scarecrow Press, Inc. (Metuchen, NJ, 1989)—Westlake contributes a chapter on Peter Rabe.

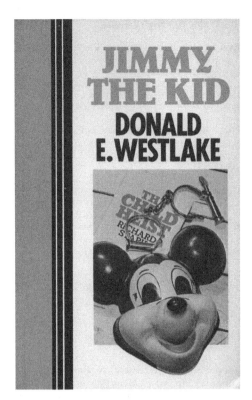

Jimmy the Kid (1974)
By Donald E. Westlake
Or, the Parker novel that never was...

A bizarre aside to the Parker saga came in 1974, after the official end of the Parker series, when Donald Westlake put John Dortmunder and his wacky gang through their third disastrous caper. The gang is made up of the serious but jinxed Dortmunder, his long-suffering wife May, the overly enthusiastic but barely reliable Kelp, the unimaginative driver Murch, and his mother the cabbie, Murch's Mom.

In **Jimmy the Kid**, Dortmunder reluctantly assents to Kelp's plan—the joke is that Kelp has read a book called **Child Heist** by one Richard Stark, starring that stolid, unsmiling master thief Parker, and now he wants to follow the plan exactly as laid out by the author. It's a sly gimmick, surely, but Westlake has the panache to pull it off, even including random chapters of the nonexistent (perhaps aborted) Parker novel written in the Stark style. The humor—and it is indeed funny—comes from seeing how

the novel's plan and the Dortmunder gang's diverge and eventually go awry. First is the fact that Jimmy Harrington is not only older than the kid in the novel, but he's smarter, too. Four years of analysis have sharpened his own analytical skills, and his IQ makes him superior to anyone in the gang. Before long, the crooks are asking him for advice.

It's gentle humor, by today's standards, built on watching goofy, uncomplicated criminals bumble their way through a caper that's more sophisticated than they are—and watching professional law enforcement personnel so misread the clues that they believe they're dealing with highly professional kidnappers.

Westlake excels at portraying the gang's serious but humorous attempts to succeed as criminals. Yet the juxtaposition of Parker's professionalism and the Dortmunder gang's lack of such creates much humor. The gang puts a misspelled Detour sign on the road, for instance ("Deture"), and then can't figure out which way it should face after the target car has driven past it. In the Parker novel the boy's limousine is driven into the back of a truck, but the Dortmunder gang manages to get a truck that's too narrow and wooden planks—which break—instead of a metal ramp. When reading instructions over the phone, Murch's Mom keeps dropping the paperback and forgetting to change the appropriate words ("Lincoln" vs "Cadillac").

Within hours of being incarcerated in a second-floor bedroom, Jimmy manages to break out of his prison both through the door and the planked-over window. After escaping into a cold and stormy night, he changes his mind and comes back—his intellect is such that he knows the Dortmunder gang is basically incapable of harming him. Even if they wanted to. Before long, kidnappers and victims are cozily watching TV together, listening to Jimmy lecture about camera angles and lighting in a James Whale picture—for Jimmy intends to be a film director, as we know from a previous brief scene with his analyst.

Murch's Mom finally guides a distracted Harrington Senior through ransom delivery instructions as from the

Stark book, which is difficult enough, and they set off for the switch. But this being a Westlake novel, all sorts of things just don't work. Whereas the Stark stories seem grittily realistic, Westlake points out that real people don't speak in clipped sentences, don't necessarily listen, and often have to repeat themselves. And various problems impede the plan from working perfectly, though it does eventually work well enough to send them back to the hideout carrying a suitcase filled with 150 grand. What they don't realize is that Jimmy, who by now has the run of the house, locates the transmitter the FBI have secreted in the suitcase and spots the waiting surveillance outside while escaping once again.

By now it's clear that Jimmy has some sort of plan of his own,
and getting the gang caught is not part of it. He leads the criminals out the
back and into the woods, from where they eventually emerge in a stolen van and head for midtown Manhattan, where they plan to release Jimmy.

His goodbye is cryptic enough that even this gang realizes there's something wrong. Sure enough, the ransom suitcase has been cleaned out. Jimmy leaves a note and $200 for each gang member, making off with his own ransom. Dortmunder is vindicated—he's had doubts about Kelp's caper all along.

A year later, a letter from Stark to his attorney requests legal action against a film comedy, *Kid Stuff*, apparently based on his novel. The response informs him that he doesn't have a case, as the producer/writer/director is a James Harrington who was himself kidnapped a year before. The kidnappers used Stark's book, but Harrington has only used the factual events which happened to him, so there's no case. In the book's final scene, Dortmunder, Kelp and Murch blow a simple truck hijacking because of Dortmunder's lack of trust in Kelp—then they head off to a movie, a comedy suggested by Kelp. **Kid Stuff**, of course.

Westlake's keen sense of humor thus skewers the gang, the authorities, the victim's affluent father, and even Stark, meaning himself. Only Jimmy, the overly

intellectual victim Dortmunder's gang has the bad luck to pick out, comes out ahead. And only Westlake (and his friend Lawrence Block) would ever consider having the kidnap victim end up with the ransom. With characteristic deftness, Westlake flips back and forth between "fact" and "fiction" and makes both seem both real and unreal on the way to offering the final twist. It might be too analytical to attribute this tendency to his desire to make a statement, but one nevertheless sneaks between the lines—never take anything for granted—your fact or your fiction.

THE TABLES WERE TURNED NOW—SUDDENLY THE HUNTED HAD BECOME **THE HUNTER**

RICHARD STARK

PERMABOOK EDITION M-4272

AN ORIGINAL EDITION

35¢

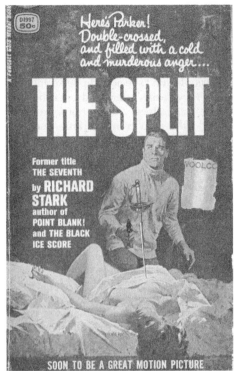

D1997 50¢

Here's Parker! Double-crossed, and filled with a cold and murderous anger....

THE SPLIT

Former title **THE SEVENTH** by **RICHARD STARK** author of **POINT BLANK!** and **THE BLACK ICE SCORE**

WOOLCO

SOON TO BE A GREAT MOTION PICTURE

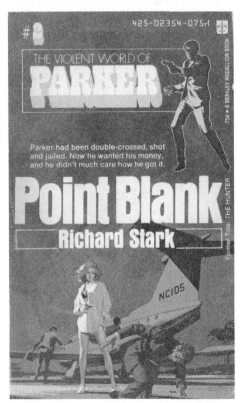

#8

THE VIOLENT WORLD OF **PARKER**

425-02354-075H

Parker had been double-crossed, shot and jailed. Now he wanted his money, and he didn't much care how he got it.

Point Blank
Richard Stark

75¢ • A BERKLEY MEDALLION BOOK

Former Title: THE HUNTER

NC105

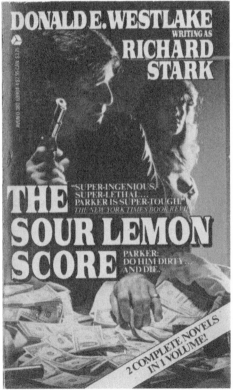

DONALD E. WESTLAKE
WRITING AS
RICHARD STARK

"SUPER-INGENIOUS, SUPER-LETHAL... PARKER IS SUPER-TOUGH" THE NEW YORK TIMES BOOK REVIEW

THE SOUR LEMON SCORE

PARKER: DO HIM DIRTY... AND DIE.

2 COMPLETE NOVELS IN 1 VOLUME!

THE METAMORPHOSIS OF THE RICHARD STARK PAPERBACK

by Peter Enfantino

In the 37 years since Perma published Richard Stark's first Parker novel as a paperback original, there have been various incarnations of the series. Perma/Pocket (the original publisher for Ed McBain's 87th Precinct) published the first seven novels, all graced by nice Harry Bennett covers. Stark was romanced away by Gold Medal (where the series really belonged) in 1966, where Parker remained for another six books (including reprintings/retitlings of **The Hunter** and **The Seventh**).

In the mid-70s, Berkley Medallion packaged Parker as a men's adventure series, complete with misleading cover art (several of the covers hint that Parker is a secret agent). This series lasted for seven numbered books. Avon re-issued all the Parker books in very unattractive packaging in the 1980s (I'd compare the cover photos to the godawful "model with a gun" photo covers that "graced" *Alfred Hitchcock's Mystery Magazine* at about the same time.

Parker's most recent pb house is Mysterious Press, which seems hell-bent on releasing the latest Parker exploits in oversized/overpriced trade paperbacks, thus ensuring no mass audience for what I feel are the two best books in the series since the Perma days.

PERMA
The Hunter
The Man with the Getaway Face
The Outfit
The Mourner
The Jugger
The Score
The Seventh

GOLD MEDAL
Point Blank! (aka **The Hunter**)
The Split (aka **The Seventh**)
The Rare Coin Score
The Green Eagle Score
The Black Ice Score
The Sour Lemon Score

BERKLEY MEDALLION
#1 **Slay-Ground**
#2 **Point Blank** (aka **The Hunter**)
#3 **The Black Ice Score**
#4 **The Outfit**
#5 **Killtown** (aka **The Score**)
#6 **Run Lethal** (aka **The Handle**)
#7 **Deadly Edge**

AVON
The Hunter
The Man With the Getaway Face
The Outfit
The Mourner
The Score
The Seventh
Slayground
The Handle
The Rare Coin Score
The Sour Lemon Score/Deadly Edge
The Green Eagle Score
The Black Ice Score
Butcher's Moon
Plunder Squad
The Jugger

MYSTERIOUS PRESS
The Man With The Getaway Face
Payback! (aka **The Hunter**)
Comeback
Backflash
Flash Fire
Firebreak
Breakout

UNIVERSITY OF CHICAGO PRESS
Nobody Runs Forever
Ask the Parrot
Dirty Money

By the time bare•bones #5 rolled around, Lawrence McCallum had contributed 14 features (spotlighting William Castle, Roger Corman, Hammer Films, and other icons of horror cinema) for TSF and bare•bones, becoming easily our most productive writer. When Lawrence first wrote me back in the late 80s, looking to contribute to The Scream Factory, *I told him I'd always liked Joe Dante's mini-reviews column for* Castle of Frankenstein. *Would he be interested in doing something like that? That birthed "The Late Show," a column that ran for 14 installments in both mags. I really looked forward to receiving his manuscripts every couple of months (McCallum's typewriter had a "period" key that was so violent it would punch a hole through the paper) and poring over his latest mini-reviews. Though he would always run subjects by me for his longer pieces (in case we had a themed issue), he always kept his Late Show spotlights a mystery. His goal was to collect them into a volume of his own writing some day. Lawrence's Edward Cahn retrospective was his swan song for us. -Peter*

HORROR RISES FROM THE PAST IN THE FILMS OF EDWARD L. CAHN!!!

by Lawrence McCallum

We've all heard, at one time or another, that the evil men do lives after them. That statement has been used as the basic premise for many horror tales, both in literature and in film. Authors such as Bram Stoker, H. P. Lovecraft, and August Derleth concentrated on stories about monstrous individuals whose personalities reached from beyond the grave and created mayhem in the world of the living. This theme was effectively delineated in many films ranging from Tod Browning's classic version of **Dracula** (1931) to the low-budget Roger Corman sleeper **The Undead** (1957). The B-chillers of Edward L. Cahn often dealt with the same premise but, unfortunately, his efforts have been given little attention in the past.

Cahn was born in Brooklyn, New York on February 12, 1899. He worked at a number of jobs in his youth before becoming a film cutter at Universal. Cahn then began working nights while attending UCLA during the day. By 1926, he had become chief film editor for Universal Studios and, in 1931, directed his first feature film entitled **Homicide Squad.**

Law and Order (1932) was Cahn's second film as director and this melodrama received generally good reviews. The film, starring Walter Huston as Wyatt Earp, was based on a novel entitled **Saint Johnson** by W. R. Burnett. Earp brought effective law enforcement to Tombstone, Arizona, even though his brutal efficiency also wiped out a large segment of the town's population. **Law and Order** emerged as an unoriginal, but fairly exciting, western adventure helped by its brisk pace and enriched by a number of rugged performances. The all-male cast also includes Harry Carey and Walter Brennan.

The simplistic struggle of good vs. evil is examined in **Law and Order**, and many of Cahn's later efforts explore the same shallow philosophical territory. Virtuous lawmen fight despicable criminals in **Radio Patrol** (1932), **Bad Guy** (1937), **Dangerous Partners** (1945), **Destination Murder** (1950), and about a dozen other melodramas directed by Cahn between 1932 and 1951. The director finally combined his cops and robbers format with an SF framework in **The Creature With the Atom**

Brain (1955), starring Richard Denning. The spotty but often foolish script concerns an alliance between a misguided scientist and a ruthless criminal who use electronically controlled "zombies" in a campaign of terror and revenge. Director Cahn provides several exciting action sequences and the film emerges as a halfway decent juxtaposition of two popular genres.

In 1956, Cahn began his association with American-International, a low-budget company that specialized in horror films and teenage movies. Such neophyte directors as Roger Corman and Bert I. Gordon were doing cheaply-made thrillers for AIP and a cost-conscious veteran like Edward L. Cahn became a welcome addition to the studio's stable of quickie filmmakers. *Runaway Daughters* and *Girls in Prison*, both released in 1956, gave a youthful slant to the clichéd gangster melodramas that Cahn once considered his specialty.

The director's first AIP horror film, *The She Creature*, is marked by impressive camerawork and a dark, brooding atmosphere. Produced by Alex Gordon, the film concerns a mysterious black-cloaked hypnotist (Chester Morris) who regresses a beautiful woman (Marla English) to her past life as a rampaging sea monster. The woman's psychic link with the creature only emerges when she is placed into a deep hypnotic trance. A series of grisly murders begins to occur during such mesmeric interludes with hypnotist Morris finally becoming the prime suspect as instigator of the mayhem. When a young psychiatrist (Lance Fuller) and a shrewd detective (Ron Randall) join forces in the police investigation, the monstrous killer makes a terrifying open appearance. Several people are killed before the hypnotist himself falls victim to the scaly horror. With the death of the sinister Morris, Ms. English is freed from his diabolical control and the female monster vanishes into a gray mist.

The grim undercurrent of sociological horror present in Cahn's gangster melodramas is successfully transposed to the horror-fantasy genre in *The She Creature*. Rather than contrast the criminal underworld with mainstream society, however, Cahn portrays the eerie intrusion of a prehistoric past into the modern world. The savagery of such a past becomes the means of revenge for the Chester Morris character, who feels that he has been scorned and neglected by the people around him. His female subject fails to share such bitter feelings and eventually rebels against his influence. The woman's deadly saurian incarnation from the dawn of time finally resists being an instrument of vengeance and instead strikes down the ruthless man who manipulated her. The film's closing moments may pose an intriguing question for each of us to answer. Has the potential for unbridled human savagery been left in the distant past or does the tendency toward bestial fury still dwell within us—ready to spring to the surface?

After the success of *The She Creature*, producer Alex Gordon was once again teamed with Edward L. Cahn for *Voodoo Woman* (1957). This rather routine AIP thriller merges jungle adventure with sf-horror melodrama and manages to generate only a few mildly frightening moments. Marla English stars as a hardened criminal transformed into a "half-human, half-animal" menace by mad scientist Tom Conway. The film is marred by heavy-handed dialogue, cheap stock shots and an outrageously hammy performance by the usually competent Conway. Mike Connors, as a rugged jungle guide, plays his role with cool conviction and the film is helped by effective black and white photography. After completing this mediocre chiller, Cahn directed several other AIP efforts with the last effort, *Motorcycle Gang*, being released near the end of 1957.

The Zombies of Mora Tau (1957) is a lively but unimaginative rehash of clichés taken from Monogram and PRC thrillers of the 1930's. Genre favorite Allison Hayes gives her typically hard-edged but sensual performance in a thinly-plotted story about the search for a cache of precious gems protected by an army of the walking dead. Director Cahn creates tension in several sequences as cold-eyed zombies move silently through darkened rooms in search of unwary victims. Unfortunately, the bleak, shadowy style of the film can't compensate for a frequent lack of excitement value.

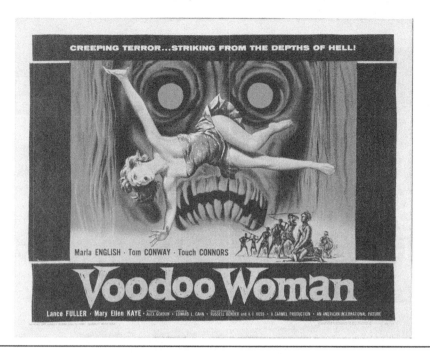

Edward L. Cahn Selected Filmography

Homicide Squad (Universal, 1931) Leo Carrillo, Russell Gleason
Law and Order (Universal, 1932) Walter Huston, Harry Carey
Radio Patrol (Universal, 1932) Robert Armstrong, Russell Hapton
Confidential (MGM, 1935) Donald Cook, Evelyn Knapp
Bad Guy (MGM, 1937) Bruce Cabot, Virginia Grey
Main Street After Dark (MGM, 1945) Audrey Totter, Edward Arnold
Dangerous Partners (MGM, 1945) James Craig, Signe Hasso
The Creature With the Atom Brain (Columbia, 1955) Richard Denning, Angela Stevens
Girls in Prison (AIP, 1956) Richard Denning, Joan Taylor
The She Creature (AIP, 1956) Chester Morris, Marla English
Runaway Daughters (AIP, 1956) Marla English, Gloria Castillo
Shake, Rattle and Roll (AIP, 1956) Mike (Touch) Connors, Fats Domino
Voodoo Woman (AIP, 1957) Marla English, Tom Conway
Dragstrip Girl (AIP, 1957) Faye Spain, Steve Terrell
The Zombies of Mora Tau (Allied Artists, 1957)Allison Hayes, Gregg Palmer
Invasion of the Saucer-Men (AIP, 1957) Steve Terrell, Floria Castillo
Motorcycle Gang (AIP, 1957) John Ashley, Russ Bender
Curse of the Faceless Man (Allied Artists, 1958) Richard Anderson, Elaine Edwards
It! The Terror From Beyond Space! (United Artists, 1958) Gerald Mohr, Lee Van Cleef
Invisible Invaders (United Artists, 1959) John Agar, Robert Hutton
The Four Skulls of Jonathan Drake (United Artists, 1959) Henry Daniell, Grant Richards
Inside the Mafia (Allied Artists, 1959) Cameron Mitchell, Elaine Edwards
Vice Raid (Allied Artists, 1959) Mamie Van Doren, Brad Dexter
Gunfighters of Abilene (United Artists, 1960) Buster Crabbe, Barton MacLane
Twelve Hours to Kill (United Artists, 1960) Nico Minardos, Barbara Eden
Operation Bottleneck (United Artists, 1961) Ron Foster, Norm Alden
The Clown and the Kid (Allied Artists, 1961) John Lupton
Beauty and the Beast (United Artists, 1963) Mark Damon, Joyce Taylor

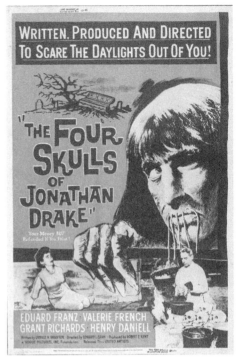

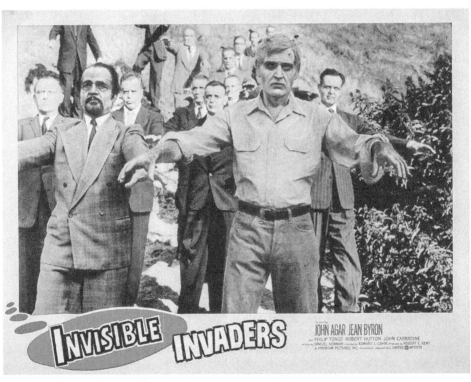

Curse of the Faceless Man (1958) also employs the "living dead" premise, but is handled with a bit more restraint and contains a few good plot twists. The story takes place in modern-day Italy, where archeologists have uncovered a petrified man from the ruins of Pompeii. A strange link soon emerges between the stone man and a woman (Elaine Edwards) who, apparently, is the reincarnation of the human artifact's sweetheart. The stone man returns from the dead, finally kidnapping the woman in an attempt to escape the disaster that is still being enacted in his mind—the cataclysmic eruption of Mt. Vesuvius. After arriving at a deserted beach, he wades into the sea with the intention of carrying his long-lost love to safety. When bullets prove powerless in stopping the ancient horror, the police are stunned to see his body dissolve in the sea water. The final scene has the heroine being rescued from drowning by her archeologist-husband (Richard Anderson).

Though marred by stilted acting, *Curse of the Faceless Man* is helped by careful plotting and good camerawork. Visual horror is kept to a minimum, but director Cahn instills a claustrophobic sense of horror in the viewer as we see a woman oppressed by deeply rooted fears that she can't begin to understand. Psychological tensions mount throughout the story until we reach the overt physical horror of the film's final sequences. This effort emerges as a satisfying example of how good work can be done on a limited budget.

Edward L. Cahn directed a pair of minor but fairly engaging thrillers for United Artists, with both films providing the basis for widely acclaimed efforts yet to come. *It! The Terror From Beyond Space!* (1958) concerns the struggle of a space crew against a seemingly invulnerable alien monster that has stowed away on board their vessel returning to Earth. The structure and characters contained in the film closely resemble that of Ridley Scott's *Alien* (1979), which was a conscious imitation. *Invisible Invaders* (1959) pits a tough marine (John Agar) against a horde of reanimated corpses inhabited by hostile alien intellects. The latter film presents nightmarish images of pasty-faced human monsters relentlessly stalking horrified victims. Such images became an integral part of George Romero's *Night of the Living Dead* (1968) nearly ten years after the release of *Invisible Invaders*. Neither of the two Cahn efforts received critical acceptance, but their influence on the creation of future cult classics cannot be ignored.

The Four Skulls of Jonathan Drake (1959) is Edward L. Cahn's last horror film. Even though many critics felt that this low-budget thriller more closely resembled a TV feature than a theatrical release, an eerie atmosphere and considerable suspense value help make the Allied Artists production emerge as a better-than-average B-chiller. The film stars Henry Daniell as the modern-day purveyor of an 18th Century Jivaro curse. Daniell, posing as a reclusive Dutch doctor, is aided by a zombie-like Jivaro Indian who kills his victims with a deadly poison and then decapitates the bodies. The subjects of this gruesome campaign of vengeance are the surviving members of the Drake family, whose ancestors were involved in the plunder and destruction of a South American Indian village.

Jonathan Drake (Eduard Franz) manages to convince a no-nonsense detective (Grant Richards) that the ritualistic killings are the result of voodoo and they head off to the doctor's gloomy mansion in search of further evidence. After they discover the shrunken heads of several murder victims, there is a violent encounter with the doctor and his cohort. Bullets have no effect on the murderous pair, but the zombie-servant is consumed by the flames of the ritual fire into which he has fallen. The detective, now armed with a poison-tipped knife, pursues the fleeing doctor. After a frantic struggle, the doctor's neck is punctured by the blade, bringing an end to his horrid existence.

After the release of *The Four Skulls of Jonathan Drake*, Edward L. Cahn directed a number of straight adventure and suspense melodramas. Between 1959 and 1962, a total of 26 Cahn efforts were released to theaters! These films covered a variety of themes, ranging from the violent World War II realism of *Operation Bottleneck* (1961) to the innocuous human interest of a mild suspensor entitled *The Clown and*

From the long ago and far away—the tale of fear and love that will never die!

Beauty and the BEAST

JOYCE TAYLOR and MARK DAMON EDUARD FRANZ

TECHNICOLOR

The Kid (1961). Though he now worked at a feverish pace that was rivaled only by Roger Corman's hectic schedule, the many screen accomplishments of director Cahn were still being ignored by most critics.

A turn in a positive direction seemed to come in 1963, when United Artists assigned Cahn to direct *Beauty and the Beast*. This ambitious period fantasy was one of several UA efforts inspired by American-International's highly successful series of Edgar Allan Poe adaptations. UA's hopes for its own string of horror-fantasies began with their release of Reginald Le Borg's *Diary of a Madman* (1963), which starred Vincent Price and was based on Guy Du Maupassant's "The Horla."

Beauty and the Beast was fairly expensive for an Edward L. Cahn film. Despite an elaborate production design, this effort is marred by an unimaginative script and the presence of a straining heroine (Joyce Taylor). The bitter-sweet love story that is so well-known receives a heavy handed treatment from Cahn, who was far more skilled as an action director. United Artists was very disappointed with the overall quality of the film, which quickly disappeared after a limited distribution in the United States.

Quite sadly, Edward L. Cahn suffered a fatal heart attack shortly after the release of *Beauty and the Beast* in 1963. Although he directed 67 films in a career that spanned 32 years, Cahn never received the recognition granted to other B-grade directors such as Roger Corman, Jack Arnold and Edgar G. Ulmer. Much like those three filmmakers, Cahn delineated tales of terror that placed a strong emphasis on the human factor. However, the average Cahn thriller is distinguished by its examination of conflicts created by the intrusion of past misdeeds into normal, present-day lives. whether it is the mayhem caused by the long-festering vendetta of a hoodlum in *The Creature With the Atom Brain* or the shocking brutality that reaches from the past life of a lovely girl in *The She Creature*, we see the destruction of quiet lives through the-emergence of vaguely remembered horrors.

Perhaps each of us has, at some time in our lives, committed acts that were destructive toward others. Such hostilities may be better left forgotten, but many people are frequently haunted by uncertain fears about the far-reaching effects of negative past behavior. The thrillers of Edward L. Cahn might make us question our own humanity when we see long-buried hostilities claw viciously at the "normal" world.

bare•bones $5

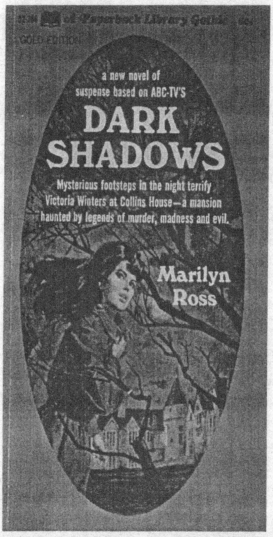

UNEARTHING VINTAGE AND FORGOTTEN
HORROR/MYSTERY/SCI-FI/WESTERN
FILM-PAPERBACKS-PULP FICTION-VIDEO

52-386 A Paperback Library Gothic 50¢

GOLD EDITION

a new novel of suspense based on ABC-TV'S

DARK SHADOWS

Mysterious footsteps in the night terrify Victoria Winters at Collins House—a mansion haunted by legends of murder, madness and evil.

Marilyn Ross

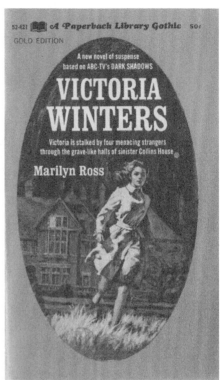

52-421 A Paperback Library Gothic 50¢

GOLD EDITION

A new novel of suspense based on ABC-TV's DARK SHADOWS

VICTORIA WINTERS

Victoria is stalked by four menacing strangers through the grave-like halls of sinister Collins House.

Marilyn Ross

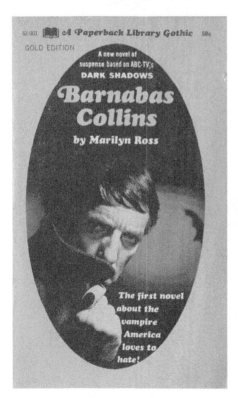

62-001 A Paperback Library Gothic 50¢

GOLD EDITION

A new novel of suspense based on ABC-TV's DARK SHADOWS

Barnabas Collins

by Marilyn Ross

The first novel about the vampire America loves to hate!

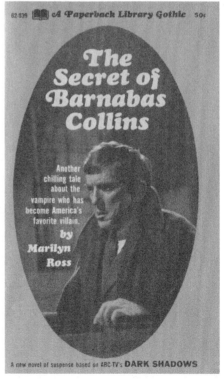

62-039 A Paperback Library Gothic 50¢

The Secret of Barnabas Collins

Another chilling tale about the vampire who has become America's favorite villain.

by Marilyn Ross

A new novel of suspense based on ABC-TV's DARK SHADOWS

220

As I'm almost four years into a five-year run blogging on the 50th anniversary of each and every episode of Dark Shadows *(all 1225 of them!), it was interesting to revisit this, knowing now just how far removed the books are from the original storylines. David Brown saves us the trouble of having to read them all—although I have to admit that I'm very tempted to dive into the one about space aliens arriving in Collinwood! If this overview piques your interest, you'll be thrilled to hear that Hermes Press has just announced that they will be reprinting all 32 volumes in the series. -John*

DARK GOTHIC
The *Dark Shadows* Novels of Dan Ross
By David Allen Brown

William Edward Daniel Ross was a writer from a very early age, although he did not make his debut as a novelist until 1961 at the age of forty-nine with the publication of **Summer Season**. But Dan Ross wrote that book, like so many others, from the shadows, under a penname. Jane Rossiter was the first of many pseudonyms for many novels to come.

As if to make up for his late start as a novelist (he had written over 600 short stories prior to the publication of **Summer Season**), Dan Ross began to publish an array of novels at a pace that is literally awe-inspiring. In the span of seven short years, 100 of his novels would see print. In fourteen more years he would reach number 300 with the publication of **Beloved Adversary** in 1982. Do the math on a calculator and you will find that his average output for both time periods comes out exactly the same—14.285714 books a year. This is truly fitting for a man who wrote all his novels with mathematical precision.

There were almost always 12 chapters with about 13 pages each. The only two *Dark Shadows* books to break this rule were **Victoria Winters** and **Barnabas Collins**, which introduced the title character to the literary world. Dan Ross even managed to adapt the novelization of *House of Dark Shadows* to this precise formula.

Writing 14 novels a year is difficult enough—that's more than a novel a month— but to write them all so that every book contained the same number of chapters and the same number of pages per chapter is a feat that is really beyond the skills of most writers. Just the thought of trying to do a novel a month for a whole year is enough to send chills down any writer's fingers as he or she pounds the typewriter keys.

Then imagine, if you could, keeping up this pace for 20 years! At the time of his death, he would have 358 novels published! Even a prolific writer seems downright lethargic in comparison.

The most infamous example of Dan Ross' speed came in 1970 when his agent telephoned on a Wednesday to say he needed a 75,000-word nurse novel by next week. Dan Ross handed in **Department Store Nurse** (written as by Rose Dana) on Monday—five days after the call! To give you an idea how difficult this is: you would have to write—on average—15,000 words a day for those five days. In that span of 120 hours, if you wrote 24 hours a day, every day, you would have to average at least 625 words every hour!

Comedic talk show host David Letterman joked about Dan Ross' accomplishment when the author appeared on *Late Night With David Letterman* on April Fools Day, 1987.

Sadly, Dan Ross spent his career writing from the shadows, under as many as 21 different pseudonyms, and the mention of his name would garner little recognition from today's readers. His work on the *Dark Shadows* novels has kept his memory and work alive to a small degree.

The pseudonyms he utilized were: Marilyn Ross, W.E.D. Ross, Dana Ross, Rose Williams, Ruth Dorset, Clarissa Ross, Jane Rossiter, Tex Steele, Jane Daniels, Rose Dana, Ann Gilmer, Dan Roberts, Sali Brenner, Ellen Randolph, Leslie Ames, Laura Frances

Brooks, Lydia Colby, Charlotte McCormack, Diana Randall, Marilyn Carter and Claude Nicole. He did occasionally write under his own name, publishing such titles as **Cliffhaven** and **Fogbound**.

On Wednesday, November 1, 1995, Dan Ross died of congestive heart failure in his hometown of Saint John, New Brunswick. He was 82 years old. He was survived by Marilyn Ross, his wife of 35 years.

•

The early *Dark Shadows* novels had Victoria Winters residing at Collinwood and romancing Ernest Collins, whose insane wife, hidden in the attic of Collinwood, tries to murder Victoria in the series' first installment. Later books brought menacing strangers to the house atop Widow's Hill, and there were varied attempts on Victoria's life.

The addition of the supernatural into the TV series caused a change in the books as well, although Dan Ross was hesitant to fully embrace the otherworldly goings-on; his novels would, more often than not, have a rational explanation and all-too-human villain, even though his characters included vampires, witches and werewolves.

The Curse of Collinwood marked the point of transition. Ernest Collins has died in a plane crash and zombies prowl the great estate. Ross does leave the reader with lingering doubts as to whether the creatures are really Derek and Esther Collins, the walking dead, or if they are merely escaped killer Tim Mooney and his girlfriend Nora Sonier.

Barnabas Collins, the next installment, plunges headlong into the abyss with the introduction of the title character to Collinwood, circa 1902. The novel spans a number of years as Barnabas falls in love with a girl named Judith, who resembles his lost love Josette, and imagines that Judith's love will save him from his vampire curse.

This theme would be repeated throughout the series of novels, each taking place in different periods, with various heroines falling in love with the tormented vampire. Victoria Winters gives way to Maggie Evans and then Carolyn Stoddard. Then there are all of the young ladies from an array of time periods. The Barnabas in the earlier novels is a much darker figure than the character later in the series. Gradually, he is transformed into a sort of supernatural crime fighter, rescuing beautiful damsels in distress. Quentin Collins would undergo a similar metamorphosis.

Quentin would make his debut in **Barnabas Collins and Quentin's Demon**. He began the series as an unsympathetic character, a rival to Barnabas Collins, even though his character is mostly a bystander in the novels, usually skulking around Collinwood in one disguise or another. There are exceptions, of course. In **Barnabas, Quentin and the Witch's Curse**, Quentin is the thoroughly evil head of a coven of witches and in **Barnabas, Quentin and the Serpent**, Quentin commits a series of murders under the guise of an ancient Aztec legend, but he would join Barnabas on the side of good with the publication of **Barnabas, Quentin and the Magic Potion**. In this installment, Barnabas refers to his werewolf cousin as his 'friendly rival.'

In the next installment, **Barnabas, Quentin and the Body Snatchers**, our titled heroes do battle with invaders from outer space who abduct humans (Roger Collins among them) and assume their likeness to sabotage the U.S. Space Program.

As with any series, the novels vary in quality. The earliest Barnabas novels rank among the best. Other top efforts include: **Barnabas Collins and the Gypsy Witch**, **Barnabas, Quentin and the Crystal Coffin**, **Barnabas, Quentin and the Frightened Bride**, **Barnabas, Quentin and the Grave Robbers** and **Barnabas, Quentin and the Vampire Beauty**.

The low points in the series: **Barnabas, Quentin and the Mummy's Curse**, **Barnabas, Quentin and the Serpent** (containing one of the dumbest revelations ever) and **Barnabas, Quentin and the Mad Magician**. The failures are usually the result of Dan Ross' refusal to employ true supernatural occurrences, or having his characters behave in such illogical ways that the novels become cartoonish, almost

Scooby-Doo-like in their unsophisticated awfulness.

Still, overall, the novels were competently written, an entertaining way for *Dark Shadows* fans to get their fix of Barnabas, Quentin and their various escapades at Collinwood.

•

The following is a summary of all of the *Dark Shadows* novels Dan Ross wrote under the pen name Marilyn Ross.

Dark Shadows (December, 1966)

Victoria Winters comes to Maine to work for the Collins family, hoping to unravel the secrets of her past, which may be tied to the Collins family. There are several attempts on her life as she becomes romantically involved with Ernest Collins, whose insane wife has taken secret refuge at Collinwood.

Victoria Winters (March, 1967)

Henry Francis, a schoolmate of Elizabeth Stoddard's, comes to stay at Collinwood with his daughters Rachel and Dorothy, who is recovering from surgery to remove a brain tumor and is in a catatonic-like state. With Ernest Collins away, Victoria is romanced by Paul Caine, a mysterious artist and Will Grant, a young lawyer. There are attempts on Victoria's life as she uncovers a sinister kidnapping plot.

Strangers at Collins House (September, 1967)

Elderly Henry Collins and his entourage—faithful companion, son, and daughter-in-law—arrive at Collinwood. Henry Collins wants to spend his final days in a room in a closed off wing of the house, a room that he has created as an exact duplicate of the suite he had occupied in the Ritz Hampton Hotel in New York City circa 1916. On Halloween night of that year, Henry's mistress, Winifred Ray, vanished, and Victoria bears a striking resemblance to the young woman. Could this be, at last, a key to her identity?

The Mystery of Collinwood (January, 1968)

Professor Mark Veno, a mentalist, and his daughter arrive at Collinwood. Victoria learns from Mark the legend of the Phantom Mariner, a skeletal figure clad in a black cape and cowl, who would appear to the wives of sailors on Widow's Hill. His sighting meant either death to those who saw him, or to someone dear to them. Victoria sees the ghostly apparition and there are mysterious attempts on her life. Could the legend of the Phantom Mariner be real?

The Curse of Collinwood (May, 1968)

Ernest Collins is killed in a plane crash and a distraught Victoria turns to Burke Devlin for comfort. She learns the legend of Derek Collins, captain of the Mary Dorn, who took a woman named Esther, daughter of the governor of a West Indies island, as his wife. When Derek began dealing in the slave trade, his enraged wife murdered him and had a witch doctor transform him into a zombie. She killed herself and the witch doctor made her a zombie as well. The bodies were shipped to Collinwood and placed in a crypt, waiting for a shaft of moonlight to touch their coffins and stir them to life. Burke and Victoria open the crypt, searching for treasure that was supposed to be buried with them. Unable to properly close the door, they leave and mysterious sightings of a man and woman are observed at Collinwood. Have Derek and Esther returned as the living dead?

Barnabas Collins (November, 1968)

Barnabas Collins comes to visit Collinwood in 1902. Margaret Collins, mistress of the great estate, learns his dark secret, but keeps quiet because her daughter Greta, who is confined to a wheelchair due to twisted, abnormal legs, is in love with him. Barnabas sees Judith, a young orphan, as his long lost Josette and plans to adopt her until she is of marrying age. As the years pass, Judith falls in love with another man. Will Margaret be able to stop Barnabas from claiming Judith as his vampire bride?

The Secret of Barnabas Collins (January, 1969)

London, circa 1870, Lady Clare Duncan falls in love with Barnabas Collins despite the protests of her father and the dark rumors about him. After Clare learns his secret, Barnabas flees London with Clare in pursuit. Her journey will take her to an abandoned Benedictine Monastery and then to Maine, where Barnabas has taken up residence at Stormcliff, a neighboring estate to Collinwood. Clare still loves Barnabas, but he is involved with Julia Conrad, wife of the captain of the Belle Corliss, a ship where the novel comes to a climax.

The Demon of Barnabas Collins (April, 1969)

Hollywood meets Collinwood as a movie company comes to the great estate to film a movie. Actress Rita Glenn falls in love with Barnabas and runs afoul of the sinister Dr. Moreno, personal physician to Clifton Kerr, her temperamental co-star. There are vampire attacks, and Barnabas and Rita suspect another vampire is on the loose. Will there be a Hollywood happy ending for Barnabas and Rita?

The Foe of Barnabas Collins (July, 1969)

1910: newly married, Christopher Jennings brings his new bride to Cranshaw, a neighboring estate to Collinwood. Paula is terrified by the strange behavior of her husband, whom she fears may be a werewolf, and is befriended by Barnabas Collins, who believes that Melissa Henry, their servant girl, is the reincarnation of Angelique. What dark design does Chris and Melissa have in store for Paula, and can Barnabas save her from a fate worse than death?

The Phantom and Barnabas Collins (September, 1969)

Maggie Evans and Barnabas Collins visit the Collins family graveyard. Barnabas takes her to the tomb of Giles Collins and shows her a hidden chamber where Valeria Norris is entombed. Maggie stares into Barnabas' hypnotic eyes and faints. She comes to, with memory loss, at Collinwood, circa 1880, where Dr. Giles Collins tells her that she was thrown from a horse. Maggie recognizes Barnabas, who befriends her, causing Giles to be jealous. Giles has a consumptive clinic on the estate, working to find a cure for a mysterious blood disease that caused his wife to wither and age before her time, and now threatens Valeria Norris, his sister-in-law. A phantom-like figure begins to visit Maggie and tries to kill her. Will Barnabas, suspected of being a vampire, be able to save her? Will Maggie regain her memory and return to her own time?

Barnabas Collins versus the Warlock (October, 1969)

The first truly awful installment has David Collins and Amy Jennings seemingly possessed by a 'shadowy stranger' who tells them to do bad things. Maggie Evans is concerned about their behavior, and about the arrival of Elizabeth's cousin Nina and her husband, Dr. Eli Bremmer, who has come to Collinwood to further his studies in psychic research. After a séance, Dr. Bremmer becomes convinced that the children are possessed by a warlock named Asaph Clay, and is obsessed with finding his skull. Will the warlock have, at last, his vengeance on the entire Collins family?

The Peril of Barnabas Collins (November, 1969)

The novel takes place in London during the reign of Queen Victoria. Heiress Diana Hastings is in love with Barnabas, but her mother is opposed and whisks her daughter off to Italy to visit upon the Count of Baraga, whom she hopes will wed her Diana. The deranged Count holds Diana and her mother captive, but Barnabas Collins comes to the rescue. They travel to Collinwood, along with sinister Dr. Padrel and his daughter Maria. Barnabas hopes Padrel will be able to cure him of his vampire curse, but does the not-so-good doctor have other plans, which center on Diana?

Barnabas Collins and the Mysterious Ghost (January, 1970)

The members of the Mary Wentworth Ballet Company are given free room and board at Collinwood while

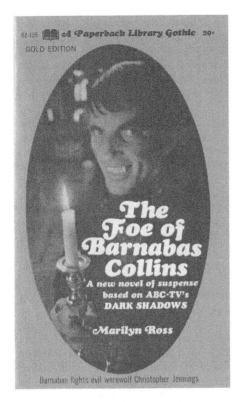

The Foe of Barnabas Collins

A new novel of suspense based on ABC-TV's DARK SHADOWS

Marilyn Ross

Barnabas fights evil werewolf Christopher Jennings

Based on ABC-TV's DARK SHADOWS

Barnabas Collins And The Mysterious Ghost

Barnabas risks losing his freedom to save the life of the woman he loves.

Marilyn Ross

Barnabas engages in mortal battle to rid Collinwood of the curse of an ancient monster

Barnabas, Quentin and the Serpent

by Marilyn Ross

Barnabas, Quentin and the Body Snatchers

Can Barnabas and Quentin rid Collinwood of the ruthless invaders from outer space?

Marilyn Ross

preparing their new ballet, Roxanna. Diana Samson, the second female lead, encounters supernatural forces, learning of the ghost of a young sailor said to haunt the chapel. The sailor had fallen in love with Anya Collins; a misunderstanding resulted in Anya hanging herself in the chapel and the sailor throwing himself off Widow's Hill. Ghostly events plague the Ballet Company and Diana in particular, as unseen forces try to kill her. Can Barnabas save the beautiful dancer from the forces that seek to destroy her?

Barnabas Collins and Quentin's Demon (February, 1970)

The story begins in May of 1895 with the arrival of Lara Balfour at Collinwood. Quentin Collins, who had corresponded with her out of admiration for the haunting waltz her late father had composed, has invited her to the estate. Lara becomes infatuated with Quentin's cousin, Barnabas, and fearful that Quentin may be a werewolf; his first wife had her throat torn out by a wild beast. Quentin claims his brother Conrad breeds savage dogs and they are to blame, but when the full moon rises there are more attacks at the great estate. Will Lara meet the fate of Quentin's first wife, or will Barnabas be able to save her from a grisly fate?

Barnabas Collins and the Gypsy Witch (March, 1970)

Roxanna Collins is alone in New York in 1895. She falls into the clutches of Sybil Makham and William Oakes, who plan to ship her off to South America, but she escapes and is taken in by Barnabas, who accompanies the young girl back to Collinwood. A Gypsy fortune teller warns Roxanna that Collinwood is under a curse and that there will be sudden, violent deaths. Roxanna's father is stabbed to death and her brother Robert is found dead on the rocks beneath Widow's Hill. Barnabas is suspected, and Roxanna is in grave danger as the killer comes after her as well.

Barnabas, Quentin and the Mummy's Curse (April, 1970)

Professor Anthony Collins and associates, including Dr. Herb Price (AKA Quentin Collins) come to Collinwood to catalog relics from the tomb of Egyptian King Rehotip. Maggie Evans is employed as a secretary and she learns that the mummy of Rehotip is actually in suspended animation and that Anthony Collins plans on reviving him. The mummy breaks lose and roams the grounds of Collinwood. The professor blackmails Maggie into remaining silent by threatening to point the blame at Barnabas. But, as some of the inhabitants of Collinwood fall to foul play, can Maggie remain quiet, and can she and Barnabas find Rehotip before it's too late?

Barnabas, Quentin and the Avenging Ghost (May, 1970)

Roger Collins was foreman of the jury that convicted murderess Harriet Barnes, who swore vengeance on Roger before taking her own life. Meanwhile, Alice Dalton (an ex-love of Roger's) comes to Collinwood with her husband, a renowned expert in the spirit world, and their daughter Celia, whose participation in her father's work has resulted in a nervous breakdown. Strange events, such as Carolyn Stoddard being choked into unconsciousness, plague Collinwood, seemingly committed by Celia, who has blackouts. Her father insists that the ghost of Harriet Barnes possesses her. Is the spirit of the murderess trying to wreak vengeance from beyond the grave?

Barnabas, Quentin and the Nightmare Assassin (June, 1970)

A car accident propels Carolyn Stoddard and Barnabas Collins back to the year 1869. Carolyn finds herself engaged to Quentin Collins, who is suspected of being a werewolf, and in love with Barnabas, who finds himself temporarily cured of his vampire affliction. Unable to take his own life, Quentin turns to Samuel Clive, the family attorney, to hire an assassin; the barrister dies before the killer's identity is revealed. Will the assassin finish the job and is Quentin really responsible for the mysterious attacks at Collinwood?

Barnabas, Quentin and the Crystal Coffin
(July, 1970)

Englishwoman Betty Ward discovers that her twin sister Georgette has eloped with American Jeremy Frene. After being rescued from the clutches of an evil count, who had been obsessed with Georgette, Betty and Quentin Collins journey to America to pay a visit to Frene Castle, a neighboring estate to Collinwood. Betty is horrified to learn that Georgette has died from some mysterious malady and that a grief-stricken Jeremy has placed her body in a glass coffin. He refuses to bury her, claiming that her ghost visits nightly, and shows Betty painting that her sister's ghost is supposed to have done. Has Jeremy gone mad, and is he responsible for her sister's death? And by remaining at Frene Castle, will Betty meet the same fate as her twin sister?

Barnabas, Quentin and the Witch's Curse
(August, 1970)

Americans Anita Burgess, her brother, and her fiancée first meet Quentin Collins in Venice of 1900. Quentin is the head of a black magic cult that worships Satan, and he wants Anita to join his coven. Her fiancée dies under mysterious circumstances, and Anita points the finger of blame at Quentin, who flees to America. Anita and her brother follow him to Collinwood, vowing to avenge the death of Anita's beloved. Aided by Barnabas Collins, Anita tries to bring Quentin and his followers to justice, but in doing so, has she placed her-and soul-in mortal jeopardy?

Barnabas, Quentin and the Haunted Cave
(September, 1970)

Harriet Turnbridge is recently widowed. Her husband was killed; his throat ripped open. As she and Barnabas try to unravel the mystery, her brother-in-law and father-in-law meet the same fate. Could it be her neighbor, whom she suspects is Quentin Collins in disguise? The answers may lay in her dreams, in which she is transported to another era, where she is menaced by Quentin's devil cult and put on trial for witchcraft; Barnabas projects himself into her dreams to try to rescue her.

The hidden cave beneath the Collins family cemetery may reveal the secret, or it may become Harriet's Tomb if she and Barnabas cannot discover the killer's identity in time.

Barnabas, Quentin and the Frightened Bride (October, 1970)

At the end of the First World War, Ann Hayward accompanies her husband John, who is suffering from shell shock, to Collinsport. They are invited to stay at Collinwood by William Collins, who resides with his spoiled son Eric. Eric's twin brother had died of a mysterious wasting disease. Already worried about her husband's fragile mental state, Ann is further distressed when learning of the Hayward Curse, in which the wives of the Hayward men often met tragic ends. There are attempts on her life; could her husband behind them, or could it be the mysterious disfigured stranger (whom she suspects may be the werewolf Quentin Collins) that resides in a nearby cottage?

Barnabas, Quentin and the Scorpio Curse
(November, 1970)

Diana Collins and her sister Carol come to Collinwood. Diana has been suffering from blackouts since the death of her father. Diana is to be treated at the nearby Turnbridge House, a psychiatric clinic where Barnabas Collins, recovering from a long time aversion to sunlight, is also a guest. The house is said to be haunted by the Lost Lady of Turnbridge, the daughter of the house's original owner, who killed herself after being jilted by her fiancée. Her ghost, clad in a hooded cloak, is said to appear to those about to die. Diana, while questioning her own sanity, begins to suspect that one of the doctors is actually Quentin Collins. During her blackouts, some of the patients are killed (a drawing of a scorpion left on their foreheads) and suspicion falls on Diana. Can she and Barnabas uncover the culprit before it is too late?

Barnabas, Quentin and the Serpent
(December, 1970)

Professor Gerald Collins inherits Collinwood in the winter of 1870. He and his daughter Irma were investigating a lost

Aztec village down in Mexico when they receive the news. After a falling out with Quentin Collins, who was in the Professor's employ, Gerald Collins packs up some rare specimens and transports them to Collinwood. Irma fears that her father has shipped a Quetzalcoatl, a feathered flying serpent of Aztec legend. Her father denies this, but soon a large feathered creature in sighted in the skies over Collinwood and mysterious deaths follow. Can Irma clear her father's good name and solve the mystery, or will become another victim of a centuries-old legend?

Barnabas, Quentin and the Magic Potion (January, 1971)

Carolyn Stoddard takes a summer job at the 'Olde Antique Barn' run by the strange Nicholas Freeze, against the wishes of her mother, who wants Carolyn to take a position at the summer theater run by Mike Buchanan. Barnabas has agreed to appear in one of Buchanan's plays. One night at the shop, while cleaning an antique desk belonging to an eighteenth century chemist, Carolyn uncovers three flasks whose contents, according to an accompanying letter, will give eternal life. The letter warns that the elixir must be administered in small doses, and that it is very dangerous. Harriet Freeze tells Carolyn that her father wants to test the elixir on her. Then Harriet dies mysteriously and she is seen walking the grounds of Collinwood. Meanwhile, a series of wolf sightings convinces Carolyn and Barnabas that Quentin has returned, but has he disguised himself as director Mike Buchanan or actor Jim Swift? Of course, Freeze is still trying to perfect and he needs a new test subject—Carolyn!

Barnabas, Quentin and the Body Snatchers (February, 1971)

Murdoch Gray, one of the space program's top scientists, and his daughter Marjorie are invited to stay at Collinwood by Roger Collins, who was an old college roommate of Murdoch. Murdoch confides to his daughter that a space warp had been discovered during the Apollo 13 mission, and that they were receiving radio transmissions from the planet Velva which they had not

been able to decode. Marjorie wonders if they were not a warning to stay away. Soon, aliens, who assume their likeness in order to sabotage the space program, abduct Roger Collins and Murdoch Gray. Quentin, alias rock idol Jim James, is Marjorie's boyfriend. After Roger and Murdoch's behavior makes the other inhabitants of Collinwood suspicious, Quentin and Barnabas uncover the alien plot, race to free their friends, and put a stop to the invaders once and for all.

Barnabas, Quentin and Dr. Jekyll's Son (April, 1971)

The tale begins in the winter of 1908. Collinwood is blanketed by blizzard-like conditions. Barnabas Collins has brought Dr. Henry Jekyll from England to stay with him at the Old House. Emily Collins has fallen in love with the doctor, who is trying to cure Barnabas of his vampire affliction. Foster daughter Ada Collins thinks Dr. Jekyll, who suffers from blackouts, may be tainted from his father, the notorious murderer. When a servant girl is killed, Jekyll is suspected. Quentin, disguised as private detective Paul Faron, and Barnabas try to clear themselves and the good doctor before the killer, who seems to have his or her sights set on Emily, strikes again.

Barnabas, Quentin and the Grave Robbers (June, 1971)

The novel begins in London in the spring of 1830. Sir Phillip Sullivan, the city's leading surgeon, finds himself at odds with the evil Nicholas Bentley, a doctor who utilized immoral and illegal means of obtaining fresh cadavers for medical experimentation. Dr. Bentley has his cohorts kidnap Paula and plan to force her into marriage. Saved by Barnabas Collins, whom she has come to love, Paula is rescued only to see her friends abducted by Bentley, and her father is brutally murdered by Bentley's hulking servant. Knowing she is unsafe as long as Bentley and his criminal companions are free, Paula accompanies Barnabas to America. But is Collinwood far enough away to escape the evil plans Dr. Bentley has in store for Paula—to transform her into a zombie.

Barnabas, Quentin and the Sea Ghost (August, 1971)

Norah Bliss and her father, who run the most successful salvage company in the United States, come to stay at Collinwood. They try to salvage the cargo of the pirate ship Jenny Swift (named after it's captain, who was disfigured trying to quell a mutiny), which was lost in Collinsport Cove over two hundred years ago. All previous attempts to salvage the ship had met with disaster. The last, led by Carson Blythe, who resides in a house atop the cliffs with his adopted daughter Grace, saw all his equipment destroyed by a storm; it was said that the ghost of Jenny Swift haunting his home caused his wife to take her own life by leaping off the cliffs. Soon, Norah comes face to face with the pirate queen's ghost as mysterious accidents and death plague their attempt to uncover the treasure.

Barnabas, Quentin and the Mad Magician (October, 1971)

Carolyn Stoddard and her friend Beth Mayberry are excited when they learn that Cabrini, the world famous magician, would be staying at nearby Kerrhaven and would be performing a magic show on the grounds of the Collinwood estate. But for Carolyn, excitement gives way to apprehension; she fears that her young friend has been placed under as hypnotic spell by the sinister magician, forced to join his troupe. Several deaths occur in and around Collinsport; the victims having their throats ripped open. The authorities suspect Quentin Collins, who is seeking treatment from Dr. Julia Hoffman, but Carolyn is convinced that Cabrini is somehow involved. Then Beth Mayberry joins the list of victims and Carolyn is determined, with the help of Barnabas and Quentin, to out trick Cabrini and break the spell of terror he has cast over Collinwood.

Barnabas, Quentin and the Hidden Tomb (December, 1971)

The novel begins in the summer of 1866. Ellen Drury and her aunt travel from Atlanta to Graywood, the estate of Stephen Gray, a man she had loved before the Civil war separated them. Ellen's aunt is suspicious of Stephen's motives, thinking he has lost his fortune in the war and was looking to replenish the coffers with the riches of the Drury estate. Ellen discovers that her beloved is actually Stephen's twin brother Louis, a vampire; Stephen was killed in a fire. Ellen's aunt is killed, but before she dies she tells her niece to go to New York to seek out the aid of Barnabas Collins, whom she knew in her days as a Broadway actress. Ellen finds Barnabas and, after rescuing her from being kidnapped by the Gray Family lawyer, he takes her to Collinwood. There are Vampire attacks in the area, but Barnabas has been cured of his affliction. Has Louis followed Ellen to Collinwood, determined to claim her as his vampire bride?

Barnabas, Quentin and the Vampire Beauty (March, 1972)

Fashion model Adele Marriot is tricked by Dr. Stefan Spivak into agreeing to an operation that will allow her to maintain a constant weight without diet or exorcise. Once she is in his isolated clinic in the Swiss Alps, Adele discovers that she has been transformed into a vampire in order to free another from the affliction, at least temporarily. Told by a nurse to seek out Barnabas Collins, Adele travels to Collinwood and enlists the aid of Barnabas, whom Dr. Julia Hoffman is trying to cure. Aided by Quentin as well, the trio finds themselves in a life and death battle with Spivak and his vampire clients, who want Adele for a second operation.

Barnabas, Quentin and the Mad Ghoul

Before the series was canceled, Dan Ross wrote an outline (due date to publishers was July 1st, 1971) for a thirty-third book. Though he never committed his storyline to paper, a synopsis of the outline is presented on the following pages.

House of Dark Shadows (October, 1970)

While not part of the book series, Dan Ross also novelized the first *Dark Shadows* film. No novelization was written for *Night of Dark Shadows*, as there had been a falling out between Dan Curtis Productions, ABC and Paperback Library.

The following is a synopsis of the story Dan Ross presented in his outline to Paperback Library. The surviving document I have adapted is faded in a couple places and impossible to discern. I have filled in the blanks, fixed errors in spelling and grammar and adapted the document by incorporating hand-written notes and other data into the text as smoothly and unobtrusively as possible.

The mocking laughter of a man dead for two centuries is the signal for a wave of terror in Collinsport. When Ellen Trecartin and her husband, Ralph, return to Collinsport and decide to restore the Old House that had originally belonged to Captain Jack Collins, located along the cliffs not far from Collinwood, there is a lot of whispering among the elders of the village.

The house had been destroyed by fire fifty years before and, at the time, the villagers had been happy about its destruction. For while it remained standing, the ghost of Jack Collins was said to appear at the estate and also in the village. The legend claimed that even in death he carried on his career as a secret villain. Though he sailed the first large schooner out of Collinsport and had been a successful trader and a pillar of the founding village, he had also been a notorious Casanova, and it was said he enjoyed winning the love of married women so he could seek out the jealous husbands, pick quarrels with them and then challenge them to duels. It was the dueling he enjoyed. He was a crack shot and always killed his opponent.

Apparently death did not diminish his charms. It was said his ghost would claim the love of any woman he desired. He would then proceed to kill the husband or cause him to die in some mysterious fashion. Every woman who had lived in his house wound up a widow.

Now Lawyer Stephen Harrod brings Ellen Trecartin and her husband to Collinsport and encourages them to build their home built on the foundation of Jack Collins' former estate. Ellen's sister, Lila, resides in the area with her banker husband, so they agree and restoration ensues. Ellen and Ralph live in a rented cottage on the Collins estate while the house is under construction.

They are invited to a house party at Collinwood and warned about the curse of Jack Collins by Roger, Elizabeth and Carolyn, but neither Ellen nor Ralph believe in such superstitious nonsense. Among those at the party is Quentin Collins, handsome cousin to Roger and Elizabeth. Ellen takes a liking to the charming young man and Quentin takes her aside, telling her not to scoff at the curse, which he believes, has some firm truth to it. She is still unconvinced.

Later, the woman working for Ellen at the cottage tells her that Quentin is a mysterious person, saying that he and another cousin named Barnabas sometimes returned to Collinwood for brief visits but Roger and Elizabeth do not welcome them. She asks why and the woman replies that Barnabas is rumored to be a vampire and Quentin a werewolf.

Ellen scoffs at this and the housekeeper agrees. She has another theory regarding Quentin Collins, thinking he is the reincarnation of Captain Jack Collins and that he may be a killer like the long-ago sea captain. Ellen begins to feel apprehensive and goes into the village. At the bottom of the steep main street she finds a huge boulder-about six feet high and wide with a plaque on it, dedicated to Captain Jack Collins as the first sea captain to sail out of Collinsport on a regular basis.

From Quentin she learns that Jack Collins was probably a slaver and a part-time pirate. Quentin is amused that the town honors him with the stone. Ellen cannot believe that Quentin is the reincarnation of Captain Jack Collins, but feels he is mysterious.

Lawyer Stephen Harrod tells Ellen not to listen to the warnings from members of the Collins family, saying they just did not want to see the rival mansion restored. Ellen and Ralph take up residence in the house and Ralph becomes annoyed at his wife as she dabbles in spiritualism, trying to get a ghostly message on an Ouija board. He also becomes strangely jealous of her friendship with Quentin.

Ellen and Quentin go to the Collins graveyard one moonlit night to search for clues at the grave of Jack Collins. Quentin is stricken by a strange malady and flees, leaving Ellen alone in the cemetery. Seconds later she sees a great wolf-like creature bounding across the field.

Ellen stands in the cemetery, alarmed and frightened, when another figure appears, a handsome man in a caped cloak. He introduces himself as Barnabas Collins and escorts her back to Collinwood. Elizabeth is alone in the mansion, and is upset by Ellen's story of Quentin's vanishing.

Upset, Ellen drives back to the house. Ralph is nowhere around and Ellen goes to bed. She awakens to the sound of maniacal laughter, but manages to fall asleep. Ralph's body is discovered in the garden the following morning, his throat torn open as if by some animal. There is much speculation about his death, the superstitious claim the ghost of Jack Collins killed him. The police call it murder or an attack by some wild animal. Ellen can only think of Quentin and that he may have become a werewolf last night in the cemetery. Recalling the housekeeper's theory that Quentin was the reincarnation of the wicked Captain Jack Collins, Ellen wonders if he killed her husband according to the legend, making her a widow just like all the other women who had lived in the house before her.

While the police investigate, Quentin comes to Ellen and tells her that he is not responsible. She doesn't know whether to believe him or not. Quentin warns her to be careful of Barnabas, who is under a curse and might harm her. A week or so later, Ellen is standing in the garden where Ralph was murdered at night.

Barnabas appears and Ellen does not understand his strange behavior. Barnabas attacks her, sinking his fangs into her throat, and she faints. She regains consciousness in her bedroom with Quentin seated beside her. He tells her not to be afraid and says she will be all right. Ellen asks about Barnabas and Quentin promises to explain everything to her the next day.

And so he does. He takes her to the Old House and shows her Barnabas in his coffin, asleep in his vampire state.

Ellen realizes that she is falling in love with Quentin. Then Lila's banker-husband is murdered in the same manner as Ralph, his throat torn open. Lila claims she heard mocking laughter before it happened. There is tension between Quentin and Ellen, who realizes that she loves him, but fears he may have insane moments and wants to protect him.

There is a strange hippie-type camping on the beach, a big, burly youth who had been caught torturing a dog and vandalizing graves and gravestones. The police had suspected him of being mad from LSD and threw him in jail. He was ordered to leave Collinsport when his sentence was finished, but he lurks in the area. Ellen hears about him and begins to wonder if he may be the murderer.

Ellen goes for a walk in the garden at night and finds Quentin stretched out on the ground, knocked unconscious from a blow to the head. Ellen is trying to get Quentin into the house in his injured state when Barnabas arrives to help. He apologizes for his previous behavior and says he has an idea who the killer is, but he will not divulge the information on mere suspicion.

Briefly, Ellen wonders if Barnabas might be a madman and the killer, but she decides against this.

Ellen decides to sell the house and leave Collinsport. Stephen Harrod tries to dissuade her, but she will not listen. She tells the lawyer that she thinks she knows the killer's identify, but does not reveal the name because she believes Quentin is the murderer.

The following night, after hearing the mocking laughter that had preceded the death of her husband, Ellen is attacked. Quentin arrives in time to scare off the attacker, who races to his car and drives off. Quentin and Ellen give chase in her car. The killer drives down steep Main Street, tries to turn the corner, and the car careens out of control, crashing into the boulder monument to Captain Jack Collins.

Quentin and Ellen go to the wrecked vehicle and discover Ellen's lawyer, Stephen Harrod, crushed to death behind the wheel. Quentin claims that the ghost of Captain Jack Collins got his revenge and cleared his name. It is discovered that Stephen Harrod had been in love with Ellen's sister, Lila, and had lost her money. To cover himself, he had to get Ellen's money, which was held in a trust fund, by killing her and her husband, and blaming Quentin. He killed Lila's banker-husband when he threatened to reveal the truth.

Ellen is still determined to sell the house. Barnabas has already left, and Quentin comes to the house to say good-bye. He tells her that he loves her, but that they must wait, saying that he would see her again when she returned to Boston.

The novel ends with Ellen wondering if Quentin meant what he told her, or if he was just telling her what she wanted to hear.

Barnabas, Quentin and the Mad Ghoul, as far as the outline indicates, would have been another standard installment in the series with its main point of interest being the emergence of Quentin Collins as the romantic hero, while Barnabas took on a smaller supporting role. Unfortunately, the series ended and Quentin was denied his starring role.

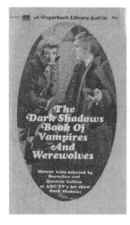

The *Dark Shadows* Book of Vampires and Werewolves edited by Barnabas and Quentin Collins (August, 1970)

Paperback Library released a few *Dark Shadows* tie-ins outside of the Dan Ross numbered series and novelization of *House of Dark Shadows*. These include **Barnabas Collins—In a Funny Vein** (pages of bad jokes and puns), **The Barnabas Collins Personal Picture Album** (a selection of portraits and behind the scenes photos of Jonathan Frid), and perhaps most interestingly, **The *Dark Shadows* Book of Vampires and Werewolves**.

This last volume is described as "Horror tales selected by Barnabas and Quentin Collins." Not Jonathan Frid and David Selby, mind you, but Barnabas and Quentin themselves.

The introduction begins:

"Rarely is the ordinary mortal granted an opportunity to know the torment and suffering that is the lot of the vampire or the werewolf. Objects of disgust, horror, and fear, we are hunted down like the lowliest of beasts and hooded to a destruction more degrading than that afforded common criminals, for the curse that makes us what we are also makes men forget that once we were as they are—happy creatures permitted the joys of sunlight, and flowers, and the simplest pleasures of life.

Here, then, is a singular collection of tales and narratives gleaned from the shelves of fiction and fact, offering readers a glimpse of the truth as it really is."

The following vampire tales are included:
"Mrs. Amworth" by E.F. Benson
"For the Blood is the Life" by F. Marion Crawford
"The Vampire Nemesis" by Dolly
"Count Magnus" by M.R. James
"The Vampyre" by John Polidori

It also includes two non-fiction pieces:
"The Vampire of Crogling Grange" by Augustus Hare
"The Vampire Legend: Its Origin and Nature" by Lewis Spence

Werewolf fans sadly get short shrift, with only two werewolf stories among the contents:
"Wolves Don't Cry" by Bruce Elliott
"Men-Wolves" (From the Polish)

While it was the only *Dark Shadows* anthology published, **The *Dark Shadows* Book of Vampires and Werewolves** is a unique tie-in that *Dark Shadows* paperback collectors will surely want to add to their collection.
—John Scoleri

A great writer is persuasive, and David J. Schow is a great writer. In what might appear on the surface to be a straightforward book review of an author's new collection, Schow manages to not only provide an introduction to Trevanian, but a concise overview of the author's unique history and body of work. I dare you to come away without having added at least one title to your want list—if not all of them. -John

AKA Trevanian
by David J. Schow

Hot Night in the City? Isn't that a bitch fuckarama HBO series about a quartet of too-precious designer whiners? Trevanian? Isn't he a pseudonym for a gang of lawyers who write spy thrillers? What the hell is this mainstream, mass-market mung doing in *bare•bones*, anyway?

Well, it isn't, he's not, and this book is a sparkling example of how a single writer with a powerful talent can cross generic lines with impunity, even obliterate them, rendering them irrelevant.

Hot Night in the City (Thomas Dunne Books/St Martin's Press, June 2000) is the first—and probably only—collection of short stories from a man who has written in multiple genres under a menu of pseudonyms for more than three decades. Blurbage will have you know Trevanian is a "New York Times bestselling author," but usually doesn't point out that he enjoys this distinction having never made a public appearance, never done an in-store signing, and, indeed, is a person who divides his writing life from his private life so cleanly and definitively that it makes you wish others would follow his example, if only because it boils away personae and publicity and soapboxing and stunts, and leaves reputation and impact to be determined

by one thing only, the thing that actually matters—writing.

Let's presuppose good writing isn't sufficient recommendation. Let's impose a few shackles of genre, and say that the writing, good or bad, must brush up against the categories of "dark fiction," or scary storytelling, or suspense, or horror, or some other damned thing, to merit your time and attention. On our way to the relevant connections, an attempt will be made to dazzle you with a dash of backstory and a bit of history.

Whereas the modern era of the intrigue thriller can be said to have begun the instant President Kennedy noted that one of his favorite books was the James Bond adventure **From Russia With Love**, by Ian Fleming (thus commencing a spy craze that still thrives today, thanks to endless recycling), Trevanian put paid to the whole genre when he wrote the be-all, end-all blowout adventure of hit men, paladins, corrupt agencies, dirty tricks, black ops, honor, betrayal, and the conflict of technology with the human spirit, **Shibumi**. Not coincidentally, this novel also brackets the trendwave begun specifically by **From Russia With Love**'s runaway success, for another reason specific to its own plot,

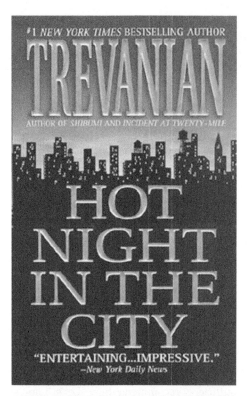

#1 NEW YORK TIMES BESTSELLING AUTHOR

TREVANIAN

AUTHOR OF *SHIBUMI* AND *INCIDENT AT TWENTY-MILE*

HOT NIGHT IN THE CITY

"ENTERTAINING...IMPRESSIVE."
—*New York Daily News*

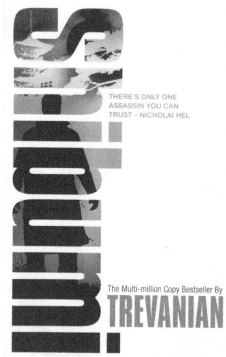

shibumi

THERE'S ONLY ONE ASSASSIN YOU CAN TRUST – NICHOLAI HEL

The Multi-million Copy Bestseller By
TREVANIAN

The Eiger Sanction

A NOVEL BY
TREVANIAN

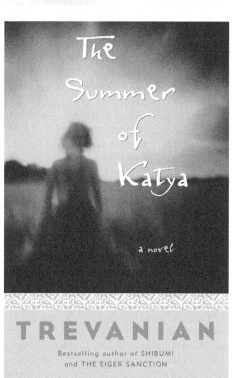

The Summer of Katya

a novel

TREVANIAN

Bestselling author of SHIBUMI
and THE EIGER SANCTION

which will be left unspecified in the hope that a reader or two might wish to uncover it for him or herself.

When **Shibumi** was published in 1979, Trevanian—an ex-University of Texas professor named Rodney Whitaker—had already published a fairly scholarly work on the texture, tone and grammar of cinema titled **The Language of Film** (as Whitaker), and, as Professor Nicholas Seare, two volumes of medieval ribaldry, **1339 Or So, Being an Apology for a Pedlar** (1975) and a bawdy re-fit of the Arthurian myth, **Rude Tales and Glorious** (1983). Intermittent with these was a string of bestselling mainstream intrigue thrillers as Trevanian: **The Eiger Sanction** (1972), **The Loo Sanction** (1973), and **The Main** (1976). For the convoluted story of how and why the Sanction books were written (as parodies, says Mr. T.) and the setback of having **The Main** published as a book by Trevanian when in fact it was intended to be yet another of Whitaker's complex pseudonym-personae (one "Jean-Paul Morin," in fact), please seek out a very illuminative *Publisher's Weekly* "interview" (done via fax in August, 1998).

Then, after a long dry spell, followed **The Summer of Katya** (1983)—barely novella length, fattened just enough to merit hard covers plus a renewed, and perceivably desperate, ballyhoo about a new Trevanian book … even though, to the Trevanian aficionado, **Katya** was clearly another non-Trevanian Trevanian book, as was **The Main**.

Katya was also, no bones about it, a psychological horror novel, something not hinted at in the flap copy or reviews. Imagine **Psycho**, re-set in a French Basque village in 1914, and you may get the idea. Not a horror novel by any sort of commercially comprehensible marketing definition, **Katya** is best summed up as a sort of nightmare romance. Nor was **Katya** a "Trevanian" novel, strictly speaking, since to write it, yet another new auctorial identity had been confected (to use one of Trevanian's favorite expressions). Neither was **Incident at Twenty-Mile**, a Western marking the return, after a fifteen-year absence, to the Western (as in Occidental) literary scene of someone whom publishers,

publicists and promoters, frantic for continuity, seem determined to nail down to the single identity known as Trevanian, no matter what he writes or how he writes it.

Even more frustratingly for pigeonholers, it turns out that this "Trevanian" entity has been publishing short fiction, infrequently, almost invisibly, since 1978 in the likes of *Playboy*, *Harper's*, the *Yale Literary Review*, *The Antioch Review*, even, amazingly, in *Redbook*—and all of these stories, plus more, are on display in **Hot Night in the City**.

Typically for the multi-faceted entity we choose to denote as Trevanian, the title story establishes an odd precedent I cannot recall having seen in any other collection, that is, "Hot Night in the City" appears *twice*, bookending the other contents. This psychological tale of stalker and stalkee is presented first from the viewpoint of one, then recapitulated from the viewpoint of the other, with differing resolutions.

The author's penchant for presenting wry nod-and-wink fables based on classically ethnic storytelling structures, principally Basque and American Indian, is exerted here in "Minutes of a Village Meeting" (from *Harper's*), "That Fox of a Beñat," and most splendidly in "How the Animals Got Their Voices: An Onondagan Primal Tale." As with the best campfire stories and folk-tale legends, these veneer deeply adult concerns in musical, almost hypnotically simple language, or, as the writer says in the voice of She-Who-Creates-By-Speaking-Its-Name, "tales meant to amuse on top and to teach underneath."

"Sir Gervais in the Enchanted Forest" is a chapter of **Rude Tales and Glorious** presented here as a stand-alone story. If you need a strong, satirical breeze to blow away the bad taste of too many bloated, gassy, airy-fairy King Arthur books, this story adequately suggests the potent antidote that is **Rude Tales**.

"The Sacking of Miss Plimsoll" (from *Redbook*, where it appeared as "The Secrets of Miss Plimsoll, Private Secretary") is another kind of rude tale, specifically, one of those writers-writing-about-writers ragouts that seems the inevitable duty of anyone who has been a writer long enough to call themselves a writer without hanging their head.

"Snatch Off Your Cap, Kid!" might have been a missing chapter from Bradbury's **The Illustrated Man**, had Bradbury leavened his juvenile enthusiasms with a teaspoon more adult cynicism.

Surely by now you get the picture. Trevanian's collection gear-shifts effortlessly from modern to period, parody to suspense, urban to sylvan, and yes, from dread to awe, with a refreshingly-honed wryness and surgical exactitude of language you may find refreshing after one too many cookie-cutter horrors. The thirteen stories here, while not the "feast for every taste" described by the inadequate jacket copy, nonetheless serve up a palette of styles and trajectories broad enough to encourage the curious reader to investigate the larger canvases this writer has created ... whoever he might or might not be.

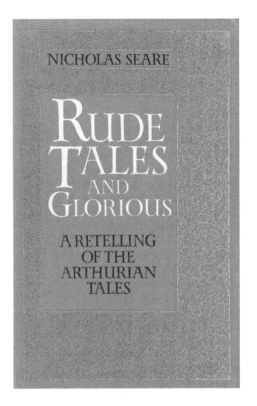

About the Contributors

David Allen Brown is the author of the novel **Web**, an ebook available through Amazon. He was born and raised in Ohio, and has lived in Florida and Nevada. He attended Ohio State University and majored in Journalism. He currently resides in Columbus, Ohio.

Thomas Deja has been writing professionally for over twenty five years. His work has appeared in the seminal Brooklyn 'zine *Inside Joke*, *The Scream Factory*, *bare•bones*, and *Fangoria*. Recently, he has been writing stories in what he calls "The Chimera Falls Universe." Thomas' passion for film has extended to maintaining *Damn Your Ears! Damn Your Eyes!*, a blog where he publishes his notorious '10 Statements About' kinda, sorta movie reviews. Thomas lives in New York City, where he struggles with his lifelong devotion to the Jets and strives to improve himself every day.

Stefan Dziemianowicz has edited more than 60 anthologies of horror, fantasy, mystery, and science fiction. He's a pulp magazine junkie, and he occasionally hits his deadlines.

Peter Enfantino is an obsessive collector of Mystery, Crime and Horror digests including *Alfred Hitchcock, Manhunt, Mike Shayne*, as well as the entire stable of Warren Magazines. He has written for all the major channels on the topics, including *Paperback Parade, Mystery Scene, The Digest Enthusiast, Paperback Fanatic, Monster Maniac, Men of Violence, Mystery File, Comic Effect*, and Peter Normanton's *From the Tomb*. He is currently working on an exhaustive critical guide to the Atlas Pre-Code Horror Comic Books. In his spare time, he writes with Jack Seabrook on DC War comics, the Warren Publishing phenomenon, and Batman in the 1980s. He Lives in Gilbert, Arizona.

Vince Fahey is a married father of two living in the Arizona wasteland where he counts the days between enjoyable seasonal weather. Vince is a partner/co-owner of a company that licenses private families to foster adults with developmental disabilities. In his spare time, Vince is an avid reader with generally 3-4 books going at the same time. He loves going to movies, reading comic books and spending time with his family.

W.D. Gagliani is the author of the Nick Lupo Series: **Wolf's Trap** (Bram Stoker Award finalist), **Wolf's Gambit, Wolf's Bluff, Wolf's Edge, Wolf's Cut, Wolf's Blind,** and the novella "Wolf's Deal," plus the thrillers **The Judas Hit** and **Savage Nights**. He has had fiction and nonfiction in numerous anthologies and publications, such as Robert Bloch's **Psychos,** and his fiction has garnered six Honorable Mentions in **The Year's Best Fantasy & Horror**. The team of W.D. Gagliani & David Benton has published **Killer Lake** (Deadite Press, 2019) plus short fiction in anthologies such as **The X-Files: Trust No One, Splatterpunk: Fighting Back, Splatterpunk Zine's Past Indiscretions, SNAFU: An Anthology of Military Horror, Dark Passions: Hot Blood 13,** etc., and some of their collaborations are available in the collection **Mysteries & Mayhem**. Find W.D. Gagliani at www.wdgagliani.com, www.facebook.com/wdgagliani, and on Twitter at @WDGagliani.

Derek Hill has written for numerous online and print publications. He is the author of the book **Charlie Kaufman and Hollywood's Merry Band of Pranksters, Fabulists and Dreamers,** and he's contributed to a number of other books. He is currently working on a crime novel while hiding out in Eugene, Oregon. He loves his cat.

Lawrence McCallum is the author of **Italian Horror Films of the 60s** (McFarland, 2004). In addition to *bare•bones*, his work has appeared in *Filmfax, Scary Monsters,* and he was a regular contributor to *The Scream Factory* beginning with issue #2. He passed away in 2010.

David J. Schow is a multiple-award-winning West Coast writer. The latest of his ten novels is a hardboiled extravaganza called **The Big Crush** (2019). The newest of his ten short story collections is a greatest hits anniversary compendium titled **DJStories** (2018). He has been a contributor to Storm King Comics' **John Carpenter's Tales for a Halloween Night** since its very first issue. In 2018 Storm King released his five-issue series for **John Carpenter's Tales of Science Fiction—"The Standoff."** DJS has written extensively for film (*The Crow, Leatherface: Texas Chainsaw Massacre III, The Hills Run Red*) and television (*Masters of Horror, Mob City, Creepshow's* "The Finger"). His nonfiction works include **The Art of Drew Struzan** (2010) and **The Outer Limits at 50** (2014). He can be seen on various DVDs as expert witness or documentarian on everything from *Creature from the Black Lagoon* to *Psycho* to *I, Robot,* not to mention the Rondo and Saturn Award-winning *Outer Limits* (Seasons 1 and 2) discs from Kino-Lorber. Thanks to him, the word "splatterpunk" has been in the Oxford English Dictionary since 2002.

John Scoleri is the author of several books on artist Ralph McQuarrie, including **The Art of Ralph McQuarrie** (Dreams & Visions Press, 2007) and **The Art of Ralph McQuarrie: ARCHIVES** (Dreams & Visions Press, 2015), and the producer of the DVDs *Ralph McQuarrie: Illustrator* (2002) and *Caroline Munro: First Lady of Fantasy* (2004). He has contributed to several books on Richard Matheson, including **Bloodlines** (Gauntlet Press, 2006), as well as **Tobe Hooper's Salem's Lot: Studies in the Horror Film** (Centipede Press, 2014; revised 2019). He curates the **I Am Legend** Archive (iamlegendarchive.com) from his home in Santa Clara, California, and is currently at work on a photographic retrospective of *Night of the Living Dead* titled **Latent Images** (Dreams & Visions Press, 2020).

David H. Smith contributed to several volumes of the *Midnight Marquee Actors Series,* including **Lon Chaney Jr., Boris Karloff, Peter Lorre** and **Bela Lugosi**. He attended Indiana University, and served four years in the US Air Force. He was a lifelong aficionado of science-fiction, fantasy and horror. In addition to *bare•bones*, his work has appeared in *Midnight Marquee*. He passed away in 2017.

Index to *bare*•bones Magazine (1997-2001)

• indicates the article is reprinted in this volume

Made in the USA
Middletown, DE
21 October 2024

62558983R00145